FINANCIAL REGULATION

The 2007 to 2009 financial crisis resulted in the re-emergence of the debate on financial regulation and its relationships with other macroeconomic policies, particularly monetary policy. In Europe, the financial crisis was followed by the sovereign debt crisis, as the bail-out of the financial sector put strains on public finances in several countries. The sequence of events called for a strengthening of the union, ranging from a common framework for supervisory policies that could minimise the risk of unforeseen bank or country defaults to a common resolution mechanism that could set equal rules across countries and reduce ex ante mis-incentives to risk-taking and moral hazard.

This analysis of the state of and prospects for financial regulation examines the lending and saving behaviour of banks and households, as well as their borrowing activities, in order to understand the conflicting priorities and complicated decisions involved in the development and implementation of financial legislation.

ESTER FAIA holds the Chair in Monetary and Fiscal Policy at Goethe University, Frankfurt am Main, Germany, and is Program Director of the Macro-Finance area at the Research Center SAFE.

ANDREAS HACKETHAL is Professor of Finance at Goethe University, Frankfurt am Main, Germany, where he is also Dean of the Faculty of Economics and Business Administration.

MICHAEL HALIASSOS holds the Chair of Macroeconomics and Finance at Goethe University, Frankfurt am Main, Germany, Director of the Center for Financial Studies, and Director of the CEPR Network on Household Finance.

KATJA LANGENBUCHER is Professor of Private Law, Corporate and Financial Law at Goethe University, Frankfurt am Main, Germany, and an affiliated professor of the Institut d'Etudes Politiques (SciencesPo) in Paris.

FINANCIAL REGULATION

A Transatlantic Perspective

Edited by
ESTER FAIA, ANDREAS HACKETHAL,
MICHAEL HALIASSOS AND
KATJA LANGENBUCHER

CAMBRIDGE
UNIVERSITY PRESS

CAMBRIDGE
UNIVERSITY PRESS

University Printing House, Cambridge CB2 8BS, United Kingdom

Cambridge University Press is part of the University of Cambridge.

It furthers the University's mission by disseminating knowledge in the pursuit of education, learning and research at the highest international levels of excellence.

www.cambridge.org
Information on this title: www.cambridge.org/9781107084261

First published 2015

A catalogue record for this publication is available from the British Library

Library of Congress Cataloguing in Publication data
Financial regulation (Faia, Hackethal, Haliassos, Langenbucher)
Financial regulation : a transatlantic perspective / edited by Ester Faia, Andreas Hackethal, Michael Haliassos and Katja Langenbucher.
pages cm
ISBN 978-1-107-08426-1 (hardback)
1. Finance – Government policy – Europe. 2. Monetary policy – Europe. 3. Financial institutions – Law and legislation – Europe. 4. Financial institutions – Government policy – Europe. 5. Financial crises – Europe – Prevention. I. Faia, Ester. II. Title.
HG186.A2F57256 2015
332.094–dc23
2015011596

ISBN 978-1-107-08426-1 Hardback

CONTENTS

List of figures *page* vii
List of tables ix
List of contributors x
Foreword – Vítor Constâncio xii
Editors' preface xxi
Acknowledgements xxiv

PART I **Micro- and macro-prudential regulation** 1

1 The road from micro-prudential to macro-prudential regulation
ESTER FAIA AND ISABEL SCHNABEL 3

2 Lessons from the European financial crisis
MARCO PAGANO 23

3 Bank stress tests as a policy tool: the European experience during the crisis
ATHANASIOS ORPHANIDES 49

4 Monetary policy in a banking union
TOBIAS LINZERT AND FRANK SMETS 61

5 Competition and state aid rules in the time of banking union
IGNAZIO ANGELONI AND NIALL LENIHAN 89

6 Bail-in clauses
JAN PIETER KRAHNEN AND LAURA MORETTI 125

7 Shadow resolutions as a no-no in a sound Banking Union
LUCA ENRIQUES AND GERARD HERTIG 150

8 A political economy perspective on common supervision in the Eurozone
TOBIAS H. TRÖGER 167

PART II **Investor and borrower protection** 193

9 Keeping households out of financial trouble
MICHAEL HALIASSOS 195

10 Financial market governance and consumer protection in the EU
NIAMH MOLONEY 221

11 Financial advice
ANDREAS HACKETHAL 245

12 U.S. financial regulation in the aftermath of the Global Financial Crisis
HOWELL E. JACKSON 271

13 Risk aversion and financial crisis
LUIGI GUISO 290

14 Household finance and the law – a case study on economic transplants
KATJA LANGENBUCHER 313

Index 336

FIGURES

1.1 Transmission channels of systemic risk 5
2.1 Two-year moving correlation between bank sector monthly stock returns and 10-year domestic sovereign debt returns and domestic sovereign exposures of banks in the euro-area periphery 27
2.2 Two-year moving correlation between bank sector monthly stock returns and 10-year domestic sovereign debt returns and domestic sovereign exposures of banks in the euro-area core 28
2.3 Bank resolution in the US and EU 36
2.4 Average reduction in the funding costs of banks due to government guarantee (basis points) 37
2.5 Book leverage ratio versus regulatory capital ratio: median of top 20 EU banks 42
2.6 Correlation between the leverage ratio and the regulatory capital ratio for listed EU banks 43
2.7 Global banks' Tier-1 capital as percentage of risk-weighted assets in 2006 45
2.8 Global systemically important banks' leverage ratios in Q2–2013 46
3.1 Economic performance in the US and the euro area 50
3.2 Credit-crunch-induced recession in the euro area 56
3.3 Policy-induced credit crunch in the periphery 57
3.4 The impact of the policy-induced credit crunch 59
4.1 Lending of last resort to markets 71
4.2 Share of the Eurosystem in Euro Area MFI main liabilities 72
4.3 Lending of last resort to individual institutions: ELA 73
4.4 Challenges and risks of financial dominance 74
4.5 Lending of last resort in a banking union 79
8.1 ECB/NCA interplay within the SSM 177
8.2 ECB supervisory decision making 185

11.1 Portfolio return and risk profiles for 3,400 online broker clients (2003–2012) 247
11.2 Comparison of stated risk preferences and average actual portfolio risk 249
13.1 Share of highly risk-averse people in the Survey of Consumer Finances 304

TABLES

4.1 The importance of banks for the ECB's monetary policy 65
8.1 Direct ECB supervisory competence according to SSM regulation 173
13.1 Evolution of the distribution of risk preferences among US households 303

CONTRIBUTORS

IGNAZIO ANGELONI is Member of the Supervisory Board of the European Central Bank.

VÍTOR CONSTÂNCIO is Vice-President of the European Central Bank.

LUCA ENRIQUES is Allen & Overy Professor of Corporate Law at the University of Oxford and fellow at the European Corporate Governance Institute (ECGI).

ESTER FAIA is Professor of Monetary and Fiscal Policy at Goethe University, Member of the Scientific Board of the Research Center SAFE, Senior Fellow at Center for Financial Studies (CFS), and Fellow at the Centre for Economic Policy Research (CEPR).

LUIGI GUISO is AXA Professor of Household Finance at Einaudi Institute for Economics and Finance (EIEF) and Fellow at the Centre for Economic Policy Research (CEPR).

ANDREAS HACKETHAL is Professor of Finance at Goethe University Frankfurt, Dean of Goethe's Faculty of Economics and Business Administration, and Director of the E-Finance Lab.

MICHAEL HALIASSOS is Professor of Macroeconomics and Finance at Goethe University Frankfurt, Director of the Center for Financial Studies, and Director of the CEPR Network on Household Finance.

GERARD HERTIG is Professor of Law at the Swiss Institute of Technology (ETH Zurich) and fellow at the European Corporate Governance Institute (ECGI).

HOWELL E. JACKSON is James S. Reid Jr. Professor of Law at Harvard Law School.

JAN PIETER KRAHNEN is Professor of Corporate Finance, Goethe University Frankfurt, Director of the Center for Financial Studies, and Director of the Research Center SAFE.

KATJA LANGENBUCHER is Professor for Private Law, Corporate and Financial Law at Goethe University and Affiliated Professor at SciencesPo/ Ecole de Droit, Paris.

NIALL LENIHAN is Senior Advisor in the Directorate-General Legal Services of the European Central Bank.

TOBIAS LINZERT is Deputy Head of Monetary Policy Strategy Division of the European Central Bank.

NIAMH MOLONEY is Professor of Financial Markets Law at the London School of Economics and Political Science and Fellow of the Center for Financial Studies.

LAURA MORETTI is a senior researcher at the Center for Financial Studies and the SAFE Policy Center at Goethe University in Frankfurt.

ATHANASIOS ORPHANIDES is Professor of the Practice of Global Economics and Management at the MIT Sloan and Senior Fellow at the Center for Financial Studies.

MARCO PAGANO is Professor of Economics, University of Naples Federico II, President of the Einaudi Institute for Economics and Finance (EIEF), and Research Fellow at CSEF and CEPR.

ISABEL SCHNABEL is Professor of Financial Economics at Johannes Gutenberg University Mainz, and Research Affiliate at the Centre for Economic Policy Research (CEPR) and at the Max Planck Institute for Research on Collective Goods (MPI) in Bonn.

FRANK SMETS is Director General of the Directorate-General Research of the ECB.

TOBIAS H. TRÖGER is Professor of Private Law, Trade and Business Law, Jurisprudence at Goethe University Frankfurt and Fellow of the Center for Financial Studies.

FOREWORD: FINANCIAL REGULATION – THE FIRST MACRO-PRUDENTIAL TOOL

Financial regulation aims to de-risk the financial system by improving resilience and taming the financial cycle. This book provides a broad overview, combining the insights of academic researchers with the knowledge of practitioners of the latest transatlantic developments in this field. It shows how financial regulation must seek to tweak the incentives around banks' private decisions to align them with social welfare. To do this, authorities must intelligently combine financial regulation and the use of broader macro-prudential policies. Financial regulation is about designing a financial system resilient to systemic risk and as such it is, in my view, the first tool of the newly established macro-prudential policy area (see Chapter 1 by Ester Faia and Isabel Schnabel for an expanded examination of the role of macro-prudential policy). Sound shock-absorption capacity needs to be assured before cyclical aspects can be brought into consideration. However, I will argue that macro-prudential policy should also be used assertively to tame the financial cycle that arises endogenously from the financial system. Ideally, financial regulation should be used to induce the banks to internalise fully the costs and benefits of their asset–liability structure. By doing so, they make the financial system more resilient to shocks.

In achieving this, the banking union project and the Single Supervisory Mechanism (SSM) will make an essential contribution (see Chapters 4 and 5 on different aspects of banking union, by Frank Smets and Tobias Linzert, and Ignazio Angeloni and Niall Lenihan, respectively). The absence of European supervision and resolution was an initial design flaw of monetary union. As the crisis developed, this became quite clear. The high degree of interconnectedness in the euro area implies that the impact of supervision affects not only the domestic banking sector but also, as an externality, other countries. With increasing financial integration, pursuing national financial policies will generally not lead to financial stability, because national policies seek to benefit national welfare while not taking into account externalities of national supervisory practices in other countries. This leads to an under-provision of financial stability as a public good.[1]

Banking union has, of course, many other goals:[2] to avoid large financial imbalances among members by taking a European perspective in monitoring the cross-border intermediation by banks; to contribute to financial integration by severing the links between banks and respective sovereigns; to overcome financial fragmentation and improve the transmission of monetary policy; and, finally, to increase the efficiency of the banking system which is the dominant source of finance for the European economy.

The SSM will be a strong and independent supervisor, enforcing supervision consistently across the participating Member States. The SSM will ensure a fully integrated approach to the supervision of cross-border banks. Compared with supervision at the national level, this integrated approach will enable the SSM to detect excessive risk-taking and the cross-border externalities associated with it, and therefore to be proactive if local financial developments threaten broader financial stability.

That said, high-standard banking supervision does not focus on preventing bank failures at any cost. In fact, to effectively perform its tasks, a supervisor must also be able to let failing banks exit the market. This is the reason why the SSM has also been given the competence to withdraw credit institutions' licences to operate. However, given the role of banks in the financial system, and in order to safeguard financial stability, the supervisor has to feel confident that the resolution of banks can be conducted in an orderly fashion. This brings me to the second pillar of the banking union, the Single Resolution Mechanism (SRM).

The establishment of the SRM was the second crucial step towards addressing financial fragmentation and breaking the bank–sovereign nexus. This is because the orderly resolution of banks, even large ones, helps avoid costly rescues by sovereigns that may endanger their own

[1] On financial stability as a public good, see, for instance, Beck, Thorsten, Diane Coyle, Mathias Dewatripont, Xavier Freixas and Paul Seabright (2010): *Bailing out the Banks: Reconciling Stability and Competition: An Analysis of State-Supported Schemes for Financial Institutions*, London: CEPR.

[2] See Vítor Constâncio: "Reflections on financial integration and stability", speech at the Joint ECB-EC Conference on Financial Integration and Stability in a New Financial Architecture, Frankfurt, 28 April 2014 and "Towards the Banking Union", speech at the 2nd FIN-FSA Conference on EU Regulation and Supervision "Banking and Supervision under Transformation" organised by the Financial Supervisory Authority, Helsinki, 12 February 2013.

finances. This will enable swift and unbiased resolution decisions, which will address notable cross-border resolution cases in an effective manner. In this respect, the SRM should be viewed as a necessary – and logical – complement to the SSM.

Banks' asset–liability structure – ensuring externalities are internalised

When banks fail, systemic consequences often arise for the rest of the financial sector and the overall economy. This can happen as a result of contagion – either directly via write-downs on exposures to the failed bank, or indirectly via confidence effects that can freeze markets and diminish access to funding. The existence of such systemic risks tends to distort the healthy functioning of the financial market. It results in pressures on authorities to save failing banks in order to avoid financial crises and the associated damage to the real economy. Ultimately, this distortion tends to exacerbate private–social incentive misalignment by creating moral hazard among bank managers and investors. Therefore, without adequate financial regulation, the financial system will tend to build excessively risky balance sheets and to grow more than efficiently. How should this problem be addressed?

Enhancing resilience – loss absorbency and asset liquidity

Firstly, rules must be imposed on banks to ensure their balance sheets are not excessively risky. On the liability side, this means that capital requirements should be strengthened. Furthermore, they could be time-variant. Strong capital build-up in good times reduces the frequency of financial crises and contributes to more sustainable economic growth and higher levels of output over the long term.[3]

Authorities must also ensure that banks' broader funding models are stable. This means that funding should be pushed towards longer-term sources that do not disappear rapidly in moments of stress. In addition, banks must hold sufficient liquid assets that can be sold to fulfil funding needs when sources of short-term finance disappear.

[3] A study by the Basel Long-Term Economic Impact Group has estimated that banking crises occur, on average, every 20 to 25 years. This estimate means that there is a 4.6% annual probability of a crisis. The study shows that a 4 percentage point increase in the capital ratio lowers this annual probability to less than 1%.

Much progress has been made in recent years in increasing minimum standards for banks' capital adequacy, funding structures, and liquidity. The agreement of Basel III is the central policy achievement in this area, and it provides a robust basis for the design of minimum requirements worldwide.

However, there is more to be done. In my view, the balance of the academic work on optimal bank capital levels suggests that there is still room for increasing requirements on banks.[4] There may be scope for also shaping the composition of the capital stock to induce more prudent risk-taking behaviour. Recent research has pointed to the importance of a banks' ownership structure in determining their overall risk profile.[5] There may be sizeable scope for designing regulation appropriately to induce a capital and ownership structure that induces prudent behaviour. I call upon researchers to help develop such mechanisms, and for the regulatory community to actively explore how they may be applied to the banking system. Additionally, I note that banks may be manipulating risk-weighting models to reduce the capital they must hold against their assets – as also described by Marco Pagano in Chapter 2. His lesson is to rely on a set of simpler and more robust indicators. I would agree with calls for a stronger leverage ratio, significantly above the initially proposed 3% level for G-SIBs, as this could play an important positive role in mitigating the risk that risk weights are manipulated.

[4] Historical evidence seems to indicate that there is no relationship between the simple ratio of book capital to total assets (or its inverse, with leverage expressed as a multiplier) and economic growth. Indeed, from a social perspective, the cost of highly capitalised banks would seem to be rather low. The relatively cheap cost of debt in comparison with the cost of equity seen currently is due, largely, to the widespread tax advantage that debt financing has over equity. See Haldane A.G. and P. Alessandri (2009): "Banking on the State" London: Bank of England; Miles, D., J. Yang and G. Marcheggiano (2011): "Optimal bank capital", *Bank of England Discussion Paper Series* 32: 6; Kashyap, A.K., J.C. Stein and S. Hanson (2010): "An analysis of the impact of 'substantially heightened' capital requirements on large financial institutions", *mimeo*: 19; Taylor A. (2012) "The Great Leveraging", *NBER Working Papers* 18290, National Bureau of Economic Research; Admati, A.R., P.M. DeMarzo, M.F. Hellwig and P. Pfleiderer (2013): "Fallacies, Irrelevant Facts, and Myths in the Discussion of Capital Regulation: Why Bank Equity is Not Socially Expensive", *Rock Center for Corporate Governance Working Paper Series* 161.

[5] See Laeven, L. and R. Levine (2009) "Bank governance, regulation and risk taking", *Journal of Financial Economics* 93(2): 259–275, who also find that bank executives before the crisis held only small amounts of their own banks' stocks.

Enhancing resolvability – reducing the systemic consequences of bank failure

Secondly, we must implement reforms to reduce the systemic consequences that arise when banks fail. To achieve this goal, a strong bank resolution framework is needed to ensure that the costs of a bank's failure fall where they belong – on its shareholders and creditors. In this vein, Michael Haliassos discusses in Chapter 9 the reason why regulation is needed and how households can be kept out of financial stress. Such an orderly resolution mechanism is an ex post measure with beneficial ex ante effects on private risk-taking decisions. Clarifying that the costs of bank failures will fall on banks' shareholders and creditors sharpens these investors' incentives to monitor and influence banks' decisions on their risk appetite. Excessive risk-taking will not be tolerated by investors who know they will be forced to pay for the negative consequences that may result from that strategy. This injection of market discipline is particularly beneficial in the modern context where deposit insurance has muted the monitoring incentives stemming originally from the risk of depositor runs.[6]

The financial crisis showed us that existing bank resolution systems were inadequate. Banks were structured in such complex ways that it was near to impossible to identify where losses would fall in a case of insolvency. Authorities lacked the necessary powers to act decisively to shut down failing institutions and apportion losses in an orderly fashion. Bail-outs resulted, and moral hazard problems intensified.

I am glad to say we have gone a substantial way to addressing these shortcomings. In Europe, the establishment of the SRM and the Bank Recovery and Resolution Directive (BRRD) are crucial steps, while the Dodd-Frank Act creates a similar resolution framework for US authorities. In this book, Gerard Hertig and Luca Enriques illustrate the details of bank resolution at the level of the EU, and its interplay with resolution at the level of Member States, in Chapter 7, whereas Tobias Tröger discusses the institutional arrangements of the SSM in Chapter 8.

Despite this positive reform, clearly there is still work to be done. Perhaps most crucially, authorities must begin using the resolution tools they have been given – thereby adding credibility to the system. The recent agreement at the FSB and G20 levels to introduce a new

[6] See Demirguc-Kunt, A. and E. Detragiache (2005): "Cross-Country Empirical Studies of Systemic Bank Distress: A Survey", *World Bank Policy Research Working Paper* 3719.

concept of Total Loan Absorption Capacity (TLAC) for Global SIBs was, in this respect, a very important step forward. European regulation now needs to adjust the concept of Minimum Requirements of Eligible Liabilities (MREL) that will be applied to all banks, in order to ensure full compatibility with the TLAC concept. In Chapter 6, Jan Pieter Krahnen and Laura Moretti highlight the need for a clear and credible pecking order when allocating losses and discuss possible formats. Both TLAC and MREL should ensure that sufficient "bail-inable" debt will always exist on bank balance sheets to insulate tax-payers from burdens in all but the most extreme crisis scenarios.

Macro-prudential policy should tame the financial cycle

Together, the measures set out above on increasing the resilience and resolvability of banks will make the banking system safer, more stable, and better equipped to allocate resources efficiently across the economy. Nonetheless, endogenous forces exist within the financial sector that still make the availability of credit pro-cyclical.[7] For instance, easier credit in a boom phase encourages investors to buy more assets, which in turn increases the value of collateral, thereby fuelling the credit boom further. Hence, the expansion of credit in good times can, by itself, lead to excessive leverage in the financial system and increase the probability of crises, only to go into reverse during a bust.[8]

To contain these pro-cyclical forces we need an assertive and pre-emptive counter-cyclical policy. Macro-prudential policy should aim at cutting short credit booms in order to prevent the risk of future financial crises. So what tools are needed to pursue this goal?

We have already discussed how capital requirements help to ensure the resilience of the financial system. However, capital requirements that vary over time are also proposed as a way to smooth the financial cycle – for example, the Basel III framework introduces the Counter-

[7] See Borio, C. (2009): "Implementing the Macro-prudential Approach to Financial Regulation and Supervision", *Banque de France Financial Stability Review* 13; Shin, H.S. (2011): "Macro-prudential policies beyond Basel III", in "Macro-prudential regulation and policy", *Bank for International Settlements BIS Papers* 60.

[8] See Kiyotaki, N. and J. Moore (1997): "Credit Cycles", *Journal of Political Economy* 105(2): 211–248; Bernanke, B.S., M. Gertler and S. Gilchrist "The financial accelerator in a quantitative business cycle framework", in: J.B. Taylor and M. Woodford (eds.), *Handbook of Macroeconomics*, Elsevier vol.1, chapter 21, 1341–1393.

Cyclical Capital Buffer (CCB) as a key counter-cyclical tool. One may be sceptical about the power of using capital buffers for macro-prudential purposes, given the long lag between the imposition, and this ultimately feeding through into lending behaviour. That makes calibration difficult, and thereby creates a bias towards a too timid approach, also to avoid action based on false alarms.

To be effective, macro-prudential policy has to be deployed aggressively and in a timely manner. Instruments with quantitative restrictions such as Large Exposures limits, Loan to Value ratios, and Debt to Income (DTI) ratios may be well suited to allowing authorities to pursue the necessary bold approach to macro-prudential policy. Where these tools have not yet been provided to macro-prudential authorities, they should be granted. Other possible extensions to the toolkit are loan-to-deposit ratios, or the anti-cyclical variation of mandatory margins and haircuts used in some financial markets. Only time will tell if these newly designed tools will be used adequately to make our financial system safe.

Another major area on which macro-prudential supervision needs to focus is so-called shadow banking. The significant expansion of this sector can present systemic risks that need to be detected, monitored and managed. Similar to the traditional financial intermediation activities of banks, "shadow bank" credit intermediation involves credit exposures, normally through purchased securities, that are of a longer maturity and less liquid in nature than short-term and liquid liabilities. Moreover, some of these entities are leveraged, although leverage differs greatly among them. For instance, the majority of the investment funds that are an important part of this sector are of the open-ended type and do not face a problem of leverage, but can become vulnerable because of the degree of maturity transformation they create. In addition, many of the open-ended funds offered by asset management firms, such as exchange-traded funds (ETFs), in essence provide a promise of daily liquidity that they may not be able to deliver under stressed conditions. These are just some examples of the new task of macro-prudential supervision regarding the transformation of the financial system by the unavoidable expansion of the new market-based credit system, also known as "shadow banking".[9]

[9] See Vítor Constâncio, speech "Beyond traditional banking: a new credit system coming out of the shadows" at the 2nd Frankfurt Conference on Financial Market Policy: Banking Beyond Banks, organised by the SAFE Policy Center at Goethe University, Frankfurt, 17 October 2014.

Challenges ahead – integrating academic research into regulatory implementation

As described above, the regulatory framework on both sides of the Atlantic has become more robust since the beginning of the crisis. These positive changes build upon the current state of academic research. Yet, to ensure financial stability in an ever-changing financial landscape, existing regulatory concepts need to be adapted and new issues addressed. This requires continuous improvements in our understanding of the regulatory mechanisms and of the incentives they shape. The interaction of regulation and academic research will therefore remain vitally important for both sides and, ultimately, for the appropriate development of effective financial policy.

A case in point is the field of macro-prudential policy, where central bankers are currently pioneering in unchartered territories. The academic literature has made enormous steps in developing the framework to assess macro-prudential instruments, but the toolkit is still incomplete. Researchers can help policy makers understand what tools to implement and activate, and into which directions to extend.

Some questions concerning regulation drill more deeply into fundamental issues in our economies. The ability of the financial sector to extract excess rents from its clients has often been seen as one of the drivers for excessive risk-taking and risk correlation. It would benefit consumers and increase the stability of the system if this rent extraction was curtailed. This will involve striking a balance between ensuring sufficient competition to reduce overall rents within the banking sector, setting appropriate incentives to reward useful innovations, and ensuring that incentives for prudent risk-taking remain in place. In addition, as Luigi Guiso illustrates in Chapter 13, risk appetite may vary over time, independently from changes in regulation. The co-operation of academic researchers, policy makers, and regulatory practitioners is well-placed to develop such frameworks.

Vítor Constâncio[10]

[10] Vice-President of the European Central Bank.

EDITORS' PREFACE

November 1, 2014: this is the date on which the European banking union entered into force with its first pillar, the SSM. This step bears two important meanings. First, it epitomises the response of European regulators and policy makers to the wave of financial crises that started in 2007–2008. Second, it represents an irrevocable step towards European integration. By setting a level playing field for all banks in Europe, it is intended to foster fairness and competition, and to eliminate the scope for strategic interaction among uncoordinated national supervisors witnessed so far. This book embarks on an assessment of the current state and future prospects of financial regulation on both sides of the Atlantic. The analysis takes a broad view, encompassing banks as well as households in their saving and borrowing activities.

The volume starts by revisiting the logical steps required to move financial regulation from a micro-prudential to a macro-prudential perspective, the necessity of which has been much emphasised following the 2007 crisis, with a view to limiting the scope for further bank panics. A number of chapters are devoted to dissecting actual experiences and crisis events that occurred in Europe, ranging from various debt and banking crises to the experiences gained by the working of bodies such as the European Systemic Risk Board or the Liikanen Group. These analyses draw lessons and conclusions, but also critiques, through the lenses of academic reasoning.

A number of chapters innovate, by blending an economic and a legal perspective when analysing aspects of financial regulation (like banking competition), while others try to envisage how economists and lawyers can work together to design efficient and fair regulations. The book does not neglect interactions between policies: to this purpose, some authors evaluate the delicate role of lender of last resort to complement financial regulation in achieving financial stability.

In its second part, the book sets a pathway for approaching a gaping hole in the current apparatus of European regulation, namely provisions for investors' protection. Indeed, while the Dodd-Frank Act in its Title IX introduces norms and regulations for investors' protection, Europe still features a quite fragmented and insufficient map for regulation of how investors and borrowers can be protected from inappropriate financial products or uninformed usage thereof.

A crucial aspect of the book is that it offers some comparison between the European experience of the financial crisis and subsequent changes in financial regulation and those of other countries, in particular Anglo-Saxon ones. The European regulatory response to the crisis took longer to be completed than that of the United States, where the Dodd-Frank Act was adopted. A good reason for this delay was that it required a massive effort to harmonise the views of different countries on how to deal with capital requirements and resolution mechanisms. In addition, regulators in Europe also had to deal with the perverse nexus that had developed between sovereign and bank risk. On the other hand, the care taken to develop these measures may strengthen their endurance in the future.

While there are differences between the reforms undertaken in Europe and those envisaged, for instance, in the Dodd-Frank Act, there are also many similarities. A strengthening of the capital and liquidity requirements as well as a shift of focus from micro- to macro-prudential regulations are common aspects of regulation in Europe and in the United States. Other similarities emerge in more specific aspects of the financial reforms. One example for this is the design of bail-in clauses. Both Europe and the United States have chosen to design their resolution mechanisms with bail-in clauses that are based on a single point of entry approach (i.e. the parent holding company of large banking groups is responsible for putting up, up-front, enough capital for all foreign activities and branches). In the case of the United States this serves the purpose of limiting the scope of regulatory arbitrage via activities overseas, while in the case of Europe it serves the purpose of limiting the scope of risk-taking in peripheral and more fragile countries.

The last part of the book deals with regulation intended to protect savers and borrowers from mistakes or unsound practices by financial advisors and marketers of financial products. In contrast to the existence of well-developed frameworks for consumer protection against low-quality products and services and against medical malpractice, a sound and comprehensive framework for investor and borrower protection is yet to be developed and widely applied. These aspects, as the ones relating to bank regulation, have very important legal implications, some of which are discussed throughout this volume.

The process of financial regulation in Europe started, and is proceeding, at a good pace. Important milestones have been set and other steps are on the way. For instance, the new SRM Regulation will be applicable from 2016. This book, co-sponsored by the Policy Center of the Research Center SAFE (on a Sustainable Architecture of Finance in Europe) and by the Center for Financial Studies, is the first to address all aspects encompassed by this evolving experience. By placing itself in the middle of this process, it aims to provide useful suggestions, which could be helpful for policy makers in the design of further steps.

ACKNOWLEDGEMENTS

The editors wish to thank the Policy Center team of the Research Center SAFE, and especially Margit Vanberg, for providing invaluable support for our efforts. We further wish to thank all contributors to the workshop we held in Frankfurt in June 2014, which brought together authors, discussants, and editors, to debate first versions of the papers included in this volume. We are especially grateful to Johannes Adolff, Rob Alessie, Tabea Bucher-Koenen, Mathias Dewatripont, Christoph Grigoleit, Reint Gropp, Cornelia Holthausen, Irmfried Schwimann, Helmut Siekmann, and Chiara Zilioli, who acted as discussants of the chapters presented in the volume conference. Research on this volume was supported by the Research Center SAFE and by the Center for Financial Studies.

PART I

Micro- and macro-prudential regulation

1

The road from micro-prudential to macro-prudential regulation

ESTER FAIA AND ISABEL SCHNABEL[1]

Introduction

One of the most important lessons from the 2007–2009 crisis was that micro-prudential regulation and supervision are insufficient to stabilize financial systems. Despite a highly sophisticated micro-prudential framework, the world experienced the most severe crisis since the Great Depression. This showed quite plainly that a focus of regulation on individual intermediaries is not enough to prevent the breakdown of the financial system, and that instead more attention has to be paid to the evolution of systemic risk. Nowadays, both academics and regulators agree that the micro-prudential focus should be complemented by a macro-prudential perspective.

The emergence of the largely micro-prudential Basel framework goes back to the 1980s. After several decades of financial calm with strongly regulated and rather closed economies worldwide after the Second World War, the 1980s and 1990s saw a wave of deregulation in many spheres, including financial markets. At the same time, globalization proceeded rapidly and evoked the need for harmonized financial regulation to create a global "level playing field." This gave rise to the Basel process, which became the global regulatory framework for banking. This framework was largely micro-prudential in nature – it tried to ensure the safety and soundness of individual institutions, putting more emphasis on the goal

[1] Ester Faia is Professor of Monetary and Fiscal Policy at Goethe University Frankfurt, and Isabel Schnabel is Professor of Financial Economics at Johannes Gutenberg University Mainz. The authors would like to thank Carmelo Salleo, Michalis Haliassos, as well as conference participants at the SAFE Workshop on Financial Regulation for useful comments and discussions.

of depositor protection than on system stability. At the same time, there was an overall consensus that financial markets were by and large efficient and that they were capable of selecting stable equilibria in which individual incentives could, in most cases, be disciplined by "the market." The regulator only had the task of limiting the scope of activities for individual intermediaries, in particular by asking for minimum capital holdings.

As the regulatory framework came increasingly under pressure due to regulatory arbitrage and financial innovation, regulation was modified in a stepwise fashion, raising the degree of complexity substantially and trying to capture risks at an ever-increasing granularity (Haldane 2012). The major innovation was the reliance on banks' internal models – first with respect to market risk, then, under Basel II, also with respect to credit risk. The formulation of value-at-risk models was left in the hands of individual intermediaries, the underlying idea being that intermediaries and financial markets were able to elaborate the optimal management of risks by themselves. This approach ignored that banks maximize profits rather than social welfare and that their behavior may entail externalities on the financial system and the real economy that a profit-maximizing bank would not take into account. Hence, the reliance on banks' internal models is inherently micro-prudential.

Consequently, unweighted capital ratios often fell to levels of no more than 2 percent and banks built up substantial off-balance sheet risks in the form of special purpose vehicles investing in structured products, such as mortgage-backed securities, while relying on short-term funding and liquidity guarantees from their sponsors.[2] In the financial crisis, the initial failures of particularly weak banks were magnified by macroeconomic repercussions in the financial system – for example, through fire sale externalities. These amplification mechanisms were not the result of an exogenous shock, but they were caused by banks' endogenous responses to such shocks. Hence, aggregate risk proved to be much more than the sum of individual risk positions.

Although the severity of the crisis, the timing, and the degree of interconnectedness of financial institutions were surprising for many observers, the underlying mechanisms were already well understood long before the crisis. Hellwig (1995) wrote about them as early as 1995. Crocket (2000) started an intensive debate on the importance of the macro-prudential dimension of financial stability at the Bank for

[2] For detailed accounts of the financial crisis, see Brunnermeier (2009) and Hellwig (2009).

International Settlements (BIS), which was continued by Borio (2003) and others. Daníelsson et al. (2001) criticized the Basel II Accord for not taking into account the endogeneity of risk and its inherent procyclicality. However, these criticisms were not taken up by policy makers.

This chapter presents our vision of an appropriate framework for macro-prudential regulation. We proceed by first identifying the transmission channels of aggregate risk, secondly by defining the different dimensions and targets of macro-prudential regulation, and thirdly by outlining the institutional framework implemented in Europe. Finally, we discuss some important issues concerning policy implementation, such as the debate on rules versus discretion and cross-border coordination, as well as possible conflicts or overlaps with other macro-policies, such as monetary policy.

Transmission channels of systemic risk

The financial system is subject to various types of shocks, including idiosyncratic and aggregate shocks. Both types of shocks can lead to systemic stress through various channels (see Figure 1.1 for an illustration). The most basic manifestation of systemic risk is a situation in which an *exogenous aggregate shock* hits many banks at the same time because they are exposed to the same type of risk. For example, the recent crisis was triggered by a sharp drop in real estate prices in the United States. Since many banks were exposed to U.S. mortgages, the price decline generated a loss of values on the asset side of many financial intermediaries at the same time.

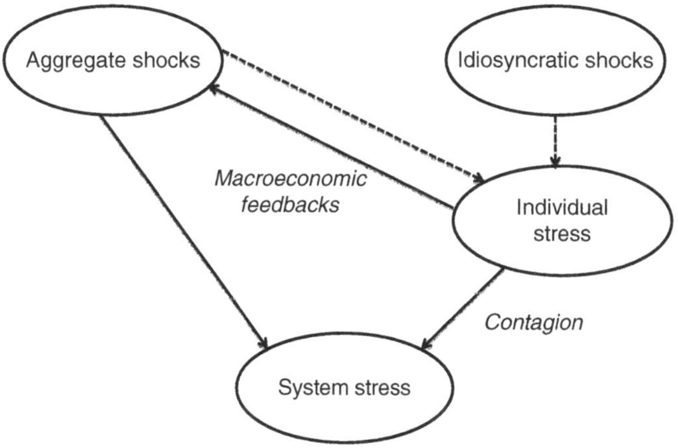

Figure 1.1 Transmission channels of systemic risk

Systemic stress can also arise from *idiosyncratic shocks* if individual stress is transmitted to other financial institutions (*contagion*). Contagion may work through three different channels: information, interconnections among banks, and macroeconomic feedbacks. Information contagion (as in Chen 1999) occurs when the failure of one institution signals the fragilities of other financial institutions. Such effects appear to have played an important role in interbank markets during the crisis.

The second channel works through banks' interconnectedness, such as lending exposures on interbank markets or inter-linkages through CDS and other insurance contracts, which lead to domino effects and default cascades. Consider the case of interbank exposures: as a single bank is hit by an idiosyncratic shock, it may be unable to meet its obligations on the interbank market. The inability of one bank to honor its debt would transmit losses to other banks, which then potentially become insolvent (as in Allen and Gale 2000). This chain of insolvencies is produced by network externalities and can induce widespread defaults even as a result of a shock to a single bank.

The third type of contagion is caused by macroeconomic feedbacks. In this case, individual stress induces banks to adjust their behavior in a way that has repercussions for the macro-economy. These *endogenous* aggregate shocks in turn affect all financial institutions, with the potential of generating vicious cycles between individual stress and the macro-economy. Such cycles may be amplified by regulation, making evident how the prescriptions of micro- and macro-prudential regulation can diverge.

For example, Basel rules prescribe that banks increase their capital or reduce their assets when they incur losses, and capital requirements are binding. Due to risk-weighting, the same reaction is required when asset risk increases, as happens in a recession. The underlying rationale is that banks shall be able to cope with increased potential losses in portfolio values. While such behavior seems prudent from the point of view of the individual intermediary, it might produce disruptive consequences at an aggregate level. Reducing assets in the middle of a recession may induce a credit crunch, exacerbating the downturn (see Angeloni and Faia 2013). A macro-prudential regulator concerned with the stabilization of aggregate credit would therefore prescribe countercyclical capital buffers, such as those featured in the Spanish dynamic provisioning or in the Basel III countercyclical capital buffers.

In the above example, the amplification works through banks' capital positions. Another type of feedback is related to bank liquidity. When a bank suffers an (idiosyncratic) liquidity shock, it may be forced to sell assets in order to produce the liquidity needed to honor its obligations. Again, this seems like a reasonable response from a microeconomic perspective. However, the fire sale may produce a fall in the market price of that asset, especially in times of market distress, leading to liquidity spirals (Brunnermeier and Pedersen 2009). In the presence of mark-to-market accounting procedures, the fall in this asset's price will inflict portfolio losses on all other banks who have invested in the same asset. But even in the absence of mark-to-market accounting it limits other banks' possibilities of generating liquidity by selling assets.[3]

Banks do not take such externalities into account when choosing their capital structure (equity versus debt) or the maturity structure of their debt. This may lead to both excessive leverage and maturity transformation, yielding a rationale for regulation, such as increased capital requirements and the introduction of liquidity requirements under Basel III.

Summing up, systemic stress can be generated either by an exogenous aggregate shock or it can propagate endogenously through bank runs, interconnections, or macroeconomic feedbacks. Micro-prudential regulation has generally neglected the possibility of endogenous self-propagation of risk and its time-varying nature. It traditionally focuses on preventing individual stress (i.e., on the dashed arrows in Figure 1.1). In contrast, macro-prudential regulation concerns contagion effects, exposures to macroeconomic risk at the system level, and macroeconomic feedback effects (as shown by the solid arrows in Figure 1.1).

The two dimensions of macro-prudential regulation

The literature distinguishes between two dimensions of macro-prudential regulation (see Borio 2003): the cross-sectional and the time series dimension. The cross-sectional dimension refers to the varying levels of systemic risk emanating from financial institutions at a given point in time. This dimension captures the strength of contagion effects as described above. The time series dimension is concerned with the evolution of systemic risk over time and is hence closely related to the evolution of macroeconomic prices and quantities (such as credit), caused by exogenous shocks or driven by the endogenous dynamics of

[3] This transmission channel results from a classical pecuniary externality. Such externalities cause distortions only in the presence of other frictions (see Hanson et al. 2011).

the financial system. Macro-prudential regulators have to be concerned with both dimensions if they want to limit systemic risk.

Appropriate definition of the policy objective, as well as instruments, is surely one of the most important aspects of macro-prudential regulation. The two dimensions manifest themselves in different objectives and instruments, some of which will be outlined in the following sections.[4] Objectives will capture the cost of aggregate externalities to be minimized: this goes beyond the mere aggregation of individual risk, capturing the endogenous risk propagation mentioned above. An obvious challenge is the measurement of such propagation mechanisms. In contrast to objectives, which may apply at the aggregate level, instruments (such as capital or liquidity requirements) should be bank-specific: due to bank heterogeneity, aggregate instruments, applied equally to all institutions, are likely to induce distortions.

The cross-sectional dimension of macro-prudential regulation

The central idea of the cross-sectional dimension is that macro-prudential regulation should be calibrated in a way that captures individual contributions to systemic risk. This necessarily implies that systemic banks should be regulated more strictly than non-systemic banks. This is a departure from traditional (micro-prudential) regulatory practices, stressing the importance of a level playing field (although the playing field was not so level after all, given implicit bail-out guarantees). An example under Basel III is the capital surcharge for systemically important financial institutions (SIFIs).

In order to measure systemic risk, supervisors may either use an indicator approach or a quantitative measure based on banks' return distributions. In the more common indicator approach, banks are categorized according to different determinants of systemic relevance. The most frequently used criterion is bank size, which is easy to measure and is seen as a proxy for many other determinants of systemic relevance.

A second criterion is interconnectedness. Theory-based measures of interconnectedness try to capture externalities within network models. While taking into account the role of interconnections, such measures are also able to identify systemically important institutions or key spreaders of risk. In this context there is a distinction between static ex-ante

[4] An extensive discussion of macro-prudential instruments is beyond the scope of this chapter.

measures versus dynamic ex-post measures. Ex-ante metrics include network centrality or input–output metrics. Centrality indices, which were first developed in graph theory, produce rankings that identify the most important nodes. The variety of centrality measures is identified by the way importance is defined. The idea behind input–output metrics is as follows: if a bank is hit by a shock, it will transmit it to the rest of the system according to the coefficient of the input–output matrix, which in a banking context represents a transformation of the interbank exposure matrix. One advantage, compared to centrality measures, is that systemically important banks emerge also in more sparse systems, which do not necessarily feature a vertex to which many banks are connected. Both centrality and input–output metrics are by their nature static as the matrix of connections is taken at a certain point in time: they can only signal the critical nodes, i.e., those institutions that are potential spreaders of risk. However, they lack predictive power as they do not indicate how risk can spread within the system.

A second type of measure is represented by the Shapley value and other measures borrowed from the literature on cooperative game theory. Given a multivariate distribution of shocks across banks, those metrics capture the contribution of each bank to the diffusion of risk by considering all possible permutations in which the same bank enters the network matrix. Those metrics capture the ex-post diffusion of risk as they indicate the contribution of each bank to total losses in the system after the shock has been spread across the network. Due to their dynamic nature they are more apt for use in crisis management. Although such network measures are well-developed theoretically, their use is often hampered by a lack of data. At the current stage, their practical application is therefore limited.

As an alternative to the indicator approach, a number of measures have been developed to capture the systemic risk of financial institutions on the basis of joint return distributions. Examples are the change in the conditional value at risk (ΔCoVaR) developed by Adrian and Brunnermeier (2011), the marginal expected short-fall (MES) by Acharya et al. (2012), the capital short-fall (SRisk) by Brownlees and Engle (2012), and the change in the conditional joint probability of default (ΔCoJPoD) developed by Radev (2012). All such measures try to capture tail risk conditional on some distress event.

Their main advantage is that they are based on data that is readily available for publicly traded firms. In Europe, many banks are not traded, which limits the usefulness of these measures. Moreover, the measures rely on the assumption that market prices have some predictive power of distress. However, as was seen before the recent crisis, markets tend to understate risks in boom times. Furthermore, the different measures of systemic risk yield widely varying results regarding the systemic relevance of different financial institutions. Hence, further research is needed in this area. The most problematic issue is the strong pro-cyclicality of such measures. For example, ΔCoVaR rose dramatically over the course of the financial crisis (see Barth and Schnabel 2013). Hence, linking capital requirements to this type of variable would introduce an additional pro-cyclical element into financial regulation. Thus, the cross-sectional and the time series dimension may be contradictory. This speaks for using through-the-cycle concepts, which are purged from cyclical factors, to capture the cross-sectional aspect of systemic risk.

The goals of macro-prudential regulation would be to make systemic banks safer, to make it less attractive for financial institutions to become systemic, and to reduce the competitive distortions caused by implicit government guarantees for systemic banks. In order to achieve these goals, various regulatory instruments can be linked to the described systemic risk measures, including capital and liquidity requirements or bank taxes. In order to achieve the desired incentive effects, it is crucial to link regulation to a bank's contribution to systemic risk rather than burdening all institutions to a similar degree. This suggests, for example, that banks' contribution to the Single Resolution Fund should be calibrated to banks' systemic risk.

In addition, changes in the financial infrastructure can help to reduce contagion effects and remove distorted incentives from implicit government guarantees. Important examples are the introduction of central counterparties (CCPs) for derivatives trading and the implementation of bank resolution procedures, as envisaged in the Single Resolution Mechanism (SRM) of the European Banking Union. Disclosure requirements can also be useful – for example, concerning the interconnectedness in interbank markets.

The time series dimension of macro-prudential regulation

The time series dimension of macro-prudential regulation focuses on two objectives: dampening the financial cycle, and preventing the emergence of bubbles in certain market segments.

In order to dampen the financial cycle, macro-prudential regulation should be adjusted over time to the evolution of macroeconomic aggregates such as total credit. The main goal is to mitigate financial accelerators inherent in the financial system (Bernanke and Gertler 1989) as well as the pro-cyclicality of traditional capital regulation, and thereby reduce the macroeconomic feedback effects from banks' deleveraging. The underlying dilemma of capital regulation is that regulatory capital is not a buffer for the bank itself because it must not be used to absorb losses if the bank wants to continue its operations.

Deleveraging is particularly strong under risk-based capital regulation (as risk weights tend to increase in a recession) and when capital requirements are low (Admati et al. 2013, Admati and Hellwig 2013). To give a simple example, consider a bank with a capital ratio of 5 percent. If such a bank incurs a loss and cannot raise additional capital, it has to reduce its assets by a factor of 20 to keep its leverage constant. If the capital ratio were 20 percent, the factor would be just 5. Hence, the most obvious macro-prudential instrument is a tightening of Basel capital ratios, which at the same time makes systemic banks more resilient (dealing with the cross-sectional dimension) and mitigates pro-cyclicality. Another useful instrument is a non-risk-weighted capital ratio, a leverage ratio. In contrast to risk-based capital ratios, the leverage ratio is not subject to a manipulation of risk weights assigned to different asset classes as it is defined in relation to total assets. This reduces the scope of financial institutions to lower capital requirements by fine-tuning their internal models and hence tackles the problem of a shrinking capital base, as observed especially for large, systemic banks before the crisis. At the same time, it removes a further pro-cyclical element of capital regulation by avoiding rising capital requirements in times of rising risks. Hence, a leverage ratio seems particularly useful from a macro-prudential perspective.

Deleveraging can also be reduced by introducing countercyclical capital buffers, as prescribed under Basel III, building up additional capital buffers in good times and allowing banks to draw them down in bad times. In theory, this has two effects: It raises the additional absorption capacity in a crisis, and hence lowers the need for deleveraging. But, even more importantly, it dampens the boom by requiring higher capital in good times and thereby limiting the excessive build-up of risk. However, the true effectiveness of countercyclical buffers is uncertain. Countercyclical buffers can be ineffective if markets require higher capital in crisis times and do not allow banks to draw down their buffers. Similarly, the buffers may not be able to limit the expansion of credit in good times if credit is substituted from other sources, be it from other countries or from outside the banking sector (see Jiménez et al. 2012 on the Spanish experience). Moreover, the successful implementation of such buffers relies on the correct timing. If the financial cycle is measured imprecisely, the buffers may easily turn out to be pro- rather than countercyclical.

Therefore, the definition of the policy target is key in order to properly implement a macro-prudential policy. An appropriate target should satisfy the following requirements. First, it should have a time-varying component that allows the policy-maker to predict the insurgence of a financial crisis. Second, it should be apt to detect the asymmetric distribution of risk across heterogeneous intermediaries and its diffusion among interconnected intermediaries.

The simplest possible objective is aggregate credit or leverage. In periods of sustained growth, credit and leverage expand. While this may raise aggregate investment, it may also induce intermediaries to take up more risk, thereby increasing the likelihood of financial instability. It would therefore seem appropriate for the prudential regulator to target a threshold for aggregate credit (or leverage) beyond which the risk of financial crisis becomes very high. However, the predictive power of simple credit and leverage aggregates may be questioned because they are by their nature backward-looking. Therefore, they can only signal the possibility of exaggerations whenever some pre-defined thresholds are reached. The regulator, however, needs metrics with high predictive power.

Several alternatives have been conceived. First, one possibility would be to monitor the evolution of CDS spreads. Under the hypothesis that markets can track risk efficiently, CDS spreads could potentially have predictive power. Second, one could monitor statistical indicators of default (Segoviano and Goodhart 2009), similar to those discussed above. Such statistical indicators could quantify the probability that several institutions default jointly and should be able to account properly for rare events (using quantile analysis based on the tails of the distribution). It has indeed been established that prior to the 2007 crisis the statistical indicators of defaults based on joint metrics or on tail risk would have assigned a much higher probability to the insurgence of the financial crisis than the standard statistical indicators used up to that point (IMF 2009). Of course, the reliability of all statistical indicators is hampered by Goodhart's Law, stating that any indicator may become useless once it is used for regulatory purposes.

Simple aggregate criteria work best as long as there are no significant differences among intermediaries and sectors. However, there is a high degree of heterogeneity within the banking sector. Hence, an aggregate capital, leverage, or liquidity requirement might indeed be appropriate for intermediaries that are excessively exposed to risk, but might impair the activity of intermediaries that are well capitalized, have low leverage, and are less exposed to risky investments. Systemic risk metrics therefore have to be more sophisticated to also capture the cross-sectional component.

Besides the dampening of the financial cycle, a second objective is the prevention of bubbles in financial markets. There is a long-standing debate on whether asset price bubbles should be tackled by monetary policy by "leaning against the wind" when a bubble emerges, as promoted strongly by the BIS (Borio and Lowe 2002, White 2004, Cecchetti 2005). The Fed's declared policy of "cleaning up the mess" – which means mitigating the consequences of bursting bubbles rather than preventing asset price bubbles when they emerge (Greenspan 1999, 2002) – received a hit by the financial crisis, which showed quite plainly how costly such a policy can be, especially when the financial system is involved. Therefore, the debate is now less focused on whether any action should be taken, and more on who should take it – monetary policy makers or (macro-prudential) financial regulators.[5] Sectoral capital requirements or loan-level restrictions (such as loan-to-value or margining requirements) are macro-prudential alternatives to central bank interventions in the form of changing interest rates or reserve requirements.

Brunnermeier and Schnabel (2015) analyze a number of historical bubbles, putting particular emphasis on the observed policy responses. No particular instrument appears to be dominant in dealing with asset price bubbles. While monetary policy instruments are less focused, they are more likely to reach all parts of the financial system. Macro-prudential instruments are more targeted, but are subject to regulatory arbitrage. Moreover, the appropriate timing is shown to be essential. Late interventions are shown to be ineffective or even harmful, which stresses the need for a continuous macro-prudential oversight trying to detect asset price bubbles early on.

Institutional framework and the supervisory mechanism in Europe

The design of the new institutional framework of supervisory policy in Europe has proceeded through subsequent steps. In each of those steps

[5] See, however, Gali (2014) and Gali and Gambetti (2014), who argue that tight monetary policy may even foster asset price bubbles.

different authorities have been established, and their tasks and scope of actions have become partly overlapping and partly conflicting. The advent of the Single Supervisory Mechanism in Europe calls for a reflection upon the appropriate number of institutions that shall be involved in the various aspects of the supervisory policy, on the scope and the extent of their roles and mandates, and on the degree of coordination of regulatory measures across different countries. In the following, we will outline the major actors concerned with macro-prudential supervision in Europe.[6]

At the level of the European Union, the major institution responsible for macro-prudential supervision is the European Systemic Risk Board (ESRB). It is complemented by macro-prudential supervisors at the national level. In addition, under the Single Supervisory Mechanism, the European Central Bank has been assigned substantial power in macro-prudential supervision for all banks located in the Euro Area. Finally, national micro-prudential supervisory authorities are also actors in macro-prudential supervision as most macro-prudential instruments have to be implemented at the bank level.

The ESRB is part of the European System of Financial Supervision (ESFS) that was established on January 1, 2011, following the recommendation from the de Larosière report. According to the ESRB regulation (Regulation (EU) No. 1092/2010, Article 3(1)), it

> shall be responsible for the macro-prudential oversight of the financial system within the Union in order to contribute to the prevention or mitigation of systemic risks to financial stability in the Union that arise from developments within the financial system and taking into account macroeconomic developments, so as to avoid periods of widespread financial distress. It shall contribute to the smooth functioning of the internal market and thereby ensure a sustainable contribution of the financial sector to economic growth.

Its most important task is the identification of systemic risks. If such risks are detected, the ESRB may issue warnings as well as recommendations for remedial action, which are subject to a comply-or-explain mechanism.

In contrast to the three European Supervisory Authorities (ESAs), the ESRB is not restricted to the oversight of a particular sector, but it is responsible for banks, insurance companies, and financial markets. It is

[6] This section is based on Gurlit and Schnabel (2014).

also not restricted to the Euro Area – it is responsible for the entire European Union. The major decision body is the General Council, consisting mostly of central bankers from the ECB and the national central banks as well as national supervisors (the latter without voting power). The General Council does not include members from the national ministries of finance. The ESRB has defined four intermediate objectives in order to achieve its overall goal of safeguarding the stability of the financial sector (see ESRB 2014): (1) credit growth and leverage, (2) maturity mismatch and market illiquidity, (3) exposure concentrations, and (4) moral hazard from implicit government guarantees.

In January 2012, the ESRB published a recommendation concerning the design of macro-prudential supervisory structures at the national level. Since then, many European countries have implemented new supervisory structures for macro-prudential supervision. As the ESRB does not have any power to use macro-prudential instruments directly, implementation at the national level is key. Therefore, the ESRB issued five "guiding principles" on how to design the macro-prudential mandate at the national level: (1) an unambiguous mandate for system stability, including all components of the financial sector; (2) a leading role for the central bank and coordination among all institutions responsible for financial stability; (3) access to information and appropriate policy tools; (4) transparency and accountability; and (5) independence from the financial industry as well as from politics.

In practice, the chosen structures for macro-prudential supervision vary widely across EU countries (see Posch and Van der Molen 2012). In most cases, the macro-prudential mandate was given to special committees or councils consisting of representatives from central banks, supervisory authorities, and the ministries of finance or economics. The weight of political representatives differs widely across countries. While in countries such as Germany and France, the councils are chaired by politicians, their role is much smaller in other countries, such as the United Kingdom. In Belgium, the central bank is itself fully responsible for macro-prudential supervision.

A third actor in macro-prudential supervision in the Euro Area is the European Central Bank, which has responsibilities in macro-prudential supervision in the context of the Single Supervisory Mechanism. Whereas the ESRB can only issue warnings and recommendations, the European Central Bank was assigned formal decision power. Article 5 of the SSM Council Regulation (Council Regulation (EU) No. 1024/2013) states that:

> 2. The ECB may, if deemed necessary, instead of the national competent authorities or national designated authorities of the participating Member State, apply higher requirements for capital buffers than applied by the national competent authorities or national designated authorities of participating Member States to be held by credit institutions . . . and apply more stringent measures aimed at addressing systemic or macroprudential risks at the level of credit institutions . . . 4. Where the ECB intends to act in accordance with paragraph 2, it shall cooperate closely with the national designated authorities in the Member States concerned.

This implies that the ECB may in effect overrule national decisions regarding macro-prudential supervision, as long as it wants to implement stricter rules than the national macro-prudential authority. Interestingly, this provision refers to all financial institutions while direct (micro-prudential) supervision by the ECB is limited to significant institutions.

The new institutional structure raises a number of issues. The large number of actors is problematic due to overlapping responsibilities, potentially giving rise to turf wars. This is all the more problematic as objectives may differ substantially, e.g., regarding a national versus international perspective, a micro- versus macro-prudential view, or the goals of financial versus monetary stability. In the following section, we discuss some particular challenges regarding the implementation of macro-prudential supervision in Europe.

Policy implementation

When implementing macro-prudential regulation, one has to tackle the typical problems inherent in macroeconomic policy, such as the debate on rules versus discretion, commitment, and policy coordination with other macroeconomic policies and across countries.

Rules versus discretion and the Lucas critique

Like any type of macroeconomic policy, prudential regulation must take into account the role of agents' expectations. According to the Lucas critique, it is not possible to predict the effect of any macro-policy based on given historical relations of economic behavior. Any policy analysis should therefore take into account how rules interact with agents' behavior and with their expectation formation process. The same type of critique applies to macro-prudential policy. Consider, for instance, the role of taxes on returns of specific assets: if agents expect that the policymaker will tax returns on those assets, they will try to undo the effect of those policies simply by reshuffling their portfolios. This dynamic dimension of the game-theoretic interaction between policy makers and economic agents was largely missing from the analysis of micro-prudential regulation and should instead become a crucial aspect of financial regulation.

An important aspect concerning the interaction between policy and agents' behavior is the role of policy commitment. As it happens for monetary policy, prudential policy should try to establish credibility with respect to ex-post interventions. This issue is particularly topical in the design of the resolution framework within the European Banking Union. As systemic defaults materialize, the regulator might be tempted to put in place widespread safety nets: those measures would in fact ignite moral hazard and undermine the credibility that the regulator will in the future enforce strict prudential rules. As for any macroeconomic policy, there is effectively a tension between the flexibility needed to face unexpected events and the application of automatic rules that reduce regulators' discretion.

The role of commitment is particularly important in the design of prudential regulation as this area is very sensitive to the calls of interest groups. Political economy problems are more likely to arise in contexts where powerful lobbies, such as the financial ones, can exert strong political pressures.

A particular issue in macro-prudential supervision is the danger of an "inaction bias." Since the success of macro-prudential policies materializes only over the long run – whereas the costs of macro-prudential measures are felt continuously – such measures are politically unpopular. This may prevent them from being implemented, especially in pre-election years. One way to avoid the inaction bias would be strict implementation rules. However, as was described above, there is too much uncertainty about systemic risk measures to implement a strict rule-based approach. Therefore, Posch and Van der Molen (2012) recommend an approach of "guided discretion," which means that supervisory authorities exercise their judgment on the basis of declared principles. The hope is that supervisors are at least mildly bound by these declared principles, which may mitigate the inaction bias.

Cross-country policy coordination

Another important aspect, which is peculiar to prudential regulation as a macro-policy, is cross-country policy coordination. Particularly in the context of high financial integration, the efficacy of macro-prudential regulation can be hampered by the possibility of cross-border arbitrage. Consider the application of capital requirements to domestic banks. As long as foreign banks are not subject to the same prudential requirements, they may counteract measures aimed at reducing aggregate credit by expanding credit to domestic firms or households. A similar reasoning applies to other types of market regulations, such as bank levies or systemic risk charges. It is therefore crucial that prudential policies are coordinated across different countries as it happens with other types of macroeconomic policies. Such coordination ensures a level playing field among domestic and foreign banks. In fact, exposures to a specific country should be subject to the same regulatory requirements independent of a bank's home country. At the European level, the cross-border coordination problem has partly been tackled under CRD IV by introducing a "reciprocity" principle with respect to countercyclical capital buffers.

Overlaps or conflicts with other macro-policies

A discussion on the optimal design of macro-prudential policy cannot neglect the possibility of overlaps or conflicts with other types of macro-policies. In the case of macro-prudential policies the most immediate overlap or conflict might occur with monetary policy (see Haldane 2013). This is particularly so since recently – albeit not explicitly – an important role has been assigned to financial stability as an additional objective for monetary policy, beyond the objective of price stability (and possibly employment).

Three considerations arise in this context. First, if monetary policy rules included the stabilization of credit and asset prices among their targets, there would be a reduced role for macro-prudential policies targeting credit aggregates and leverage ratios.

Secondly, certain types of monetary policy might increase systemic risk and therefore enter into conflict with macro-prudential objectives. Financial crises are mostly followed by recessions, which can be protracted, as happened after the 2007 crisis. In this context, a monetary authority concerned also with the unemployment stabilization objective might need to undertake expansionary actions, such as lowering interest rates and/or injecting liquidity. Those actions feature a typical trade-off: while they reduce the danger of systemic default by improving intermediaries' ability to honor debts, they also ignite risk-taking in the form of search-for-yield behavior and hence may give rise to asset price bubbles in some market segments, thereby requiring stricter prudential regulations in the future. Similarly, it has been argued that prior to 2007 expansionary monetary policy had played an important role in generating the build-up of risk, which culminated in the financial crisis.

Lastly, the design of macro-prudential policies requires an appropriate set-up with regard to the mandate, accountability, and independence from the monetary authority. On the one hand, the choice taken in many countries has been that of giving central banks a leading role in macro-prudential policies. This is also the case in the European Union. This choice may be advantageous since the monetary authority possesses extensive and immediate information on financial markets and financial variables, which facilitates the task of monitoring, as well as independence, which also reduces political interference in macro-prudential policy. However, as mentioned above, macro-prudential supervision can at times conflict with the mandate of monetary policy, which may harm the credibility and transparency of monetary policy and reduce accountability by adding a much more blurred objective. It is necessary to strike the optimal balance between the benefits of acquiring easy access to information and the detrimental effects arising from the overlap of two conflicting mandates, potential reputational spillovers, and an overburdened central bank.

Conclusion

The 2007–2009 financial crisis has led to a reorientation of financial regulation and supervision toward a macro-prudential perspective, which is now being implemented under the new European institutional structure, consisting of the ESRB, national micro- and macro-prudential authorities, and the European Central Bank. The main rationale behind the adoption of macro-prudential policies on top of and beyond the micro-prudential ones lies in the existence of collective externalities. The latter can be triggered by common risk exposures of banks, which tend to amplify the correlation of risk in crisis times, by contagion effects among financial institutions, and by macroeconomic feedback effects through lending or fire sales. In some cases, externalities can also result from the interactions of individual behavior and policy actions, as is the case when banks increase their risk-taking behavior in response to low policy rates or when pro-cyclical lending is amplified by capital regulation.

Macro-prudential regulation is distinguished along the cross-sectional and time series dimensions. While both dimensions are important, at times they might provide conflicting prescriptions and require a multifaceted definition of objectives and instruments. Finally, macro-prudential policy differs from its micro-prudential counterpart in that it has to tackle the typical problems inherent in macroeconomic policy, related to the debate on rules versus discretion, commitment, and coordination with other macro-policies as well as across countries. Our chapter has left unexplored the important role of bank resolution mechanisms in mitigating the problem of banks being too systemic to fail. The design of such mechanisms, including functioning bail-in rules, will be one of the greatest challenges for the upcoming years.

References

Acharya, Viral V., Lasse H. Pedersen, Thomas Philippon, and Matthew P. Richardson (2012). "Measuring systemic risk." *CEPR Discussion Paper* 8824.

Admati, Anat and Martin Hellwig (2013). *The bankers' new clothes.* Princeton University Press.

Admati, Anat R., Peter M. DeMarzo, Martin F. Hellwig, and Paul C. Pfleiderer (2013). "Fallacies, irrelevant facts, and myths in the discussion of capital regulation: Why bank equity is not expensive." *Max Planck Institute for Research on Collective Goods* 2013/23.

Adrian, Tobias and Markus K. Brunnermeier (2011). "CoVaR." *NBER Working Paper* 17454.

Allen, Franklin and Douglas Gale (2000). "Financial contagion." *Journal of Political Economy* 108(1): 1–33.

Angeloni, Ignazio and Ester Faia (2013). "Capital regulation and monetary policy with fragile banks." *Journal of Monetary Economics* 60(3): 311–324.

Barth, Andreas and Isabel Schnabel (2013). "Why banks are not too big to fail – evidence from the CDS market." *Economic Policy* 28(74): 335–369.

Bernanke, Ben S. and Mark Gertler (1989). "Agency costs, net worth, and business fluctuations." *American Economic Review* 79(1): 14–31.

Borio, Claudio (2003). "Towards a macroprudential framework for financial supervision and regulation?" *BIS Working Paper* 128.

Borio, Claudio and Philip Lowe (2002). "Asset prices, financial and monetary stability: Exploring the nexus." *BIS Working Paper* 114.

Brownlees, C. and R. Engle (2012). "Volatility, correlation and tails for systemic risk management." *Working Paper*, Available at SSRN: http://ssrn.com/abstract=1611229.

Brunnermeier, Markus K. (2009). "Deciphering the liquidity and credit crunch 2007–2008." *Journal of Economic Perspectives* 23(1): 77–100.

Brunnermeier, Markus K. and Isabel Schnabel (2015). "Bubbles and central banks: Historical Perspectives." *CEPR Discussion Paper 10528.*

Brunnermeier, Markus K. and Lasse H. Pedersen (2009). "Market liquidity and funding liquidity." *The Review of Financial Studies* 22(6): 2201–2238.

Cecchetti, Stephen G. (2005). "The brave new world of central banking: The policy challenges posed by asset price booms and busts." *Czech National Bank Working Paper Series* 14.

Chen, Yehning (1999). "Banking panics: The role of the first-come, first served rule and information externalities." *Journal of Political Economy* 107: 946–968.

Crocket, Andrew (2000). "Marrying the micro- and macro-prudential dimensions of financial stability." *BIS Speech*, 21 September.

Daníelsson, Jón, Paul Embrechts, Charles Goodhart, Con Keating, Felix Muennich, Olivier Renault, and Hyun Song Shin (2001). "An academic response to Basel II." *FMG Special Paper* 130.

European Systemic Risk Board (ESRB) (2014). *The ESRB Handbook on Operationalising Macro-Prudential Policy in the Banking Sector.* Available at: www.esrb.europa.eu/pub/html/index.en.html.

Gali, Jordi (2014). "Monetary policy and rational asset price bubbles." *American Economic Review* 104(3): 721–752.

Gali, Jordi and Luca Gambetti (2014). "The effects of monetary policy on stock market bubbles: Some evidence." *NBER Working Paper* 19981.

Greenspan, Alan (1999). *Testimony of Chairman Alan Greenspan before the Committee on Banking and Financial Services.* U.S. House of Representatives, July 22.

Greenspan, Alan (2002). "Economic volatility." *Speech at a symposium sponsored by the Federal Reserve Bank of Kansas City*, Jackson Hole, Wyoming, August 30.

Gurlit, Elke and Isabel Schnabel (2014). "Makroprudentielle Bankenaufsicht." *Unpublished working paper.*

Haldane, Andy (2012). "The dog and the frisbee." *Paper presented at the Federal Reserve Bank of Kansas City*, 366th Economic Policy Symposium Jackson Hole Wyoming.

Haldane, Andy (2013). "Macroprudential policies. When and how to use them." *IMF Rethinking Macro Policy II Conference, First Steps and Early Lessons*, April 16–17.

Hanson, Samuel G., Anil K. Kashyap, and Jeremy C. Stein (2011). "A macroprudential approach to financial regulation." *Journal of Economic Perspectives* 25(1): 3–28.

Hellwig, Martin F. (1995). "Systemic aspects of risk management in banking and finance." *Schweizerische Zeitschrift für Volkswirtschaft und Statistik* 131(IV): 723–737.

Hellwig, Martin F. (2009). "Systemic risk in the financial sector: An analysis of the subprime-mortgage financial crisis." *De Economist* 157: 129–207.

International Monetary Fund (IMF) (2009). *Global financial stability report. Assessing the systemic implications of financial linkages.* Washington, DC.

Jiménez, Gabriel, Steven Ongena, José-Luis Peydró, and Jesús Saurina (2012). "Macroprudential policy, countercyclical bank capital buffers and credit supply: Evidence from the Spanish dynamic provisioning experiments." *National Bank of Belgium Working Paper* 231.

Posch, Michaela and Remco Van der Molen (2012). "The macro-prudential mandate of national authorities." *Macro-prudential Commentaries* 2, European Systemic Risk Board (ESRB).

Radev, Deyan (2012). "Systemic risk and sovereign debt in the euro area." *Working Paper*, Gutenberg School of Management and Economics Discussion Paper 1207, Johannes Gutenberg University Mainz.

Segoviano, M. and Charles Goodhart (2009). "Banking stability measures." *International Monetary Fund Working Paper* 09/04.

White, William R. (2004). "Making macroprudential concerns operational." *Speech delivered at a Financial Stability Symposium organised by the Netherlands Bank in Amsterdam* on October 25–26, 2004.

2

Lessons from the European financial crisis

MARCO PAGANO[1]

"Every cloud has a silver lining": just as going through a serious illness may vividly impress on us the need for a healthier lifestyle, there is nothing like the frightening turbulence and the social costs of a financial crisis to focus our minds on the flaws of financial regulation and supervision that triggered it, and on the need for financial reform. This chapter is precisely such a stock-taking exercise: it attempts to identify some of the regulatory failures that contributed to the severity of the euro debt crisis of 2009–12, and to suggest how such failures might be remedied or assess whether ongoing reforms are moving in the right direction and are likely to go far enough.

Without making any claim to completeness, this chapter focuses on three main features of the 2009–12 euro debt crisis, and traces the roots of each to flaws in European financial regulation. The first section ("Bank-sovereign feedback loop and regulation of banks' sovereign exposures") highlights the key role that sovereign debt exposures of banks have played in the feedback loop between bank and fiscal distress, and inquires how the regulation of banks' sovereign exposures in the euro area could be

[1] Professor of Economics, University of Naples Federico II, CSEF, EIEF and CEPR. I am grateful to Mathias Dewatripont, Andrew Ellul, Ester Faia, Cornelia Holthausen and participants in the workshop on "Financial Regulation: A Transatlantic Perspective" organised by the Research Center SAFE for their insightful comments and suggestions. The paper draws extensively on material contained in previous co-authored work; specifically, "Bank-sovereign feedback loop and regulation of banks' sovereign exposures" draws on the 2014 article "Systemic Risk, Sovereign Yields and Bank Exposures in the Euro Crisis"; "Bank forbearance, regulatory forbearance and bank resolution" and "Bank leverage and capital requirements" draw on the ESRB Advisory Scientific Committee (ASC) Reports on "Forbearance, resolution and deposit insurance" (No. 1, July 2012) and "Is Europe Overbanked?" (No. 4, June 2014); the third section also draws on an internal ASC note on the 2014 Bank Stress Test. Hence, this paper owes much to all the co-authors of these papers and reports: the members of the ESRB ASC (particularly Viral Acharya, Martin Hellwig and André Sapir), Niccolò Battistini, Sam Langfield and Saverio Simonelli.

changed to mitigate this feedback loop in the future. The second section ("Bank forbearance, regulatory forbearance and bank resolution") explores the relationship between the forbearance of non-performing loans by European banks and the tendency of EU regulators to rescue rather than resolve distressed banks, and asks to what extent the new regulatory framework of the euro-area "banking union" can be expected to mitigate excessive forbearance and facilitate resolution of insolvent banks. The third section ("Bank leverage and capital requirements") argues that basing capital requirements on the ratio of Tier-1 capital to risk-weighted assets created regulatory loopholes that large banks exploited to expand leverage, and that simpler and more robust indicators – such as the leverage ratio – might be a better gauge of banks' capital shortfall.

Bank-sovereign feedback loop and regulation of banks' sovereign exposures

The feedback loop between sovereigns and banks has been the hallmark of the euro-area debt crisis. The sovereign exposures of banks to high-yield, high-risk sovereign debt have contributed to this feedback loop: drops in the price of debt issued by distressed governments lowered the equity value of banks with large exposures to such debt; this threatened their solvency, and induced investors to expect governments to bail them out, which in turn exacerbated stress in sovereign debt markets.

The initial trigger differed across countries. For instance, in Greece the initial trigger was the investors' concern over sovereign solvency in November 2009, when the new government revealed that the fiscal deficit was twice as large as previously believed; this triggered a collapse of Greek debt prices, reflecting concerns of a sovereign default, which in turn led to the distress of Greek banks. Conversely, in Ireland the crisis originated in the banking sector and spilled over to the sovereign debt market, as the government bailed out several Irish banks; by the end of 2010 the spread on Irish sovereign debt rose sharply, and eventually the government lost access to private markets, with spreads over German bunds reaching 600 basis points.

Another feature of the euro-area debt crisis is its international contagion dimension: first, banks were exposed to the sovereign risk of other countries; second, distress from one sovereign lead investors to reassess the risk of other sovereigns. For instance, in March 2010 investors became increasingly concerned that a default by the Greek government would undermine the stability of euro-area banks holding Greek sovereign debt; at the same time, the news from Greece acted as a "wake-up call", leading investors to reassess the credit risk of other euro-area sovereigns with less severe but similar fiscal problems, such as Portugal and Ireland, and even Italy and Spain – the entire so-called "euro-area periphery". This re-pricing of all periphery debt in turn had further repercussions on the solvency of euro-area banks, both because of their direct exposures to periphery sovereigns and because rating downgrades of this debt crippled the euro interbank lending market, for fear that the European Central Bank (ECB) would no longer accept it as collateral from banks.

Indeed, cross-border contagion during the crisis was so strong that it started raising doubts about the very survival of the euro: under the rules of the monetary union, euro-area distressed sovereigns cannot resort to money creation to bail out banks in their jurisdictions (unlike, say, the US and the UK), and therefore investors started fearing that one or more of them would eventually break away from the Economic and Monetary Union (EMU) and restore national currencies. The risk of euro-area breakup and devaluation of periphery countries' future currencies vis-à-vis those of core countries determined a strong co-movement in sovereign yield differentials and CDS sovereign premia (Battistini, Pagano and Simonelli 2014). Media, investors and academics repeatedly voiced concerns about the possible breakup of the EMU. Between late 2010 and 2011 four issues of *The Economist* featured cover illustrations referring to its breakup. In November 2011 the managers of several multinational companies disclosed euro-breakup contingency plans. Between April 2010 and July 2012, Paul Krugman regularly prognosticated the collapse of the euro from his columns in *The New York Times*. At the 2012 World Economic Forum meeting in Davos, Nouriel Roubini predicted that Greece would leave the euro-area in the subsequent 12 months, followed by Portugal, and assessed at 50 per cent the chance that the euro area would break up in the subsequent three to five years. Even ECB President Mario Draghi pointed to the effect of redenomination risk on sovereign yield differentials when he stated in a speech given on 26 July 2012 that "the premia that are being charged on sovereign states borrowings . . . have to do more and more with convertibility, with the risk of convertibility".

Sovereign exposures and bank risk

This brief account highlights the extent to which systemic risk during the crisis was amplified by the exposure of euro-area banks to euro-area sovereigns, and especially by the exposure of banks in the euro-area periphery towards their domestic sovereign. Due to this strong home bias, the price drop of periphery sovereign debt in 2010–12 inflicted severe losses upon the banks in those countries (and, conversely, the post-2012 price recovery of periphery sovereign debt paid them handsome profits).

This is illustrated by the fact that, during the crisis, time-varying correlations between the returns on bank stocks and the returns on the respective country's domestic sovereign debt are associated with the aggregate size of the respective banks' domestic sovereign exposures, scaled by total assets. Figures 2.1 and 2.2 present the resulting evidence, for periphery and for core banks respectively. Each graph in the figures shows two lines. The solid line is the moving correlation between banking sector monthly stock returns and the 10-year domestic sovereign debt return for that country, from January 2001 to May 2011 (both drawn from Datastream). The observation for each date is the correlation computed using the returns for the 24 months centred on that date (the 11 previous months, the current month and the 12 subsequent months). This correlation is measured on the left axis of each graph on a common scale for all countries. The dashed line in each graph plots instead the domestic sovereign debt exposures of the banks in that country from January 2001 to March 2012 (drawn from the Statistical Data Warehouse [SDW] of the ECB). Sovereign exposures are measured on the right axis, again on a common scale for all countries (except Greece), and are scaled by total bank assets.

Figure 2.1 shows that in the euro-area periphery the correlation between bank stock returns and sovereign debt returns is typically negative or zero before 2009, when in this area banks were reducing their domestic sovereign exposures. The correlation turns positive (and statistically significant) in late 2008 in Greece, Ireland, Italy and Portugal, and in 2009 in Spain, and subsequently tends to increase, as banks in these countries increase their domestic sovereign exposures. From June 2010 to May 2011, the correlation between stock and sovereign debt returns becomes on average 37 per cent in Greece, 28 per cent in Ireland, 39 per cent in Italy, 37 per cent in Portugal, and 53 per cent in Spain,[2] all significantly different from zero at the 1 per cent confidence level.

[2] The only instance in which the correlation is positive and large before 2008–09 is in Portugal during 2004, when Portuguese banks' sovereign holdings were still below 2 per cent.

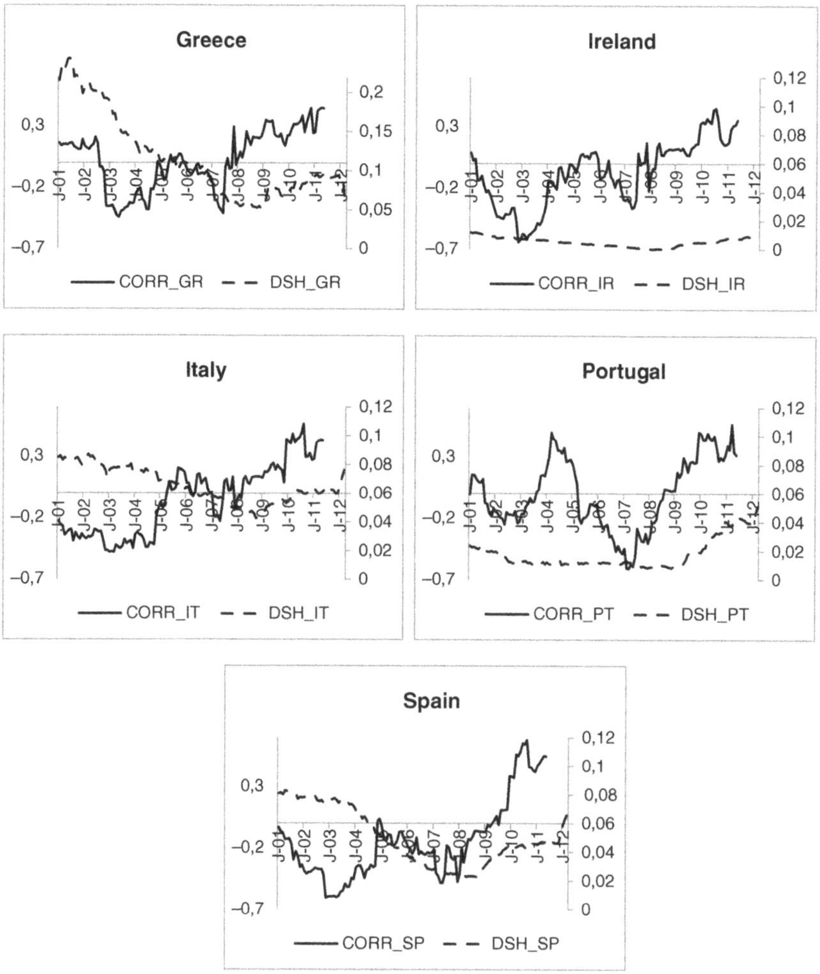

Figure 2.1 Two-year moving correlation between bank sector monthly stock returns and 10-year domestic sovereign debt returns (left axis, 2001–11) and domestic sovereign exposures of banks in the euro-area periphery (right axis, 2001–12)

Figure 2.2 shows that instead the correlation between core-country bank stock returns and core sovereign debt returns is negative or zero throughout the sample period, while the sovereign exposures of core-country banks stay small throughout the sample period, except in Belgium. The only case in which the correlation turns large and positive is Belgium in late 2010 and early 2011, when it is on average 44 per cent between January and April 2011. Interestingly, in this period Belgium is

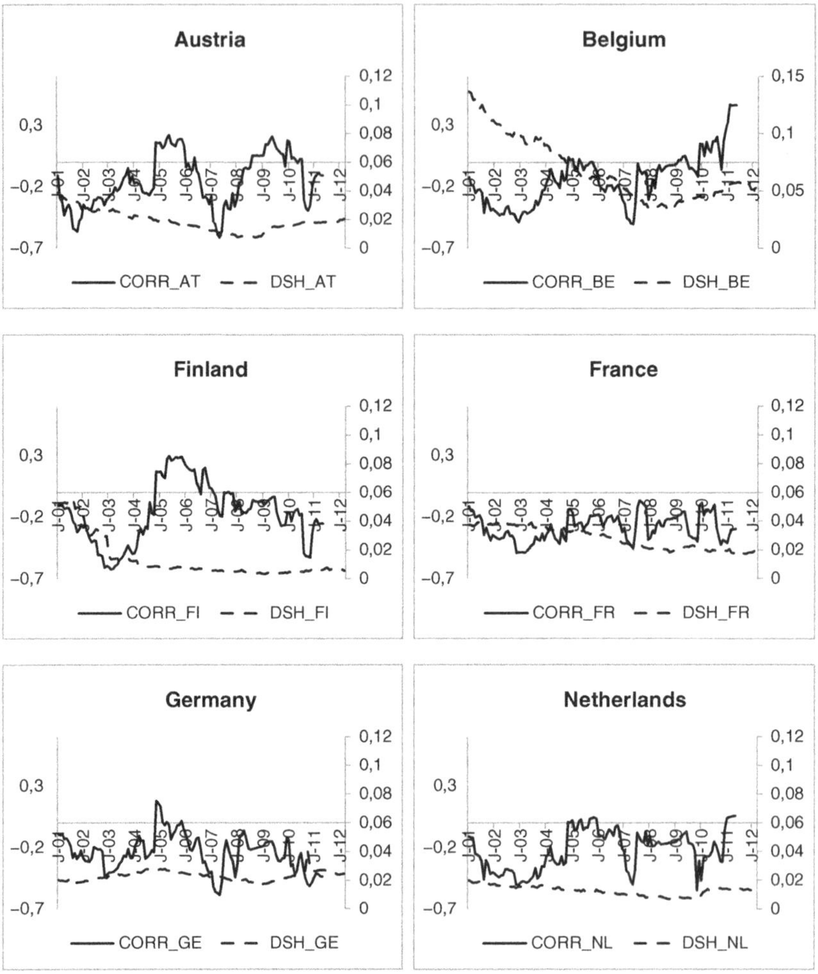

Figure 2.2 Two-year moving correlation between bank sector monthly stock returns and 10-year domestic sovereign debt returns (left axis, 2001–11) and domestic sovereign exposures of banks in the euro-area core (right axis, 2001–12)

the only core country whose banks increase their domestic sovereign exposures above the 5 per cent mark.

This evidence is consistent with the findings of Acharya and Steffen (2015), who find that the factor loadings of bank-level returns on the difference between periphery and core sovereign debt returns are positively correlated with cross-sectional snapshots of sovereign exposures for a sample of 50 publicly listed banks subjected to the stress tests of the

European Banking Authority (EBA) in July 2010, July 2011 and December 2011. More specifically, they find that Greek, Italian and Spanish banks with higher sovereign holdings at the date of the EBA stress test have stock returns that load more heavily on the bond return of their respective sovereign.

Of course, banks' sovereign exposures are not the only factor explaining the correlation between bank and sovereign distress. Other obvious sources of connection are (i) the reliance of banks, especially systemically important ones, on their respective sovereigns as ultimate backstops in case of insolvency, and (ii) the severe recession, especially in the euro-area periphery, which obviously worsened both the performance of banks' loan portfolios and the fiscal position of the corresponding sovereigns. But the evidence shown in Figures 2.1 and 2.2 suggests that banks' domestic sovereign exposures did play a specific role, especially in the countries of the euro-area periphery.

Changes in banks' sovereign exposures and in sovereign yields

Figures 2.1 and 2.2 also show that, at the aggregate level, the domestic sovereign exposures of euro-area banks (shown as the dashed lines) have changed considerably since the inception of the euro: in both groups of countries, they were considerably larger at the inception of the EMU than they are now, but increased again after 2008, and more so in periphery countries than in core ones. Indeed, as argued above, the post-2008 increase in the home bias of banks' sovereign exposures in the euro-area periphery strengthened the impact of sovereign price shocks on their asset values.

Were these changes in the domestic sovereign exposures of banks related to the concomitant changes in sovereign yield differentials? Battistini, Pagano and Simonelli (2014) find that, in general, they were: banks invested more in their home sovereign's debt when its yield increased. They also explore how the changes in domestic exposures responded to two components of yield differentials: a common (or systemic) component, which they interpret as reflecting mainly the risk of euro collapse (i.e., a redenomination risk premium), and a country-specific component, driven mainly by country-level changes in sovereign risk. This decomposition allows them to discriminate to some extent between three different reasons why banks may have changed their domestic sovereign exposures in response to a widening differential between the domestic yield and the euro-area swap rate:

1. Distressed sovereign issuers may exert "moral suasion" on the banks in their jurisdiction to increase their domestic sovereign holdings, in order to support demand for sovereign debt when it is low and thus yields are comparatively high.
2. Undercapitalised banks may bet for resurrection by engaging in "carry trades" whereby they go long on high-risk, high-yield sovereign debt, and fund such exposures either by going short on low-yield debt or by borrowing from the ECB, consistently with the bank-level evidence in Acharya and Steffen (2015) and Drechsler et al. (2013): insofar as most undercapitalised banks are in periphery countries, this may result in a home bias in the sovereign portfolios of periphery-country banks.
3. In the event of a collapse of the euro, bank liabilities in each country would be redenominated into new national currencies, and so would their holdings of domestic sovereign debt. Hence, domestic banks are better hedged than foreign ones against the redenomination risk of domestic sovereign debt: they have a "comparative advantage" in bearing this risk. Thus, banks' home bias should be correlated with the common component of sovereign risk, but not with its purely country-specific component, which instead should equally affect domestic and foreign investors.

All three stories – the "moral suasion", the "carry-trade" and the "comparative advantage" hypothesis – share a common prediction: the home bias in banks' sovereign portfolios should be positively correlated with sovereign yield differentials. However, the first two hypotheses predict that this correlation should arise irrespective of whether changes in yields are generated by country-level or common risk; in contrast, the third predicts that this correlation should arise *only* from changes in common risk – that is, the risk of collapse of the euro. Moreover, since during the crisis sovereign risk and yields increased appreciably only in the euro-area periphery, the first two hypotheses can only apply to periphery-country banks, while the third may also apply to core countries.

As already mentioned, Battistini, Pagano and Simonelli (2014) found that the sovereign exposures of euro-area banks responded positively to increases in yields in most countries – except for in Belgium, France and the Netherlands. But this pattern stems from a very different response of sovereign exposures to the country risk factor in the core and in the periphery:

(i) in most periphery countries, banks respond to increases in the country risk factor by *raising* their domestic exposure, while in core countries they do not;
(ii) in contrast, in almost all countries banks increase their domestic exposures in response to an increase in the common risk factor.

Finding (i) suggests that, for periphery-country banks, and only for those, there is also evidence in support of the "moral suasion" and/or the "carry-trade" hypothesis, since these banks increase their exposures in response to increases in country-level sovereign risk, not just in response to systemic euro-area risk. Periphery banks appear to behave as if they were less risk-averse than other investors, reflecting either government-dictated or opportunistic risk-taking incentives.

Finding (ii) indicates that, when systemic risk increases, most banks – both in core and in periphery countries – increase their domestic sovereign holdings. This suggests that increased risk of euro collapse and currency redenomination has contributed to the increase in the home bias of banks' sovereign portfolios – in core countries being its only determinant.

Implications for the regulation of banks' sovereign exposures

Suppose that finding (i) were to reflect moral suasion by their regulator, concerned by the domestic sovereign's distress. Under this interpretation, regulators themselves prompted banks to increase their domestic sovereign exposures in situations where government solvency was already in danger, thus enhancing the feedback loop between fiscal solvency and bank solvency deterioration. This problem, if present, should be mitigated by the introduction of the Euro Area Banking Union: the ECB acting as "single supervisor" should be more insulated from the pressures of national governments than national prudential supervisors. The rationale for this impending policy change is reinforced by the fact that it has become clear that, when euro-area governments are fiscally distressed, they are no longer the only ultimate backstops of their domestic banks, as illustrated by the contribution of the European Stability Mechanism (ESM) to the recapitalisation of Spanish banks since late 2012: it is then consistent that, ex ante, an euro-area bank supervisor should constrain the bets that euro-area banks can take on the bonds issued by their distressed sovereign.

Finding (i) by Battistini et al. (2014) could also be interpreted as indicating that periphery banks increased their sovereign exposures to search for yield, especially since most of these banks were undercapitalised and could borrow cheaply from the ECB: if successful, their sovereign-debt carry trades would help them to shore up their capital ratios. Indeed, Acharya and Steffen (2015), as well as Buch et al. (2013) provide evidence that banks that were less capitalised and more dependent on wholesale funding invested more in sovereign debt than others. A variant of this carry-trade story, popular among euro-area bankers, goes as follows: "if my sovereign defaults, also my bank does, so I can ignore my own sovereign's default risk". This argument may contribute to explaining why carry trades by banks have been far more prevalent in fiscally distressed countries than in fiscally sound ones. While such behaviour may appear rational from a bank's individual standpoint, it is no less inefficient for society than if it were motivated by plain moral hazard: it leads the banks of the fiscally distressed country to overexpose themselves to sovereign risk, and thus it also makes them more likely to require a bailout in the event of an increase in domestic yields. Insofar as this increases their demands on the public finances of their country in bad states of the world, it also exacerbates the chances that their sovereign will be distressed. In other words, however motivated, banks' carry trades strengthen the feedback loop between financial instability and fiscal distress.

Discouraging carry trades would require revising the prudential regulation of sovereign exposures in the euro area, by scrapping the current preferential treatment of sovereign exposures: currently, euro-area banks face no capital requirement (a "zero risk weight") for holdings of sovereign euro-area debt, irrespective of its issuer; moreover, sovereign holdings are exempted from the "large exposures regime", which limits exposures to a single counterparty to a quarter of their eligible capital. Such regulation makes it particularly attractive for euro-area banks to invest in high-yield euro-denominated sovereign debt, especially considering that they can fund such investments by borrowing at low rates from the ECB.

In principle, such carry trades can be discouraged by imposing either positive risk weights on sovereign debt in computing banks' capital or limits on banks' exposure towards each single sovereign issuer, thus requiring them to diversify their sovereign portfolios. Each of these two choices has its own problems: on the one hand, the responsiveness of banks' portfolio choices to risk weights on sovereign exposures is unknown, and in practice may be quite low in the presence of very profitable carry trades; on the other hand, setting limits to exposures vis-à-vis each single sovereign issuer may require most euro-area banks to undertake substantial portfolio adjustments, which may result in gyrations in relative yields in the euro-area sovereign debt market.

However, there are ways to guide the banks' portfolio reallocation process smoothly in the direction of greater diversification: for instance, the limit on sovereign exposures could be phased in very gradually; moreover, euro-area banks may be exempted from this limit altogether if they invest in a well-diversified portfolio of euro-area sovereign bonds rather than in those issued by a specific sovereign. In this respect, the portfolio reallocation process could be made smoother by the introduction of European Safe Bonds, as proposed by the Euro-nomics Group[3]: a European Debt Agency (EDA) could buy a GDP-weighted portfolio of bonds from euro-area sovereigns, and use them as collateral to issue two securities. The first security, European Safe Bonds (ESBies), would be a senior claim on the payments from the sovereign bonds held in the portfolio. The second security, European Junior Bonds, would be a junior claim on these payments – that is, it would be first in line to absorb losses arising from the pool of sovereign bonds that serve as collateral for these issues. Owing to the diversification of country-specific risk and to their seniority, ESBies would have virtually no exposure to sovereign risk, and therefore would be an ideal asset for euro-area banks to diversify their sovereign portfolios.

Finally, it is worth asking which are the policy implications of finding (ii) described above – namely, that even in core countries euro-area banks have responded to greater common (or redenomination) risk by increasing the home bias of their sovereign portfolios. As already mentioned, this response would appear completely consistent with economic rationality and market equilibrium: in the event of euro breakup, the banks of each country would be better positioned to bear the brunt of redenomination of domestic sovereign debt in the new national currency, as their deposits would also be redenominated in the new currency. Insofar as redenomination risk gives them a "comparative advantage" in holding domestic debt relative to foreign banks, home bias in the euro-area sovereign debt market is an equilibrium phenomenon.

The only way to address this source of segmentation of euro-area sovereign bond markets – and more generally of euro-area debt markets – is to address the credibility of the EMU, as was done by Draghi with his well-known "whatever-it-takes" speech in July 2012 and with the subsequent inception of the Outright Monetary Transactions (OMT) programme: by creating the credible threat that the ECB could buy the

3 See http://euronomics.princeton.edu/

sovereign debt of distressed euro-area countries, the ECB reduced investors' estimate of the probability of a possible euro breakup.

Nevertheless, the degree of segmentation of euro-area debt markets remains high: in each member country, domestic banks are still a key source of funding for both the domestic sovereign and the local private sector. Currently, the home bias of euro-area banks is close to its peak in recent years; even though this has enabled banks in periphery countries to benefit from the drop in their domestic sovereign yields since mid-2012, it now leaves them more exposed to the risk of a rebound in these yields than they were at the breakout of the crisis in 2008. Right now, investors appear to consider a snapback in the risk premia on periphery sovereign debt as a low-probability event; yet, it might be more destabilising than before – the typical features of tail risk. This risk is to some extent driven by changing political factors: the German government has recently expressed opposition to future ECB sovereign bond-buying that is part of the OMT programme;[4] the European elections of May 2014 have recorded decreasing popular support for EU institutions and in particular for the EMU; moreover, the fiscal imbalances of several euro-area countries are larger than they were during the financial crisis. At some point, these factors may revive investors' concerns about the survival of the euro, and lead sovereign yield differentials to spike again.

Bank forbearance, regulatory forbearance and bank resolution

Faced with a non-performing loan, a bank may exercise forbearance – that is, may agree to renegotiate and restructure the loan, for instance by extending its maturity ("evergreening"). While this practice is perfectly justified when the bank's customer is facing a liquidity shock – and indeed is part of the insurance role that banks are supposed to play in their lending activity – it is not when the borrower is not solvent and the forbearance reflects the bank's attempt to avoid the recognition and allocation of losses that have occurred, and possibly to game its supervisors so as to avoid its own resolution. As noted in ESRB (2012), from a regulatory perspective the problem is whether these decisions by banks

[4] On 21 March 2014, the German finance minister Wolfgang Schäuble stated that the ECB cannot decide on OMT bond purchases "because it has bound them to conditions that are beyond its control". Schäuble said that these conditions are decided by the ESM (the European Stability Mechanism bailout fund), which is controlled by governments, and "ESM decisions are subject to a unanimous vote and we will not approve of such a programme as announced by the ECB".

are distorted by risk-shifting incentives. In particular, banks may wish to delay the recognition of losses if their capital position is weak and loan collateral values are depressed, or if their stock prices are depressed, so that a recapitalisation could only occur at unattractive terms.

Renegotiating loans with high-risk customers is effectively a gamble on the borrower's ability or willingness to repay. If the gamble does not pay off and the bank is eventually insolvent, some of the costs are borne by creditors and possibly by taxpayers, who will fund resolution of the bank. This gamble also wastes resources that could be more productively lent to more solid, new customers rather than to old, high-risk ones, and therefore tends to lower aggregate profitability and growth.

The problem is worsened if the forbearance of banks towards their borrowers is itself tolerated by supervisors – namely, if there is also forbearance of supervisors towards banks. In this case, there is not only moral hazard by banks but moral hazard by supervisors. The latter may engage in forbearance towards banks because they fear the fiscal consequences of cleaning up their balance sheets and taking control of them. This can be a first-order determinant of systemic risk, because it raises the banks' incentives to engage in excessive forbearance, delays the recognition of their losses, and allows them to mount. To be effective, intervention must be swift and consist either of (i) recapitalisation with effective imposition of control by the authorities to clean up the bank's books, or (ii) resolution of the bank, to get rid of "zombie banks".

In the European context, the problem of forbearance can be complicated by cross-border externalities. Suppose that banks in country A exercise excessive forbearance towards their borrowers, and this is tolerated by their supervisors. If the banks in country A are heavily indebted with banks in country B, these are damaged by the lack of transparency about the true solvency position of banks in country A.

Regulatory forbearance and bank resolution: the European record

The European record before and during the crisis appears to feature a considerable degree of regulatory forbearance, especially when benchmarked with that of the US. National supervisors in the EU appear to have been far less inclined to shut down and liquidate distressed banks than the FDIC in the US, which has acquired a reputation for swift and efficient bank resolution. This transatlantic discrepancy is highlighted by Figure 2.3, which shows that far fewer EU banks have failed since 2008 compared with the number of banks that have been resolved by the FDIC

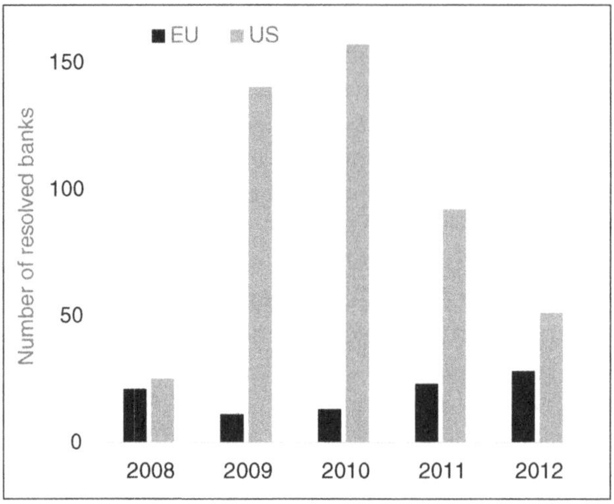

Figure 2.3 Bank resolution in the US and EU

in the US. A low propensity to resolve distressed institutions suggests a greater degree of regulatory forbearance by supervisors towards under-capitalised banks.

Most European responses to banks' difficulties in the crisis have been based on a desire to avoid intervention. Banks were given capital, loans and guarantees without any effective imposition of control by the authorities. Much capital was given in the form of hybrid securities, which are basically debt, except that they can absorb some losses under certain circumstances; this loss absorption capacity gave supervisors a rationale for treating these hybrids as equity even though in fact they are not. When capital was given in the form of equity, governments required seats on the banks' board but did not exert control to clean up their books.

European authorities have often preferred to rescue distressed banks by favouring acquisitions by (or mergers with) other domestic banks, rather than resolving them. During the financial crisis, governments and supervisors facilitated several mergers or acquisitions involving distressed banks, despite concerns regarding excessive concentration and lack of competition. Between August 2008 and February 2014, the EU Commission received 440 requests from EU member states to provide state aid to financial institutions. The Commission did not object to the vast majority (413) of these requests, although state aid approvals often entail bank restructuring requirements, which in some cases are substantial (EU Commission 2011).

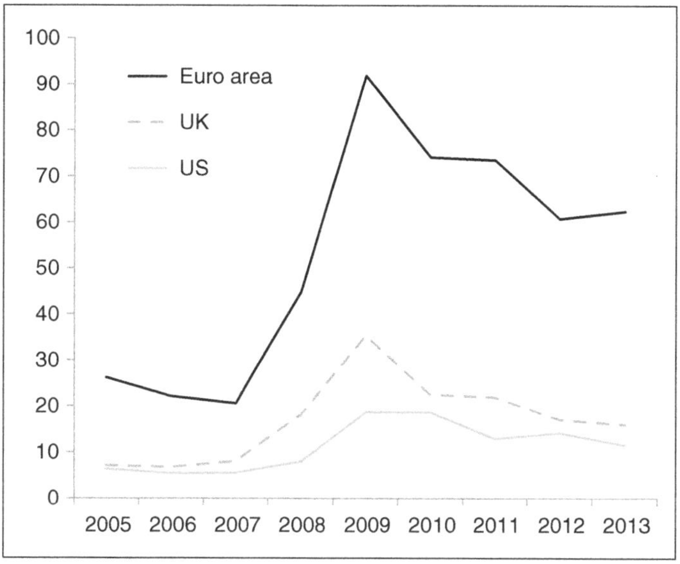

Figure 2.4 Average reduction in the funding costs of banks due to government guarantee (basis points)

Lambert et al. (2014), who estimate the implicit government subsidy received by US, UK and euro area banks as a result of public implicit bailout guarantees, find that the size of this subsidy has declined somewhat from crisis peaks, but remains substantial, especially in the euro area. This is captured in Figure 2.4, which shows the average benefit (in terms of reduced funding costs) for banks in receipt of government support. Importantly, euro-area banks continue to benefit from a greater reduction in funding costs owing to government support than US or even UK banks. This reflects not only the weaker state of euro area banks' balance sheets, but also differences in the bank resolution frameworks. Moreover, Lambert et al. (2014) show that bank subsidies are more evenly distributed across banks in the euro area, whereas in the US they tend to be more selectively targeted at systemically important banks. This strong government support is likely to correlate also with greater risk-taking by banks: Marques, Correa and Sapriza (2013) conclude that the intensity of government support is positively related to measures of bank risk-taking, especially in 2009–10.

What can explain the greater public support provided to distressed banks in the EU, compared with the US? One can think of several reasons:

1. In Europe, the ties between politics and banks are in some respects tighter than in the US. European governments have nurtured the growth of banks that could act as "national champions" in the competition with foreign banks – an attitude that Véron (2013) labels "banking nationalism". Véron points out that this tendency of European governments has ironically been enhanced by European financial integration: as the protection afforded by national boundaries diminished, politicians felt that they had to facilitate domestic banks' quest for size.
2. In the US, the legal and institutional tradition of bank resolution is long and strong: since its creation in 1934, the Federal Deposit Insurance Corporation (FDIC) has resolved 4,063 banks, of which 3,471 have resulted in outright bank failures, and just 592 in FDIC-assisted mergers. The law gives the FDIC full powers to intervene promptly, with a system of graduated responses depending on the severity of the solvency problem, and to take control if the situation seems to require it. The European institutional setup and track record in bank resolution is strikingly different, as shown by Figure 2.3: since 2008, around 50 euro-area banks have been resolved, compared with about 500 in the US (see Sapir and Wolff, 2013). The EU Directive on Bank Recovery and Resolution (and the Single Resolution Mechanism for euro-area banks) is expected to enter into force only in 2015 (see section "Regulatory forbearance and bank resolution: the ongoing European reforms"). The lack of such legal tools in the pre-crisis era may have contributed to the expectation that distressed banks would be bailed out, encouraging EU banks to indulge in excessive forbearance.
3. Banking supervision in parts of Europe has been less effective than in the US. Until 2014, bank supervision in Europe was a national concern, even though the span of European mega-banks' operations was international. This mismatch may partly explain the tendency to avoid resolution of distressed banks: so far, the EU lacked a procedure for integrated resolution of the parents and subsidiaries of banks with large cross-border operations by a single authority capable of maintaining integrated operations of the corporate entity during resolution and avoiding harmful repercussions on the whole financial system. Moreover, as suggested by Shin (2012), the earlier and more comprehensive take-up of Basel 2 in the EU (compared to the US) allowed EU banks to expand more aggressively, given excessively low risk weights on securitisation activity and the procyclicality of the Basel 2

framework. In some countries, the sheer speed of banks' expansion may have outpaced national supervisors' ability to scale up their personnel and operations. For instance, in Iceland prior to 2007, financial supervision became inadequate to deal with the rapid expansion of domestic banks (see Benediktsdottir et al. 2011).

4. In Europe, the universal banking business model is pervasive. Universal banks' securities trading arm can obtain funding at interest rates that reflect the public subsidies associated with their deposit-taking arm, increasing their incentive to take excessive risk in securities markets. The econometric analysis in Annex A4.2 of the Commission's report on implicit state guarantees to EU banks (EU Commission 2014a) finds that the European banks that receive a larger implicit public subsidy are larger, riskier, more interconnected, less capitalised and rely more on the wholesale market for funding, which are all typical features of universal banks.

Regulatory forbearance and bank resolution: the ongoing European reforms

The euro debt crisis has heightened European policy-makers' concerns about excessive forbearance by both banks and regulators, about the cross-border externalities that such forbearance may generate, and about the lack of an integrated resolution mechanism for distressed banks with extensive cross-border operations. The EU Commission and Parliament have attempted to address these problems with a drastic overhaul of both the system of bank prudential supervision and that of bank resolution, especially for systemically important banks.

In November 2013, the "Single Supervisory Mechanism (SSM) regulation" – conferring bank-supervisory powers on the ECB – entered into force. The SSM creates a new system of financial supervision comprising the ECB and the national competent authorities of participating EU countries. The centralisation of bank supervision should help to eliminate or at least mitigate the risk of regulatory forbearance, by (i) setting homogeneous standards to monitor banks' forbearance throughout the euro area, and (ii) shifting the power over banks' loss recognition and resolution into the hands of an authority removed from national concerns and political pressures.

In April 2014, the European Parliament adopted the Bank Recovery and Resolution Directive (BRRD). The Directive requires EU member states to ensure that their national supervisory and resolution authorities have a minimum set of common tools and powers to avert and, where necessary, manage the orderly failure of a bank. It gives national resolution authorities powers to resolve branches of banks based in third countries in certain circumstances, and provides a framework for improved cooperation and coordination between national supervisory and resolution authorities. Moreover, from 2016 the BRRD will enable authorities to "bail-in" the eligible liabilities (including unsecured creditors) of banks subject to resolution. Authorities will have powers to intervene ex ante in banks which are deemed irresolvable. This should help reduce the government subsidy given to EU banks, and therefore their incentive to indulge in excess forbearance ex ante.

In April 2014, the European Parliament also adopted a regulation establishing a Single Resolution Mechanism (SRM). The SRM implements the BRRD in the euro area, and therefore complements the SSM. A new EU body, the Single Resolution Board, will guide the resolution process for financial institutions in the euro area and in other EU countries signing up to it. The final decision on whether to resolve a bank will, however, be entrusted to the EU Commission, usually on the basis of a proposal by the Board. As part of the SRM regulation, a Single Resolution Fund, financed ex ante by banks, will help to provide "bridge financing" for resolved banks – although this fund will not reach its target level of 1 per cent of bank deposits (about €55tn) until 2023.

As pointed out by several scholars, this resolution mechanism suffers from three serious weaknesses. First, it entrusts the decision to shut down a bank to a collection of too many authorities: the ECB (as prudential regulator), the Board of the SRM (which comprises the Commission, the Council, the ECB and national resolution authorities) and the EU Commission itself, while it leaves the implementation of the resolution to national authorities. Second, the Single Resolution Fund is widely considered as too limited to support the resolution of systemically important financial institution (SIFI): "the Fund, as it is proposed today, will not be credible to support the resolution of a SIFI. The possibility to borrow on the capital market is insufficient, in particular since such loans will not be endorsed by governments, nor will the Fund be able to tap the European Stability Mechanism ESM" (Gordon and Ringe, 2014, p. 31). Third, the EU resolution mechanism is not complemented by a centralised deposit insurance mechanism, unlike the FDIC in the US; hence, bank runs may occur in countries where banks are perceived as distressed, as depositors try to rescue their deposits by moving them to the banks of countries whose legal arrangements they trust more. This type of behaviour may obviously interfere with the orderly resolution of a distressed bank.

These three flaws – the complexity of the resolution mechanism, the insufficient scale of its funding, and the absence of a centralised deposit insurance mechanism – may therefore hinder the prompt and orderly resolution of large, systemically important banks in the EU. This may in turn hurt the credibility of the Single Supervisor, as the lack of a credible resolution mechanism may force even the Single Supervisor to engage in forbearance in prudential supervision. If so, the euro-area tendency to excessive forbearance may eventually persist to some extent, despite these extensive reforms.

Bank leverage and capital requirements

By their very nature, banks are highly levered institutions: most of what they lend is borrowed either from depositors, bondholders or the central bank. Such high leverage creates risk-shifting incentives for banks' shareholders and managers, especially because a considerable fraction of their funding comes from unsophisticated and dispersed depositors. This incentive is further enhanced by the opacity of banks' assets: for outside investors, it is hard to evaluate the riskiness of a bank's loan portfolio. Yet another source of risk-shifting arises from deposit insurance: intended to address the intrinsic fragility stemming from banks' maturity transformation, it effectively enables banks to unload also on taxpayers the losses arising from non-performing loans or security positions. On top of explicit deposit insurance schemes, systemically relevant banks can count on the government's implicit bailout guarantee – an additional source of moral hazard, as already noted above (see section on "Bank forbearance, regulatory forbearance and bank resolution").

The main counterweight to such risk-shifting incentives comes from the equity capital of banks, which plays a double role: ex ante, it reduces the risk-taking incentives of banks' shareholders by ensuring that they have enough "skin in the game"; ex post, equity acts as a loss-absorbing buffer, being the first claim that is wiped out when losses arise, and thus gives protection to debtholders (including depositors) and taxpayers.

However, the equity capital requirements imposed by prudential regulation are often circumvented by banks, especially large ones, by exploiting loopholes in regulation. The behaviour of large European banks before the financial crisis is a good case in point. In the late 1990s, the largest 20 listed banks in the EU had a median "book leverage ratio"

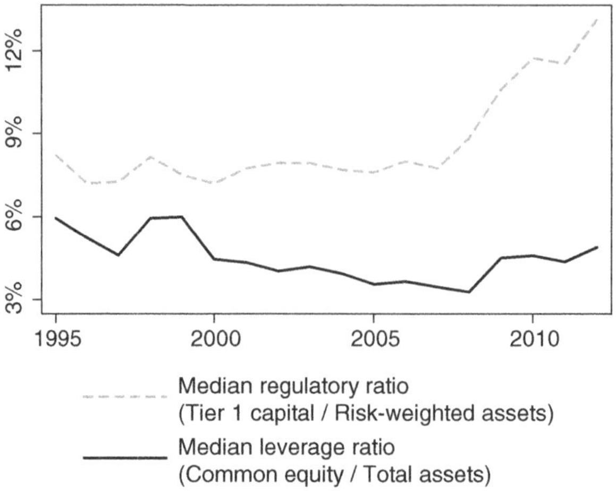

Figure 2.5 Book leverage ratio versus regulatory capital ratio: median of top 20 EU banks

(defined as the book value of equity divided by the book value of total assets) of around 6 per cent (Figure 2.5). By 2008, the median leverage ratio of these banks had dropped to just over 3 per cent. All of the largest 20 listed EU banks reduced their leverage ratios before 2009. In the late 1990s, only a few of them had ratios below 4 per cent; 10 years later, for most of them it was below this mark. Banks that in 2003 had ratios above 8 per cent – such as HSBC and BBVA – had by 2008 reduced them by around half. The two banks that began the decade with ratios below 3 per cent – Commerzbank and Dexia – finished the decade being bailed out by governments.

While the leverage ratios of banks fell between 2000 and 2007, their regulatory ratio – that is, Tier 1 capital divided by risk-weighted assets – remained relatively stable. The median regulatory capital ratio was around 8 per cent in each year between 1997 and 2007 – a period over which the median book equity-asset ratio fell by half (Figure 2.6). Hence, there was an increasing divergence between book and regulatory capital/asset ratios. These two measures, which were highly and positively correlated in the 1990s, became no longer correlated in the early 2000s for the largest banks. In fact, by 2012 the correlation became negative and statistically significant: banks that were more capitalised according to the regulator had lower book equity relative to total assets!

Large banks managed to achieve this by acting both on the numerator (Tier 1 capital) and on the denominator (risk-weighted assets) of the

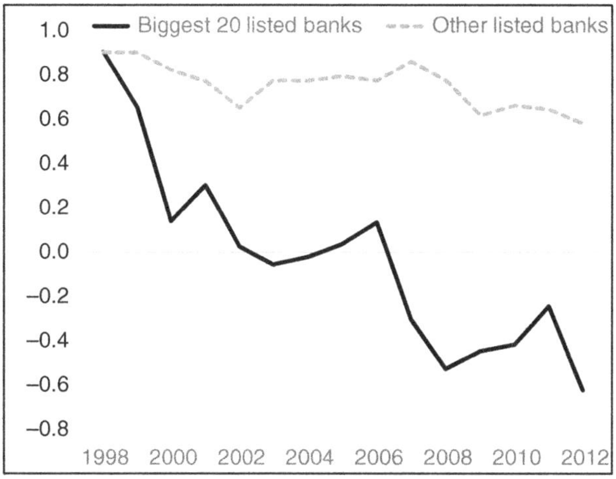

Figure 2.6 Correlation between the leverage ratio and the regulatory capital ratio for listed EU banks

regulatory capital ratio. On both sides, they engaged in massive regulatory arbitrage, made possible by the mistaken design of prudential regulation.

On the numerator's side, they replaced a considerable amount of equity capital with hybrid securities (such as conditional convertible bonds): these qualify as regulatory capital but have certain properties of debt – for example, their cash flow is treated as interest and is thus tax deductible. Many banks issued hybrid capital as a cost-effective means of meeting their Tier 1 and Tier 2 capital requirements, although in the crisis many of these hybrid securities did not absorb losses as expected, as governments bailed out their holders alongside their depositors.[5]

On the denominator's side, banks managed to keep the growth of risk-weighted assets far below that of their total assets (hence exposing themselves to undercapitalised risks), in three ways:

(i) Insofar as euro-area banks invested in euro-denominated sovereign debt, they did not add to their risk-weighted assets, as these

[5] Boyson et al. (2013) study trust preferred securities (TPS), a hybrid security issued by US bank holding companies since 1996 to replace equity in their Tier 1 capital. They document that US banks issued TPS mainly to maintain their Tier 1 capital ratios in periods of rapid growth, and argue that this regulatory arbitrage allowed banks to expand their leverage too much in the 2000s, leading to a deterioration in their performance during the financial crisis.

securities carry a zero risk weight in the computation of risk-weighted assets (as explained in section "Implications for the regulation of banks' sovereign exposures").

(ii) Banks – especially large ones – exploited the latitude conferred to them by the Basel II treaty, by which they could devise their own internal risk models to determine the risk weights to be applied to their assets, based on the idea that this would make capital charges more sensitive to risk. But banks often tweaked ("optimised") these models to systematically reduce the capital charges relative to those commensurate to the actual risks they were taking. Using German loan-level data, Behn et al. (2014) show that the internal risk estimates produced for regulatory purposes systematically under-predict default rates, and that reliance on internal risk models allowed large banks to reduce their capital charges and thus expand their lending more than smaller banks that did not rely on internal risk models. Also, Beltratti and Paladino (2013) document that banks exploited the latitude allowed by internal risk models, using an unbalanced panel data set of 548 banks from 45 countries over the period 2005–11: banks with a higher cost of capital and better growth opportunities were more aggressive in reducing risk weights.

(iii) Banks used securitisation to reduce regulatory capital, exploiting the lower risk weights that regulators attached to asset-backed securities than to the underlying loan pools: before the financial crisis of 2007–09, they increasingly relied on securitisation methods that allowed them to retain risks on their balance sheets and yet achieve a reduction in regulatory capital, as documented by Acharya et al. (2013) for asset-backed commercial paper conduits.

Notably, these regulatory arbitrage activities were performed mostly by large banks, which were better equipped to engage in them than smaller ones: for instance, they had the technical expertise to develop and tweak internal risk models. Moreover, large banks had the greatest incentive to do so: given their scale, achieving even a small reduction in the leverage ratio without affecting their regulatory capital ratio would translate in a massive increase in assets, more than sufficient to cover the costs of the quants and lawyers required to plan and carry out the regulatory arbitrage. As a result, especially for large banks, the regulatory capital ratio has become less and less useful as an indicator of future distress probability (Danielsson 2002). Figure 2.7 crystallises this notion: Tier 1 capital ratios

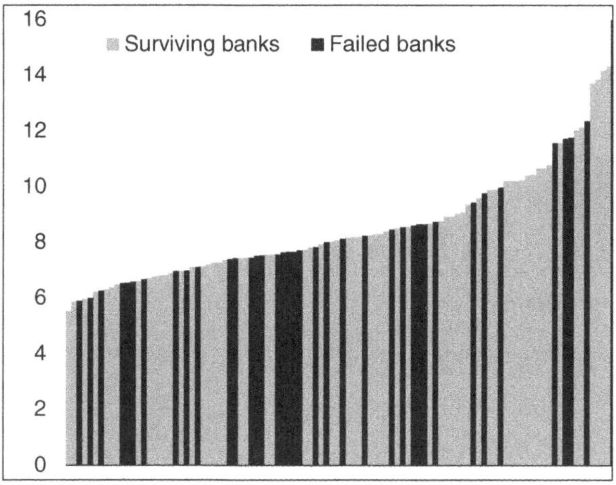

Figure 2.7 Global banks' Tier-1 capital as percentage of risk-weighted assets in 2006

in 2006 were uninformative about the respective banks' true default probabilities. Several large banks with high regulatory capital ratios in 2006 subsequently failed; conversely, several banks with low regulatory ratios in 2006 did not.

Recently, European banks have started to increase their regulatory capital ratios, but again this has been largely by reducing average risk weights rather than by increasing their leverage ratio. Without risk-weighting, some EU banks remain thinly capitalised compared with international peers. As shown by Figure 2.8, the average leverage ratio of EU globally systemically important banks stood at 3.9 per cent in the second quarter of 2013, versus 4.5 per cent for US G-SIBs (using IFRS-equivalent accounting standards).

This highlights the importance of relying on a set of equity capital requirements that cannot be easily gamed, unlike what has apparently been the case so far. One possible solution would be to require banks to compute capital based on uniform risk weights set by regulators for each type of asset (the so-called "standardised approach"), rather than on their own internal models. Basel III has not adopted this solution, as it keeps relying on the ratio of Tier 1 capital to risk-weighted assets and on internal risk models. But Basel III tries to correct the problem by its concomitant requirement of a minimum book leverage ratio. Since no regulatory ratio is perfect, adopting multiple ratios does guard against the weaknesses of each while benefitting from the strengths of each, and helps to address the "regulatory arbitrage" by banks of a single choice of

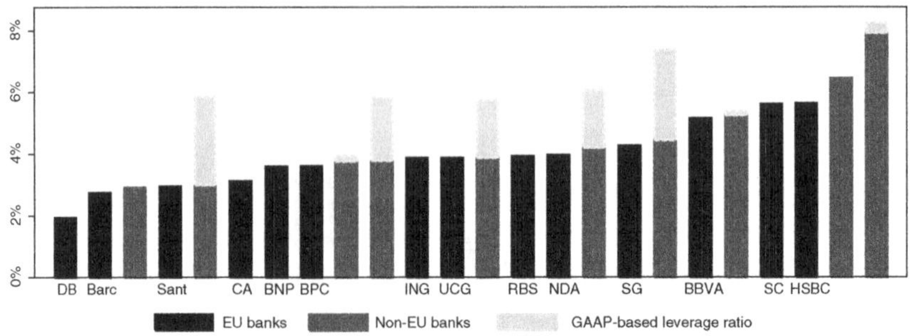

Figure 2.8 Global systemically important banks' leverage ratios in Q2-2013

capital requirement: it helps identify banks that look healthy under one capital requirement but not under an alternative reasonable benchmark, such as the book leverage ratio.

Regulators would also benefit from comparing the rankings of capital shortfalls based on capital ratios with benchmark rankings of capital shortfalls arising from market-based assessment of the capital condition of the banks whose stocks are traded on sufficiently liquid markets. For such banks, the regulator could use as benchmarks (i) the market leverage ratio – that is, the market value of equity divided by tangible assets minus derivative liabilities, and (ii) the stressed market leverage ratio, which accounts for the loss to market value of equity under stress, as, for example, in the SRISK measure produced by the NYU VLab. Prudential supervisors should monitor and investigate significant discrepancies between market-based and book-based measures of capital shortfalls, especially in the context of stress tests, as such discrepancies typically arise when investors suspect that asset valuations in banks' books do not reflect the full extent of their losses.

Conclusions

This chapter has highlighted serious flaws in three aspects of European financial regulation which contributed to the crisis that Europe experienced in the 2009–12 period, and which, unless corrected, will remain a source of persistent fragility of European banks. The EU legislators are aware of this, and have started a vast overhaul of bank supervision and resolution in the euro area (the epicentre of the crisis) – the "banking union" project. But this vast regulatory overhaul also suffers from some vulnerabilities, as noted in the second section ("Bank forbearance, regulatory forbearance and bank resolution"). In other key areas, the reform process is much further behind. As noted in the first section ("Bank-sovereign feedback loop and regulation of banks' sovereign exposures"), the current regulation of the sovereign exposures of banks is still a serious source of fragility of the euro-area banking system. Similarly, it is alarming that banks' capital regulation keeps assigning a central importance to the ratio of Tier 1 capital to risk-weighted assets, and keeps relying on banks' internal risk-based models, considering how susceptible to gaming these aspects of regulation have proved in the run-up to the crisis. Even the Asset Quality Review recently conducted by the ECB and the EBA in preparation of the 2014 stress tests still assigned a central role to the ratio between Tier 1 capital and risk-weighted assets, although it required banks to disclose also their leverage ratio for information purposes only – that is, without binding value or impact on the measurement of capital shortfalls (ECB 2014).

References

Acharya, V., P. Schnabl and G. Suarez (2013). "Securitization Without Risk Transfer". *Journal of Financial Economics* 107: 515–536.

Acharya, V. and S. Steffen (2015). "The Greatest Carry Trade Ever? Understanding Eurozone Bank Risks". *Journal of Financial Economics* 115: 215–236.

Battistini, N., M. Pagano and S. Simonelli (2014). "Systemic Risk, Sovereign Yields and Bank Exposures in the Euro Crisis". *Economic Policy* 30(78): 183–231.

Behn, M., R. Haselmann and V. Vig (2014). "The Limits of Model-Based Regulation". *mimeo*.

Beltratti, A. and G. Paladino (2013). "Why Do Banks Optimize Risk Weights? The Relevance of the Cost of Equity Capital". *mimeo*.

Benediktsdottir, S., J. Danielsson and G. Zoega (2011). "Lessons from a Collapse of a Financial System". *Economic Policy* 26(66): 183–231.

Boyson, N. M., Rüdiger Fahlenbrach and René M. Stulz (2013). "Trust Preferred Securities and Regulatory Arbitrage". *mimeo*.

Buch, C., M. Koetter and J. Ohls (2013). "Banks and Sovereign Risk: A Granular View". *Deutsche Bundesbank Discussion Paper* 29/2013.

Danielsson, J. (2002). "The Emperor Has No Clothes: Limits to Risk Modelling". *Journal of Banking and Finance* 26: 1273–1296.

Drechsler, I., T. Drechsel and D. Marques-Ibanez (2013). "Who Borrows from the Lender of Last Resort?" *mimeo*.

ECB (2014). "Note on the Comprehensive Assessment". July 2014.

ESRB Advisory Scientific Committee (2012). "Forbearance, Resolution and Deposit Insurance". *Reports of the Advisory Scientific Committee* 1, July.

ESRB Advisory Scientific Committee (2014). "Is Europe Overbanked?" *Reports of the Advisory Scientific Committee* 4, June.

EU Commission (2011). "The Effects of Temporary State Aid Rules Adopted in the Context of the Financial and Economic Crisis". *Commission Staff Working Paper*.

EU Commission (2014a). "Size and Determinants of Implicit State Guarantees". Annex 4.2 to the impact assessment of a regulation on structural reform of EU banks.

EU Commission (2014b). "Economic Review of the Financial Regulation Agenda". *Commission Staff Working Document* 2014/158.

Gordon, J. N. and W.-G. Ringe (2014). "Resolution in the European Banking Union: A Transatlantic Perspective on What It Would Take". *University of Oxford Legal Research Paper* 18/2014.

Lambert, F. J., K. Ueda, P. Deb, D. F. Gray and P. Grippa (2014). "How Big Is the Implicit Subsidy for Banks Considered too Important to Fail?" In International Monetary Fund, *Global Financial Stability Report*, chapter 3.

Marques, L. B., R. Correa and H. Sapriza (2013). "International Evidence on Government Support and Risk Taking in the Banking Sector". IMF Working Paper no. 13/94.

Sapir, A. and G. Wolff (2013). "The Neglected Side of Banking Union". Note presented at the informal ECOFIN, September 14, 2013, Vilnius.

Shin, H. S. (2012). "Global Banking Glut and Loan Risk Premium". Mundell-Fleming Lecture, *IMF Economic Review* 60(2): 155–192.

Soussa, F. (2000). "Too Big to Fail: Moral Hazard and Unfair Competition?" In L. Halme, C. Hawkesby, J. Healey, I. Saapar and F. Soussa (eds.), *Financial Stability and Central Banks: Selected Issues for Financial Safety Nets and Market Discipline*. Bank of England, chapter 1.

Véron, N. (2013). "Banking Nationalism and the European Crisis". Bruegel blog, www.bruegel.org/nc/blog/detail/article/1175-banking-nationalism-and-the-european-crisis/.

3

Bank stress tests as a policy tool: the European experience during the crisis

ATHANASIOS ORPHANIDES[1]

Introduction

A comparison of the evolution of real output in the United States (US) and euro area since the beginning of the global financial crisis in 2008 reveals a startling difference (see Figure 3.1). Following a deep recession in late 2008 and early 2009 that affected the two economies similarly, the US economy has grown steadily while the euro area economy returned into recession in 2011 and has languished since then. What explains this difference? A short answer could be the policy response of the euro area governments which gave rise to the "euro area crisis." A more informative answer, however, would identify specific differences in policy decisions in the two economies and trace out their consequences.[2] This paper focuses on one critical difference in the policy response to the crisis relating to the handling of the banking systems of the two economies: the design and implementation of system-wide bank stress tests.

During the initial phase of the global crisis in late 2008 and early 2009, policymakers faced similar challenges in the US and the euro area and adopted similar responses. Monetary and fiscal policy was eased and government interventions in a few troubled financial institutions stabilized the economy. The initial responses by US and euro area authorities, in late 2008 and 2009, were comparable. Consistent with sound crisis

[1] Athanasios Orphanides is a Professor of the Practice of Global Economics and Management at the MIT Sloan School of Management. The author would like to thank the organizers and participants of the "SAFE Workshop on Financial Regulation: A Transatlantic Perspective," Frankfurt, June 6, 2014, for useful comments and discussions.

[2] Extensive comparisons are available that cover numerous aspects of the response to the crisis. Hoshi and Kashyap (2014) compare the responses of the US and Europe to that of Japan's lost decade, focusing on banking. Orphanides (2014b) compares the monetary policy of the Fed and the ECB. De Grauwe and Ji (2013) offer a critical review of fiscal policy.

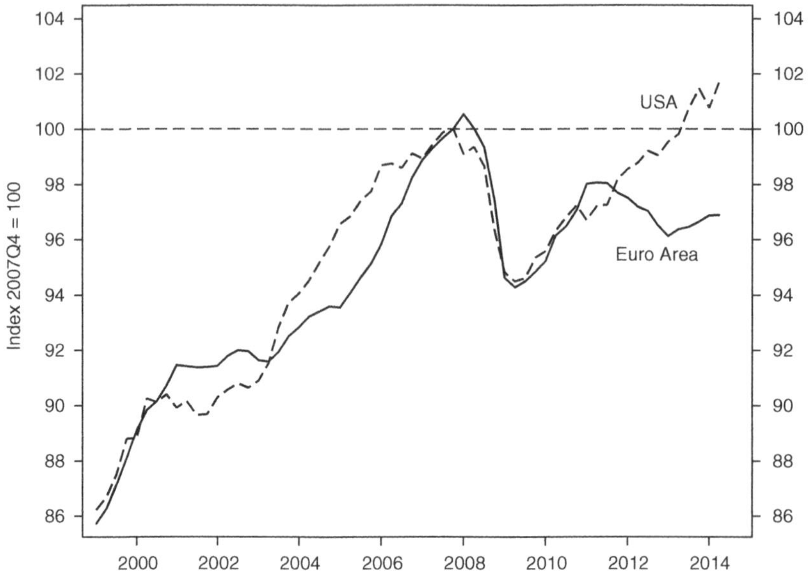

Figure 3.1 Economic performance in the US and the euro area
Note: GDP per capita in the US and the euro area.

management principles, the focus was on providing support to help the economy avoid a protracted slump. The sharp recession, however, weakened the balance sheets of banks in both economies, feeding lingering doubts about the overall state of the banking systems of the two economies. Lack of confidence in the banking system became a crucial common challenge. Restoring overall confidence in the banking system became a key objective to facilitate the return to sustained growth.

The subsequent responses to the common challenge of restoring confidence in the banking system diverged dramatically. Stress tests were used in both economies with the same objective – to restore confidence – but key elements in the design and implementation differed. In the US, a system-wide stress test was performed in 2009 (Supervisory Capital Assessment Program) and succeeded in restoring confidence. In the euro area, a series of system-wide stress tests and associated government decisions undermined confidence further. The result in the euro area was a credit crunch and policy-induced recession in 2011 and continuing weakness of the economy to date.

This chapter reviews elements that can account for the success and failure of stress tests in restoring confidence in the banking system and identifies the policy decisions that can account for the difference in the experiences of the US and the euro area in the past few years. A key difference that is identified is the absence of a well-defined backstop in the case of the euro area. As a consequence, the euro area stress tests contributed to a retrenchment in credit supply. The decision to inject credit risk to sovereign debt markets in the euro area, and then force banks to raise capital buffers to account for possible sovereign debt default, was another important factor.[3] The combined effect of these decisions was equivalent to a massive increase in capital requirements during the crisis, especially in the periphery of the euro area whose sovereign markets were viewed as more vulnerable. The overall result of the flawed design and implementation of the stress test exercises in the euro area was a policy-induced credit crunch that led to a severe slowdown of economic activity, particularly in the euro area periphery.

Successful vs. destructive stress tests

When properly employed, bank stress tests can be effective as a supervisory tool to strengthen the resilience of a banking institution or a banking system overall. In this context, stress tests have been an integral part of bank supervision frameworks for some time. In the regulatory framework developed under Basle, individual bank stress tests were meant to serve as an integral part of the micro-supervisory toolkit. Adverse scenaria can check the resilience of a bank in a forward-looking manner to severe but plausible stresses. This can help identify how much capital a bank should be required to hold under Pillar 2 of the Basle II framework, beyond the Pillar 1 regulatory requirement that is meant to serve as the absolute minimum benchmark.

When used as part of the supervisory review process to assess Pillar 2 capital, potential capital needs identified for a specific bank following a stress test are corrected in a confidential manner, as for other micro-supervisory matters. The lack of disclosure of the details of a stress test performed on an individual institution under this framework is part of the design. The confidentiality of the process allows regulators to test quite severe scenaria and check the resilience of a specific institution

[3] This was particularly harmful because both before and during the crisis the regulatory framework in place had encouraged banks to maintain substantial exposures to sovereign debt and to treat them as zero-risk-weight assets. Interestingly, despite other regulatory changes, this preferential treatment of sovereign debt continues to be in effect, as reflected in the Capital Requirements Directive.

without the risk that the outcome might be misinterpreted as a forecast of the capital position of an institution, which it is not. Since the adverse scenaria employed can be considerably more severe than what would be normally expected, the outcome of a stress test could easily suggest that the bank involved would be undercapitalized under the stress scenario, in the sense of having projected capital ratios below the Pillar 1 benchmark, in the event that the stress scenario were to materialize. Preserving the confidentiality of such results avoids the risk of misinterpretation that could put a banking institution at a disadvantage vis-à-vis its peers whenever it is under regulatory review. At the same time, this framework allows easier access to raising capital by an institution for which the result suggests that Pillar 2 capital should be adjusted upwards. Raising capital for one bank in isolation is not disruptive to the economy so micro-supervisory stress tests, as envisioned in the Basle framework, need not examine any broader macroeconomic implications of the exercise.

In contrast to the purpose of micro stress tests, macro stress tests, which examine the banking system in an economy as a whole, serve a very different purpose. In the aftermath of the global financial crisis in 2008, macro stress tests were developed in the US and the EU (with particular attention to the euro area) with the aim of solving the generalized confidence problem that emerged during the crisis. Because of this purpose, and unlike the micro-supervisory stress tests, the communication of the results and associated policies acquired critical importance.

Subjecting the whole banking system to a macro stress test examines the impact of severe but plausible stresses that could potentially further weaken the banking system during a crisis. The objective is to ensure that the banking system will be able to withstand these stresses. To succeed in restoring confidence, the stress scenaria and results are communicated in public, but the communication aspect makes two elements critical: first, the stress test must be sufficiently severe to incorporate plausible adverse scenaria that reflect concerns that may sap public confidence; second, to the extent that capital needs are found in particular institutions that "fail" the test, a credible mechanism must be in place that ensures that the necessary capital will be replenished with no disruption – that is, a credible backstop must be in place.

In the absence of a backstop, concerns about capital needs that may trigger resolutions later on, in the event that the stress scenario were to materialize, add to the uncertainty and become counterproductive. Rather than restore confidence, a stress test may then lead to the deterioration of a system-wide crisis. When confidence is shattered and it is expected that a severe stress test will uncover some capital needs in the system, the most crucial aspect of rebuilding confidence is the knowledge that these needs will be covered in the aggregate through a clear ex ante identified backstop. The key to restoring confidence is ensuring that a credible solution is available for any problem that might be identified in the process.

The absence of a credible backstop adversely impacts the credibility of the exercise and the economy even before a macro stress test is performed. Knowledge by market participants that the regulatory agency performing the stress test does not have a credible backstop creates concerns that the regulator will fail to disclose potential problems for fear of igniting a crisis for specific institutions. Without a credible backstop, the regulatory agency tasked to perform and communicate the macro stress test cannot allay such concerns.

The availability or not of a credible backstop can thus become the determining factor for success or failure of a macro stress test. In the absence of a credible backstop that clearly explains in advance how any capital needs might be covered, the very announcement of a macro stress test can be damaging and counterproductive. To protect the bank's interests, the management of a bank undergoing a stress test will have an incentive to engage in capital preservation, such as by tightening credit standards and deleveraging. This would be the optimal response, from the bank's perspective. The perceived risks for the bank are asymmetric. A public disclosure suggesting that the bank "failed" the test and needs to raise additional capital may be quite detrimental for existing shareholders. Deleveraging protects against such a risk. The effect may be especially acute when there is lack of clarity on what workout the bank might be forced to go through in case it "fails" to pass the test. Although this may be the optimal response by an individual bank, the resulting credit supply tightening can have undesirable effects for the economy as a whole.

In contrast to micro stress-testing exercises, bank capital in a macro stress test should be seen as a public good, as explained in Kashyap et al. (2008). Communication of the availability of capital, in case it is needed, becomes crucial for the success of such an exercise.

Stress tests and the overall economy

Policy decisions which encourage banks to engage in capital preservation and deleveraging during a crisis, when credit supply is already tighter than desirable, can be destructive for the macroeconomy. Such policy decisions effectively induce a credit crunch in the economy. Banks may become far less willing to extend credit and the resulting disruption in the flow of credit supply can cause a recession. In turn, the recession could lead to a deterioration of bank balance sheets and weaken the capital position of banks for numerous reasons. A recession increases the incidence of non-performing loans (NPLs) requiring provisions. Further, a recession leads to a decline in the valuations of assets pledged as collateral, implying both that additional provisions will be required for existing NPLs, and that larger provisions will be required for future NPLs.

Overall, the successful design of a macro stress test differs fundamentally from micro-supervisory stress tests. As Greenlaw et al. (2012) point out, the goal of a macro prudential stress test should be to contain the adverse effects of a crisis on the economy as a whole. Part of the design should be to limit the likelihood and costs of a credit crunch and prevent aggregate fire sales and systemic defaults. This is why the success of a macro stress test rests on the certainty that the capital needs that might be identified for the banking system will not cause any disruption. In effect, bank managements must be reassured ex ante that the "solution" to whatever capital "problem" is identified is already provided. This can be achieved if a credible backstop is identified together with the announcement that a macro stress test will take place.

In the absence of a credible backstop, the announcement of a stress test should be expected to cause a credit supply retrenchment with all the adverse consequences that would be expected of any policy-induced credit crunch. The announcement of a macro stress test, without clarity on the availability of a capital backstop, can trigger a self-fulfilling adverse feedback loop: a credit crunch would weaken the economy, lead to a further deterioration in the bank's capital conditions, and potentially drive the economy into a severe depression.

Macro stress tests: The experience in the US and the euro area

Coming out of the global financial crisis in 2009, US and European authorities faced the common challenge of restoring confidence in the banking system. In both economies, macro stress tests were used as a tool to achieve this objective.

In the US, a macro stress test was employed with success. The Supervisory Capital Assessment Program was coordinated by the Federal Reserve and the Treasury and succeeded in restoring confidence.[4] The test was properly designed. Emphasis was given to ensuring that a credible backstop was available and would be used to cover any shortfall that might materialize. Incentives were given to banks to raise capital, and confidence provided to investors that uncertainty was resolved, increasing willingness to invest in banks.

This critical aspect of the backstop in the exercise was explained at the time by the Chairman of the Federal Reserve, Ben Bernanke:

> We have strongly encouraged institutions requiring additional capital to obtain it through private means, including, for example, new equity issues, conversions, exchange offers, or sales of businesses or other assets. To ensure that all of these firms can build the needed capital cushions, however, the Treasury has made a firm commitment to provide contingent common equity, in the form of mandatory convertible preferred stock, as a bridge to obtaining private capital in the future (Bernanke 2009).

The US Treasury, which enjoyed high credibility and the ability to raise resources at low cost, provided a credible backstop.

In contrast to the US experience, in the European Union decisions were made at a political level to go ahead with similar stress test exercises, but without a coherent plan for the availability of a credible backstop. This omission became particularly critical in the euro area following the decision in Deauville, on October 18, 2010, to inject credit risk in euro area sovereign debt. As a result of the Deauville decision, the credibility of the governments of many member states to serve as a backstop to banks based in their states was shattered.[5] A series of macro stress-testing exercises have been implemented since then, with the predictable results of a deterioration of the euro area economy because of the policy-induced credit crunch. The adverse consequences can be seen in Figure 3.2, which compares real GDP growth in the euro area with the real growth of credit to non-financial corporations and households.

The aggregate behavior of credit growth obscures important heterogeneity across member states. As a result of the Deauville agreement, the sovereigns of periphery member states were disproportionately challenged by uncertainty regarding the possibility that other governments might force them to default. Banks in these member states who were holding substantial quantities of periphery sovereign debt found themselves without any assurances that in case of difficulties they might be able

[4] An overview of the exercise is provided in Board of Governors of the Federal Reserve System (2009).

[5] Orphanides (2013) provides an analysis of the implications of the Deauville blunder.

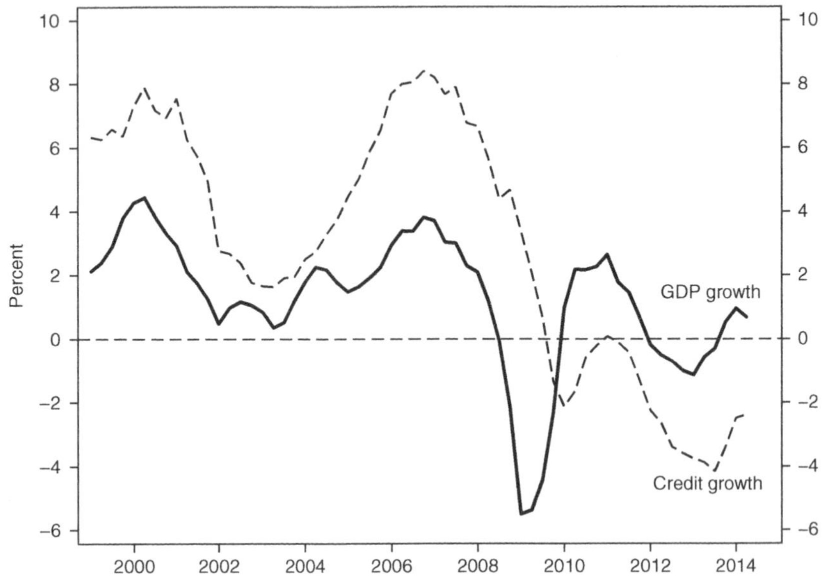

Figure 3.2 Credit-crunch-induced recession in the euro area
Note: Credit growth reflects loans extended to NFCs and households, deflated by HICP inflation. GDP growth deflated with GDP deflator.

to secure temporary public support on terms equal to those of banks in member states whose sovereign debt was not facing similar pressures. In effect, the macro stress test exercises became a vehicle for amplifying the unequal playing field that developed across the euro area after the Deauville blunder. This favored banks based in member states perceived as strong and punished banks in member states perceived as weak, through the dynamics explained in Orphanides (2012).

The results of the unequal playing field generated by the combination of these factors can be seen in Figure 3.3. The figure compares the lending rates to corporations in the four largest member states of the euro area – Germany, France, Italy, and Spain – which together account for about 80 percent of euro area GDP. Of these four, Germany benefited from the injection of risk in sovereign markets, while Italy and Spain suffered significant deteriorations in the perceived credit-worthiness of their sovereign debt, which was transmitted to the economy through increases in lending rates to corporations and households.

The importance of a credible backstop was recognized in Europe while the implementation of the macro stress tests was still under discussion in

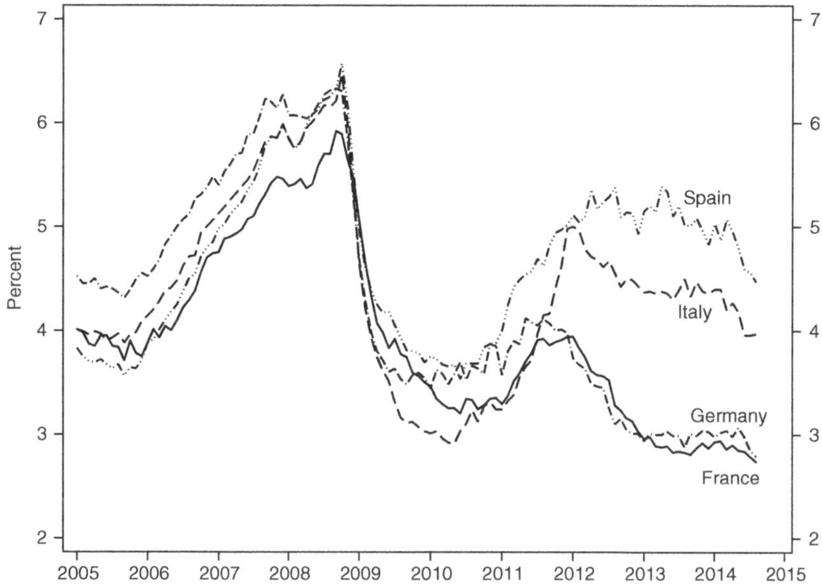

Figure 3.3 Policy-induced credit crunch in the periphery
Note: Lending rates to corporations for loans under 1 million.

2010. In the case of the euro area, an effective backstop could have been provided by the activation of the EFSF and later the ESM, the two facilities that were created to serve the management of the crisis. This was proposed and actively discussed in the period leading to the decision to implement macro stress tests, and was even discussed at European Council meetings – for example, in July and October 2011. Unfortunately for the euro area, the governments failed to reach an agreement to make these facilities available to serve as a common backstop while at the same time deciding to proceed with the implementation of macro stress test exercises.

A significant tension in the case of the euro area was the government's ambivalence as to whether they should collectively treat sovereign debt as risk free or retain the option to force a default, through the so-called Private Sector Involvement (PSI), whenever a euro area government needed temporary liquidity support. The governments oscillated between alternatives, failing to provide certainty to banks that held that debt and to provide clarity about the availability of a backstop. This resulted in incoherent decisions regarding stress test exercises, as highlighted, for example, in the decision taken at the Euro Summit on

October 26, 2011 (European Commission 2011). The statement made by euro area governments at that summit simultaneously reaffirmed that member states such as Spain and Italy should not be considered as facing the possibility of default, but at the same time confirmed the decision to subject the banking system to a stress test exercise that reflected substantial default probabilities for Italy and Spain and forced banks to raise capital to provision for the associated default risk. The result was the intensification of the crisis, with catastrophic consequences for the euro area economy – a European Lehman event, as described afterwards by the President of the ECB, Mario Draghi:

> The ideal sequencing would have been to first have a firewall in place, then do the recapitalisation of the banks, and only afterwards decide whether you need to have PSI. This would have allowed managing stressed sovereign conditions in an orderly way. This was not done. Neither the EFSF was in place, nor were banks recapitalised, before people started suggesting PSI. It was like letting a bank fail without having a proper mechanism for managing this failure, as it had happened with Lehman (Draghi 2011).

The consequences of the mishandling of the macro stress tests in the euro area were entirely predictable. The credit crunch that would have been expected under the circumstances materialized, especially in the member states perceived as weak. The credit crunch depressed real economic activity and resulted in sustained losses in growth prospects.

As can be seen in Figure 3.4, real GDP per person has been stagnant in the periphery. Whereas the crisis may have benefited Germany, as shown by the rapid recovery in GDP per person following the global financial crisis, it has been catastrophic for Italy and Spain.

Going forward

A comparative analysis of how macro stress tests were used in the US and the euro area during the crisis illustrates one dimension of mishandling of the crisis by euro area governments. Specific policy decisions led to the deterioration of the crisis in some member states, while benefiting others. The construction of the euro and the segmentation of the financial sector across member states were effectively exploited by member states enjoying a relative position of strength, at a huge cost to the euro area as a whole. The proper design and implementation of solutions in the euro area requires a level of political cooperation that has been absent. Member-state politics have dominated over economics in the management of the crisis (Orphanides 2014a). The flawed design of macro stress

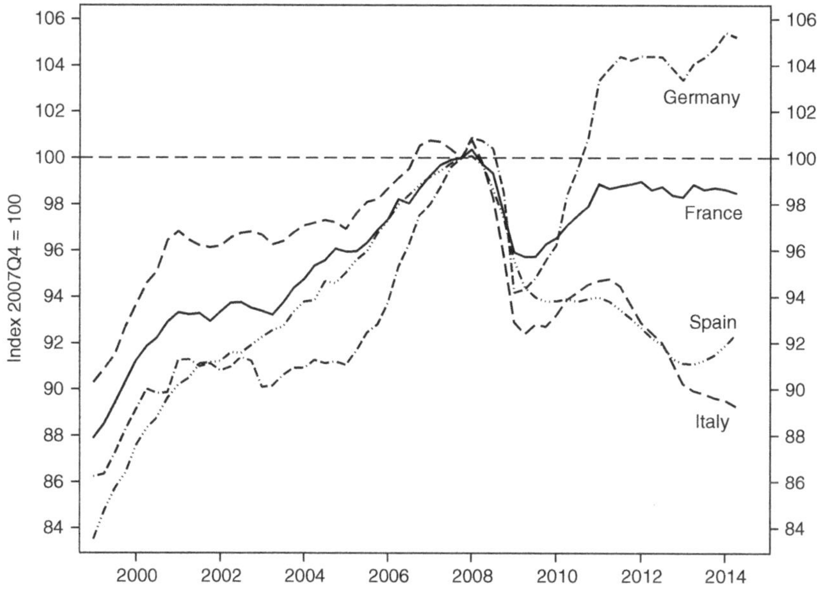

Figure 3.4 The impact of the policy-induced credit crunch
Note: GDP per capita in four largest member states.

tests in the euro area during the crisis is simply a manifestation of the broader political difficulties exposed during the crisis.

Going forward, European governments are faced with difficult choices. Either the euro area should be unwound or its financial sector be fully unified. Following the disastrous experience with the stress test exercises in 2011, it has been recognized that the creation of a true banking union could help resolve some fundamental tensions. A true banking union requires common supervision, common deposit guarantees, and a common resolution mechanism. This is available in the US, where the Federal Reserve is responsible for bank supervision and the FDIC ensures a level playing field across states with a common deposit guarantee and resolution framework. In this context, discussions for the formation of a banking union in Europe in 2012 offered some reason for optimism. Unfortunately, following protracted negotiations, euro area governments rejected the formation of a true banking union, at least for the next several years (Hellwig 2014). Instead, they agreed to unify bank supervision under the ECB, but kept deposit guarantee and bank resolution fragmented across national lines. Only one of the three elements needed for a true banking union has been achieved.

Remarkably, in 2013 a new stress test without a common backstop was decided upon in the euro area. The test was conducted during 2014, as part of the implementation of the decision to unify bank supervision. Once again, the importance of a credible backstop was recognized and discussed, but once again it was rejected. Predictably, the stagnation of the euro area continued.

References

Bernanke, Ben (2009). "The Supervisory Capital Assessment Program." *Speech*, May 11.

Board of Governors of the Federal Reserve System (2009). The Supervisory Capital Assessment Program: Overview of Results. May 7.

De Grauwe, Paul and Yuemei Ji (2013). "From Panic-Driven Austerity to Symmetric Macroeconomic Policies in the Eurozone." *Journal of Common Market Studies* 51(S1): 31–41, September.

Draghi, Mario (2011). Interview with the Financial Times. December 14. European Central Bank.

European Commission (2011). Euro Summit Statement. Brussels, October 26.

Greenlaw, David, Anil Kashyap, Kermit Schoenholtz, and Hyun Song Shin (2012). "Stressed Out: Macroprudential Principles for Stress Testing." *Chicago Booth working paper* 12–08, January.

Hellwig, Martin (2014). "Yes Virginia, There Is a European Banking Union! But It May Not Make Your Wishes Come True." *Max Planck Institute for Research on Collective Goods, Preprint* 2014/12, August 2014.

Hoshi, Takeo and Anil Kashyap (2014). "Will the U.S. and Europe Avoid a Lost Decade? Lessons from Japan's Postcrisis Experience." *IMF Economic Review*, forthcoming.

Kashyap, Anil, Raghuram Rajan, and Jeremy Stein (2008). "Rethinking Capital Regulation." In *Maintaining Stability in a Changing Financial System*, Federal Reserve of Kansas City Jackson Hole Conference.

Orphanides, Athanasios (2012). State Aid in the Banking Market and the Euro Area Crisis: Towards a Banking Union. Presented at the at the conference on State Aid in the Banking Market – Legal and Economic Perspectives, jointly organized by the House of Finance Policy Platform and the Institute for Monetary and Financial Stability (IMFS), June 21.

Orphanides, Athanasios (2013). "The Sovereign Debt Crisis in the Euro Area." *Ekonomia* 15(2) and 16(1),45–64.

Orphanides, Athanasios (2014a). "The Euro Area Crisis: Politics Over Economics." *Atlantic Economic Journal* 42(3), September.

Orphanides, Athanasios (2014b). "European Headwind: ECB Policy and Fed Normalization." *MIT Sloan Research Paper* 5119–14, November.

4

Monetary policy in a banking union

TOBIAS LINZERT AND FRANK SMETS[1]

Introduction

The original architecture of the Economic and Monetary Union (EMU), as laid out in the Maastricht Treaty of 1993, was very much influenced by the realization that imprudent fiscal policy in a monetary union with many national fiscal authorities could unduly affect the conduct of monetary policy and endanger price stability, a phenomenon sometimes described as "fiscal dominance."[2] Accordingly, the ECB was set up as an independent central bank, with the primary objective of maintaining price stability, and several safeguards (such as the prohibition of monetary financing and the Stability and Growth Pact) were built into the institutional architecture of EMU to protect the central bank from fiscal dominance.[3]

[1] Tobias Linzert is Head of the Policy Assessment Section of the ECB and Frank Smets is Adviser to the President at the ECB. We are grateful to Anna Rogantini and Irene Pablos Nuevo for helpful assistance. We are also grateful to Ulrich Bindseil, Ester Faia, Athanasios Orphanides, and Fatima Pires for helpful comments and suggestions.

[2] Fiscal dominance refers to a regime where monetary policy is forced to ensure the solvency of the government (see Sargent and Wallace, 1981). In fact, historical experience shows that excessive levels of government debt may put undue pressure on the central bank to lower the value of nominal debt in contribution to fiscal sustainability (monetization of government debt), risking compromise on the objective of central banks to maintain price stability, ultimately leading to episodes of higher inflation (see Reinhardt and Rogoff, 2010, and Reinhardt and Sbrancia, 2011).

[3] The price stability mandate is stipulated in Art. 127(1) and the ECB's independence in Art. 130 of the EU Treaty. Further safeguards on the central banking side include the monetary financing prohibition, which prohibits the central bank to directly or indirectly finance euro-area governments (Arts. 123 and 124 of the Treaty). And, on the side of governments, there are several institutional provisions to foster fiscal discipline, such as through the no-bail out provision of the Treaty (Arts. 125 and 126) and the provisions contained in the Stability and Growth Pact (see Arts. 125 and 126 of the Treaty).

In contrast, the EU Treaty was largely silent on provisions relating to the safeguarding of euro-area-wide financial stability and the possibility that financial imbalances and systemic instability may also unduly affect monetary policy, often coined as "financial dominance" (see Brunnermeier and Sannikov, 2012).[4] The responsibility for financial stability arrangements and financial sector policies were left largely at the national level. Moreover, most countries lacked adequate provisions for bank resolution. At the euro-area level, crisis management arrangements prior to the crisis were largely based on non-binding frameworks of cooperation and information exchange (see Fonteyne and Van der Vossen, 2007, and ECB, 2006). Also, lending of last resort arrangements (i.e., the provision of emergency liquidity assistance) remained a tool under national responsibility, consistent with the allocation of supervisory and regulatory responsibilities, and the procedures and modalities were left unspecified, in line with the principle of constructive ambiguity (see Padoa-Schioppa, 1999, and ECB, 2006).

The financial and sovereign debt crises that have unfolded since August 2007 have shown that the significant increase in the integration of financial markets must be accompanied by a commensurate increase in the integration of financial sector policies and crisis management arrangements. Existing financial stability and crisis management arrangements were insufficient to deal with crises of such magnitude.

From the outset, the ECB stepped in as a key player in euro-area crisis management. The ECB not only provided monetary accommodation by reducing policy rates to historical lows, the flexible expansion of the Eurosystem's balance sheet proved to be a powerful tool to prevent liquidity shortages in the euro area banking sector and to address an impaired monetary policy transmission mechanism, and thereby ultimately to safeguard price stability. This balance sheet expansion, including through banks' recourse to emergency liquidity assistance, also proved to be crucial in safeguarding the stability of the banking sector. In this sense, the central banks' balance sheet has played a dual and complementary role, ensuring monetary policy transmission to maintain price stability and safeguarding financial stability (see also Tucker, 2004). This dual role is, however, not without risk, in particular in situations where financial sector imbalances combined with a vicious feedback loop between the financial and sovereign sectors can undermine monetary dominance.

[4] Brunnermeier and Sannikov (2012) provide a joint framework for analyzing the risk of fiscal and financial dominance for the conduct of monetary policy; see also Smets (2014).

This chapter first describes the foundations and the experience of the ECB as a crisis manager ("The ECB's role as crisis manager"). The set-up of the Eurosystem included from the outset the possibility of stepping in as lender of last resort in exceptional circumstances, on a case-by-case basis, for temporarily illiquid, but solvent institutions.

"Challenges and risks of financial dominance" then discusses the challenges the ECB faced during this crisis in its role as lender of last resort, and the associated risk of "financial dominance." The three challenges relate to (i) the lack of an adequate bank crisis management and resolution framework in the euro area; (ii) the emergence of the sovereign-bank nexus; and (iii) the difficulty of distinguishing between illiquidity and solvency. "Lending of last resort in a banking union" argues that the establishment of a banking union that includes the Single Supervisory Mechanism (SSM) and the Single Resolution Mechanism (SRM) fills an important institutional gap, which will help to preserve monetary dominance and ensure that the ECB's role as lender of last resort does not unduly affect its monetary policy responsibilities.

Finally, "What's next? What's missing?" discusses whether the banking union institutional set-up will require a re-thinking of the role of the ECB as crisis manager. In particular, the chapter asks whether the existing lending of last resort arrangements, based on national responsibilities and the principle of "constructive ambiguity," are commensurate to and consistent with a centralized banking union. The chapter argues that there are good reasons for establishing a homogenous framework based on clear criteria and eligibility conditions. However, pinning down the role of the lender of last resort cannot be made without clarity on the ultimate fiscal responsibility. Lending of last resort activity must not compromise the integrity of the central bank's balance sheet and its role as monetary policy authority in the pursuit of price stability.

The ECB's role as crisis manager

Banking with banks

Historically, most central banks were founded in order to provide financing to governments or to provide a stable source of financing to banks. In fact, most central banks were established after severe government debt or banking crises.[5] As central banks were given the monopoly power to

[5] The Bank of England was established in 1694 to finance the war debt of William III and Mary II (see Haldane, 2012). The US Federal Reserve, in turn, was founded after the

issue money backed by the respective governments, over time their role moved away from focusing on preserving financial stability to the tasks of issuing money and to maintaining the stability of its value (see Goodhart, 2010). Indeed, today the prime task of central banks is to maintain price stability, which is manifested in their respective statutes and mandates.

The euro area is a bank-based economy, where the banking system is at the heart of conducting monetary policy. This is also reflected in the fact that the ECB deals with banks in order to implement its desired monetary policy stance in the short-term money market.[6] To satisfy banks' demand for central bank money, the ECB conducts credit operations in the form of repurchase agreements with banks that are sound and can pledge adequate collateral.[7] The liquidity provided to banks via these repo operations determines the liquidity conditions in the short-term money market, thereby steering the overnight rate EONIA to the desired level set by the ECB's Governing Council.

Indeed, credit operations are the predominant instrument for the ECB to implement its monetary policy: see Table 4.1. Specifically, the ECB conducts its main credit operations with over 1,500 eligible counterparties, compared with 21 primary dealers in the US. Moreover, refinancing operations prior to the crisis amounted up to over 50 percent of the Eurosystem's balance sheet and up to around 80 percent of the ECB's outstanding monetary policy operations. In comparison, the Fed lends only on a small scale and conducts its monetary policy mainly via outright purchases of US Treasury bonds from its set of primary dealers.

Central banks as lender of last resort

The importance of the banking sector for the conduct and implementation of monetary policy provides central banks, and the ECB in

banking crisis of 1907 by the Federal Reserve Act in 1913. The Sveriges Riksbank, established in 1668, was chartered to lend the government funds and to act as a clearing house for commerce. Similarly, the Banque de France was established by Napoleon in 1800 to stabilize the currency after the hyperinflation of paper money during the French Revolution, as well as to aid in government finance; see also Goodhart (2010).

6 The demand for central bank money arises from (i) the convertibility of commercial money or deposits into banknotes, (ii) the function of central bank money as a final settlement asset, and (iii) the requirement to hold reserves with the central bank.

7 According to Art. 18(1) of the Statute of the ESCB and the ECB, the ECB conducts credit operations with counterparties that are sound and against adequate collateral; see also ECB (2011) for details on counterparty eligibility and the ECB's procedures for implementing its monetary policy. Note that the ECB's monetary policy is implemented via the ECB and the Eurosystem National Central Banks (NCBs).

Table 4.1 *The importance of banks for the ECB's monetary policy*

	No. of counterparties	Size of collateralized lending operations with banks (in % of total size of balance sheet)		
	Today	Pre-crisis	Post-Lehman	End-2014
ECB	Standard tender operations: 1749 Marginal lending facility: 1979 Deposit facility: 2455	51%	60%	45%
Fed	Primary dealers: 21	2%	28%	0%
BoE	Open market operations: 55 Discount window facility: 96 Reserves accounts and standing facilities: 117	60%	83%	0%
BoJ	Outright: 35–47 Loan: 66–257 Repurchase: 26–46	24%	41%	22%

particular, with a legitimate role as crisis manager, both from a monetary policy and financial stability perspective. Safeguarding the stability of the banking sector is a key ingredient for ensuring the smooth transmission and implementation of monetary policy in the pursuit of price stability. In fact, as argued by Goodhart (1999), financial stability is a public good jointly produced by governments and central banks, providing a legitimate case for central banks to step in to provide liquidity as lender of last resort. Therefore, even though the focus of central banks is on the management of macroeconomic stability, in particular price stability, most central banks maintain an implicit or explicit mandate as lender of last resort.

Moreover, the role of central banks as lender of last resort originates from their unique ability to create universally acceptable means of settlement in the form of central bank money by flexibly expanding their balance sheet.[8] In this regard, the central bank's balance sheet can play a

[8] It has been argued, however, that central bank balance sheet expansion can ultimately impact the financial strength of the central bank, thereby undermining its credibility with respect to its ability to preserve price stability. In this regard, the strength of the central bank's balance sheet would be ultimately linked to the potential backing by the fiscal authority; see also Goodhart (1999) and Sims (2004).

unique dual role. It can implement the desired monetary policy stance in the market as well as function as a liquidity backstop. Hence, conducting operations with banks using the central bank's balance sheet has implications for both monetary and financial stability.

There is a long history of central banks providing lending of last resort facilities during banking panics (see Laeven and Valencia, 2012). The design of such facilities has remained largely unaltered since the early central banking days, going back to the well-established prescriptions of Thornton (1802) and Bagehot (1873) in the nineteenth century to lend freely against adequate collateral at a penalty rate to banks. Yet, the question arises of why lending of last resort interventions by central banks are needed in times of well-developed money and capital markets, in sharp contrast to the nineteenth-century circumstances of Thornton and Bagehot.[9]

The need for lending of last resort can emerge from severe macroeconomic shocks, from market failures, or from failures of individual institutions, which can threaten financial stability and, thereby, overall macroeconomic stability. Market failures stemming from externalities or asymmetric information can trigger disturbances in financial markets, bank runs, or more generalized banking panics, which can lead to sudden large-scale withdrawals of liquidity (see, for example, Diamond and Dybvig, 1983, and Gorton, 1988). In this situation depositors may "run" on the bank because they cannot evaluate its "true" financial health. This could render the bank illiquid, as access to funding markets may be denied and liquidating assets may take time or may only be possible at fire-sale prices. In this case, lending of last resort can overcome the coordination failure, preventing the bank from insolvency.

Moreover, illiquidity of an individual bank may propagate to other banks or the banking system more generally, threatening the overall functioning of the financial system and ultimately causing a systemic crisis: see, for example, Aghion, Bolton, and Dewatripont (2000); Allen and Gale (2000); and Goodhart and Huang (2000). In this case, a generalized systemic shock can impact individual banks' business independently of their current strength and creditworthiness, thereby justifying lending of last resort action by the central bank to prevent unwarranted economic costs incurred on society.

[9] Indeed, Goodfriend and King (1988) argued that in an uncollateralized interbank market, peer monitoring would suffice to ensure adequate market discipline.

Lending of last resort can be to markets and/or to individual institutions (see Freixas et al., 1999). The first case relates to an injection of liquidity into the money market as a whole to counter a general dry-up of liquidity, preventing excessive volatility in liquidity conditions and the respective money market rates. The second case relates to the provision of liquidity to an *individual institution* which faces a temporary liquidity shortage and which, despite being considered solvent, cannot raise sufficient funds from the market or via the standard monetary policy operations of a central bank. In this case, central banks typically offer special lending of last resort facilities.

The ECB's pre-crisis crisis management framework

While the primary mandate of the ECB is to maintain price stability, the EU Treaty provides the ECB with the responsibility for contributing to a smooth functioning of payment systems and to the safeguarding of financial stability.[10] The Eurosystem had accordingly set up appropriate procedures to contain the potential systemic effects of a financial disturbance: see ECB (2006).[11] In particular, prior to the crisis, the crisis management framework to contain market turbulences caused by liquidity shortages and general disturbance to the interbank market comprised three main tools.

First, in line with the notion of market lending of last resort (i.e., in case of a general market liquidity shortage), the operational framework provided the ECB with the opportunity to conduct so-called fine-tuning operations. These operations allowed the ECB to inject liquidity into the aggregate money market outside the framework of its regular open market operations.[12]

Second, in the case of a liquidity shortage by an individual bank, the ECB's operational framework also included the possibility of providing a liquidity backstop via recourse to the marginal lending facility. The use of

[10] Art. 127 (5): "5. The ESCB shall contribute to the smooth conduct of policies pursued by the competent authorities relating to the prudential supervision of credit institutions and the stability of the financial system."

[11] See ECB Financial Stability Review, December 2006 and ECB Monthly Bulletin, February 2007, which lay out the EU arrangements for financial crisis management and the ECB's role therein. See also Prati and Schinasi (1999) for a critical review of the crisis management arrangements at the outset of EMU, also with respect to the allocation of lender of last resort and banking supervision responsibilities.

[12] Prior to the crisis the ECB has conducted its main refinancing operations (MROs) and longer-term refinancing operations (LTROs) on a regular basis, fulfilling the euro-area banking sector's liquidity needs.

the marginal lending facility is at the discretion of banks – that is, unless banks were constrained by the availability of eligible collateral, a bank could borrow any desired amount, at a rate of 100 basis points above the main refinancing rate prior to the crisis.[13]

Third, a specific tool to address a bank's liquidity shortages is the provision of emergency liquidity assistance (ELA). ELA is a tool for temporary emergency lending in exceptional circumstances and on a case-by-case basis to illiquid, but solvent banks, which cannot obtain liquidity either through market sources or through the ECB's regular monetary policy operations (see ECB, 2006).

ELA up to now is founded on three cornerstones, namely (i) national competence, (ii) the principle of "constructive ambiguity," and (iii) the non-interference with monetary policy.

The first cornerstone relates to the fact that, unlike the ECB's monetary policy instruments and operations, ELA is a competence of the Eurosystem national central banks (NCBs). ELA, therefore, remains outside the confines of the ECB's single monetary policy (including the soundness and collateral requirements), even though it uses the Eurosystem's balance sheet for liquidity extension in a similar manner as the ECB's monetary policy operations. The access to ELA is at the full discretion of the NCB. Hence, the NCB assesses the factors that can justify the provision of ELA and sets the respective conditions in terms of collateral, maturity, and interest rate. The NCB also remains fully liable for ELA provision – that is, potential losses arising out of the ELA operations are not shared within the Eurosystem.[14]

When the ECB was established in 1998, there were several good reasons for this choice. First, banking supervision, including the assessment of a bank's solvency, was a national competence, which in many cases was placed under the roof of the NCB. Therefore, having access to first-hand information about the banks, the NCBs were in a better position to assess the rationale and the creditworthiness of the requesting illiquid bank. And second, the national responsibility for ELA minimizes the risk that potential errors in the provision of ELA, with potential detrimental effects for the central bank balance sheet, would create

[13] During the crisis, the ECB has narrowed the corridor, in various steps, down to 25 basis points in June 2014.

[14] Indeed, Goodhart (1999) stresses the heightened risk through lending of last resort, as the bank turns to the central bank precisely for the reason that it ran out of good collateral that is accepted for collateralized interbank loans.

reputational spill-overs to the ECB's monetary policy function and ensuring the ECB's financial independence.

The second cornerstone is that ELA has been set up according to the principle of "constructive ambiguity," whereby the exact arrangements, procedures, and conditions were not laid down explicitly and were left largely unspecified vis-à-vis the banking sector (see Padoa-Schioppa, 1999).[15] The rationale for this was based on the notion that leaving open the conditions under which the central bank could intervene was an adequate tool to contain the moral hazard associated with the lending of last resort safety net and to discipline markets accordingly (see Freixas et al., 1999).[16] Still, to some extent this also reflected the belief that by implementing monetary policy in a corridor system, where the marginal lending facility would provide a natural overdraft facility, emergency lending outside of this framework would be a rather unlikely phenomenon. Indeed, in 1999 the late Tommaso Padoa-Schioppa wrote that "the probability that a modern bank is solvent, but illiquid, and at the same time lacks sufficient collateral to obtain regular central bank funding, is, in my view, quite small."

And finally, the third cornerstone relates to the fundamental condition that ELA should not become a constraint for monetary policy. In this regard, the Statute of the ECB and the EU Treaty contain two important safeguards. First, according to Article 14.4 of the ECB's Statute, ELA should not be seen as interfering or being in conflict with the objectives and tasks of the Eurosystem, most notably with the ECB's primary objective to maintain price stability in the euro area. Should this be the case, the Governing Council could object to the provision of ELA.[17] Therefore, the provision of ELA is assessed on a regular basis to ascertain whether the liquidity provided is in line with the desired liquidity conditions in the money market and would not interfere with the ECB's

[15] The principle of "constructive ambiguity" was brought forward by Governor Gerald Corrigan of the Federal Reserve Bank of New York in a Statement before the US Senate Committee on banking, housing and urban affairs, Federal Reserve Bank of New York Bulletin (1990).

[16] More specifically, Freixas (1999) has characterized the principle of constructive ambiguity in a model where the central bank commits to a mixed strategy for lending of last resort, which reduces ex-ante risk, shifting incentives on to the side of banks.

[17] Art. 14.4 of the Statute of the ESCB and the ECB: "National central banks may perform functions other than those specified in this Statute unless the Governing Council finds, by a majority of two thirds of the votes cast, that these interfere with the objectives and tasks of the ESCB. Such functions shall be performed on the responsibility and liability of national central banks and shall not be regarded as being part of the functions of the ESCB."

control over setting the appropriate monetary policy stance.[18] Second, ELA must also be provided in full respect of the monetary financing prohibition, laid out in Art. 123 of the EU Treaty. This also includes extending any form of credit to the government, such as, for example, by taking over a government function such as solvency support.

The ECB as lender of last resort during the crisis: three facts

During the crisis, the ECB and the Eurosystem NCBs stepped in as lender of last resort both for the interbank market and for individual institutions. In doing so it used instruments that went beyond the ones laid out in the previous section. Three facts about the ECB's role as crisis manager stand out.

Fact No. 1: The ECB provided substantial liquidity support to the euro-area banking sector (see Figure 4.1). In summer 2007 the ECB started off with a series of fine-tuning operations (FTOs), which injected extra liquidity into the money market. This soon turned out to be insufficient to adequately stabilize money market conditions, which led the ECB over time to increase its extra liquidity provision in amount and tenor. Most notably, in October 2008, the ECB switched to providing unlimited funding to banks, conducting its refinancing operations in a fixed-rate full allotment mode, satisfying fully banks' demand for central bank liquidity subject to the availability of eligible collateral.[19] In this

[18] Procedures were put in place that ensured an adequate information flow within the Eurosystem to the ECB's decision-making bodies, which ensured overall control over aggregate liquidity conditions, consistent with the maintenance of the appropriate single monetary policy stance (see ECB, 2007). This information includes (1) the counterparty to which the ELA has been/will be provided; (2) the value date and maturity date of the ELA that has been/will be provided; (3) the volume of the ELA that has been/will be provided; (4) the currency in which the ELA has been/will be provided; (5) the collateral/guarantees against which the ELA has been/will be provided, including the valuation of, and any haircuts applied to, the collateral provided and, where applicable, details on the guarantee provided and the terms of any contractual safeguards; (6) the interest rate to be paid by the counterparty on the ELA that has been/will be provided; (7) the specific reason(s) for the ELA that has been/will be provided (i.e., margin calls, deposit outflows, etc.); (8) the prudential supervisor's assessment, over the short and medium term, of the liquidity position and solvency of the institution receiving the ELA, including the criteria used to come to a positive conclusion with respect to solvency; and (9) where relevant, an assessment of the cross-border dimensions and/or the potential systemic implications of the situation that has made/is making the extension of ELA necessary. See ELA Procedures, published by the ECB on October 17, 2013.

[19] Soon after the outbreak of tensions in the money market in August 2007, the ECB increased the liquidity provision via its three-month longer-term refinancing operations (LTROs) and started to provide liquidity at a maturity of six months. In May 2009, the ECB announced

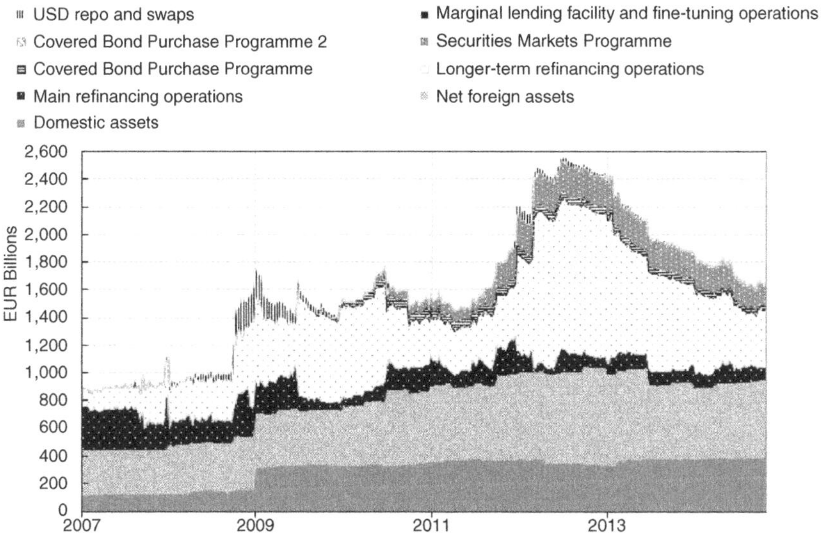

Figure 4.1 Lending of last resort to markets
Source: ECB
Latest observation: September 2014

regard, the balance sheet of the Eurosystem was used in an elastic manner to stabilize funding conditions in the euro-area money market.

Fact No. 2: The ECB largely replaced interbank intermediation and became – at times – a major source of funding for the euro-area banking sector. With the euro-area money market drying up, banks turned to the ECB as a stable source of funding. As shown in Figure 4.2, the borrowings were particularly pronounced in the periods following the default of Lehman Brothers in October 2008 and the height of the euro-area sovereign debt crisis in 2012.

Fact No. 3: The Eurosystem NCBs stepped in with sizable emergency liquidity assistance to individual institutions. As evident from Figure 4.3, which shows an approximation of the consolidated ELA provision by Eurosystem NCBs as of April 2012, ELA became an important source of funding for euro-area banks. While under national competence, ELA has contributed significantly to the overall increase in

further six-month operations and LTROs with a maturity of one year (ECB, 2010). In December 2011 and February 2012, the ECB conducted two three-year LTROs.

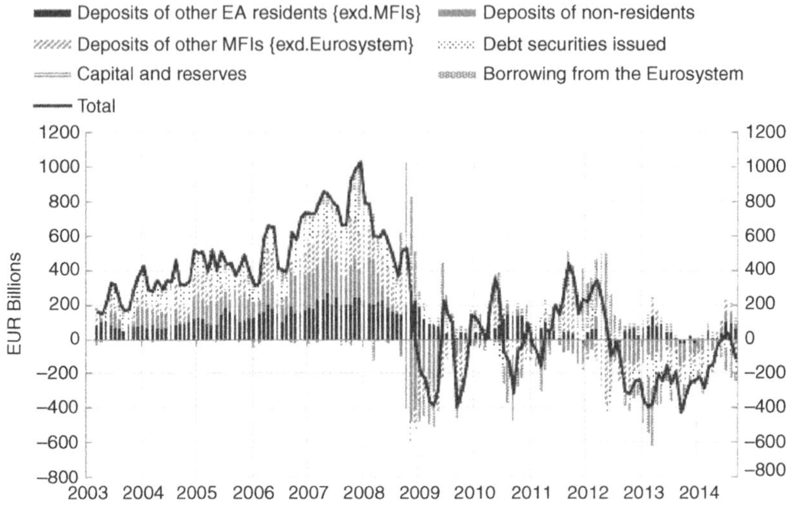

Figure 4.2 Share of the Eurosystem in Euro Area MFI main liabilities
Source: ECB
Latest observation: September 2014

the Eurosystem balance sheet and has been an integral part of the ECB's crisis management.

Challenges and risks of financial dominance

The experience of the financial crisis has shown that central banks' crisis management was essential to preserve both financial and price stability. However, with the provision of lending of last resort of the scale and duration experienced during the crisis, the question of possible risks and side effects naturally arises.

Brunnermeier and Sanikov (2012) have argued that central banks may be trapped in a situation of financial dominance, conducting monetary policy foremost in the interest of financial stability. In the extreme this could imply that the central bank tolerates higher inflation than the price stability objective of the central bank would command for the sake of safeguarding financial stability.

Financial dominance, however, in the context of the central bank using its balance sheet for lending of last resort activity, may take a more subtle form, without necessarily compromising the central bank's inflation objective. Lending of last resort can imply unduly distorting the borrowing costs

Figure 4.3 Lending of last resort to individual institutions: ELA[20]
Note: monthly data. In the week ending April 20, 2012, an accounting reclassification took place in order to harmonize the disclosure of the Emergency Liquidity Assistance (ELA) provided by Eurosystem central banks to domestic credit institutions under the Eurosystem balance sheet item "other claims on euro-area credit institutions denominated in euro" (asset item 6); see ECB press release from April 24, 2012.
Source: ECB
Latest observation: October 2014

of banks, thereby impacting the allocation of resources in the financial sector and the behavior of banks in the market. Moreover, the provision of lending of last resort may prevent the necessary adjustment of banks' balance sheets, thereby making banks' reliant on central bank liquidity provision and challenging the temporary nature of lending of last resort actions. Ultimately, financial dominance becomes fiscal dominance. In this case, the central bank could be forced to take on government tasks, such as by recapitalizing banks or providing liquidity to insolvent banks.

[20] Note that the figure displays the Eurosystem balance sheet item A6 "other claims on euro-area credit institutions denominated in euro," which only as of April 20, 2012 includes a consolidated reporting of ELA provided by Eurosystem NCBs. In this regard, the figure provides only an approximation of the ELA provision of the Eurosystem NCBs, where the shown series overestimates to some extent the actual total ELA provision.

Even without direct effects of lending of last resort on inflation, financial dominance may have serious consequences for the integrity of the central banks' balance sheet and for the central bank's credibility and reputation, ultimately compromising the central bank's ability to maintain price stability.[21] Such undue lending of last resort, resulting from using the central banks' balance sheet for more risky operations with banks, can be perceived as a threat to the financial strength of the central bank. Economic agents may, therefore, cast doubt on the inflation-fighting capability of the central bank when operating under balance sheet constraints (see Jeanne and Svensson, 2007, Gil Park, 2012, and Goodhart, 1999).

Conceptually, the respective roles of central banks and governments in a financial crisis situation can be cast into differentiating between illiquidity and insolvency of a bank (see Figure 4.4). As described in the section "Challenges and risks of financial dominance," in case a bank is temporarily unable to fulfill its liquidity needs via the market or normal central bank facilities, but is still considered as solvent, the central bank may step in as lender of last resort. Conversely, if the bank is insolvent, it

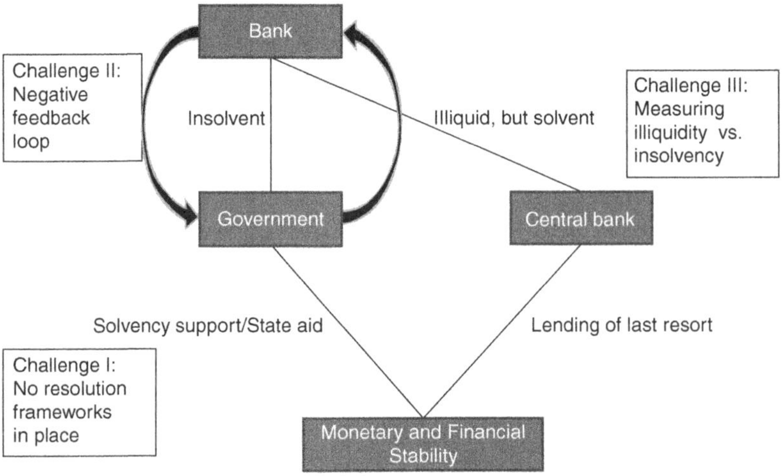

Figure 4.4 Challenges and risks of financial dominance

[21] In fact, as in the case of fiscal dominance, Davig, Leeper, and Walker (2011) show that if households consider it probable that the central bank balance sheet is used to stabilize government debt, this will lead to an upward shift in inflation expectations and increase inflation. Similar effects seem possible under financial dominance, if economic agents perceive the central bank to imprudently use its balance sheet to stabilize the banking sector.

is for the government (i.e., the finance ministry and/or resolution authority) to deal with the ailing bank, which should decide whether to liquidate, resolve, or bailout the bank.[22]

In practice, however, the process of dealing with an ailing bank is less straightforward. In the specific case of the euro area, three particular challenges stood out that could imply making the risk of financial dominance more imminent. These challenges relate to (i) the lack of adequate bank crisis management and resolution frameworks in the euro area, (ii) the emergence of the sovereign-bank nexus, and (iii) the difficulty of distinguishing between illiquidity and insolvency (see Figure 4.4).

Regarding the first challenge, the euro-area countries lacked adequate legal frameworks for banking resolution and were, therefore, insufficiently equipped to deal with an ailing bank in an orderly manner. Moreover, euro-area-wide resolution responsibilities comparable to the Federal deposit insurance and resolution authority (FDIC) in the US were non-existent. Without a clear legal framework and an appropriate toolkit to resolve banks, and with the risk of ensuing financial stability risks from a disorderly liquidation, the risk of forbearance and the use of tax-payers money to rescue an insolvent bank is very high. In addition, faced with an inadequate resolution framework, the pressure for supervisors to forbear is also heightened due to not only reputational issues (that they failed to supervise the bank properly), but also due to financial stability concerns. Indeed, in such situations, supervisors may be reluctant to let a bank fail as this could have an adverse financial stability impact and could raise concerns of possible contagion.

Regarding the second challenge, the absence of a banking union with common bank supervision and resolution led to a strong link between the health of euro-area sovereigns and their respective banking sectors. During the crisis, in the absence of bank resolution frameworks, euro-area governments financed large bank rescue operations. With fiscal discipline having been weak in the run-up to the crisis and increasingly large government deficits as a result of the crisis, government debt rose significantly in the period between 2008 and 2010. As a consequence, generalized banking sector problems in combination with a lack of fiscal space triggered a loss in market confidence. Indeed, markets began to cast doubt on the capability of euro-area governments to provide sufficient backstop to their banking sectors, impeding the sustainability of

[22] The provision of government support would need to comply with state aid rules.

government budgets and thereby triggering a substantial increase in government bond risk premia in some euro-area countries, making the sovereign sector itself a source of financial instability (see Acharya, Drechsler, and Schnabl, 2011). Given the strong financial links between euro-area governments and their respective banking sectors, this created a deep interconnection between the health of euro-area sovereigns and their respective banking sectors.[23]

Regarding the third challenge, the difficulty in distinguishing between an illiquid and an insolvent bank came to the fore in the crisis. Ultimately, the case for lending of last resort rests on the ability to distinguish problems of illiquidity from insolvency. The solvency of a bank is a complex concept, whose measurement is more an art than a science. While the regulatory framework provides legal solvency requirements that banks need to meet, in a crisis situation the regulatory capital ratios are quickly outdated. Moreover, the assessment of whether a bank is solvent is not only point-in-time, but should also encompass a forward-looking assessment as to whether the bank has a sustainable business model. Therefore, the assessment of whether a bank is solvent is not an easily quantifiable concept that one can pin down by assessing a number of clearly defined indicators, but ultimately requires discretionary supervisory judgment.[24]

Insolvency can typically arise for two reasons. First, from a balance-sheet perspective, liabilities of the bank exceed its assets, as measured by the future discounted value of the bank's assets and liabilities. Second, a bank can simply lack the means of payments or liquidity to honor its debt obligations as they fall due. This two-tier concept of insolvency is also reflected in the new EU legal framework on bank recovery and resolution, whereby the criteria to assess a bank as "failing or likely to fail" comprises both the determination of the current and future net worth of the bank and its capacity to honor current and future payment obligations.[25]

[23] Indeed, most of the sovereign debt holdings on banks' balance sheets in the euro area are held in form of domestic sovereign debt, with the fraction of these being over 80 percent in some euro-area jurisdictions; see Uhlig (2013) and Chapter 2 in this book by Marco Pagano.

[24] Indeed, supervisory solvency assessments go beyond the quantifiable criteria that, for example, underlie supervisory risk assessments, such as the CAMELS ratings (capital, asset quality, management, earnings, and liquidity) used by US supervisors.

[25] In fact, Article 27 (2) of the BRRD reads as follows:

"(b) the assets of the institution are or there are objective elements to support a determination that the assets of the institution will be, in the near future, less than its liabilities;

From this it becomes clear that illiquidity and insolvency are intricately interlinked. For example, a bank can have positive net worth, but be considered illiquid (i.e., unable to meet its debt obligations). This situation could arise if, for example, deposits are withdrawn (e.g., due to market distress), which depletes the banks cash holdings and central bank reserves. If the bank is unable to raise short-term funding in the market or liquidate its assets (e.g., due to a distressed situation in the market), the bank would be considered as illiquid, rendering the bank ultimately insolvent. Also, illiquidity can spiral off into insolvency as the bank may be forced to fund itself at prohibitive prices or sell its assets at unfavorable prices, thereby ultimately causing the bank's net worth to turn negative.

From the perspective of the lender of last resort, it is crucial to assess the underlying sources for illiquidity – namely, whether related to a market failure causing temporary illiquidity or whether it reflects valid concerns about the sustainability of a bank's balance sheet. However, to distinguish between illiquidity and insolvency might be challenging in a crisis situation. First, there are limits to measuring the net worth of a bank over time, as future asset and liability market values are uncertain and difficult to predict over a reasonable period of time.[26] Second, not all assets and liabilities have market values. These valuation challenges are even greater in a distressed environment, when the "fair price" of banks' assets and liabilities are subject to even greater uncertainty. And third, in a crisis, the lender of last resort has to act swiftly, making thorough asset quality reviews a challenging task.

Given the uncertainty over the true state of a bank, a central bank generally faces a type 1/type 2 error problem (see Sveriges Riksbank, 2003). Type 1 error occurs if the central bank provides ELA to a bank that was wrongly assessed as solvent. Conversely, type 2 errors occur when the central bank refuses to provide ELA to an institution that was erroneously assessed as insolvent.

Regarding type 1 error, the consequences of this would be possible risks to the central bank balance sheet, reputational damage, and the risk

(c) the institution is or there are objective elements to support a determination that the institution will be, in the near future, unable to pay its obligations as they fall due."

26 The uncertainty of the valuation of bank assets and liabilities will depend also on the projection horizon. Moreover, the point in time assessment may be further complicated by lags in banks' accounting data, which is typically collected on a quarterly basis. Hence, in more stressed market environments and with fast-changing asset prices, even an accurate point in time assessment might be challenging; see also Sveriges Riksbank (2003).

of moral hazard on the side of banks. In particular, any doubts about the integrity of the central bank's balance sheet can have serious consequences for the reputation and credibility of the central bank, ultimately entailing the risk of compromising its price stability mandate.

As regards type 2 errors (i.e., being unduly restrictive in the provision of ELA), these are also not without serious risks. The consequences of this type of error are incurring unnecessary costs to the economy and reduced social welfare stemming from the liquidation or resolution of a solvent institution. In the worst case, such resolution can trigger contagion, with systemic implications for the banking sector and the overall economy.

Lending of last resort in a banking union

In the euro area, the mismatch between single monetary policy and national banking sector policies has been, in the recent crisis, a destabilizing factor. The joint occurrence of a banking and sovereign debt crisis has threatened the effective conduct of monetary policy in the euro area and overall macroeconomic stability.

The banking union consisting mainly of the Single Supervisory Mechanism (SSM) and the Single Resolution Mechanism (SRM) is essential for ensuring an effective monetary policy transmission. It will also be instrumental in supporting a smooth implementation of monetary policy and shielding the central bank's role as lender of last resort (see Figure 4.5).

From the start of the SSM on November 4, 2014, the ECB, in its capacity as supervisor, is directly responsible for the solvency assessment of the significant banks under its direct supervision, which represent around 85 percent of the euro area's banking assets.

As the ECB conducts monetary policy mostly through collateralized credit operations with euro-area counterparties, first-hand information about the banks' creditworthiness is of key importance, also in view of protecting the central banks' balance sheet (see Folkerts-Landau and Garber, 1992).[27] Especially in crisis times, when collateral values may degrade, the soundness of counterparties becomes even more relevant as

[27] In fact, Repullo (2000) argues that the supervisory function in the hands of the central bank can avoid the duplication of supervisory activities and can be a means to reduce the moral hazard problem associated with lending of last resort. But conflicts of interest between the monetary policy and the supervisory function of the central bank may arise if lending of last resort distorts the effective implementation of monetary policy, distorts the allocation in the banking sector by undue subsidizing of the liquidity provision to a

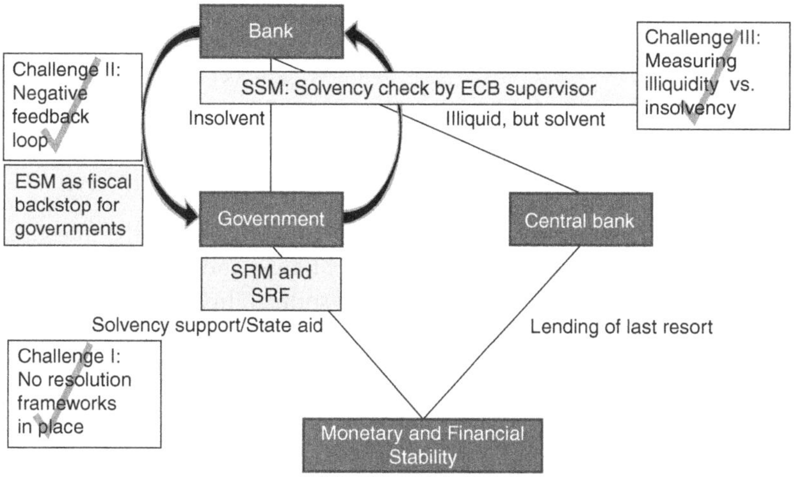

Figure 4.5 Lending of last resort in a banking union

a safeguard to the Eurosystem's balance sheet. Indeed, in a framework with about 1,800 banks being eligible in the ECB's monetary policy operations, evaluating soundness on a more robust set of information appears absolutely crucial. Also in the case of ELA, when the requested amount exceeds EUR 2 billion, the Governing Council will assess both the provision of ELA and the counterparty's solvency (in case it is a significant bank).[28]

The banking union will provide the euro area with an effective shock absorption mechanism. In fact, in case of failure of a bank, and if considered to be in the public interest, the SRM – on the basis of the resolution tools contained in the resolution framework laid out in the EU bank recovery and resolution directive (BRRD), and backed by a common resolution fund – will ensure bank resolution in an orderly manner. This provides assurance to the SSM as the banking supervisor to judge banks as insolvent without being concerned that this may trigger adverse

specific bank, or supports the financing of the banks maturity mismatch position; see Goodhart and Schoenmaker (1995).

[28] See "Emergency liquidity assistance (ELA) and monetary policy," ECB press release, October 2013. Also, in the case of the US Fed, its supervisory assessment crucially determines the counterparties' access to the Fed's liquidity facilities. Indeed, the access to the different facilities (i.e., the credit via discount window) depends on the soundness of the borrowing institution, based, for example, on the supervisory CAMELS rating. The access then differs with respect to interest rate charged, credit limits, and tenor.

financial stability implications. At the same time, it provides an insurance against erring on the strict side.

What's next? What's missing?

An effective lending of last resort framework for the euro area

As the new banking union framework is being put in place, the question arises whether the original cornerstones of the lending of last resort framework, specifically those of national responsibility and constructive ambiguity, are still adequate.

Regarding the principle of constructive ambiguity, one may claim that the crisis has not altered its underlying rationale as a deterrent of moral hazard.[29] Constructive ambiguity also avoids the reputational risk that publically pre-announced procedures and conditions drawn up in tranquil times are broken in crisis times. In fact, according to Padoa-Schioppa (1999) lending of last resort implies by its very nature an exceptional circumstance, which may require departure from rules and procedures.

However, the problem of ambiguity is discretion. Exercising discretion can lead to a more, not less, lenient provision of lending of last resort, thereby increasing the risk of moral hazard, rather than containing it. In this case, the principle of "constructive ambiguity" can turn out to be time-inconsistent and will achieve the opposite effect, once market participants build up expectations that central banks will step in in case of a crisis.

Brunnermeier and Sannikov (2012) argue that, as in any insurance scheme, the risk of moral hazard will depend on the underlying conditions and institutional arrangement. Pre-announced procedures and conditions may in fact be effective in limiting moral hazard if they are well designed and credible.[30] Freixas, Parigi, and Rochet (2004) show that making the

[29] Maintaining uncertainty about the procedures and conditions of lending of last resort will induce banks to act prudently, as they will remain uncertain over whether they will be rescued or not; see Freixas et al. (1999). Similarly, Crocket (1996) argues that managers and shareholders should remain uncertain about the costs and conditions of liquidity support, thereby deterring them from imprudent behavior.

[30] In fact, Goodfriend and Lacker (1999) argue that in order to limit moral hazard on the side of banks, the central bank has to build up a reputation for limited lending by actual prudent lending behavior. The authors stress that the central banks' commitment to limited lending is key, as otherwise banks will revise their expectations with regard to the central banks' willingness to lend, thereby inducing greater risk-taking behavior on the side of banks. The authors see an analogy to the case of central banks building up an

conditions for ELA access known in advance will provide banks with a strong incentive to reduce the probability of insolvency. In a similar vein, Brunnermeiner and Sannikov (2014) show that clear rules that discriminate by health of the bank help to overcome ex-ante moral hazard. Moreover, the stigma effect associated with lending of last resort (i.e., the fact that accessing lending of last resort will durably impact the banks reputation as a sound borrower in the interbank market) should serve as an additional deterrent against moral hazard (see, for example, Furfine, 2001).[31]

Daniel et al. (2005) argue that the best way to control moral hazard is the establishment of a strong supervisory framework, providing the appropriate incentives to financial institutions.[32] The ECB's new role as supervisor will give the ECB the tools at hand with which to control moral hazard, thereby preventing imprudent behavior on the side of banks, by, for example, taking ex-ante supervisory measures on controlling balance-sheet risk, including strict provisions for the management of liquidity risk, and ultimately holding the power to declare a bank as failing or likely to fail.[33]

A few central banks (such as the Sveriges Riksbank, the Swiss National Bank, and the Bank of Canada) have started making their lending of last resort frameworks public. Moreover, the Dodd-Frank Act in the US has also specified more clearly the role of the Fed as lender of last resort.[34] These frameworks provide clarity as to the punitive conditions and terms under which banks can expect liquidity support from the central bank, providing the appropriate incentives for banks to fulfill their liquidity needs in private markets.[35]

inflation-fighting reputation in the early 1980s, which ultimately brought down inflation expectations and actual inflation.

31 According to the ELA framework of the Sveriges Riksbank, the provision of ELA would be made public. Given the likely resulting stigma effect, this should incentivize to refrain from asking for emergency liquidity assistance; see Sveriges Riksbank (2003).

32 According to Daniel et al. (2005), banks also have an incentive to avoid recourse to ELA as they would be subject to increased supervisory attention and monitoring.

33 In fact, according to Repullo (2005), the central banks' role as lender of last resort could reduce the incentives to hold a sufficient level of liquid assets. This could be ensured ex-ante by the supervisor.

34 The Dodd-Frank Act (Section 13.3) specifies that the Fed is prohibited in acting as lender of last resort to individual institutions. The Fed can only draw up market lending of last resort facilities in the event of systemic crisis, following the approval of the US Treasury. Moreover, the Fed will be obliged to make such lending of last resort activity public.

35 In addition to the solvency criterion and the collateral requirements, the frameworks by the Swiss National Bank and the Sveriges Riksbank also include the criterion of systemic importance in the overall assessment of emergency liquidity assistance.

As regards the adequacy of ELA being a national responsibility, this ultimately depends on the degree of integration and interconnection of the respective banking sector, and the degree of centralization in financial sector governance.

The crisis has shown that, in an integrated euro-area banking system with significant cross-border exposures, financial shocks and turbulences stemming from bank failure can easily spread to banks in other euro-area member states. A more centralized lending of last resort framework could clearly internalize this aspect better than decentralized models. Moreover, homogenous arrangements of lending of last resort will ensure a level playing field in an integrated financial market.

A credible lender of last resort should have full information about the banks it lends to and, therefore should act in close cooperation with the banking supervisor. In the words of Padoa-Schioppa (1999: 303), "in normal circumstances central banking and prudential supervision have an arm's length distance between them. In crisis situations, however, they need to act closely together, often in co-operation with other authorities as well." In fact, as already argued by Folkerts-Landau and Garber (1992), the institution that puts its resources at stake through lending of last resort should also be in charge of establishing the solvency assessment (and vice versa) to avoid potential inter-agency conflicts of interest. With the introduction of the SSM, the ECB will be responsible for assessing the solvency of ECB counterparties. As the responsible bank supervisor, the ECB will have reliable "in house" information on bank solvency and collateral at hand, facilitating informed decisions on lending of last resort action.

While much speaks in favor of overhauling the lending of last resort in the euro area toward a more unified and more centralized framework, the question arises of who would take the ultimate fiscal responsibility.[36] The new banking union arrangements will provide ample safeguards against undue lending of last resort on the side of the central bank. Yet, the ultimate fiscal responsibility for banks will remain – despite the creation

[36] Of course, financial buffers and the central banks' capital provide a backstop against losses incurred on monetary policy operations as well as lending of last resort. Moreover, the financial strength of the central bank is not only determined by its point in time buffers and capital, but by its discounted value of future seignorage income stemming from the central banks' role as monopoly issuer of money. However, according to Goodhart (1999) and Sims (2004), it is ultimately the fiscal anchor given by the taxing power of the government that matters as back-up to the central bank's liabilities, which, as Goodhart (1999), notes goes back to the early works of both Thornton (1802) and Bagehot (1873).

of the European Stability Mechanism (ESM) – with the euro-area member states. It remains, therefore, an open question as to whether the fiscal precautions are sufficient to fully break the link between sovereigns and banks and can thereby sufficiently insure against the risk of financial dominance.

Does the design of the banking union really break the link between sovereigns and banks?

The new financial sector architecture should largely prevent the re-appearance of the negative feedback loop between the sovereign and banks. This is achieved, foremost, by a new pecking order for bank rescue, which will adequately tap private sector resources before turning to the public sector.[37] Only once these sources are exhausted can national governments come to the rescue with public funds.[38] These public funds will remain a national fiscal responsibility without a euro-area-wide fiscal backstop being in place to act as a "firewall" against contagion.

At the euro-area level, the ESM can act in case bank rescue action would compromise the fiscal sustainability of a member state. However, in the case of supranational responsibility for supervision and resolution, the typical ESM logic of holding member states liable for their banking sectors may not perfectly apply any more. In fact, conditions for bank resolution and fiscal support should uniformly apply across the euro area, ensuring a level playing field, independent of the fiscal backing of the particular member state. But, as yet, there is no union-wide public fiscal backstop for bank resolution in the euro area in line with the commitment of the European Council from December 2012.[39]

[37] Indeed, for dealing with an ailing bank, the new EU resolution framework foresees primarily the use of private sector bail-in of 8 percent of total bank liabilities. Once the possibilities for bail-in are exhausted, the privately funded resolution fund might contribute with an additional 5 percent of total liabilities.

[38] According to Article 50 of the EU Bank Recovery and Resolution Directive, government stabilization tools may be used as last resort in very extraordinary situations (to be assessed by the European Commission) and under the condition that shareholders and creditors have contributed to the loss absorption.

[39] Indeed, according to the Council conclusions, "The single resolution mechanism should be based on contributions by the financial sector itself and include appropriate and effective backstop arrangements. This backstop should be fiscally neutral over the medium term, by ensuring that public assistance is recouped by means of ex post levies on the financial industry."

Why is this still needed? First, from the perspective of the tax-payer, a fiscal backstop to the resolution fund – for example, on the basis of a credit line given by the collective of euro-area governments – is preferable over the existing fiscal arrangements underlying the banking union.[40] In fact, such an arrangement will reduce possible fiscal costs. If national governments or the ESM via its direct bank recapitalization instrument come to the rescue, there is the risk that such fiscal engagement will render losses if the bank ultimately defaults or the shares do not recover in value. To the contrary, rescue action by the resolution authority and the resolution fund can always be recouped from the financial industry. Indeed, the resolution authority, unlike the ESM when directly engaged in a bank, can impose future levies on the banking industry to recoup possible financial losses from its resolution engagements. Ultimately, such an arrangement would be cost-neutral to the tax-payer, whereby all possible rescue actions would be covered by the private sector.

Second, from a monetary policy perspective, a fiscal backstop to the resolution fund is needed, arising from the resolution fund's responsibility for resolution funding. Despite orderly resolution tools in place, this may not prevent depositors from withdrawing bank deposits, particularly if the resolution process cannot be concluded in a very short time frame. In this case, banks will also require funding during the resolution process to conduct payments, honor short-term liabilities, and pay out depositors.

The single resolution fund of around EUR 55 billion may not suffice to stem the possible risk of deposit outflows. A fiscal backstop would, therefore, be needed as an additional line of defense against the risk of financial dominance. Such fiscal backing could also be complemented by a joint euro-area-wide deposit guarantee scheme.

Conclusion

Central banks in general, and the ECB in particular, have played a major role in the management of the crisis. In the euro area, the crisis has not

[40] There are several options for the design of a fiscal backstop. The SRF might be given the possibility to raise funds in the market by issuing paper in a similar fashion as the ESM. Another option is to establish a credit line of the resolution fund to a common fiscal resource of the euro-area governments, just like the US FDIC has a credit line with the US Treasury. In the case of the euro area, such common fiscal resource could be provided by the already established ESM.

only threatened overall macroeconomic and financial stability, but also the integrity of the Economic and Monetary Union. While the ECB stepped in as effective crisis manager, the crisis revealed the incompleteness of the EMU architecture.

The crisis has shown that the Eurosystem's role as lender of last resort and the elastic use of its balance sheet is deeply linked to its responsibility for both monetary and financial stability. The banking union with the establishment of the SSM and the SRM and the establishment of the ESM are major stepping stones toward a more robust monetary union, providing effective tools for crisis prevention and resolution, safeguarding overall financial stability in the euro area. For monetary policy, this implies reduced threats to monetary stability and less likely calls for lending of last resort.

At the same time, a more complete EMU architecture with a banking union also opens up the opportunity to reassess the crisis management role of the ECB. There are good reasons in place for a more homogeneous lending of last resort approach based on clear eligibility criteria, conditions, and procedures. This would ensure setting clear boundaries to lending of last resort vis-à-vis other external stakeholders, namely the banking sector, the supervisor, and the resolution authority. Moreover, transparent rules and procedures combined with a high degree of accountability would support the independence and democratic legitimacy of the lending of last resort function.

Given the more centralized approach to financial sector policies and institutions established by the banking union, the case can also be made for a more centralized approach to euro-area lending of last resort. Yet, the banking union misses an important cornerstone: the fiscal backstop to the resolution fund.

Absent such fiscal backstop, the risk of financial dominance may not be entirely eliminated. More robust fiscal backing is called for, which can eliminate the risk of fiscal financial feedback loops and shields the central bank as lender of last resort.

References

Acharya, Viral, Itamar Drechsler, and Philipp Schnabl (2011). "A Pyrrhic Victory? Bank Bailouts and Sovereign Credit Risk." *Journal of Finance* 69(6): 2689–2739.

Aghion, Philippe, Patrick Bolton, and Mathias Dewatripont (2000). "Contagious Bank Failures in a Free Banking System." *European Economic Review* 44(4–6): 713–718.

Allen, Frankling and Douglas Gale (2000). "Financial Contagion." *Journal of Political Economy* 108: 1–33.

Bagehot, Walter (1873). *Lombard Street: A Description of the Money Market.* London: H. S. King & Co.

Brunnermeier, Markus K. and Yuliy Sannikov (2012). "Redistributive Monetary Policy." Federal Reserve Bank of Kansas, Jackson Hole Symposium.

Brunnermeier, Markus K. and Yuliy Sannikov (2014). "A Macroeconomic Model with a Financial Sector." *American Economic Review* 104(2): 379–421.

Crocket, Andrew (1996). "The Theory and Practice of Financial Stability." *De Economist* 144(4): 531–568.

Daniel, Fred, Walter Engert, and Dinah Maclean (2005). "The Bank of Canada as Lender of Last Resort." *Bank of Canada Review* Winter 2004–2005.

Davig, Troy, Eric M. Leeper, and Todd B. Walker, (2011). "Inflation and the Fiscal Limit." *European Economic Review* 55(1): 31–47.

Diamond, Douglas and Philip Dybvig (1983). "Bank Runs, Deposit Insurance, and Liquidity." *Journal of Political Economy* 91: 401–419.

ECB (2006). "Financial Stability Review." December 2006: 171–172.

ECB (2007). Monthly Bulletin. February 2007: 73.

ECB (2010). "The ECB's Response to the Financial Crisis." Monthly Bulletin, October.

ECB (2011). "The Implementation of Monetary Policy in the Euro Area: General Documentation on Eurosystem Monetary Policy Instruments and Procedures." September.

Folkerts-Landau, David and Peter M. Garber (1992). "The European Central Bank: A Bank or a Monetary Policy Rule." *NBER Working Paper* 4016.

Fonteyne, W., and J. W. van der Vossen (2007). "Financial Integration and Stability." In J. Decressin, H. Faruqee and W. Fonteyne (eds.), *Integrating Europe's Financial Markets.* Washington, DC: International Monetary Fund.

Freixas, Xavier (1999). "Optimal Bail-Out Policy, Conditionality and Creative Ambiguity." *Economics Working Papers* 400, Universitat Pompeu Fabra.

Freixas, Xavier, Curzio Giannini, Glenn Hoggarth, and Farouk Soussa (1999). "Lender of Last Resort: A Review of the Literature." *Financial Stability Review:* November.

Freixas, Xavier, Bruno M. Parigi, and Jean-Charles Rochet (2004). "The Lender of Last Resort: A 21st Century Approach." *Journal of the European Economic Association* 2: 1085–1115.

Furfine, Craig (2001). "The Reluctance to Borrow from the Fed." *Economics Letters* 72: 209–213.

Gil Park, Seok (2012). "Central Banks Quasi-Fiscal Policies and Inflation." *International Journal of Central Banking* 11(2): 199–236.

Goodfriend, Marvon and Jeffrey M. Lacker (1999). "Limited Commitment and Central Bank Lending." *Federal Reserve Bank of Richmond Working Paper* 99–02, January.

Goodfriend, Marvin and Robert King (1988). "Financial Deregulation, Monetary Policy, and Central Banking." In W. Haraf and R.M. Kushmeider (eds.), *Restructuring Banking and Financial Services in America.* Lanham, MD: UPA. AEI Studies 481.

Goodhart, Charles (1999). "Myths about the Lender of Last Resort." *International Finance* 2(3): 339–360.

Goodhart, Charles (2010). "The Changing Role of Central Banks." *LSE Financial Markets Group Paper Series* 197, December.

Goodhart, Charles and Haizhou Huang (2000). "A Simple Model of an International Lender of Last Resort." *IMF Working Paper*, April.

Goodhart, Charles and Dirk Schoenmaker (1995). "Should the Functions of Monetary Policy and Banking Supervision Be Separated?" *Oxford Economic Papers* 47: 539–560.

Gorton, Gary (1988). "Banking Panics and Business Cycles." *Oxford Economic Papers* 40(4): 751–781.

Haldane, Andrew G. (2012). "The Bank and the Banks." Speech, October.

Jeanne, Olivier and Lars E. O. Svensson (2007). "Credible Commitment to Optimal Escape from a Liquidity Trap: The Role of the Balance Sheet of an Independent Central Bank." *American Economic Review* 97(1): 474–490.

Laeven, Luc and Fabián Valencia (2012). "Systemic Banking Crises Database: An Update." *Working Paper* WP/12/163, June.

Padoa-Schioppa, Tommasso (1999). "EMU and Banking Supervision." *International Finance* 2(2): 295–308.

Prati, Alessandro and Gary S. Schinasi (1999). "Financial Stability in European Economic and Monetary Union." *Princeton Studies in International Finance* 86.

Reinhardt, Carmen M. and Kenneth Rogoff (2010). "Growth in Time of Debt." *American Economic Review: Papers & Proceedings* 100: 573–578.

Reinhardt, Carmen M. and M. Belen Sbrancia (2011). "The Liquidation of Government Debt." *NBER Working Paper* 16893, March.

Repullo, Rafael (2000). "Who Should Act as Lender of Last Resort? An Incomplete Contracts Model." *Journal of Money, Credit, and Banking* 32: 580–605.

Repullo, R. (2005). "Liquidity, Risk Taking, and the Lender of Last Resort." *International Journal of Central Banking* 1(2): 47–80.

Thornton, H. (1802). *An Enquiry into the Nature and Effects of the Paper Credit of Great Britain. Britain* (London, 1802), ed. with intro. by F. A. von Hayek. London: George Allen and Unwin.

Tucker, Paul M. W. (2004). "Managing the Central Bank's Balance Sheet: Where Monetary Policy Meets Financial Stability." Speech, July.

Sargent, T. J. N. Wallace (1981). "Some Unpleasant Monetarist Arithmetic." *Federal Reserve Bank of Minneapolis Quarterly Review* 5: 1–17.

Sims, Christopher (2004). "Fiscal Aspects of Central Bank Independence." In Hans-Werner Sinn, Mika Widgrén, and Marko Köthenbürger (eds.), *European Monetary Integration*. MIT Press, 103–116.

Smets, Frank (2014). "Financial Stability and Monetary Policy: How Closely Interlinked?" *International Journal of Central Banking* 10(2): 263–300.

Sveriges Riksbank (2003). "The Riksbank's Roles as Lender of Last Resort." *Financial Stability Report* 2: 57–73.

Uhlig, Harald (2013). "Sovereign Default Risk and Banks in a Monetary Union." *NBER Working Paper* 19343.

5

Competition and state aid rules in the time of banking union

IGNAZIO ANGELONI AND NIALL LENIHAN[1]

Introduction

European bank regulation underwent a head-to-toe overhaul recently. In just four years, new rules to calculate and establish capital buffers were introduced (the Capital Requirements Directive (CRD) and Capital Requirements Regulation (CRR), 2013); national rules to restructure or resolve ailing banks were harmonised (the Bank Recovery and Resolution Directive (BRRD 2014)); a new euro-area-wide banking supervisor, the Single Supervisory Mechanism (SSM), was set up (2014); and a novel euro-area-wide restructuring and resolution authority, the Single Resolution Mechanism, was established, alongside a single bank resolution fund (SRM/SRF 2014). If this wasn't enough, in preparation for assuming its new supervisory responsibility, the European Central Bank (ECB) has undertaken a review of the balance sheets of all major euro-area banks: the so-called comprehensive assessment. This regulatory tour de force is not merely a translation of international rules but has a distinct European imprint, owing much to the initiative and drive of the European Commission (EC) in its composition prior to the last European elections.

It is not difficult to predict that, after this reform, the competitive playing field of European banking will not be the same. Gauging the

[1] Ignazio Angeloni is Member of the Supervisory Board and Niall Lenihan is Senior Adviser in the Directorate General Legal Services of the European Central Bank. We are grateful to Barbara Attinger, Mathias Dewatripont, Charles Goodhart, Cécile Meys, Danièle Nouy, Marguerite O'Connell, Petra Senkovic, Marek Svoboda, Pedro Teixeira, Andres Tupits, Nicolas Véron, and all participants at the conference organised by the Center of Excellence SAFE at Goethe University Frankfurt from 6–7 June 2014, for helpful comments and encouragement. The views expressed here are personal and do not necessarily reflect those of the ECB.

direction of change, however, is less easy. On the one hand, the move towards common rules and supervisory practices will strengthen competition, particularly by facilitating cross-border banking activities of all sorts. On the other hand, competition among national jurisdictions propelling national banking "champions", a pervasive phenomenon in recent European Union (EU) history, should become less relevant. Such competition often featured the active participation of national supervisors, which, in the new regulatory regime, will no longer be autonomous but will contribute as members of a single policy-making body, the SSM. A transition from jurisdictional-based competition towards a more bank-based, less oligopolistic one, in the context of a more levelled playing field, should promote efficiency and benefit European consumers of banking services. What needs to be understood is what competition rules are best suited to serve the new environment.

Somewhat surprisingly, this impressive reform process was not accompanied by a systematic and broad-based rethinking of the EU bank competition and state aid framework. Certainly, some steps were undertaken. In the mid-2000s, the Commission's Directorate General for Competition launched a "State aid action plan" aimed at achieving "less and better targeted State aid" (Lowe 2006). Legal and economic arguments were taken into account to assess market distortions arising from the existence of externalities and market failures, and to identify circumstances where public intervention was justified for "social reasons". However, the case of banking was not specifically considered, though such failures are particularly relevant in banking as a result of information asymmetries. More recently, the Commission has issued a sequence of "communications" to help clarify its own interpretation of the competition and state aid rules under the Treaty on the Functioning of the European Union (TFEU) in the evolving circumstances (Pisani-Ferry and Sapir 2010). In the absence (until recently) of a European bank supervisor, it has also played a central role in reviewing and approving bank restructuring plans implemented under adjustment programmes negotiated with the "Troika" (IMF, EC and ECB). The Commission has maintained, over the years, a basic tenet that competition rules in banking should be the same as in other sectors, but de facto has repeatedly recognised the special nature of banking and has used its authorisation powers generously in many specific cases, especially after the failure of Lehman Brothers (September 2008) and during the ensuing financial crisis. As we will illustrate, more recently the Commission has changed its emphasis by focusing more on limiting the scope of state aid in the interest of taxpayers, notably by setting up burden-sharing arrangements among bank stakeholders.

Against this background, our aim is to provide elements to rethink how the competition and state aid framework should respond to the new environment created by the banking union. These elements should accompany and become an integral part of the progressive establishment of a proper banking union. We use the word "progressive" on purpose because we consider that any changes to the existing arrangements along the lines proposed should not happen immediately, but only once some key initial milestones of the banking union have been reached. This includes, first and foremost, the operational start of the SSM and the completion of the comprehensive assessment, as well as any follow-up actions – a process that should not, in our opinion, be disturbed by a changeable regulatory environment.

This paper is structured as follows. "Bank competition and state aid rules in the EU" revisits the European experience of applying competition rules to the banking sector, taking stock of arguments from the economic literature on the "special nature" of banking vis-à-vis other sectors. In "The US experience" we examine the experience of the United States, a country that has a long experience in applying antitrust and banking legislation in a federal context. In "State aid control" we focus on state aid, highlighting a number of issues which emerged in recent applications of the EU framework during the crisis. Finally, in "Elements for a new framework" we pull the strings together and present a list of elements that we believe should be taken into consideration in discussions going forward.

Bank competition and state aid rules in the EU

Background on general competition and state aid rules (not specific to banking)

Competition law is a cornerstone of EU policy. The opening articles to the Treaty on European Union (TEU) state that the Union shall work for the sustainable development of Europe based on, inter alia, a highly competitive social market economy. According to the TFEU, economic policy is to be conducted in accordance with the principle of an open market economy with free competition, favouring an efficient allocation of resources. The treaties foresee rules to ensure that competition within the Internal Market is not distorted, which apply to undertakings (Articles 101–106, TFEU), including prohibitions on cartels, restrictive practices and any abuse of a dominant position, as well as rules restricting state aid (Articles 107–109, TFEU).

Prohibitions on cartels and restrictive practices (Article 101) cover all agreements which may affect trade between member states with the objective of preventing, restricting or distorting competition within the Internal Market, in particular by (a) fixing purchase or selling prices or any other trading conditions; (b) limiting or controlling production, markets, technical development, or investment; (c) sharing markets or sources of supply; and (d) applying dissimilar conditions to equivalent transactions with other trading parties. Acts that contain such practices are automatically void, unless they entail certain social benefits – improving the production or distribution of goods, promoting technical or economic progress, and so forth. Any abuse of a dominant position (Article 102), taking the form of practices such as the ones just listed, is prohibited as incompatible with the Internal Market. In this context, all concentrations of undertakings with a Union dimension – that is, determined by reference to thresholds relating to the worldwide turnover of the undertakings concerned and the Union-wide turnover of the two largest undertakings concerned – are subject to the EC Merger Regulation (Council Regulation (EC) No 139/2004 on the control of concentrations between undertakings).

The above provisions are not dissimilar to ones prevailing in other advanced economies (see the US case described in "The US experience"). By contrast, the notion of controlling state aid by law is unique to the European Union and was already a core plank of the Rome Treaty of 1957, a fact that can be explained by the Union's highly decentralised political structure. In a Union composed of a plurality of largely autonomous and potentially competing countries, competition among undertakings and the very notion of an internal market would be distorted if states were allowed to provide financial support to companies (Lista 2013). Accordingly, any aid by a Member State or through state resources which distorts or threatens to distort competition by favouring certain undertakings or the production of certain goods, insofar as it affects trade between member states, is seen as incompatible with the Internal Market (Article 107(1)). Exceptions are: (a) aid having a social character, granted to individual consumers, provided that such aid is granted without discrimination related to the origin of the products concerned; and (b) aid to make good the damage caused by natural disasters or exceptional circumstances (Article 107(2)). In addition, the following may be considered compatible with the Internal Market: (a) aid to promote the economic development of areas where the standard of living is abnormally low or where there is serious underemployment, and certain specified disadvantaged regions; (b) aid to promote the execution of an important project of common European interest or to remedy a serious disturbance in the economy of a Member State; (c) aid to facilitate the development of certain economic activities or of certain economic areas, where such aid does not adversely affect trading conditions contrary to the common interest; (d) aid to promote culture and heritage conservation, again, where such aid does not affect trading conditions and competition in the Union; and (e) other categories of aid, such as may be specified by a decision of the European Council based on a proposal of the Commission (Article 107(3)).

State aid is subject to notification and clearance by the Commission, which has the power to require a Member State to abolish or alter aid that it finds to be incompatible with the Internal Market, subject to the review of the Court of Justice (Articles 108–109 and Council Regulation (EC) No 659/1999 laying down detailed rules on the application of Article 93 of the EC Treaty). On application by a Member State, the Council may, acting unanimously, decide that aid which that state is granting or intends to grant shall be considered as compatible with the Internal Market, in derogation from the applicable EU state aid rules, if such a decision is justified by exceptional circumstances (see paragraph 3 of Article 108(2)).

Application to banking

A long-established practice in the application of EU competition law is that the same rules apply to all sectors of the economy. This means that banking is considered in the same way as any other sector and there is no special treatment of banks under EU competition law. On this basis, an extensive jurisprudence has built up regarding the application of EU competition rules to the banking and financial services industry, including to concerted practices in respect of pricing, multilateral interchange fees charged in connection with payment card systems, non-price competition issues arising within the context of payment systems (rules relating to access to essential facilities, agreements relating to operational issues, membership rules), mergers and acquisitions in the banking sector, clearing and settlement services, and so forth (Lista 2013, Ritter and Braun 2004).

Although the Commission initially seemed open to the idea that monetary policy requirements might delimit the application of the

Treaty provisions on competition in the banking sector (Commission 1973), the basic principle that the Treaty provisions on competition apply as a rule to the banking sector has been upheld in concrete decisions by the Court of Justice and the Commission.

In *Gerhard Züchner v. Bayerische Vereinsbank AG* (1981) the Court of Justice rejected the argument that because of the special nature of the services provided by banking undertakings and the vital role which they play in transfers of capital, they must be considered as "undertakings entrusted with the operation of services of general economic interest" within the meaning of the applicable Treaty provisions, and thus are not subject to the Treaty rules on competition. Although the transfer of customers' funds from one Member State to another is an operation which falls within the special tasks of banks, that was not considered sufficient to make banks "undertakings entrusted with the operation of services of general economic interest", unless it can be established that, when performing such transfers, banks are operating a service of general economic interest with which they have been entrusted by a measure adopted by the public authorities.

In its "Lombard Club" decision (2004), involving a group of Austrian banks, the Commission rejected the argument that banks must not be exposed to the free play of market forces or assessed on the basis of market economy criteria, since this would result in insolvencies and hence disastrous consequences for the economy. The Commission stated that it is desirable for unprofitable banks to exit the market. Member states have adequate instruments at their disposal to ensure the orderly liquidation of even a large credit institution and to prevent a crisis in the system. Community legislation covers the eventuality of the market exit of credit institutions which are in crisis, given the adoption of the Directive on the reorganisation and winding up of credit institutions (Directive 2001/24/EC). Somewhat prophetically, the Commission stated that, if a major insolvency should in fact threaten to develop into a crisis affecting the whole system, the member states can provide direct support within the limits set by the rules governing state aid.

By and large, these orientations match reasonably well with the orientation taken by the economic and financial literature. In a seminal contribution, Carletti and Hartmann (2002) examine the relationship between financial stability and market structures as well as competition policies in banking, concluding that "the idea that competition is something dangerous in banking, since it generally causes instability, can be dismissed. In the light of the importance of the market mechanism for allocational efficiency and growth, competition aspects need to be carefully considered in industrial countries, also in banking" (p. 6). However, they also warn that "beyond this it is very hard to draw any strong conclusions, because both the theoretical and the empirical literature suggests that the stability effects of changes in market structures and competition are extremely case-dependent" (p. 6).

The basic message of this strand of literature is summarised in a report from the Centre for Economic Policy Research (CEPR) by Beck et al. (2010):

> Competition policy should apply, but conditions on bailouts must reflect the specifics of banking. . . . There is no case for applying weaker competition policy criteria to banks, because competition and stability are not incompatible. The data show that the share of profits of financial institutions, in GDP, had been growing steadily over time until 2008. Even if some of this was an unsustainable bubble, it was not a situation in which trouble would have been unavoidable whatever the design of regulation. The problem was clearly not one of competition leading inevitably to banking fragility. Proper prudential regulation should therefore be sufficient to allow standard competition policy principles (Articles [101] and [102] and merger regulations) to be applied: there is no need to weaken standard competition policy for banks. Nor should competition policy be applied more strictly in a crisis; it should be applied with sensitivity to the circumstances that distinguish banks from other kinds of state-aided firms (p. 3).

To understand the specific nature of banking, it should be considered that, in other industries, a company that receives assistance from the state is clearly securing a competitive advantage over its competitors. In the banking sector, however, a bail-out often favours the bank's competitors. This is because of two factors. First, due to the interconnectivity of the banking sector, a bail-out increases the chances of competitors exposed to the bank of being paid by the bank itself. In other industries, the main counterparts of companies are not their competitors. Moreover, financial stability, which involves positive externalities for all players in the banking sector, plays an important role. There are "network externality" elements in banking that are absent in manufacturing and most other services. These features would seem to support adjusting the competition assessment that the Commission undertakes in the banking sector.

In Commission practice, the interaction between competition and prudential rules in the banking and financial services sector is explicitly recognised in the area of merger control (for an empirical economic analysis, see Carletti, Hartmann and Ongena (2007); for a legal perspective, see Kerjean (2008)). In general, under the EC Merger Regulation, the Commission, subject to review by the Court of Justice, has sole jurisdiction to take decisions to approve, attach conditions to or block concentrations with a Community dimension, and national legislation on competition may not be applied to any such concentration. However, member states may take "appropriate measures to protect legitimate interests other than those taken into consideration by the EC Merger Regulation and compatible with the general principles and other provisions of Community law". For these purposes, "prudential rules" are regarded as legitimate interests. In its BSCH/Champalimaud decision (1999), the Commission clarified that prudential interests should be understood to cover measures addressed, for example, to ensure the good reputation of individuals, the honesty of transactions and the rules of solvency. The Commission also noted that the ongoing process of harmonisation of prudential rules at the Community level should also be taken into account in order to determine the Community notion of prudential interest, which should include those interests protected by the harmonisation directives.

The application of this prudential carve-out has generated controversy in a number of proposed cross-border acquisitions in the European banking industry where there have been allegations that national prudential authorities have used their powers as a means of advancing national interests by blocking takeovers initiated by foreign banks, most notably with regard to the Banco Bilbao Vizcaya Argentaria (BBVA, Spain)/ Banca Nazionale del Lavoro (BNL, Italy) and the ABN AMRO (the Netherlands)/Banca Antoniana Popolare Veneta (Banca Antonveneta, Italy) cases in 2005. Against this background, it has been suggested that a more systematic procedure for notification to the Commission of legitimate interests relating to prudential rules might, in the context of banking mergers with a Community dimension, remove potential conflicts between the rules derived from the EC Merger Regulation on the one hand, and those derived from prudential requirements contained in EU law on the other hand (Kerjean 2008). This matter acquires greater urgency given the transfer of competences for the prudential supervision of credit institutions from the national to the EU level, raising the question of whether the EC Merger Regulation needs to be adapted to extend the prudential carve-out from the Commission's exclusive jurisdiction in order to authorise the ECB to take appropriate measures to protect legitimate prudential interests.

Summing up

- Legal doctrine and practice concur with economic analyses in suggesting that competition rules (regarding dominant positions and their implications, merger control, and so forth) should apply to banking, broadly in keeping with other sectors.
- Nonetheless, a "carve-out" specific to banking has been envisaged in the area of merger control to cater for cases where the protection of legitimate interests is necessary, including, specifically, prudential rules.
- In a number of prominent cases the "prudential carve-out" has given rise to allegations of abuse and excess by national banking supervisors, with these being accused of blocking takeovers by foreign firms in order to promote or defend national banking "champions".

The US experience

General background

The United States is arguably the country where the scope of market forces in the economy is broadest, and it possesses the largest financial market in the world. For these reasons, its historical experience – regardless of how successful one may judge it to be – is highly relevant in guiding the design of an appropriate body of bank competition legislation for Europe.

Though early forms of anti-collusion norms were present already in ancient Rome, a comprehensive body of competition legislation, the Sherman Act, was first introduced in the US in 1890. The vast accumulation of wealth and power in the hands of corporations and individuals and the enormous development of corporate organisations with the ability to combine into trusts were, around the end of the nineteenth century in the US, matters of grave political concern.

The Sherman Act combats restrictive agreements and misuses of monopoly power, rendering illegal contracts, combinations or conspiracies in restraint of trade as well as attempts or conspiracies to monopolise trade or commerce. This basic law was later supplemented by the more targeted Clayton Act (1914), which, for example, outlawed (1) price discrimination between different purchasers of commodities of similar quality, (2) sales conditional on the purchaser's agreement not to deal in competitors' goods and other exclusive dealing arrangements, (3) acquisitions of share capital or assets of competitors where the effect may be to substantially lessen competition, and (4) certain interlocking directorates and officers across competing corporations. The Clayton Act explicitly targeted mergers and acquisitions that were not covered by the Sherman Act. In the same year (1914), the Federal Trade Commission Act outlawed unfair methods of competition and unfair or deceptive acts or practices in or affecting commerce. For our purpose, it is noteworthy that the Clayton Act, though it was adopted shortly after the devastating 1907 banking crisis in which bank monopolists (led by J.P. Morgan) had played a dominant role, did not cover bank monopolies at all: the US legislator had dealt with the implications of that crisis one year earlier, by founding the Federal Reserve.

Unlike the provisions on the role of the public sector in the economy, which were completely overhauled in the 1930s, competition laws, as interpreted strictly, went relatively unscathed through the reforms following the Great Depression.

Since the early twentieth century, US antitrust laws have been enforced through legal proceedings instituted before the country's courts by the Antitrust Division of the United States Department of Justice (DoJ; see DoJ 2015) and the Federal Trade Commission (FTC), including both civil and criminal proceedings in the case of the DoJ, supplemented by civil actions instituted by injured private parties and by state attorney generals.

Application to banking

The jurisdiction and allocation of responsibilities for implementing bank competition rules in the US are complex, and not always clear-cut.

As a matter of principle, under US antitrust laws, most activities by banks have been treated similarly to comparable activities by other unregulated institutions. Thus, if banks engage in price-fixing, concerted refusals to deal or other prohibited conduct, no systematic exemption from US antitrust laws exists and the conduct will be tested by the generally prevailing standards applied under these laws (Kintner and Bauer 1989 and 2012).

The US Supreme Court, in its seminal bank merger decision in the case of *United States v. Philadelphia National Bank* (1963), held that "immunity from the antitrust laws is not lightly implied", reflecting the "indispensable role of antitrust policy in the maintenance of a free economy". The Court also stated that "competition is our fundamental national economic policy, offering as it does the only alternative to the cartelization or governmental regimentation of large portions of the economy".

Notwithstanding this robust defence of the application of US antitrust laws to the banking industry, the Court did, critically, recognise that there may be circumstances where US antitrust laws would need to be relaxed for financial stability reasons:

> Section 7 [of the Clayton Act] does not exclude defenses based on dangers to liquidity or solvency, if to avert them a merger is necessary. Thus, arguably, the so-called failing-company defense might have somewhat larger contours as applied to bank mergers because of the greater public impact of a bank failure compared with ordinary business failures.

Under the failing-company doctrine, for example, a proposed acquisition may be approved despite its anticompetitive effect, if the resources of the target company are so depleted and the prospect of rehabilitation so remote that it faces the grave probability of business failure. Since companies reorganised through the US Bankruptcy Code often emerge as strong competitive companies, the failing-company doctrine does not apply unless the acquired corporation's prospects of such reorganisation are dim or non-existent (American Jurisprudence 2013, second edition). In view of the "larger contours" of the doctrine envisaged by the Supreme Court when applied to bank mergers, it would seem that it might come into play whenever a merger is necessary to avert dangers to the liquidity or solvency of a bank and to preserve the public interest.

The application of US antitrust laws to commercial banking, defined under *United States v. Philadelphia National Bank* (1963) as denoting a cluster of products, including various kinds of credit and services (such as deposit-taking and trust administration), is well established. It is interesting to note that a different conclusion has been reached in the context of investment banking activities. In *Credit Suisse Securities (USA) LLC v. Billing* (2007) the Supreme Court held that US securities laws implicitly precluded the application of the country's antitrust laws to alleged anticompetitive agreements among underwriting syndicates in initial public offerings (IPOs) by technology companies, because the US securities laws were clearly incompatible with the application of the US antitrust laws in this context.

Relevance of the regulatory framework for banking to the application of US antitrust laws

The fact that banking is subject to a high degree of governmental regulation does not render it immune from US antitrust laws. Nonetheless, the country's courts have striven to apply US antitrust laws within the broad framework of governmental regulation for the banking industry.

The specific treatment of banking in this respect must be seen in the context of the structural changes that occurred in the US banking sector during the post-war period. Historically, commercial banking had been dominated by a very large number of independent, local banks regulated by state law. Some states prohibited branching altogether, while others enabled a bank to extend itself to state lines only, and often not even that far. Bank holding companies enabled banking groups to expand across state lines. However, it was not until the 1980s and 1990s that the internal US banking market was opened up. By the mid-1990s, almost all states allowed interstate banking, and only one or two states prohibited state-wide banking (Garrett, Wagner and Wheelock 2003). With the Riegle-Neal Interstate Banking and Branching Efficiency Act (1994), interstate merger transactions were allowed as of 1997. As a result, the structure of the US banking industry changed considerably from 1980 to 2010, with the number of institutions declining dramatically and concentration among the largest institutions increasing. In 1980, the ten largest banking organisations held 13.5 per cent of banking assets; this figure increased to 36 per cent by 2000 and was about 50 per cent by 2010 (Adams 2012). It is noted that while this institutional change had substantial consequences, a systematic analysis of these goes beyond the scope of this paper.

Against this very specific historical background, the Supreme Court made it clear in its decisions on *United States v. Marine Bancorporation, Inc.* (1974) and *United States v. Citizens & Southern National Bank* (1975) that, when applying US antitrust laws to banking, careful account must be taken of the pervasive federal and state regulatory restraints on entry into that line of commerce. The key principle underpinning the Court's decisions has a wider contemporary resonance: when applying the country's antitrust laws to banking, the courts must take into consideration the extensive federal and state regulation characteristics of the banking industry.

The special treatment of bank mergers under US antitrust laws

A number of key banking activities have been deemed to affect the balance between the twin goals of insuring the safety of banking institutions and their depositors and promoting the goals of competition, such that variations from the otherwise prevailing US antitrust standards have been considered appropriate in respect of the banking industry. Most notably, the US Congress has intervened to insulate mergers and acquisitions by banks and bank holding companies from the full reach of the country's antitrust laws (Kintner and Bauer 1989 and 2012). Part of the rationale is that, since certain mergers can strengthen banks and promote collective well-being by fostering or preserving financial stability, the existence of these circumstances should be assessed by the authorities responsible for bank supervision.

Specifically, the Bank Merger Act (1960, as amended) stipulates that a merger, consolidation, asset acquisition or assumption of deposit liabilities by a depository institution whose deposits are insured by the Federal Deposit Insurance Corporation (FDIC) requires the approval of the responsible US banking agency, namely the Comptroller of the Currency, the Board of Governors of the Federal Reserve System or the FDIC. The Act confers a limited role to the Antitrust Division of the DoJ regarding the administration of US antitrust laws, instead vesting this authority directly in the responsible banking agency. The Bank Holding Company Act (1956, as amended) incorporates virtually identical procedures and standards with respect to bank holding company transactions approved by the Federal Reserve as those applicable under the Bank Merger Act. In practice, the control of mergers and acquisitions is performed largely by the Federal Reserve, in collaboration, to a limited extent, with the DoJ (Blinder 1996).

As regards the criteria governing the merger, the banking agency must not approve a merger which would result in, or facilitate, a monopoly, or whose effect may be to substantially lessen competition or restrain trade, unless it finds that the anticompetitive effects of the proposed transaction are clearly outweighed in the public interest by the probable effect of the transaction in meeting the convenience and needs of the community to be served. In each case, the responsible agency must take into consideration the financial and managerial resources and future prospects of the existing and proposed institutions as well as the risk to the stability of the US banking or financial system.

More importantly, the Bank Merger Act establishes a balance between antitrust and prudential considerations, setting out the criteria for interaction and collaboration among the respective authorities, so that the twin goals of antitrust and prudential policy can be effectively attained and priorities can be established. The US Supreme Court explained the important financial stability considerations at stake in its decision on *United States v. Third National Bank in Nashville* (1968):

> the purpose of the Bank Merger Act was to permit certain bank mergers even though they tended to lessen competition in the relevant market. Congress felt that the role of banks in a community's economic life was such that the public interest would sometimes be served by a bank merger even though the merger lessened competition ... Congress was also concerned about banks in danger of collapse – banks not so deeply in trouble as to call forth the traditional "failing company" defense, but nonetheless in danger of becoming before long financially unsound institutions. Congress seems to have felt that a bank failure is a much greater community catastrophe than the failure of an industrial or retail enterprise, and that a much smaller risk of failure than that required by the failing company doctrine should be sufficient to justify the rather radical preventive step of an anticompetitive merger.

Significantly, it is the responsible banking agency, often the Federal Reserve, which must undertake the antitrust assessment, and, if the merger is considered anticompetitive, then decide whether the undesired competition effects of the proposed transaction are clearly outweighed in the public interest by the probable effect of the transaction in meeting the convenience and needs of the community. In order to ensure an appropriate system of institutional checks and balances, the DoJ is given a specific role in the process: it reports on the competitive factors involved and has the authority to initiate legal proceedings challenging the banking agency's approval of a transaction within specified deadlines; that is, unless the banking agency must act immediately to prevent a bank failure.

Another element reflecting this balance between competition and prudential considerations can be seen in the general requirement that the responsible banking agency may not approve an interstate merger transaction if the resulting insured depository institution (including all affiliated insured depository institutions) would control more than 10 per cent of the total amount of deposits of insured depository institutions in the United States upon completion of the transaction. This restriction does not apply to an interstate merger transaction that involves one or more insured depository institutions in default or receiving support from the FDIC.

Other adaptations to US antitrust laws in the banking area

Three additional specific areas where adaptations to US antitrust laws have been made in the banking area concern: (1) interlocking directorships (Clayton Act; the Depository Institution Management Interlocks Act (1978), administered and enforced by the responsible banking agencies, including the Federal Reserve; (2) conditional transactions, including tying arrangements, exclusive dealing arrangements and reciprocal dealing arrangements (Section 106 of the Bank Holding Company Act (1970) and Section 331 of the Garn-St. Germain Depository Institutions Act of 1982) – note that the Federal Reserve's Board of Governors is granted authority to permit exceptions to the prohibitions under the Bank Holding Company Act that it considers will not be contrary to the purposes of the legislation; and (3) the exclusion of the banking sector from the jurisdiction of the FTC.

Summing up

This overview suggests that the US approach is based on three main pillars:

- There is no reason to exclude banking from the reach of US antitrust laws. Market distortions arising from cartels, agreements, dominant positions and their exploitation, and so forth, are in banking potentially as damaging to collective welfare as they are elsewhere.
- However, competition rules must be applied with due regard for the specificities of banking, originating from the fact that externalities here are more pervasive and complex. In particular, policy-makers need to be mindful of the potential implications for systemic risk and financial stability.
- For this reason, an important role in enforcing specific competition legislation in the banking sector should be played by banking supervisory authorities. In bank mergers, banking supervisors approve anticompetitive transactions where clearly necessary in the public interest, taking into consideration the risk to the stability of the banking or financial system. The role of the antitrust authority is by no means excluded: it must report on the competitive factors involved and may initiate legal proceedings challenging the banking supervisor's approval of a transaction within specified deadlines, unless the banking supervisor must act immediately to prevent a bank failure.

State aid control

Background: the nexus between state aid and competition

At first glance, state aid control may appear to be a natural extension of competition enforcement; the dominant role to be controlled being not that of a private market participant, but that of the dominant player *par excellence* – the state. The analogy is only apparent, however, since while the exercise of economic dominance by a private entity is necessarily and always market-distorting and detrimental from a welfare perspective (if one abstracts from second-best considerations), that of the state need not be so, if public intervention is justified ex ante by the presence of externalities or market failures. In fact, the very existence of the state finds its ultimate justification in those failures; its role is precisely to correct externalities and to provide public goods that would otherwise be under-produced.

Therefore, at least as a matter of principle, there would seem to be no reason *whatsoever* for the existence of state aid control as a policy function if the state, and the persons who represent it, act in good faith when exercising their function.[2] To keep the role of the state within appropriate boundaries, one needs to ensure that its intervention is guided by a proper interpretation and assessment of the market imperfection to be corrected, and that the use of taxpayer resources is minimised. While the first goal requires rigorous cost-benefit analysis, taxpayer protection is an area that typically calls for parliamentary control. There is no apparent rationale for linking it to a competition authority.

For this reason, it comes as no surprise that the existence of State aid control as part of the competition authority in the EU is an exception in the international comparison, not – to our knowledge – matched in any country in the world. As already noted, this *unicum* is justified by the highly decentralised structure of the Union, where national governments and institutions, including banking authorities, can – and often do – act to protect national interests and foster the competitive ability of national firms, including banks. The risk that states may act to prop up national "champions" against competitors located in other member states, hence distorting market competition, places the state aid control function fully and justifiably in the camp of the European competition authority. By the same reasoning, were those risks to subside, for example, because member states lose policy prerogatives to European institutions, EU control of state aid in the banking sector would need to place much greater reliance on the competent European institutions.

The role played by this authority in the EU banking sector during recent decades has been important and mutable, varying in modality and intensity depending on economic and other conditions. To understand

[2] Of course, good faith cannot always be assumed; but if it is not there, the responsibility to intervene belongs to the judiciary, not to the competition regulator.

it, in this section we first briefly describe its evolution, distinguishing between three phases: the period preceding the financial crisis, the crisis period (up to 2013) and the most recent period. We then focus in particular on two specific aspects: burden-sharing (namely, the sharing of costs stemming from bank rescues and failures between bank shareholders, bank creditors and the taxpayer) and the link between state aid and the central bank's performance of the lender of last resort function.

Pre-crisis experience: the case of Crédit Lyonnais

The Commission's decision in the Crédit Lyonnais I case (1995) is a landmark one in relation to the conduct of state aid control by the European authority in that period. It deserves to be examined in some detail, not just because of its importance – it involves the biggest bank in a major country and, by some standards, the largest European bank at the time – but also because it exemplifies well an approach that would remain valid in subsequent rulings.

To illustrate the approach taken, several passages of that decision are worth mentioning. In the first stage of its analysis, the Commission considered the applicability of state aid rules to banks and the assessment of the existence of state aid:

> In examining State measures to support banks, it must first be borne in mind that the Treaty contains no specific rules governing State aid for credit institutions. The Commission is aware, however, of the special nature of the banking sector and of the great sensitivity of financial markets, even where difficulties are limited to one or other institution; this has to be borne in mind in applying the State aid rules . . . State measures which have the effect of giving financial support to banks in difficulty to enable them to satisfy Community prudential standards may also contain State aid components. The Commission must therefore establish whether the State aid rules in the Treaty are being complied with in order to prevent any incompatible distortion of competition (Section 3.1).

Following the letter of the Treaty, the Commission applies the same standard to capital injections by the state into banks as for any other company (see Commission Communication, 1993). Based on a "private market economy investor" test, the presence of state aid can be presumed where the financial position of the company is such that a normal return in dividends or capital gains cannot be expected within a reasonable time from the capital invested, or where the risks involved in such a transaction are too high or extend over too long a period. In the same way, the

Commission takes the view that there is a presumption of state aid in a state guarantee if the guarantee is necessary to the survival of the company and if it lasts for an exceptional length of time or entails a very high level of risk.

If the Commission determines that the measures do indeed constitute state aid, it will then assess whether that aid is compatible with the Single Market, including if it is justified "to remedy a serious disturbance in the economy of a Member State" (as per Article 107(3)(b) of the TFEU):

> Where circumstances outside the control of the banks cause a crisis of confidence in the system, the State may need to give its support to all credit institutions in order to avoid the negative impact of such a systemic crisis. In the case of a true systemic crisis, therefore, the derogation provided for in point (b) of Article [107] (3) may be invoked in order "to remedy a serious disturbance in the economy of a Member State". . . . In assessing whether or not aid granted to large banks is compatible with the common market, the Commission checks that the aid does not adversely affect trading conditions to an extent contrary to the common interest, in accordance with point (a) or (c) of Article [107] (3) . . . [I]n certain situations special measures may be needed to prevent the undesirable repercussions which the failure of a large bank could have on financial markets. The need to ensure that measures are in line with the common interest may require the impossibility of an institution becoming bankrupt to be offset by major restrictions on its competitive strength (Section 3.2).

Drawing on the Commission Guidelines on State Aid for rescuing and restructuring firms in difficulty (1994), the Commission set some specific principles regarding the scope of such aid by stating that:

> in order not to undermine the common interest and therefore to be declared compatible with the common market, State aid ha[s] to comply with the following four principles: (a) the aid must restore the viability of the firm within a reasonable timescale; (b) the aid must be in proportion to the restructuring costs and benefits and must not exceed what is strictly necessary; (c) in order to limit distortions of competition for competitors, aid measures must have the least distorting effect on competition possible and the firm must make a significant financial contribution to the restructuring costs; (d) measures must be taken to compensate competitors as far as possible for the adverse effects of aid. The Commission takes the view that these four principles can be applied to banks provided that account is taken of any undesirable negative effects of applying them on the financial system and on public confidence in the banking sector and of the need to comply with Community rules in the banking sphere (Section 3.2).

These passages express, in our view, a well-balanced approach which aims at combining the unavoidable tension between supporting a market player for prudential reasons (and a major one, like in this case) and maintaining good competitive standards in the market.

In relation to this specific case, eventually the Commission did not conclude that the aid granted was designed to remedy a serious disturbance in the economy, since it was intended to remedy the difficulties of the bank itself and not those of all enterprises in the sector. The Commission judged that the problem did not stem from a systemic banking crisis in France (although other French banks were facing difficulties), but was specific to Crédit Lyonnais and largely connected to its aggressive lending and investment policy. Although the Commission stated that it was aware of the special sensitivity of financial markets and of the negative consequences that the bankruptcy of Crédit Lyonnais might have, it did not consider the aid to be of common European interest.

Instead, the Commission decided to clear the aid under Article 107(3)(c) (i.e. "aid to facilitate certain economic activities or of certain economic areas"). The decision not to invoke Article 107(3)(b) (i.e. "remedy a serious disturbance in the economy") is striking in view of the Commission's own acknowledgement that the bankruptcy of the bank – the then leading European banking group in terms of total assets – would have had an undesirable and disproportionate negative impact on other credit institutions and on the financial markets.[3] By refusing to apply Article 107(3)(b), the Commission created a sort of intermediary situation between a bank in difficulty due to its wrong business strategy and a systemic failure concerning, or potentially impacting, all financial institutions (Gebski 2009). What is relevant, in fact, is the possibility that the failure of an individual bank, for whatever reason, may trigger a serious disturbance in the economy through the interconnection of exposures with other banks because of contagion effects, or through other multiple channels, as emphasised by the modern banking literature.[4] In a later decision the Commission argued that "the objectives of competition policy and those of prudential banking policy cannot be

[3] In the subsequent WestLB decision (2008), the Commission confirmed that a serious economic disruption is not remedied by aid that "resolve[s] the problems of a single recipient . . ., as opposed to the acute problems facing all operators in the industry".

[4] An excellent survey of the modern banking literature is provided by Freixas and Rochet (2008). Contagion risks potentially leading to systemic crises are discussed, in the context of the recent crisis, by Goodhart and Avgouleas (2014).

mutually incompatible, since both are designed to achieve a common end, namely the development of a competitive, healthy banking sector".[5] Conflicts between the two policies can indeed arise – for example, if macro-prudential concerns are taken into consideration or if short-term risks to financial stability coexist with longer-term benefits from competition; see, again, Carletti and Hartmann (2002) and Beck et al. (2010).

The Commission continued to maintain its traditional approach in the period directly preceding October 2008, stretching the boundaries of the normal state aid rules to their limits in the face of financial stability concerns (see the Bradford & Bingley decision (2008), Lista 2013). It was not until the international financial crisis precipitated by the collapse of Lehman Brothers in late 2008 that the Commission finally chose to invoke its power to allow state aid to remedy a serious disturbance in the economy of a Member State.

The crisis period

The crisis period (2008–13) was one of intense and growing involvement by the Commission in the banking sector. This involvement took essentially two forms. First, starting in 2008, the Commission established a temporary framework for coordinated state aid in support of the financial sector, in order to ensure financial stability while minimising distortions in competition between banks located in different member states as well as between banks which receive public support and those which do not. Reflecting a dynamic and responsive attitude to the changing market and regulatory environment, this framework has constantly evolved in a series of seven communications – the so-called Crisis Communications (2008–13). Second, the Commission handed down around 400 individual state aid decisions due to the financial crisis, affecting 104 banks across the EU and 44 schemes, including the countries undergoing adjustment programmes with support from the IMF and the EU.

In its first Banking Communication (2008), which has since expired, the Commission set out the general principles governing state aid to remedy a serious disturbance in the economy of a Member State (as per Article 107(3)(b) of the TFEU). The Commission reaffirmed its position that Article 107(3)(b) necessitates a restrictive interpretation of what can be considered a "serious disturbance" of a Member State's economy,

[5] Commission Decision 98/490/EC of 20 May 1998 concerning aid granted to the Crédit Lyonnais group, OJ 1998, L 221.

while at the same time considering it a proper legal basis for aid measures to be undertaken in the light of the severity of the crisis. It stated that this applies, in particular, to aid provided in the form of general schemes available to several or all financial institutions in a Member State. The Commission further clarified that, should the Member State's authorities responsible for financial stability – presumably the finance ministry, central bank and financial supervisor(s) – declare to the Commission that there is a risk of such a serious disturbance, this would be of particular relevance to its assessment. Ad hoc interventions by member states are not excluded in circumstances fulfilling the criteria of Article 107(3)(b).

Furthermore, the Commission emphasised that the use of Article 107(3)(b) cannot be envisaged as a matter of principle in crisis situations in other sectors in the absence of comparable risks involving the economy as a whole. As regards the financial sector, invoking this provision is possible only in genuinely exceptional circumstances where the functioning of the entire financial sector is jeopardised. The treatment of illiquid but fundamentally sound financial institutions should be distinguished from that of financial institutions characterised by "endogenous" problems. In the first case, viability problems originate from outside the financial institution itself, having to do with stressed market conditions. Distortions to competition resulting from support to such institutions will normally be more limited and require less substantial restructuring. By contrast, other financial institutions affected by losses stemming from faulty internal management or strategies would fall under the normal framework of rescue aid, requiring, in particular, a far-reaching restructuring as well as compensatory measures to limit distortions to competition. In all cases, however, in the absence of appropriate safeguards, distortions to competition may be substantial as they could unduly favour the beneficiaries to the detriment of their competitors, also in other member states.

The Crisis Communications provided more detailed guidance regarding the compatibility with state aid rules of guarantee schemes, recapitalisations and asset relief schemes (including schemes for the segregation of impaired assets through the establishment of asset management companies or similar entities). These Communications also explain how the Commission will examine aid for bank restructuring operations.

In line with the general principles underlying the state aid rules of the TFEU, which require that the aid granted does not exceed what is strictly necessary to achieve its legitimate purpose and that distortions to competition are avoided or minimised as far as possible, all support measures have to be (1) well-targeted in order to be able to achieve effectively the objective of remedying a serious disturbance in the economy, (2) proportionate to the challenge faced, not going beyond what is required to attain this effect, and (3) designed in such a way as to minimise negative spillover effects.

While a thorough assessment of the conduct of state aid control during the crisis goes beyond the scope of this chapter, we tend to concur with the prevailing view in the economic literature that the Commission responded with the necessary decisiveness and flexibility. This conclusion is remarkable, particularly considering the lack of an adequate normative framework for addressing systemic bank risks. Pisani-Ferry and Sapir (2010) place the role played by the competition arm of the Commission in administering public sector support to banks in this phase alongside that of the ECB in providing timely liquidity support: according to the authors, due to the prompt response of these two authorities, Europe averted a potentially much more disruptive systemic crisis (see also Schiavo 2014). Beck et al. (2010) note that, while allowing for large volumes of public funds to be temporarily channelled to the banking system (in the year following the Paris summit of 12 October 2008, in which the euro-area leaders committed to guarantee bank debt with a maturity of up to five years and to provide Tier 1 capital to banks to the extent needed, the total volume of state aid approved in the EU amounted to nearly 50 per cent of GDP), the Commission was able to administer conditionality so as to avoid major negative consequences for competition.

The 2013 Banking Communication, burden-sharing and bail-ins

The 2013 Banking Communication marks a sharp turn in the direction of a more restrictive approach, with tighter conditions, in particular regarding burden-sharing, which the Commission considers can help to ensure a smooth passage to the future regime under the BRRD. While applicable only as of 1 August 2013, this change had been in the air for some time, being hinted at as early as the Prolongation Communication of 7 December 2010. At that time, based on the assumption that the banking crisis was receding, tighter conditions were applied to state guarantees, removing the distinction between sound and distressed banks for the purposes of submitting a restructuring plan so that each beneficiary of a new recapitalisation or impaired asset measure would be required to submit a restructuring plan. Considering the timing, it is tempting to relate this change in direction to the "Deauville doctrine" announced at the Franco-German summit of 18 October 2010, which introduced the notion of "private sector involvement" in sovereign rescues.

Unfortunately, the assumption of improved conditions for euro-area banks was to prove premature, as subsequent events in Spain and elsewhere would show. The first Banking Communication (2008) had enabled member states to put rescue schemes in place while at the same time not excluding the availability of ad hoc interventions. However, given the changed market conditions by the time of the 2013 Banking Communication (which repealed the previous one), the Commission considered that there was less need for structural rescue measures. While such an approach helped prevent the irremediable collapse of the financial sector as a whole, the Commission considered that the restructuring efforts of individual beneficiaries were often delayed and that late action to address banks' problems had resulted, in some cases, in a higher final bill for taxpayers. Against this backdrop, the 2013 Banking Communication established the principle that recapitalisation and impaired asset measures would be authorised only once the bank's restructuring plan is approved. Only in exceptional emergency situations where financial stability is endangered can recapitalisation or impaired asset measures be taken on a temporary basis before a restructuring plan is approved.

Furthermore, the 2013 Banking Communication provides more detailed guidance on burden-sharing by shareholders and subordinated creditors. Since the start of the crisis, when examining the compatibility of aid to banks, the Commission did not set ex ante thresholds for burden-sharing (e.g. absorbing losses with available capital) relative to the amount of aid received by the banks concerned. The Commission noted that, in the first phases of the crisis, member states did not generally go beyond the minimum requirements set by state aid rules with regard to burden-sharing ex ante, and creditors were not required to contribute to rescuing credit institutions for reasons of financial stability. However, the Commission stated that the sovereign crisis had made it clear that such a policy could not ensure financial stability in the long term, particularly for member states where the cost of bank bail-outs had significantly weakened the underlying fiscal position. Indeed, some member states had to go beyond minimum requirements under state aid rules and, by introducing new legal frameworks, enforce stricter ex ante burden-sharing requirements. That development led to diverging approaches to burden-sharing across member states – namely, there are those that have limited themselves to the minimum requirements under state aid rules and those which have gone beyond the said requirements, requiring bail-in of creditors. Such differences led to divergent funding costs between banks, depending on the perceived likelihood of a bail-in as a function of a Member State's fiscal strength. The Commission concluded that these differences pose a threat to the integrity of the Single Market and risk undermining the level playing field which state aid control aims to protect.

Hence, the Commission decided that the minimum requirements for burden-sharing should be raised. But before granting any kind of restructuring aid, all capital-generating measures, including the conversion of junior debt, should be exhausted. As restructuring aid is needed to prevent the possible disorderly demise of a bank, in order to reduce the aid to the minimum level, burden-sharing measures should be respected regardless of the initial solvency of the bank. Contributions from hybrid capital and subordinated debt holders can take the form of either a conversion into Common Equity Tier 1 or a write-down of the principal of the instruments. The Commission will not require contribution from senior debt holders (in particular from insured deposits, uninsured deposits, bonds and all other senior debt) as a mandatory component of burden-sharing under state aid rules. The underlying assumption is that, where the capital ratio of a bank with an identified capital shortfall remains above the EU regulatory minimum, the bank should be able to restore the capital position on its own, in particular through capital-raising measures.

Exceptions can be made where implementing such measures would endanger financial stability or lead to disproportionate results. These exceptions have yet to be defined precisely, but could cover cases where the aid amount to be received is small in comparison to the bank's risk-weighted assets and the capital shortfall has been reduced significantly, in particular through capital-raising measures. In the context of implementing these requirements, fundamental rights must also be respected and the "no creditor worse off" principle should be adhered to – that is, subordinated creditors should not receive less in economic terms than what their instrument would have been worth if no state aid were to be granted.

Going forward, the application of state aid rules to the banking sector will, de facto, take place within the legal framework of the BRRD, which is scheduled to come into force on 1 January 2015 (Schiavo 2014).

Resolution authorities may take resolution action only if a number of conditions are met, including, crucially, that a determination of whether an institution is failing or likely to fail has been made by the competent supervisory authority (or, under certain circumstances, the resolution authority). An institution would be deemed failing or likely to fail in a number of specified circumstances, including – and this is of relevance in the state aid context – where extraordinary public financial support is required. There are a number of exceptions to this rule,[6] but also conditions applicable before extraordinary public financial support can be granted without a bank being deemed to be failing or likely to fail, potentially triggering a resolution of the bank. Based on these provisions, there is clearly a greater likelihood that in the future a bank will be restructured pursuant to a resolution process before any extraordinary public financial support will be provided.

Once resolution of a credit institution is decided, the authorities have a broad range of resolution tools at their disposal, which are specified in detail in the Directive. The burden-sharing requirements under the Commission's state aid rules should become practically irrelevant once the BRRD provisions for the bail-in of bank liabilities take effect on 1 January 2016 (they will, in fact, lose much of their practical relevance once the capital write-down provisions under the Directive come into force on 1 January 2015, except for subordinated debt instruments not qualifying as capital instruments). Once the bank's assets and liabilities have been mandatorily transferred to an external entity pending sale to a third party purchaser, no state aid should be necessary for the rump entity to be liquidated.

The introduction of automatic and stringent burden-sharing provisions for "going concern" banks (in particular, banks that fulfil the minimum regulatory capital standards and yet require a capital injection for prudential reasons, as ascertained by the supervisor) has been subject to criticism recently by several authors; see, in particular, Dewatripont (2014) and Goodhart and Avgouleas (2015). Their argument emphasises the conflict between, on the one hand, the potential beneficial effects of bail-in provisions in setting ex ante correct incentives and fostering

[6] Specifically, when, in order to remedy a serious disturbance in the economy of a Member State and preserve financial stability, the extraordinary public financial support takes any of the following forms: (i) a state guarantee to back liquidity facilities provided by the central bank according to the central bank's conditions; (ii) a state guarantee of newly issued liabilities; or (iii) an injection of own funds or purchase of capital instruments at prices and on terms that do not confer an advantage upon the institution.

market discipline, and thereby reducing moral hazard, and, on the other hand, the risk that such provisions may become themselves a factor of instability in a crisis, potentially undermining confidence and triggering bank runs and systemic crises. The semi-automatic mechanisms incorporated in the 2013 Banking Communication, made even more binding in the BRRD and the SRM regulation, are such that these risks will clearly be present in certain circumstances. This literature demonstrates that a solvent bank (i.e. one fulfilling the regulatory minima) cannot in all circumstances obtain the necessary capital from private sources, especially if markets are under stress.

The supervisory authority, supported in the relevant circumstances by the resolution authority, has in its mandate to independently assess the safety and soundness of individual banking intermediaries from a micro-prudential perspective. The supervisor and the macro-prudential authorities at both the EU and national levels are best placed to judge the potential systemic implications stemming from the weakness of individual banks. This places the responsibility for assessing the need for state support with these authorities, which will need to carefully coordinate their efforts with the fiscal authorities providing any support. The establishment of a new euro-area-wide supervisory authority, the Single Supervisory Mechanism, complemented by the Single Resolution Mechanism, is relevant in this context. The ECB, in its supervisory function, is institutionally free from national bias, and hence does not require a specific state aid control framework, such as that in place to prevent member states from distorting the level competitive playing field in the euro area. It should be emphasised, however, that the state aid framework operates at the level of the EU as a whole, and not only at the level of the member states participating in the SSM/SRM. Consequently, a level playing field for both SSM/SRM member states and EU member states outside the SSM/SRM still needs to be ensured, in order to preserve the integrity of the Internal Market. For this reason, the Commission has been given a mandate under the BRRD to control "Union aid" by the Single Resolution Fund, in order to ensure the level playing field, and State aid rules will continue to apply to the provision of state aid to the banking sector by member states.

In its 2013 Banking Communication the Commission acknowledged that exercising state aid control for the financial sector sometimes interacts with responsibilities of supervisory authorities in member states. The Commission noted, for example, that, "in certain cases, supervisory authorities might require adjustments in matters such as corporate governance and remuneration practices which for banks benefiting from State aid are often also set out in restructuring plans". The Commission acknowledged that:

> in such cases, whilst fully preserving the Commission's exclusive competence in State aid control, coordination between the Commission and the competent supervisory authorities is of importance. Given the evolving regulatory and supervisory landscape in the Union and, in particular, in the euro area, the Commission will liaise closely as it does already today with supervisory authorities to ensure a smooth interplay between the different roles and responsibilities of all the authorities involved.

In this respect, it is noted that both the Commission and the ECB are required to practise mutual sincere cooperation with each other under the Treaty on European Union, including in connection with the state aid tasks of the Commission and the specific tasks conferred on the ECB within the framework of the SSM concerning the prudential supervision of credit institutions, also as regards significant credit institutions.

To move in this direction under the existing Treaty, a more formalised role could be assigned to supervisory authorities in state aid procedures, insofar as they relate to credit institutions – for example, foreseeing that the supervisory authority should formally be heard before a final decision is taken by the Commission.

State aid and lending of last resort

The approach taken by the 2008 Banking Communication (broadly confirmed by the 2013 Banking Communication) is that central bank financing measures open to all comparable market players, involving lending on equal terms, are outside the scope of the state aid rules and do not need to be notified to the Commission. This is the case, for example, with traditional open market transactions and standing facilities. Conversely, dedicated support through the provision of central bank funds to a specific credit institution in the form of emergency liquidity assistance (ELA) does not constitute aid *only* when four conditions are met: (1) the credit institution may be temporarily illiquid but is solvent at the moment of the liquidity provision, which occurs in exceptional circumstances and is not part of a larger aid package; (2) the facility is fully secured by collateral to which haircuts are applied, in function of its quality and market value; (3) the central bank charges a penal interest rate to the beneficiary; and (4) the measure is taken at the central bank's own initiative, and in particular is not backed by any counter-guarantee of the state.

These criteria are surprising for two reasons. First, they imply a distinction between "normal" liquidity operations, which fall within the acceptable perimeter of central bank functions, and direct lending of last resort operations, which fall outside this, except under stringent conditions. Reputed scholars usually consider both types of operations as part of the essential toolkit of central banks, as the following quote from Goodhart (2010) suggests:

> The Essence of Central Banking . . . the traditional focus of stabilisation has been the Central Bank's capacity to lend, and thus to create liquidity, either to an individual bank, as in the Lender of Last Resort, or to the market as a whole, via open market operations (OMO). It would cause massive complications if liquidity management remained the sole province of the Central Bank while a separate financial stability authority was to be established without any command over liquidity management (p. 19).

The second surprising element involves the conditions used for distinguishing lending of last resort from state aid. The first three criteria coincide with the classic Bagehot requirements for sound last resort lending. The fourth implies that such lending is always considered state aid, regardless of other considerations, if it is guaranteed by the state. While tautologically true, this statement seems to overlook the fact that most central bank balance sheets are directly or indirectly guaranteed by the state – as was, by the way, that of the Bank of England when Bagehot wrote "Lombard Street" (1873), where no mention of state guarantees is made. More fundamental still, the extent to which lending of last resort distorts competition, if it ever does, is unlikely to depend on whether such lending is guaranteed or not.

Euro-area credit institutions can receive last resort lending through ELA, which consists of the provision by a national central bank (NCB) of central bank money to solvent financial institutions facing temporary liquidity problems. Responsibility lies with the NCB concerned, meaning that any costs and risks are incurred by the relevant NCB. The ECB Governing Council can restrict ELA operations if it considers that they interfere with the objectives and tasks of the Eurosystem – essentially, with monetary policy. The ECB also monitors the compliance of ELA with the monetary financing prohibition under the EU treaties, which forbids central banks in the European System of Central Banks (ESCB) from financing public sectors (including their obligations to third parties). In particular, the ECB considers that financing by an NCB of credit institutions other than in connection with central banking tasks, specifically the support of insolvent credit and/or financial institutions, would be incompatible with the monetary financing prohibition. In the case of ELA backed by collateral security in the form of a state guarantee, more restrictive criteria apply: (i) it must be ensured that the credit provided by the NCB is as short-term as possible; (ii) there must be systemic stability aspects at stake; (iii) there must be no doubts as to the legal validity and enforceability of the state guarantee under applicable national law; and (iv) there must be no doubts as to the economic adequacy of the state guarantee, which should cover both the principal and interest on the loans (ECB 2013).

Under Article 271(d) of the TFEU, the powers of the ECB in monitoring NCB compliance with the prohibition of monetary financing are the same as those conferred upon the Commission in respect of member states by the treaties. Given the exclusivity of those powers in their respective fields of competence, it would seem that the criteria used by the Commission and the ECB in the application of state aid and monetary financing rules should follow a uniform approach. In particular, an NCB providing ELA should not be considered as acting on the instruction of the government or in support of the state's functions merely due to the fact that its operation is concurrent with measures of a different nature undertaken by the state. Also, the acceptance by an NCB of a state guarantee – a blanket guarantee stemming from explicit provisions of national law or a specific one targeting a given credit institution – should not in itself be regarded as jeopardising the NCB's capacity to take an independent decision on whether to grant ELA, although it is acknowledged that more stringent criteria are applied by the ECB in such cases.

While the different perspectives of the state aid and monetary financing assessments are recognised, the core purpose of the prohibition of monetary financing is to prohibit central bank financing of the state's functions. Hence, central bank operations that the ECB considers to be compliant with the monetary financing prohibition – that is, undertaken by the central bank within its legitimate liquidity provision role, and not in lieu of the state's functions – should also benefit from a presumption of compliance with state aid rules. This approach would also facilitate the timeliness of ELA operations – an important consideration in crisis situations, when ELA becomes relevant. While under normal circumstances competition and stability goals coexist, in extreme conditions financial stability should prevail. It would also be more respectful of the independence of the Eurosystem, since any influence by the Commission on the decision to provide ELA indirectly affects monetary policy as well (O'Connell 2013).

Looking further ahead, it is important to note that any contiguity between ELA and state aid – perceived or real – depends on the fact that under present arrangements, ELA, albeit provided by independent NCBs, is a national responsibility. Such arrangements were established in 1999, when banking sector policies were still firmly in national hands, implying that lending of last resort should be so as well. Fifteen years later the banking union changed this logic, making it plausible to expect that at some future stage this function too will be centralised. Such a development would not only simplify the performance of this essential central bank function, but also provide for a more orderly separation between it and state aid and competition considerations.

Summing up

In synthesis, the following conclusions can be drawn from this section.

- In recent years, the intervention by the Commission in the area of state aid control has been extensive, but of variable intensity, especially before and after 2013.
- Flexibility in granting authorisations and the conditions attached (notably, regarding bail-ins) have varied over time, mainly in response to financial developments and risk; less attention has been devoted to the need of providing, on a structural basis, a stable backstop to the system, hence preserving trust in the bank sector and controlling systemic risks.
- Rules and practices have not yet internalised the new regulatory environment inherent in the banking union, in which banking authorities move from the national to the European level.
- Finally, the approach regarding liquidity provision by the central bank does not seem to recognise lending of last resort as a fundamental central banking function, of *structural* nature, whose role – alongside state intervention – is to contribute to bank systemic stability.

Elements for a new framework

Our goal in this chapter was to review the competition and state aid rules in the European banking sector in the light of the transition to the banking union. We have let legal and economic thinking, as well international experience, guide our examination of the implications of that reform for the correct balance between competition and stability in banking and the allocation of the respective policy responsibilities. We did not analyse in detail the legal instrument necessary to enact the changes that we recommend; in particular, we did not discuss the need for Treaty changes or whether the changes could instead be implemented by means of "lighter" procedures or inter-institutional cooperation.

We wish to stress that we consider our ideas to be applicable only after the SSM is well established. In particular it would not be wise, in our view, to disturb the existing arrangements regarding bank competition and state aid in the period covered by the ECB's comprehensive assessment of the banking sector and the related follow-up actions.

Our main conclusions can be summarised as follows:

a) As a general principle, banking and finance should remain covered by the EU competition framework. In the classic area of competence of the competition authority (cartels and restrictive practices, abuses of a dominant position, merger authorisations) and in the context of State aid control described in the fourth section, more systematic consideration should be given to the specificities of banking by bringing externalities and financial stability considerations more formally into the picture.
b) From this should derive new policy allocation and cooperation modalities for supervisors (the SSM and others in non-participating member states), the secondary regulator (the European Banking Authority, EBA), the resolution authorities (the SRM and others in non-participating member states) and the competition authority (the Commission). Drawing upon the US experience mentioned in the third section, consideration should be given to whether the decision-making role of supervisors should be strengthened in merger authorisation procedures, with mandatory and transparent consultation procedures with the competition authority, emphasising the potential significance of financial stability considerations in this area.
c) If the perimeter of the EU and that of the banking union (SSM/SRM) coincided, resulting in a truly integrated pan-European banking sector, there would be no compelling case for continuing to apply EU state aid rules to the banking sector. Unless or until this happens, as described in the fourth section, the Commission retains a legitimate role to ensure that state aid to the banking sector does not disturb the level playing field within the Internal Market, with specific reference to issues arising between participants and non-participants

of the SSM/SRM – notwithstanding the common banking and resolution rules applicable across the Union.

d) Given the distinctive but complementary responsibilities of the Commission and the SSM/SRM authorities elaborated in the fourth section, consultation procedures should be established whereby the supervisory authority is formally heard before a decision is taken by the Commission, and, conversely, the Commission is heard when the SSM/SRM authorities act in situations of urgency generated by present or potential financial distress. Procedures laying down how differences in views between both authorities are to be resolved should also be foreseen.

e) The EU state aid control process should not cover the lender of last resort function of the central bank. Central banks should bear full responsibility in this area, and act by means of transparent assessments and decision-making procedures. This issue would become largely irrelevant if ELA were to be treated as a centralised Eurosystem function at some point in the future.

f) In any case, the move to the new framework should be gradual, and be prepared, in the initial stage, by enhanced collaboration procedures among the authorities involved.

References

Adams, R. M. (2012). "Consolidation and Merger Activity in the United States Banking Industry from 2000 through 2010." *Finance and Economics Discussion Series*. Available at: www.federalreserve.gov/pubs/feds/2012/201251/201251pap.pdf.

American Jurisprudence (2013). "Monopolies, restraints of trade, unfair trade practices." *American Jurisprudence*, second edition.

Bagehot, W. (1873). *Lombard Street: A Description of the Money Market*. London: Henry S. King and Co.

Beck, T., D. Coyle, M. Dewatripont, X. Freixas and P. Seabright (2010). "Bailing out the banks: reconciling stability and competition; an analysis of state-supported schemes for financial institutions." *Centre for Economic Policy Research (CEPR)*. Available at: http://dev3.cepr.org/pubs/other/Bailing_out_the_banks.pdf.

Besley, T. and P. Seabright (1999). "The effects and policy implications of state aid to industry: an economic analysis." *Economic Policy* 14(28): 13–53.

Blinder, A. S. (1996). "Antitrust and banking." *The Antitrust Bulletin* 41(2): 447–452.

Bomhoff, A., A. Jarosz-Friis and N. Pesaresi (2009). "Restructuring banks in crisis – overview of applicable state aid rules." *Competition Policy Newsletter* 3: 3–9.

Carletti, E. and P. Hartmann (2002). "Competition and stability; what's special about banking." *ECB Working Paper Series* 146.

Carletti, E., P. Hartmann and S. Ongena (2007). "The economic impact of merger control; what's special about banking." *ECB Working Paper Series* 786.

Case 172/80 Case 172/80, *Gerhard Züchner vs. Bayerische Vereinsbank AG* [1981] ECR 2021 (Judgement of the Court of Justice of the European Union).

Commission Communication to the Member States on the application of Articles 92 and 93 of the EC Treaty and of Article 5 of Commission Decision 80/723/EEC to public undertakings in the manufacturing sector, [1993] O.J. C 307.

Commission Communication on the application of State aid rules to measures taken in relation to financial institutions in the context of the current global financial crisis, [2008] O.J. C 270/8 (2008 Banking Communication).

Commission Communication on the recapitalisation of financial institutions in the current financial crisis: limitation of aid to the minimum necessary and safeguards against undue distortions of competition, [2009] O.J. C 10/2 (Recapitalisation Communication).

Commission Communication on the return to viability and the assessment of restructuring measures in the financial sector in the current crisis under the State aid rules, [2009] O.J. C 195/9 (Restructuring Communication).

Commission Communication on the treatment of impaired assets in the Community financial sector, [2009] O.J. C 72/1 (Impaired Assets Communication).

Commission Communication on the application, from 1 January 2011, of State aid rules to support measures in favour of financial institutions in the context of the financial crisis, [2010] O.J. C 329/7 (2010 Prolongation Communication).

Commission Communication on the application, from 1 January 2012, of State aid rules to support measures in favour of financial institutions in the context of the financial crisis, [2011] O.J. C 356/7 (2011 Prolongation Communication).

Commission Communication on the application, from 1 August 2013, of State aid rules to support measures in favour of banks in the context of the financial crisis, [2013] O.J. C 216/1 (2013 Banking Communication).

Commission, Community guidelines on State aid for rescuing and restructuring firms in difficulty, [1994] O.J. C 368/12.

Commission Decision 95/547/EC of 26 July 1995 giving conditional approval to the aid granted by France to the bank Crédit Lyonnais, [1995] O.J. L 308 (Crédit Lyonnais I Decision).

Commission Decision 98/490/EC of 20 May 1998 concerning aid granted by France to the Crédit Lyonnais group, [1998] O.J. L 221 (Crédit Lyonnais II Decision).

Commission Decision of 20 July 1999 relating to a proceeding pursuant to Article 21 of Council Regulation 4064/89 of 21 December 1989 on the control of concentrations between undertakings (Case no IV/M.1616–BSCH/A. Champalimaud). Available at: http://ec.europa.eu/competition/mergers/cases/decisions/m1724_19990720_1290_en.pdf, paras. 35–37.

Commission Decision of 11 June 2002 relating to a proceeding under Article 81 of the EC Treaty (Case COMP/36.571/D-1: Austrian banks – 'Lombard Club') (2004/138/EC), [2004] O.J. L56/1.

Commission Decision NN 70/2007 of 5 December 2007 Northern Rock, [2007] O.J. C 135.

Commission Decision NN 25/2008 of 20 April 2008 WestLB riskshield, [2008] O.J. C 1628.

Commission Decision 41/2008 of 1 October 2008, Rescue aid to Bradford & Bingley, [2008] O.J. C 290.

Commission, "Second Report on Competition Policy" (1973). Available at: http://ec.europa.eu/competition/publications/annual_report/.

Council Regulation (EC) No. 659/1999 of March 22, 1999 laying down detailed rules for the application of Article 93 of the EC Treaty, [1999] O.J. L83/1.

Council Regulation (EC) No. 139/2004 of January 20, 2004 on the control of concentrations between undertakings, [2004] O.J. L24/1 (the EC Merger Regulation).

Council Regulation (EU) No 1024/2013 of 15 October 2013 conferring specific tasks on the European Central Bank concerning policies relating to the prudential supervision of credit institutions, [2013] O.J. L287/63.

Credit Suisse Securities (USA) *LLC vs. Billing*, 551 U.S. 264 (2007) (Judgment of the United States Supreme Court).

Dewatripont, M. (2014). "European banking: bailout, bail-in and state-aid control." *International Journal of Industrial Organization* 34: 37–43.

Directive 2013/36/EU of the European Parliament and of the Council of 26 June 2013 on access to the activity of credit institutions and the prudential supervision of credit institutions and investment firms, amending Directive 2002/87/EC and repealing Directives 2006/48/EC and 2006/49/EC, [2013] O.J. L 176/338.

Directive 2014/59/EU of the European Parliament and of the Council of 15 May 2014 establishing a framework for the recovery and resolution of credit institutions and investment firms and amending Council Directive 82/891/EEC, and Directives 2001/24/EC, 2002/47/EC, 2005/56/EC, 2011/35/EU, 2012/30/EU and 2013/36/37, and Regulations (EU) No 1093/2010 and (EU) No 648/2012, of the European Parliament and of the Council, [2014] O.J. L173/190 (the "BRRD" or Bank Recovery and Resolution Directive).

European Central Bank (2013). "Convergence Report." 29–30. Available at: www.ecb.europa.eu/pub/convergence/html/index.en.html.

European Central Bank/ Eurosystem (2014). "ELA Procedures (the procedures underlying the Governing Council's role pursuant to Article 14.4 of the Statute of the European System of Central Banks and of the European Central Bank with regard to the provision of ELA to individual credit institutions)." Available at: www.ecb.europa.eu/pub/pdf/other/201402_elaprocedures.en.pdf.

Freixas, J. and J. C. Rochet (2008). *Microeconomics of Banking*. MIT Press.

Garrett, T. A., G. A. Wagner and D. C. Wheelock (2003). "A Spatial Analysis of State Banking Regulation." *Federal Reserve Bank of St. Louis Working Paper* 2003-44 C.

Gebski, S. (2009). "Competition first? Application of State Aid Rules in the Banking Sector." *Competition Law Review* 6(1) 89–115.

Goodhart, C. A. E. (2010). "The changing role of central banks." *BIS Working Papers* No. 326.

Goodhart, C. and E. Avgouleas, (2015) "Critical reflections on bank bail-ins." *Journal of Financial Regulation* 1(1).

Kerjean, S. (2008). "The legal implications of the prudential supervisory assessment of bank mergers and acquisitions under EU law." *ECB Legal Working Paper Series* 6.

Kintner, E. W. and J. P. Bauer (1989 and 2012). *Antitrust Exemptions: Specific Industries and Activities. Federal Antitrust Laws*: Vol. 9. Anderson Publishing Co.

Lenihan, N. (2014). "Antitrust, competition and state aid rules in banking: an EU/U.S. comparison from a financial stability, banking supervisory and central bank liquidity perspective." *ECB Legal Services*, forthcoming.

Lista, A. (2013). *EU Competition Law and the Financial Services Sector*. Routledge (an Informa Law series book).

Lowe, P. (2006). "Some reflections on the European Commission's State Aid Policy." *Competition Policy International* 57.

O'Connell, M. (2013). "The Legal Framework for the provision of Emergency Liquidity Assistance within the ESCB." *Zeitschrift für Europarechtliche Studien (ZEuS)*: 261–328.

Pisani-Ferry, J. and A. Sapir (2010). "Banking crisis management in the EU: an early assessment." *Economic Policy* 25: 341–373.

Regulation (EU) No 575/2013 of the European Parliament and of the Council of 26 June 2013 on prudential requirements for credit institutions and investment firms and amending Regulation (EU) No 648/2012, [2013] O.J. 176/1.

Regulation (EU) No 806/2014 of the European Parliament and of the Council of 15 July 2014 establishing uniform rules and a uniform procedure for the resolution of credit institutions and certain investment firms in the framework of a Single Resolution Mechanism and a Single Bank Resolution Fund and amending Regulation (EU) No 1093/2010, [2014] O.J. L225/1 (the Single Resolution Mechanism/ Single Bank Resolution Fund Regulation).

Ritter, L. and W. D. Braun (2004). *European Competition Law: A Practitioner's Guide*. Kluwer Law.

Schiavo, G. L. (2014). "State aids and credit institutions in Europe: what way forward?" *European Business Law Review* 3: 427–457.

Summit of the Euro Area Countries, Declaration of a Concerted European Action Plan of the Euro Area Countries, October 12, 2008. Available at: http://ec.europa.eu/economy_finance/publications/publication13260_en.pdf.

Treaty on European Union (TEU) (consolidated version), Publications Office of the European Union, Luxembourg, 2010.

Treaty on the Functioning of the European Union (TFEU) (consolidated version), Publications Office of the European Union, Luxembourg, 2010.

United States v. Citizens & Southern National Bank, 422 U.S. 86 (1975) (Judgment of the United States Supreme Court).

United States v. Marine Bancorporation, Inc., 418 U.S. 602 (1974) (Judgment of the United States Supreme Court).

United States v. Philadelphia National Bank, 374 U.S. 321 (1963) (Judgment of the United States Supreme Court).

United States v. *Third National Bank in Nashville*, 390 U.S. 171 (1968) (Judgment of the United States Supreme Court).

U.S. Bank Holding Company Act of 1956, 12 U.S.C. § 1841, *et seq.*

U.S. Bank Holding Company Act of 1970, Section 10, 12 U.S.C. §§ 1971–1978.

U.S. Bank Merger Act of 1960, 12 U.S.C. § 1828(c).

U.S. Clayton Act of 1914, 15 U.S.C. §§ 12–27, 29 U.S.C. §§ 52–53.

U.S. Department of Justice, Antitrust Division, "History", available at: www.justice .gov/atr/about/index.html.

U.S. Depository Institution Management Interlocks Act of 1978, 12 U.S.C. §§ 3201–3207.

U.S. Federal Trade Commission Act of 1914, 15 U.S.C. §§ 41–58.

U.S. Garn-St. Germain Depository Institutions Act of 1982, Section 331, 12 U.S.C. § 1464(q).

U.S. Riegle-Neal Interstate Banking and Branching Efficiency Act of 1994, codified in scattered sections of 12 U.S.C.

U.S. Sherman Act of 1890, 15 U.S.C. §§ 1–17.

6

Bail-in clauses[1]

JAN PIETER KRAHNEN[2] AND LAURA MORETTI[3]

Introduction

"To bail-in or not to bail-in" emerges as the core theme of the recent crisis experience in Europe, 2007–2013. Creditor bail-outs of large financial institutions with taxpayers' money, prompted by fears of contagion and systemic consequences, have been some of the defining experiences of these years. However, eager to move away from a model so expensive for taxpayers, regulators have transitioned towards the bail-in of a bank's creditors. Bringing this standard instrument of corporate restructuring back to the banking industry is one of the central concerns of the legislation surrounding the euro area banking union project.

The basic approach of bail-in versus bail-out could also be phrased in terms of ex-ante versus ex-post. If bail-in is the rule, then creditors have incentives to look out for prudent behavior of bank management ex-ante, while these incentives are weak, at best, if creditors can expect a government bail-out. As we will argue, bail-in is neither easy[4] nor cost-free. It is not easy because multiple provisions have to be fulfilled in order to ensure bail-in effectiveness. Establishing and monitoring these provisions requires supervisory action, and thus has real costs ex-ante. Direct bail-out costs, on the other hand, are primarily ex-post. But there are also indirect bail-out costs, such as the misallocation effects

[1] This paper was presented at the "SAFE Workshop on Financial Regulation: A Transatlantic Perspective." We would like to thank our discussant, Johannes Adolff, workshop participants, as well as Ester Faia, the editor, and Margit Vanberg for helpful comments on earlier drafts of the paper.

[2] Professor of Corporate Finance at Goethe University Frankfurt, Director of CFS and SAFE.

[3] Senior researcher at the Center for Financial Studies and the SAFE Policy Center at Goethe University in Frankfurt.

[4] Or, to quote Mathias Dewatripont, in a comment on this paper: "If you love simplicity, you don't love bail-in."

resulting from the government embedded in the bail-out assurance, which are ex-ante. A comparison of the costs of bail-in versus bail-out, therefore, is difficult as it involves hard-to-estimate opportunity costs.

This chapter deals with the design of bail-in instruments for banks – that is, special financial contracts capable of absorbing sudden losses in asset value. Such instruments were regrettably missing when the global financial crisis started in 2007. Even today, seven years later, the European Union, home to the world's largest banking system by assets, has only started to realize how difficult a task it is to set up a credible bail-in mechanism. The banking system in the US is in no better shape with regards to the implementation of a credible bail-in policy. We will argue that the design of dedicated bail-in debt instruments, which are available for loss absorption, is crucial to render bail-in credible ex-ante, thereby reducing the likelihood of experiencing a crisis in the first place. As such, properly designed bail-in-able instruments are a precondition for the functioning of a market-oriented banking system.

To be effective, however, bail-in needs an appropriate institutional support system. Important elements of that support system are not yet in place in Europe – indeed, EU policymakers are not even fully cognizant of what is still missing. In the policy section of this chapter, we will describe what is needed to render a bail-in not only possible, but also actually credible. This chapter answers three questions: Why is bail-in crucial? How does it become effective? What needs to be done?

The recent financial crisis has highlighted the instability of highly interconnected financial systems and the need to specify explicitly, and well in advance, the policies to be implemented in case of bankruptcies of financial institutions. At the climax of the financial crisis, policy makers were faced with the dilemma of bailing out financial institutions in distress at the expense of the taxpayers, as in the case of Ireland, or letting them fail and risking a systemic crisis, as in the case of Lehman Brothers. The third option – that is, bailing-in shareholders, bondholders and, in some circumstances, even uninsured depositors – was for a long time not even on the table.[5] Based on the experiences surrounding the Lehman crisis, authorities around the world have concluded that once a systemic event is imminent, the state must intervene – be it through liquidity support by central banks, or through capital support by governments. The EU Bank Restructuring and Resolution Directive of 2014 (BRRD),

[5] See Calello and Ervin (2010).

however, has firmly anchored bail-in in the new EU framework for managing bank failures.

In fact, were there no systemic risk, supervisors would not be required to bail-out any individual bank when the latter gets in trouble. Instead, creditors would be available to do it. This is the common practice in the world of non-bank corporates.[6] In banking, systemic risk is endemic, emerging endogenously from the structure and operation of today's financial markets. It is due, at least in part, to a high degree of bank interconnectedness and asset correlation. This in turn explains why regulators are reluctant to allocate losses promptly to bank creditors when a large bank is suddenly on the brink of failure: the latency of contagion leads to fear of systemic risk, which in turn impedes bail-in measures.

This is the diagnosis underlying much of the euro area banking union project: systemic risk is an externality in the sense of an un-priced, and therefore unconsidered, side effect of banks' day-to-day operations. Internalizing the externality is therefore the objective of an effective regulatory reform project. For example, the externality could be overcome by charging banks a suitable price for contributing to the emergence of systemic risk – a systemic risk charge is in the spirit of a Pigou-tax. Another instrument that may help to reduce the common fear of systemic risk is a high-enough level of minimum equity capital requirement.[7] Finally, a system of bail-in practice will bring back market discipline to banks' debt markets – and the standard arguments in favor of creditor pressure in the corporate governance of firms regain their effectiveness, even for banks.

In this chapter, we present and discuss how a system based on bail-in would operate. The second section, "Existing regulation," reviews how the bail-in principle has been implemented in the European Union, and in the euro zone in particular. "Desirable features of the Bail-in tool" discusses the design of bail-in instruments. The fourth section ("Discussion") introduces the concept of loss absorbing capacity, comprising equity and debt. The fifth section concludes.

[6] If in trouble, non-bank corporates rely on their respective national bankruptcy code.

[7] The debate about the appropriate level of minimum equity capital requirement has intensified recently with a forceful argument developed in Admati and Hellwig (2013a). The authors argue in favor of a 20–30 percent risk unweighted equity ratio. While we sympathize greatly with a much larger loss absorption capacity (LAC) in bank balance sheets, we emphasize the added value of having bail-in debt as part of LAC, besides equity. The added value of bail-in debt as part of LAC is discussed in the fourth section of this chapter.

Existing regulation

BRRD

General issues

To address banking crises in a timely manner, safeguard financial stability and minimize the use of taxpayers' money, the European Commission in 2012 proposed the establishment of a single framework for the recovery and resolution of banks and financial institutions for the European Union. The resulting Bank Recovery and Resolution Directive (BRRD[8]), finalized in 2014, grants the dedicated resolution authorities the power to request and verify recovery and resolution plans from institutions under their supervision, and to intervene at an early stage when the financial situation or solvency of an institution is deteriorating. More importantly, it grants the power to resolve a financial institution when it "is failing or it is likely to fail."

In particular, the resolution authorities are provided with various resolution tools, including powers to sell parts of the business without the previous consent of shareholders, to create bridge institutions, and to separate "good" from "bad" assets. Conceptually, the most important tool is the bail-in tool, which grants the resolution authorities the power to unwind a distressed financial institution by allocating losses to the claims of unsecured creditors and converting debt claims to equity.[9]

Final agreement on the BRRD was reached between the Council and the European Parliament in April 2014; it will be applied in all 28 EU Member States starting from 2015, while the bail-in rules are set to enter into force in 2016.[10]

The adoption of BRRD is important also because it provides a common framework for the potential resolution of cross-border groups. In this case, BRRD requires the establishment of resolution colleges (see Articles 79a and 80) to carry out the group resolution plans and to coordinate among member states, balancing the need for timely and fair actions and the necessity to protect financial stability in all member states in which the group operates.

[8] Proposal for a Directive of the European Parliament and of the Council establishing a framework for the recovery and resolution of credit institutions and investment firms and amending Council Directives 77/91/EEC and 82/891/EC, Directives 2001/24/EC, 2002/47/EC, 2004/25/EC, 2005/56/EC, 2007/36/EC and 2011/35/EC and Regulation (EU) No 1093/2010.

[9] See also Huertas and Nieto (2013) and Moody's (2013) for comments on the BRRD.

[10] Two years earlier than proposed by the ECOFIN Council.

In establishing a resolution plan, each group can choose a multiple-point-of-entry-approach or a single-point-of entry-approach, and the minimal requirement for own funds and eligible liabilities (MREL) should reflect this choice. However, since the resolution action is applied at the level of the individual legal person, the Directive requires that the loss absorbing capacity is located in, or is accessible to, the legal person within the group in which losses occur, and the minimum requirement necessary for each individual subsidiary should be separately assessed. Moreover, regardless of the approach chosen, a different approach from the one contained in the plan might be implemented in order to reach the resolution objectives more efficiently.[11]

The waterfall principle and exceptions

The focal point of the Directive is the bail-in mechanism, which will force losses on shareholders, bondholders and on uninsured depositors in case of a bank resolution or restructuring. However, bail-in will not apply to insured deposits, short-term interbank lending or claims of clearing houses and payment and settlement systems (with a maturity lower than seven days), client assets, or liabilities such as salaries, pensions, or taxes (see Article 38(2)).

The liability classes exempted from bail-in are among the most liquid financial claims, like interbank loans, or short-term derivatives. This creates the risk that once BRRD is implemented, market participants may increasingly rely on those instruments. Such a potential flight to short-term and systemically important contracts runs counter to the intention of the Directive. Additional regulatory innovations, however, seek to address the issue of liability substitution, at least indirectly. In particular, the European Market Integrity Regulation (EMIR) has introduced central counterparties in important areas of securities and derivatives trading, thereby introducing collateral into the system. Furthermore, the re-use of collateral in interbank lending, called rehypothecation, has been restricted to one time only (Basel Committee/IOSCO).

In "exceptional circumstances," the resolution authority retains the power to exclude certain liabilities from the application of the write-down and conversion powers (for exemption rules, see Article 38, par. 3c). There are no clear guidelines to these exemption rules, leaving wide discretion to the responsible authority and raising the specter of a partial return to bail-outs, or even, in extreme cases, industrial policy on the

[11] See Directive 2014/59/EU.

national level. After all, national resolution agencies might be tempted to define systemic risk (and thereby exempt certain liabilities from bail-in) according to what is convenient or politically desired in the context of the national banking market, rather than judging by economic fundamentals. However, the BRRD sets a guiding principle that no creditor should be worse off than in the case of an outright liquidation (as, for example, in the case of formal bankruptcy proceedings), otherwise they are eligible for compensation (see Article 38(3caa)).

Moreover, the existing seniority structure among all liabilities at the time of crisis needs to be reflected in the bail-in decisions. That is, the most junior claim needs to participate in the loss allocation before any more senior claim is experiencing a loss. In one interpretation of the waterfall principle, a junior claim is fully reduced to zero before the next more senior claim is touched at all. A softer version would require junior claims to lose a larger share of their initial wealth than more senior claimants. The latter may be valuable because it partly insures against type-2 errors in bail-in initiations – that is, against the situation when a bail-in-worthy situation is diagnosed when there is actually no need. A less than 100 percent write-down then gives the claimant an opportunity to catch up in terms of wealth. Moreover, one could argue that with less than full write-down of junior claims, a certain degree of continuity in the governance of the firm is conceivable.

Finally, the underlying basic BRRD principles need to be respected – namely the pari passu rule, according to which creditors of the same category should be treated equally, and the no-worse-off rule, according to which no creditor (or shareholder, for that matter) should be worse off under a bail-in than he or she would have been under an insolvency plan. Both principles are not easily reconciled with the bail-in rules just mentioned. First, there is some ambiguity concerning the pay-off estimates under the no-worse-off rule, so the counterfactual (the insolvency proceedings) will remain hard to pin down with any degree of precision ex-post or ex-ante. Moreover, it remains to be seen how any exemption, as decided by the national regulator, will square with the more general principle of equal treatment among creditors (par conditio creditorum). Both points will almost surely require court rulings.[12]

As to the amount involved, the BRRD requires at least 8 percent of total liabilities to be bailed-in. After this compulsory threshold, the BRRD

[12] We thank Johannes Adolff for pointing this out to us.

specifies that national resolution funds can be used to cover losses exceeding the 8 percent of total liabilities, up to a maximum of an additional 5 percent. (See Article 38(3cab)). In extraordinary circumstances, for losses exceeding those 13 percent (8+5) the resolution authority may seek further funding from alternative sources.

The resolution funds will be set up on a national basis and they are financed via annual, pro rata contributions by all financial institutions authorized in that member state (see Articles 38(3cab (a)) and 94). The banks' contributions will be proportionate to their liabilities and adjusted for their risk profile. If the available funds are not sufficient at any given time, extraordinary ex-post contributions are raised from institutions authorized in the member state within a period of three years (Articles 38 par. 3cab (b) and 95). In "extraordinary circumstances," when the previous sources are not sufficient, the resolution authorities may seek further funding from alternative sources (Article 96), including European funds.

Some reservations

While the BRRD is a very important step in the direction of ending moral hazard and the "too big to fail" principle, the Directive still has some limitations that might create uncertainties. In particular, there is no clear definition of the trigger of an intervention by the resolution authorities: the Directive simply states (e.g. Article 27) that the resolution authorities shall intervene when an "institution is failing or likely to fail," without specifying further. Deciding where to draw the line, however, is far from clear. For example, not meeting the requirements for authorization should not automatically imply the entry of a particular bank into resolution, especially if the institution is still viable. Moreover, even the use of Emergency Liquidity Assistance (ELA) from national central banks, or the use of extraordinary public financial support (which need to be approved by the Commission under the state aid framework) should not constitute any sort of automatic threshold for putting a bank into resolution, thereby setting limits on any attempts by the resolution authority to conduct a purely national rescue policy under the auspices of the rescue fund.

In addition, as already noted, the new legislation gives considerable discretion to the (national) resolution authorities concerning the liabilities to be excluded, or partially excluded, from bail-in, and allows the use of temporary transfers from the government to support a financial institution in trouble. Questions regarding state aid rules, and the definition of state aid, remain: for example, to what extent will transfers from the taxpayer to bank creditors during a wind-down operation be considered state aid?

Contrary to the Liikanen Commission's suggestion, there is no clear requirement of the issuance of specific bail-in debt instruments, or an explicit holding ban for banks in the BRRD. The lack of such a regulation may be attributed to a general hesitation to interfere in bank funding markets. Switzerland is the exception as it has adopted a minimum bail-in-able debt regulation as part of its capital requirements. Its minimum requirement puts bail-in debt at par with equity, amounting to 19 percent of risk-weighted assets as capital.

Finally, the BRRD also leaves many implementation issues largely unresolved, relegating them to the European Banking Authority (EBA) (see Art. 39(4)). It falls to the EBA, within eighteen months after the date of entry into force of the BRRD, at the latest, to develop guidelines to promote the convergence of supervisory and resolution practices regarding the interpretation of the different circumstances when an institution is "failing or liking to fail," and thus to make sense of this very vague condition.

SSM and SRM

While the BRRD defines the framework for handling troubled financial institutions in all 28 EU Member States, the newly created banking union ensures the implementation of those rules in the Eurozone (and in other member states that opt to participate). The first component of the banking union is the Single Supervisory Mechanism (SSM),[13] set up under the ECB and set to become operational in November 2014. The ECB will directly supervise all systemically important banks in the euro area – that is, all those having assets of more than EUR 30 billion, or constituting at least 20 percent of their home country's GDP: this adds up to 128 banks. However, the SSM will also be indirectly responsible for the remaining 6,000 banks, by monitoring the national authorities responsible for supervising them.

In preparation for the entry into force of the SSM, the ECB and the national competent authorities responsible for conducting banking supervision will carry out a comprehensive assessment of the banks'

[13] Regulation (EU) No 1022/2013 of the European Parliament and of the Council of October 22, 2013.

balance sheets and risk profile. This review aims to enhance the transparency on banks' conditions, and therefore to build confidence by assessing the soundness of banks. If capital shortfalls against a capital benchmark[14] are identified, banks will be required to adopt corrective measures under the supervision of the ECB. The comprehensive assessment comprises a supervisory risk assessment, an asset quality review, and a stress test.[15] The second component of the banking union, the so-called Single Resolution Mechanism (SRM),[16] set to become operational in 2015, will ensure the effective management of bank resolution through a Single Resolution Board and a Single Resolution Fund. The SRM is directly responsible for the resolution of the same subset of banks supervised by the SSM. Decisions on bank resolution will be taken by a Single Resolution Board composed of the permanent members, as well as representatives from the Commission, the Council, the ECB, and the national resolution authorities. The ECB, as supervisor, will inform the Single Resolution Board of any bank that it identifies as "failing or likely to fail," which will prompt the Board to assess the presence of a systemic threat and adopt an appropriate plan for its resolution.[17]

The institution of a Single Resolution Fund proved more controversial[18] and was agreed only in time for the last plenary session of the

[14] The capital adequacy threshold for the baseline scenario will be 8 percent Common Equity Tier 1 (CET1) capital, whereas a threshold of 5.5 percent CET1 will apply in case of the adverse scenario (see ECB 2014).

[15] See ECB (2013) for further details.

[16] The SRM will be governed by two texts: an SRM regulation covering the main aspects of the mechanism and an intergovernmental agreement related to some specific aspects of the Single Resolution Fund.

[17] The Board includes the Executive Director, four permanent members and the representative of the national resolution authorities of all participating members, while the ECB and the Commission would be permanent observers. The plenary session would be responsible for the decisions that involve a significant use of the resolution fund (e.g. liquidity support exceeding 20 percent of the capital paid into the fund, or bank recapitalization exceeding 10 percent of the funds and any decision requiring the use of the fund once a total of EUR 5bn has been reached in a given calendar year) and it would take decisions by a two-thirds majority of the board members representing at least 50 percent of contributions. On the other hand, decisions involving a smaller use of the fund will be taken in executive sessions, composed by the Director, the four permanent members and the representatives from the member states potentially affected by the resolution. However, "the Council can object to the resolution scheme on a proposal from the Commission or can ask the Board to amend it." Nevertheless, if State aid is entailed, the Commission has to approve it before the adoption by the Board of the resolution scheme. The procedure involves several committees and risks severely slowing down the decision process.

[18] A compromise was reached only after a record 17-hour negotiation session.

European Parliament in April 2014 before the electoral recess. It will be built up to account for 1 percent of the covered deposits (around EUR 55 billion) over 8 years. Initially, the banks' contributions will be paid into national compartments, which will then be progressively mutualized over the period of 8 years, starting with 40 percent of these resources in the first year. In case of insufficient funds, the Single Resolution Fund is allowed to borrow from the markets. However, the absence of a public guarantee (backstop) might undermine the credibility of the fund, especially during a financial crisis. Huertas and Nieto (2014) argue instead that the limited resources available in the Single Resolution Fund reinforce the principle that investors, and not taxpayers, should bear the cost of banks' resolutions, and that therefore the funds only need to provide liquidity and not solvency support to banks.

If capital shortfalls are identified before the bail-in tool enters into force (2016), and if a bank is not able to raise sufficient capital on the markets, public funds can be used, subject to the updated state aid rules. In particular, according to the strengthened "burden-sharing" requirements, shareholders and junior creditors are required to be bailed-in before any public funds are used. Moreover, banks must present a sound plan for their restructuring or orderly winding down ("living wills") before they receive any public money. In case national backstops are not sufficient, other instruments at the European level, including the European Stability Mechanism, may be used. If banks are not viable, they may be put into resolution according to the respective national legislation.[19]

Selected experiences

As the euro crisis has progressed, there has already been an increasing move towards using existing bank capital structures to address capital gaps, and away from resorting to government funds for bail-outs. Particularly striking is the difference between the handling of the banking crisis in Ireland in 2008–10, and the one in Cyprus in 2013. In Ireland, the government extended a blanket guarantee to its six main banks in 2008, and used public funds to recapitalize the three largest banks (Anglo Irish Bank, Bank of Ireland and EBS). Despite having entered the crisis with a low level of government debt, the emergence of higher than announced

[19] See European Commission MEMO/14/294, 15/04/2014.

bank losses triggered a loss of market confidence and a dramatic increase in sovereign bond yields, forcing the Irish government to seek an EU-IMF bail-out.

In Cyprus, on the other hand, when similar banking sector problems emerged and the Cypriot government similarly sought a bail-out, the EU and IMF made the imposition of losses (i.e. bailing-in) on shareholders, bondholders and even depositors above EUR 100,000 in the troubled Laiki Bank one of the main preconditions for even agreeing to grant the bail-out. The application of the bail-in principle subsequently became the centerpiece of the European Bank Restructuring and Resolution Directive (BRRD).

Duebel (2013b) analyzed this evolution using eight case studies of troubled European banks and their handling by the respective national governments. He tracks the emergence of creditor participation in bank losses, and the corresponding reduction of bail-outs using public funds, over the course of the crisis, culminating in the restructuring of Cypriot banks (Bank of Cyprus and Laiki) and of the much less reported Dutch SNS Reaal, all three of which were financed largely through bail-ins. Yet despite this progressive implementation of bailing-in of private investors, there have been several missteps and contrasting announcements that have, at times, risked unravelling the whole process. The handling of the Cyprus case in particular laid bare the shortcomings of the current institutional structure, and provided an impetus for devising a plan for the future.

A more recent example is provided by the case of Banco Espirito Santo, S.A. (BES) of Portugal. It was widely seen as a litmus test of the rules developed in the BRRD and related regulation. After the bank had disclosed unexpectedly large losses in their statement of July 30, 2014, it missed its minimum capital requirement. The Central Bank (acting also as national supervisor) suspended access to central bank liquidity and client financial transactions on August 1. Due to its systemic importance (BES is Portugal's largest banks by assets), the Central Bank intervened and applied BRRD resolution measures to BES, involving a Novo Banco (good bank) as a going concern entity with new equity from the resolution fund (which in turn received a loan from the government of Portugal). Novo Banco takes over all sound assets from BES. Total assets, including the equity injection from the resolution fund, cover fully all deposits and all unsubordinated debt. Problem assets remain with BES, matched by BES equity and subordinate debt, as well as liabilities of other Espirito Santo group members.

Desirable features of the bail-in tool

Despite some shortcomings, the adoption of the BRRD for all European members and the establishment of banking union for the Eurozone, with the establishment of a SSM and a SRM, are significant steps forward in the prevention and management of future financial crises.

A fundamental issue for the success of the envisaged mechanism, as we see it, is the credibility of the bail-in instrument as an alternative to the use of public funds. Given the speed necessary in the decision-making process during a bank resolution, this depends crucially on the background work done by the supervisor. There must be ex-ante a viable resolution plan for each bank, as well as an assessment concerning the volume and the quality of available "bail-in-able" instruments (a minimum of 8 percent of the total liabilities is required, after all). The quality of these instruments will be regulated for each institution based on size and risk, according to the so-called minimum requirements for own funds and eligible liabilities (MREL). In 2016, the Commission plans to introduce a harmonized MREL standard, based on recommendations by the EBA.

In the following section, we will discuss three design elements of market-friendly bail-in instruments: conversion (rather than write-downs), trigger (exogenous or not) and loss absorptive ability (managed or not).

Market-friendly bail-in design I: conversion

The term *market-friendly* refers to the view of investors and their ability to properly price a security. The more complex a product, the less transparent its design features, and the more prone it is to manipulation by the recipient of the funds, the more difficult will be the pricing of the instrument, the less liquid the market will be, and, quite likely, the lower the market value of the asset will eventually be.[20] Therefore, it makes sense to think profoundly about how to design bail-in instruments before implementing the new bank capital standards.

There is more than one way to implement bail-in – for example, by writing down face value of debt, or by converting debt into equity. In the

[20] There is a growing literature on the effects of ambiguity (in the sense of not knowing the probability distribution of a particular asset) on its perceived value by investors. The literature shows that, on average, the value of the asset decreases with the level of ambiguity, intransparency, and risk endogeneity.

first case, the regulator depreciates the face value of equity, mezzanine instruments (hybrid, or Tier 2 capital), and subordinate and uncollateralized liabilities to the extent required by the capital shortfall. In this case, the write-down will be complete up to the amount of the required capital shortfall, respecting the seniority structure of the liabilities. Thus, a claim X is only affected if all claims junior to X are completely wiped out. If the available subordinate debt instruments are of equal seniority, then all these instruments will share equally in the write-downs.

In the second case, the regulator converts existing debt instruments into equity. In principle, the rates at which debt is swapped for equity will respect the waterfall principle, giving more senior claims higher conversion rates than junior claims. These seniority-dependent conversion rates may entail limited or unlimited dilution. In the latter case, like in the case of write-downs, conversion of a senior claim happens only after all more junior claims have been fully diluted, with zero option value retained by junior claim holders. In contrast, with limited dilution, sequential conversion of more and more senior claims will lead to progressively stronger dilution rates. That way, even the most junior claimholder will retain a positive option value, which is tied to his diluted equity holdings.

There are incentive-related arguments that help to distinguish among available bail-in options. In general, if there is uncertainty about the "right" moment to trigger the bail-in (which is very likely the case), a bail-in strategy is superior if it generates some risk sharing between old and new residual claimholders of the (banking) firm. This argument speaks against an unconditional write-down and also against conversion with unlimited dilution.

In financial markets, debt instruments with pre-arranged conditional conversion clauses are known under the name CoCo: contingent convertible debt instrument. CoCos are discussed in Flannery (2005), speaking of *reverse convertible debentures*; in Flannery (2009), analyzing *contingent capital certificates*; and as *regulatory hybrid securities* in Squam Lake Group (2009). Flannery (2005) proposes an instrument that would convert to common equity when a bank's market capital ratio falls below a pre-stated value. This would offer the right incentives to private investors to monitor and influence large banking firms and to help them overcome moral hazard, thus reducing the likelihood of a government intervention. Flannery (2009) revises and extends the concept, proposing *contingent capital certificates* as instruments to solve TBTF and to overcome the difficulties of supervisors in requiring institutions to sell new shares after having incurred losses.

The Squam Lake Group (a group of leading US financial economists offering advice on financial regulation reforms) likewise proposed a hybrid security that would convert from debt to equity when two trigger conditions are met simultaneously: a declaration by regulators that the system is suffering from a systemic crisis, and the violation of a bank-specific trigger. As pointed out by the Liikanen Commission, these instruments can be successful only if there is enough demand by the private sector and a liquid market has developed. As described in Murphy et al. (2012), this requires transparency about the trigger and the conversion, tractability (i.e. ease of modelling, pricing and risk managing) and liquidity of the instruments. However, there might be limitations for potential investors due to mandates that preclude investment in equities.

Market-friendly bail-in design II: triggers

The earlier proposals suggest the use of a trigger based on accounting measures (the Squam Lake Group 2009; D'Souza et al. 2009; and Glasserman and Nouri 2012).[21] However, others (Flannery 2005, 2009; Hart and Zingales 2011; Calomiris and Herring 2011; and McDonald 2013) propose the use of market-based indicators since accounting measures are subject to manipulation and suffer from a time lag; moreover, they failed to provide any warning signals prior to the onset of the recent financial crisis.[22] Martynova and Perotti (2012) show the existence of a trade-off between choosing a market trigger, which produces more conversions, some unnecessary (type II error), and a book value trigger subject to supervisory discretion, which converts too infrequently (type I error) and is thus subject to regulatory forbearance.

Hart and Zingales (2011) propose instead the use of CDS spreads on long-term debt as a better indicator than equity, because equity price also captures the upside and thus might disguise the probability of default. However, as pointed out by Calomiris and Herring (2011), the CDS market is still shallow and could be subject to manipulation. Moreover, the pricing of risk is not constant over time. Instead, they propose the use of stock price movements but, in order to avoid the criticism that stock market prices might not always reflect the institution's true value, they suggest using a quasi-market value of equity ratio (i.e. the 90-day moving

[21] In particular, D'Souza et al. (2009) suggest the use of the US stress test.

[22] See Sundares and Wang (2011) for an extensive discussion on the choice of security on which to place the market trigger.

average of the ratio of the market value of equity relative to the sum of the market value, plus the face value of debt – this serves to smooth fluctuations in share prices and reduce the noise in the market value signals). Their proposal is consistent with Sundares and Wang (2011), who note that a security with a trigger must be *junior* to contingent capital – thus ruling out CDS price signals relating to the same seniority level as the designated bail-in security, leaving only equity as a possible choice.

Though a market-based trigger is more transparent than one based on accounting measures, it might lead to multiplicity or absence of equilibria. In particular, Sundaresan and Wang (2011) show that a unique equilibrium exists only when there is no transfer of value between bond- and shareholders at conversion.[23] They conclude that only an exogenous conversion trigger can guarantee the equilibrium uniqueness.[24] From a practical standpoint, market-based triggers can work only for listed banks, as pointed out in Berg and Kaserer (2014) and Acharya and Steffen (2014). This is by no means a minor concern – even for systemically important institutions – since only 41 of the 124 banks subject to SSM supervision in the euro area are actually publicly listed.

A last point related to trigger design is the exogenous or endogenous character of the trigger event. Sundaresan and Wang (2011) argue that the regulator would be subject to political pressure and may therefore be reluctant to declare a crisis to be systemic, being wary of false alarms.[25] Moreover, including an element of discretion would increase uncertainty and introduce an element of opacity to the trigger.

To summarize, when designing the trigger it is important to consider the trade-offs between setting a strict, exogenous rule and a rather discretionary decision by the supervisor. In fact, while discretionary decisions allow adaptation to different situations, the supervisor is likely to be under political or lobbying pressure and might be reluctant to declare a crisis on time. Moreover, the transparency of a strict, exogenous rule might increase the credibility of the trigger and therefore will be

[23] In the case in which the conversion heavily dilutes the existing shareholders there is a multiplicity of equilibria, while there are no equilibria in the absence of dilution. There should be absence of transfer value not only at maturity but also at any trigger price on some days before maturity. Even extending the model with the inclusion of the possibility of equity issuance does not solve the problem.

[24] Multiple equilibria incur also in Albul et al. (2010), while in Pennacchi (2010) a closed form solution is ensured if the trigger relates to the asset-to-deposit ratio.

[25] The reputational cost could be very serious in the case of coincidence of supervisory and monetary policy authority as in the Eurozone and in the UK.

preferred by investors because, as it has lower ambiguity, it facilitates pricing on markets. A second dimension of the trigger choice relates to the accounting versus market measures. In fact, while accounting measures are not subject to sudden swings or computer glitches, they may also be subject to manipulations, and they are, by and large, backward-looking only. On the other hand, market-based triggers might lead to multiplicity of equilibria and they are feasible only for listed banks.

Berg and Kaserer (2014) survey the recent issuing of CoCo-bonds of European banks and find that observed triggers are based on regulatory ratios, with the ratio between Core Tier 1 capital and Risk Weighted Assets (CT1/RWA-ratio) being the most frequently used trigger.

Market-friendly bail-in design III: access restrictions

Credibility of bail-in announcement is not simply the result of a legal rule, unless it is believed to be true by market participants. As was observed many times during the crisis years since 2007, even if the regulator has the intention to apply creditor liability – that is, to practice bail-in – the fear of creating a systemic risk event may change her mind quickly, leading back to the classical bail-out policy. Clearly, in those cases, the initial bail-in announcement proved to be time-inconsistent as it turned out to be false ex-post.[26] Since market participants are learning over time, they will anticipate more bail-outs to come, should any systemically important bank be on the brink of failure. There is empirical evidence that markets firmly believed in bail-outs, rather than bail-ins, ever since mid-2007, as the price of creditor protection was significantly lower than was justified by market default expectations (Schweikart and Tsesmelidakis 2013).

The most obvious reason why a potential bail-in may not be executed in a crisis moment is due to interbank holdings of such subordinate debt. In fact, if the bailed-in creditor is herself a bank, the risk of spreading default to other institutions in the banking market is evidently large. As a response, regulators may insist on disallowing banks to invest in other banks' subordinate debt.[27] Conversely, we may ask what are the characteristics of a good investor, in the sense of minimizing the emergence of systemic risk. Here the answer is straightforward: an ideal investor in bank subordinate (bail-in-able) debt is an institutional investor pursuing

[26] See Duebel (2013a) for a collection of bailout case studies during the years 2008–2011.

[27] This was first suggested as a structural regulatory measure for bank soundness by the Liikanen report in 2012; see European Commission 2012.

a long-long strategy – that is, long-term investments funded by long-term deposits.[28] Long-only investment companies are, for example, pension funds, life insurance companies, and private equity funds.

If market access is limited to long-only institutional investors, and if market participants know that this holding restriction is effective, then a bank creditor bail-in is time-consistent – that is, it can be executed should a need arise, without regard to systemic risk repercussions. The deeper reason for restricting bail-in debt market access is to enforce true risk transfer of bank default risk to investors outside the banking system, thereby strengthening overall stability.

Of course, restricting market access is not a sufficient condition for the bail-in credibility. What is needed additionally is the confidence that the actual holder of the claim can weather a potential loss in asset value (caused by a bail-in) without getting into existential troubles herself. For example, a life insurance company holding high return bail-in debt should build up buffers in good times that mitigate excessive balance sheet damage in a potential bail-in. Such buffers can be built up from the coupon payments.[29]

Market-friendly bail-in design IV: the role of the supervisor

A final point in designing an environment in which government bail-outs of banks are only extreme exceptions, and the bail-in of bank creditors is the norm, relates to the key role of the supervisor. These authorities are expected to monitor the state of the bail-in *ability* of banks' subordinate creditors. If bail-in ability is met, then subordinate debt can be priced correctly, largely eliminating the implied funding subsidy inherent in an implicit government bail-out guarantee. The supervisor may need to develop the necessary tools required for monitoring bail-in ability.

Examples of additions to the supervisory task list are: monitoring access restrictions and the identity of bail-in debt investors, including

[28] Long-long investment companies do not face liquidity funding risk since they do not allow (or disincentivize) investors to withdraw their funds at short notice.

[29] Note that bail-in debt coupons are expected to be relatively elevated, because of the relatively high default risk they carry, coupled with a high expected loss given default. For example, the junior (CoCo) bonds issued by Swiss banks in 2013 offered an expected return several hundred basis points above that of senior bonds of the same issuer. The coupon, therefore, reflects not only a risk premium, but also a loss expectation. The latter should not lead to distributions to shareholder, unless a sufficiently large loss provisioning has been booked in the annual accounts.

risk re-transfers via CDS markets; monitoring loss absorptive ability for bail-in debt investors, including the build-up of sufficiently large loss buffers; and monitoring the liquidity of markets for subordinate bank debt instruments.

As a final point, we want to mention the possible integration of bail-in monitoring (the role of the supervisor), bail-in execution (the role of resolution agency), liquidation and resolution (the role national resolution agencies, like FMSA in Germany) and deposit insurance (the role of national deposit insurances and international resolution funds) into a single institution. Such a deposit-and-resolution insurance agency could be modelled after the FDIC (Federal Deposit Insurance Corporation) in the US market.[30]

Discussion

In this section we want to take a broader look at the bail-in topic by reviewing the academic debate on subordinate debt. We focus on the relationship between subordinate debt and plain equity. Both aspects are broader than the implementation-oriented view taken in the earlier sections of the paper as they do not take the bail-in concept as a regulatory given. The sub-section entitled "Equity and bail-in debt: substitutes or complements?" focuses on the comparison between equity and bail-in debt, and the widely held view of a superiority of the former over the latter, in terms of controlling risk incentives. In the section on "Towards the more general concept of loss absorbing capacity" we will suggest a rather pragmatic view by advocating a reasonable mix of both instruments – equity and bail-in debt – in an attempt to reach a sufficiently high level of loss absorptive capacity.

Equity and bail-in debt: substitutes or complements?

The discussion on the merits of more equity versus bail-in debt has been settled in the policy arena, and a compromise has been achieved. While the new Basel accord (Basel III), and subsequently the CRD IV, has raised the equity capital requirements and thus increased shareholder's "skin in the game" to a certain extent, the banking union project in the EU has

[30] This is not the place to go into any detail for a proposed DRIC, but we expect significant synergies to emerge.

focused mostly on creditor liability as a complementary tool. By advocating bail-in, junior creditors of banks are effectively reminded of their own "skin in the game." There is, however, an active debate on the academic side questioning the benefits of (new) bail-in instruments and favoring a further, significant increase of minimum bank equity capital instead. In fact, the excessive reliance on short-term financing and the consequent exposure to rollover risk were prominent features of the recent financial crisis. The main points of this debate are summarized below.

It is not clear why banks issue so much short-term debt. The traditional view, first presented in Calomiris and Kahn (1991), argues that the use of debt for funding, in particular short-term debt, has a disciplining effect on managers. Indeed, the possibility that creditors (depositors and short-term creditors) may withdraw their funds at any time acts as a disciplinary tool inducing the bankers to behave and not to divert funds.

Admati and Hellwig (2013b) challenge this view by pointing out the inconsistencies and the lack of realism of some assumptions in these models. First, these models usually assume, for example, the absence of the free-rider problem, and that all creditors invest time and energy in monitoring the bank. However, in the presence of deposit insurance (or implicit government guarantees), the incentives to do so are less strong. More importantly, the precision of the information and the cost of its acquisition – crucial variables in determining whether creditors can provide discipline – are not analyzed with sufficient depth.

Second, these models usually do not analyze the costs for the bank, or for society, of a sudden withdrawal of funds. In fact, in these models, all creditors are well informed and sudden collective withdrawals – that is, bank runs – occur only if the banker diverts funds. Hence, there are no inefficient bank runs. However, in the presence of asymmetric information, a run might force a bank to fail even if it would have been more efficient for it to remain active.

Finally, Admati and Hellwig (2013b) argue that, instead of being a disciplining device, excessive reliance on (short-term) debt might be the result of distorted incentives. They suggest that, contrary to the debt-discipline hypothesis, high indebtedness of banks is due to a *lack* of discipline. In fact, the reliance on short-term debt might be due to a debt overhang problem and the result of a maturity rat race that induces investors to shorten the maturity of debt to protect themselves. Moreover, the reliance on debt is exacerbated by the presence of implicit or explicit government guarantees or other subsidies. In a similar vein, Repullo et al. (2013) show in a theoretical model that the magnitude of the disciplinary effect of short-term debt is likely to be small, and that, from a social welfare point of view, higher capital requirements are a superior regulatory instrument.[31] Another common argument to explain the reliance on debt instead of equity is that the latter is more expensive. Calomiris and Herring (2011) explain that equity is costlier than debt due to asymmetric information and the negative signalling effect of offerings. However, Admati et al. (2011) dismiss the argument that equity is more expensive than debt as a "myth," emphasizing the important insight originally presented by Modigliani and Miller (1958). They, too, claim that an increase in equity requirements would not increase the funding costs for banks because the higher return on equity, which includes a risk premium, would decline with the increase in equity.

Overall, Admati and Hellwig reject the proposed use of contingent capital or "bail-in" mechanisms to increase cushions available to banks, because they are complicated to design and evaluate. They argue that regulators should focus instead on equity. They could also encourage a (re)building of capital by imposing temporary limits on distributions to shareholders. A related strand of the literature suggests contingent capital instruments, i.e. insurance contracts involving the commitment to inject cash when needed (Rochet and Sigrist-Zargari 2013). However, contingent capital contracts face other problems, such as restrictions imposed by any basic limited liability rule, and are therefore not a panacea either.

In a recent paper on optimal compensation of bank managers, Aptus et al. (2014) propose a "crisis contract," which effectively is a retroactive tax on manager past earnings (i.e. manager wealth) in case of a banking crisis. A crisis (compensation) contract partly dis-aligns the incentives of shareholders and managers, and aligns more closely the incentives of debt holders and management. As a consequence, excessive (from the standpoint of the society) risk taking is reduced and welfare is improved. Aptus et al.'s crisis contract can be re-interpreted as a bail-in bond, which is part of the management compensation scheme.[32] In their model, the retroactive liability of management re-aligns their risk-taking incentives in a more balanced way, considering the wealth position of both shareholders and debt holders.

[31] See McAndrews et al. (2014) for an analysis of the benefits of long-term debt versus equity.

[32] Compensating managers with bail-in debt, in order to better align incentives of creditors and management, is one of the recommendations contained in the Liikanen report of 2012; see European Commission 2012.

On a concluding note, the discussion in the theoretical literature is still incomplete insofar as the attention focuses mainly on the single banking firm, and externalities with respect to the emergence of systemic risk and the pricing of bank debt are not sufficiently incorporated. Clearly, the paper by Aptus et al. (2014) comes closest to what we have in mind when discussing the pros and cons of bail-in debt. Their paper supports a complementary role of bail-in debt and equity capital in designing management incentives – a position shared by us.

Towards the more general concept of loss absorbing capacity (LAC)

While many of these arguments carry significant weight, there are further aspects to consider that strengthen the concept of the more general term "loss absorbing capital" (including equity and bail-in-able debt) as opposed to relying exclusively on "equity." First and foremost, the role of long-term debt (as opposed to the short-term debt considered in the earlier literature) in the process of market discipline in a world characterized by systemic risk, implicit government guarantee and implied debt mispricing needs to be considered. A properly priced debt instrument,[33] particularly junior debt, will convey valuable information about a bank's asset risk to bank managers – irrespective of whether the bank is a listed company or not. Marginal borrowing costs are hard costs, and thus play an important role in guiding the bank's risk-taking decisions. For example, the issue costs of new debt will tell management how external observers perceive the business model of the institution. As explained earlier, a large enough portion of junior debt that offers loss absorption capacity in a credible way is instrumental in establishing a functional bank funding market. It is also a precondition for the emergence of market discipline. Further arguments against an exclusive focus on equity in discussing loss absorption capacity in banking relates to moral hazard in the form of asset substitution, which will not level off unless very high equity ratios are reached – say, near to 100 percent.[34]

That said, all arguments in favor of introducing bail-in debt as an additional line of defense with positive side effects should by no means

33 "Properly" means internalizing externalities.

34 When discussing the leverage of bank, i.e. the amount of equity it is required to hold against its asset side, one has to consider the determination of risk weights. For large banks, the Basle capital rules allow banks to use their own internal models to determine the risk level of its different asset classes.

diminish the importance of equity as the first line of defense against losses. Therefore, a high level of equity is "of course" a very desirable policy tool. On its own, and without the assistance of bail-in debt, however, the risk-shifting incentive for shareholders remains unchallenged. In contrast, with both layers of loss absorption in place – that is, equity *and* "bail-in-able" debt – the downside risk will become relevant for management decision-making as well, either directly via management compensation (Aptus et al. 2014), or indirectly via debt-holder activism. Bail-in debt holders may even be invited to be part of the governance system of the bank – for example, a seat on the supervisory board, or some other form of first-hand information.

Finally, putting all loss absorption weight on equity, and thus imposing a relatively low leverage ratio, will limit the ability of banks to engage in one of their main economic functions, according to some – namely, the supply of a safe asset and, by implication, the supply of liquidity to investors. Both features – safety and liquidity – are closely connected. While the latter is the basis for the Diamond and Dybvig model of banking, the former is key for a theory of securitization – and a bank may be interpreted analytically as an institutionalized structured finance transaction (see deMarzo 2005; Franke and Krahnen 2007).

Conclusion

In the previous sections, we have described the potential role of a properly designed bail-in debt market for improving welfare in financial markets. Its primary role is to repair bank risk-taking incentives in the direction of improved downside risk consideration.[35]

The role of the supervisor in this picture is that of a guard who enforces the rules of the game. He is *not* attempting to be a better risk manager at the level of individual banks than their management teams. We maintain, however, that a positive role for bail-in is tied to a strict precondition: the credibility of a future bail-in needs to be actively designed and monitored. While bail-in as a possibility is a simple consequence of a legal decree (as in the BRRD or the Dodd-Frank Act[36]), it is not automatically

[35] Even if everything is in place as suggested in this chapter, there is still uncertainty about the level of basic (or exogenous) systemic risk in the financial industry. Its monitoring and curtailing remains a major additional task of the supervisor – beyond the scope of this chapter.

[36] Dodd–Frank Wall Street Reform and Consumer Protection Act (2010). 111th Congress Public Law 2013.

credible –that is, rationally expected by market participants to be put into effect – unless adequate provisions are in place.

We have discussed such adequate provisions relating to the design of bail-in instruments, in order to make them attractive for investors and to encourage the development of secondary markets.

In all of these design features, the role of the supervisor has to be (re-)considered: its main operative objective, in our opinion, should be *to ensure bail-in-ability at all times.*

In particular, the banking supervisor, in conjunction with the agency responsible for the SRM process, will need a clear mandate for checking, on a regular basis, that banks are sufficiently staffed with loss absorbing capital – that is, equity *and* bail-in debt. For both types of loss absorbing capital, the supervisor has to ensure at any time that a necessary bail-in can actually be carried out without the fear of systemic risk repercussions. This requires thorough knowledge of the whereabouts of the equity and bail-in debt positions – that is, which investor is long in these assets, whether they are located inside or outside the banking system, and whether there is any prospect of re-transfer of risk into the banking system via CDS or other forms of insurance. Furthermore, are those particular investors subject to run risk?

In general, is a bail-in in the foreseeable future credible, if needed? If this question can be answered strongly in the affirmative, then there is new hope for an effective market discipline in banking. The banking union and its ambitious – though as yet incomplete – bail-in program is worth the effort.

References

Acharya, V. and S. Steffen (2014). "Falling short of expectations? Stress-testing the European banking system." Available at: Voxeu.org.

Admati, A. R., P. M. DeMarzo, M. F. Hellwig and P. Pleiderer (2011). "Fallacies, irrelevant facts, and myths in the discussion of capital regulation: why bank equity is not expensive." *Rock Center for Corporate Governance at Stanford University Working Paper Series* 86.

Admati, A. R. and M. F. Hellwig (2013a). *The bankers' new clothes: what's wrong with banking and what to do about it.* Princeton University Press.

Admati, A. R. and M. F. Hellwig (2013b). "Does debt discipline bankers? An academic myth about bank indebtedness." *mimeo*, available at: www.gsb.stanford.edu.

Albul, B., D.M. Jaffee and A. Tchistyi (2010). "Contingent convertible bonds and capital structure." *mimeo.*

Aptus, E., V. Britz, and H. Gersbach (2014). "On the economics of crisis contracts." *ETH-Zurich Working Paper.*

Berg, T. and C. Kaserer (2014). "Does contingent capital induce excessive risk?" *Systemic Risk, Basel III, Financial Stability and Regulation 2011, mimeo.*

Calello, P. and W. Ervin (2010). "From bail-out to bail-in." *The Economist*, January 28.

Calomiris, C. W. and R. J. Herring (2011). "Why and how to design a contingent convertible debt requirement." *mimeo*, available at: http://ssrn.com/abstract=1815406.

Calomiris, C. W. and C. M. Kahn (1991). "The role of demandable debt in structuring optimal banking arrangements." *American Economic Review* 81(3): 497–513.

DeMarzo, P. (2005). "The pooling and tranching of securities: a model of informed intermediation." *Review of Financial Studies* 18: 1–35.

Diamond, D. W. and P. H. Dybvig (1983). "Bank runs, deposit insurance, and liquidity." *Journal of Political Economy* 91(3): 401–419.

D'Souza, A. et al. (2009). "Ending 'too big to fail'." *Goldman Sachs Global Markets Institute.*

Duebel, H. (2013a). "Creditor participation in banking crisis in the eurozone – a corner turned?" Study commissioned by the Bundestagsfraktion Bündnis90/ Die Grünen and The Greens/ European Free Alliance in European Parliament.

Duebel, H. (2013b). "The capital structure of banks and the practice of bank restructuring." CFS *Working Paper* 425.

European Central Bank (2013). Note on comprehensive assessment, October.

European Central Bank (2014). Note on comprehensive assessment, February.

European Commission (2012). High-level Expert Group on reforming the structure of the EU banking sector (Liikanen Commission).

European Parliament and of the Council (2014). Directive 2014/59/EU of the of 15 May 2014 establishing a framework for the recovery and resolution of credit institutions and investment firms and amending Council Directive 82/891/EEC, and Directives 2001/24/EC, 2002/47/EC, 2004/25/EC, 2005/56/EC, 2007/36/EC, 2011/35/EU, 2012/30/EU and 2013/36/EU, and Regulations (EU) No 1093/2010 and (EU) No 648/2012, of the European Parliament and of the Council.

Flannery, M. J. (2005). "No pain, no gain? Effective market discipline via 'Reverse Convertibility Debentures'." In H. S. Scott (eds.), *Capital Adequacy beyond Basel: Banking, Securities, and Insurance.* Oxford University Press.

Flannery, M. J. (2009). "Stabilizing large financial institutions with contingent capital certificates." *mimeo*, available at SSRN: http://ssrn.com/abstract=1485689.

Franke, G. and J. P. Krahnen (2007). "Default risk sharing between banks and markets: the contribution of collateralized debt obligations." In Mark Carey and René M. Stulz (eds.), *The Risks of Financial Institutions*, National Bureau of Economic Research: 603–634.

Glasserman, P. and B. Nouri (2012). "Contingent capital with a capital-ratio trigger." *Management Science* 58(10): 1816–1833.

Hart, O. and L. Zingales (2011). "A new capital regulation for large financial institutions." *American Law and Economics Review* 13(2): 453–490.

Huertas, T. and M. J. Nieto (2013). "A game changer: The EU banking recovery and resolution directive." Available at: VoxEU.org, published 19 September.

Huertas, T. and M. J. Nieto (2014). "How much is enough? The case of the Resolution Fund in Europe." Available at: VoxEU.org, published 18 March.

Martynova, N. and E. Perotti (2012). "Convertible bonds and bank risk-taking." *mimeo*, available at SSRN: http://ssrn.com/abstract=2176191.

McAndrews, J., D. P. Morgan, J. Santos and T. Yorulmazer (2014). "What makes large bank failures so messy and what to do about it?" *Economic Policy Review*, Federal Reserve Bank of New York.

McDonald, R. L. (2013). "Contingent Capital with dual price trigger." *Journal of Financial Stability* 9(2): 230–241.

Modigliani, F. and M. H. Miller (1958). "The cost of capital, corporation finance and the theory of investment." *American Economic Review* 48(3): 261–297.

Moody's (2013). "EU bank resolution: draft directive offers clarity on future support framework, but important questions remain unanswered." September 30.

Murphy, G., M. Walsh and M. Willison (2012). "Precautionary contingent capital." *Bank of England Financial Stability Paper* 16.

Pennacchi, G. (2010). "A structural model of contingent claims." *Federal Reserve of Cleveland Working Paper* 10–4.

Repullo, R., J. Rochet and Q. A. T. Vo (2013). "Optimal debt maturity." *National Centre of Competence in Research Financial Valuation and Risk Management Working Paper* 783.

Rochet, J. C. and Y. Sigrist-Zargari (2013). "How to finance SIFIs?" *Swiss Finance Institute Discussion paper.*

Schweikart, F. and Z. Tsesmelidakis (2013). "The impact of government interventions on CDS and equity markets." *Working Paper, Goethe University, mimeo.*

Squam Lake Working Group on Financial Regulation (2009). "An expedited resolution mechanism for distressed financial firms: regulatory hybrid securities." *Council on Foreign Relations Press, Working Paper*, April.

Sundaresan, S. and Z. Wang (2011). "On the Design of Contingent Capital with Market Trigger." *Federal Reserve Bank of New York Staff Report* 448.

7

Shadow resolutions as a no-no in a sound Banking Union

LUCA ENRIQUES AND GERARD HERTIG[1]

Introduction

The credit crisis has generated much debate on the bailout or resolution of larger banks. By contrast, little attention has been paid to resolution procedures being generally circumvented when it comes to smaller banks. In fact, supervisory leniency and political considerations often result in public officials incentivizing viable banks to acquire smaller, failing banks, which weakens supervision, distorts competition, and gives resolution a bad name. Fortunately, recent reforms have provided EU authorities with significant incentives to follow formal resolution procedures rather than to operate in their shadow.

The 2014 Regulation on a Single Resolution Mechanism (SRM) and Single Bank Resolution Fund (SBRF)[2] empowers a Single Resolution Board (SRB) to closely monitor the situation of all banks and their compliance with so-called early intervention measures – i.e. measures taken by supervisory authorities in the presence of financial or other difficulties that may lead to insolvency. More importantly, the SRB is competent for adopting a resolution scheme when a bank is likely to fail and resolution action is in the public interest.[3] However, before doing so,

[1] Luca Enriques is Allen & Overy Professor of Corporate Law at the University of Oxford and Gerard Hertig is Professor of Law at ETH Zurich. Both are fellows at the European Corporate Governance Institute (ECGI).

[2] Council Regulation (EU) No 806/2014 of July 15, 2014, [2014] OJ L225/1 establishing uniform rules and a uniform procedure for the resolution of credit institutions and certain investment firms in the framework of a Single Resolution Mechanism and a Single Resolution Fund (hereafter SRM Regulation).

[3] Resolution schemes are administrative procedures that permit management of a bank failure without (direct) court involvement. For an overview of the relationship between early intervention measures and resolution within the Banking Union, see Micossi et al. 2013.

the SRB must establish the lack of reasonable prospect that any alternative private sector measures would prevent a failure within a reasonable timeframe.

In other words, private sector solutions are favored over resolution schemes, an approach that reflects two basic assumptions: whenever possible, bank reorganizations should be market-driven, and have no cost implications for taxpayers. It logically follows that a private sector solution should neither be motivated by state interests nor be based on the exercise of state powers. In the real world, however, what is called a "private" sector solution often goes hand-in-hand with state involvement. When that is the case, such a scheme, a private solution only in form, is better termed a "shadow" resolution.

Shadow resolutions can be defined as mergers and other acquisition transactions that are coerced or informally subsidized via threat of supervisory action or promise of a benevolent supervisory stance at some future time. Prototypical examples of threats include capital adequacy reassessments, regulatory investigations, and limitations in the scope of authorized activities. Prototypical examples of informal subsidies include merger assistance, facilitated market access, and compliance leniency.

While reliable data is not publicly available, shadow resolutions are a common phenomenon. Cases are regularly reported in the media and the practice is widely acknowledged in the literature. It has been documented that shadow resolutions were systematically practiced throughout Italy's banking history and for decades post-World War II in Japan. There is also turn of the millennium evidence of restructuring mergers being frequently induced by public officials in Germany and occasionally in Switzerland. More recently, the credit crisis has prompted regulators across the world to impose mergers and acquisitions to avoid insolvency filings by larger banks.

There are similarities between shadow and formal resolutions. As indicated, shadow resolutions are often done via mergers. Likewise, formal resolutions are frequently conducted using purchase and assumption (P&A) approaches,[4] which leads to resolution transactions that are functionally similar to M&A transactions. In addition, there is state involvement in shadow as well as in formal resolutions. Shadow

[4] The formal resolution of a non-viable bank is generally done using four different methods: (i) liquidate all assets; (ii) pay a third party to reimburse depositors; (iii) get an acquirer to purchase some/all assets and to assume some/all liabilities (purchase and assumption); (iv) set-up a bridge bank that include some/all assets and liabilities and continues to conduct business until an acquirer is found. See, e.g., for the US, Carnell et al. 2009: 730–1.

transactions involve state coercion or subsidies, whereas state loss sharing guarantees are an essential component of P&A transactions.

Quite obviously, there are also differences between the two types of transactions. First, no or limited information is available regarding state involvement in shadow transactions, whereas P&A transactions involve relatively transparent steering by state authorities. Second, formal resolutions require proper state authority and are subject to established review procedures. By contrast, shadow resolution participants essentially face diffuse moral suasion and informal complaint avenues. Third, official resolutions formally affect shareholder and creditor rights, while this only occurs informally in shadow resolution situations.

The remaining of this contribution is organized as follows. The costs and benefits of shadow resolutions are discussed in the section on "Costs and benefits of shadow resolutions," whereas "The appeal of shadow resolutions" documents their rampant presence in the banking sector. On that basis, the fourth section, "Making formal resolutions the dominant approach," makes the case for a more formal approach, while "Getting rid of shadow resolutions under the Banking Union framework" argues that European institutions have both the incentives and the power to impose a shift to such an approach within the (evolving) Banking Union context.

Costs and benefits of shadow resolutions

Shadow resolutions have clear advantages in common with private workouts:[5] they allow for more flexible and timely restructurings and are likely to be less disruptive in terms of business continuation. In addition, they prevent disorderly changes in the rights of the failing firm's counterparties and avoid costly judicial involvement. When it comes to banks, timely shadow resolutions remove the risk that depositors and investors massively withdraw their cash or sell their debt and equity stakes at the first sign of financial trouble, and that the bank's counterparties stop doing business with it. These reactions would, in turn, increase the failing bank's problems, which is likely to result in a botched resolution and, when it comes to larger banks, may lead to a financial crisis.

Because shadow resolutions take those risks off the table for the time being, it is easy to understand why politicians, supervisors, practitioners, and bankers are inclined to consider bank shadow resolutions as the

[5] See also Garrido 2012: 9–14.

lesser evil. Supervisory authorities, often under politicians' pressure, thus have strong incentives to push for an acquisition of the failing institution by another bank in a timely fashion, not least because it will cover up their possible prior failure to take prompt corrective action[6] and avoid having taxpayers' money being spent on bailouts.[7]

However, saving failing banks via shadow resolutions can also be costly. To begin with, the practice often goes hand-in-hand with supervisory forbearance and introduces new forms of moral hazard. Bank supervisors may adopt a laid-back approach as they know there is a palatable way out should their laxity fail to prevent a bank from getting insolvent. Bank creditors have lower monitoring incentives, given that their losses tend to zero when failures are prevented via third party takeovers. Managers and directors will avoid the reputational costs and the liability risks that a formal resolution may entail, while shareholders will have either no say in the matter or have it because they are dominant shareholders, in which case they will be directors or managers most of the time. The acquirers of failing banks, for their part, can expect their cooperation to go hand-in-hand with reduced supervisory scrutiny, which in turn increases the probability of their own failure.[8]

More importantly, shadow resolutions distort competition. Banks that are closer to regulators or have superior political contacts are likely to benefit from various shadow competitive advantages.[9] Weak but well-connected banks will be able to take more risks than their rivals as they are confident of being quietly rescued if their business strategy turns out to be a failure. Strong and well-connected banks have better chances than their rivals to acquire the most interesting among the failing banks or, at least, to get rich state support for taking over a to-be-rescued bank.

Last but not least, the availability of shadow resolutions gives formal resolutions a bad name. This is an environment where it will prove almost impossible to suddenly formally resolve any established bank. Such a move is likely to cause creditors and investors to panic and prompt financial intermediaries to expect the worse (what else could justify a departure from the shadow resolution model?) and immediately

[6] On the unwillingness of national supervisory authorities to intervene quickly and resolutely when a bank is struggling, see Ferran 2014.

[7] See Hoggarth et al. 2004 and Garicano 2012.

[8] This issue is especially significant because rescue mergers normally take place among banks incorporated in the same jurisdiction, even within the European Union. See, e.g., Sapir and Wolf 2013.

[9] Milhaupt 1999: 427.

stop transacting with the bank in resolution. At the very least this makes any formal resolution difficult to handle and is likely to require public funds, and thus, ex ante, be unpalatable to supervisors and politicians. This, in turn, will make even unsound and desperate shadow resolution mergers look a viable option, with the potential of creating more serious problems further down the road.

The appeal of shadow resolutions

In the real world, shadow resolutions are often favored over formal ones.

To begin with, state-driven mergers aiming to rescue an ailing bank (hereafter: rescue mergers) are common in times of financial crises, in particular when authorities deem them to be prudentially superior to bailouts.[10] For example, following the 1997 East Asian financial crisis, government-induced mergers proved to be one of the most effective restructuring tools for failing banks in Indonesia, Malaysia, Thailand, and South Korea.[11] Several jurisdictions adopted a similar approach following the 2007 credit crisis.[12] To name but a few well-known cases: in Germany, Sal. Oppenheim was acquired by Deutsche Bank; in Spain, Bankia resulted from the merger of seven failing state-controlled banks; in the UK, Lloyds acquired HBOS; in the US, Wachovia was absorbed by Wells Fargo.

Rescue mergers also occur in normal (non-financial crisis) times, but they are more difficult to document, essentially for two reasons. First, the supervisor in charge has an interest in keeping things quiet, to avoid claims that the rescue is due to its improper oversight of the failing bank.[13] Second, the involved parties generally prefer not to disclose the dire state of the acquired bank to minimize overreactions by investors and markets. It is, however, generally recognized that troubled banks are frequently merged with financially healthy ones,[14] with banking supervisors playing an active coordination or even guiding role.[15] In addition, many countries favor rescue mergers over resolution not only for larger banks but also for smaller ones.[16]

While there are significant incentives to keep shadow resolutions of failing banks out of the public eye, they are not always kept secret. For

[10] Perotti and Suarez 2002. [11] Claessens et al. 1999. [12] Hall 2009.

[13] For a detailed comparative description of the corrective measures available to supervisors of banks that face financial trouble, see Hüpkes 2003.

[14] Carletti and Hartmann 2002. [15] Drummond et al. 2007.

[16] Hawkins and Turner 1999: 36.

example, official records made available for (then) all German banks reveal that, in any given year during the 1995–2006 period, between 25 and 76 German banks were subject to shadow resolution – with a number of additional banks (between 88 and 193) being bailed out via recapitalization by their deposit insurance funds.[17] Interestingly, Switzerland adopted a somewhat different approach during the same period, even though many of its banks were also in financial trouble. While the bailouts and rescue mergers of state-owned cantonal banks in Basel, Bern, Geneva, and Solothurn were given extensive publicity and generated heated debates,[18] the controversial 1991 bankruptcy of the Spar- und Leihkasse Thun prompted Swiss supervisors to adopt a much more secretive approach to rescue mergers for privately held banks.[19]

Italy provides another, more recent transparency example. Efforts to arrange rescue mergers in Italy, where many of the country's 680 lenders are saddled with bad loans, were discussed in the media even before transaction completion. For example, Reuters reported on January 8, 2014 that the Bank of Italy had asked Veneto Banca to consider a rescue merger after conducting an audit of its loans.[20] Even more specifically, Reuters reported on May 29, 2014 that Banca Popolare di Vicenza had plans to acquire Banca Etruria, which had been told by the Bank of Italy to find a buyer, given its shaky loan portfolio.[21]

These differences in transparency show that there is variance in the appeal of bank restructurings. It appears that shadow resolutions are often unattractive in times of financial crisis, a state of the world where (larger) failing banks have to be openly bailed out and the resolution of (smaller) failing banks generally occurs in broad daylight. That occurs because it is almost impossible to hide restructuring efforts due to the magnitude of losses occurred in the banking sector. Moreover, the stigma effect of capital injections or resolution procedures is significantly reduced because of the large number of banks involved – which, incidentally, is also the reason why supervisory authorities often subject all major banks to rescue programs, regardless of whether they individually need help.[22]

17 Dam and Koetter 2012. 18 See Nobel 2002: 508.

19 See Swiss Federal Banking Commission 2008: 5–6.

20 *Reuters* (January 8, 2014): "Bank of Italy tells troubled Veneto Banca to consider merger."

21 *Reuters* (May 29, 2014): "Popolare Vicenza plans $295 million takeover of Banca Etruria."

22 There is also empirical evidence that it could be cheaper to bail-out smaller banks rather than to resolve them when larger banks generally benefit from state capital injections. See Croci et al. (2014).

Second, there is also evidence that shadow resolutions are not necessarily attractive in non-crisis times. The German and Swiss restructuring cases mentioned above provide a good example. They took place during a period of increasing competition in the banking industry. It was generally acknowledged that this evolution meant that bank profitability would decrease and everyone (including small investors) assumed that a number of banks would have to be restructured. As a result, supervisors had limited incentives to hide bailouts or the rescue character of many mergers. On the one hand, they could count on not being considered "at fault." On the other, the risk of investor panic or market crash was limited as long as restructurings were conducted in a discrete and orderly fashion. In fact, this is precisely what happened. The stigma effect traditionally associated with bank restructurings was only relevant when depositors could expect a financial loss (a good example being the Spar- und Leihkasse Thun) or put a high value on financial stability (as was the case for Switzerland's private banking clients).

Summing-up, shadow resolutions are more attractive, and thus pervasive, when one or several conditions are fulfilled: banks are not too big to fail; deposit insurance (as such or in the form of state guarantees) is perceived as insufficient; formal resolution is not justifiable by the presence of a financial crisis. The case for replacing shadow resolutions with formal resolutions is thus strongest for smaller banks that are failing in good times: this is an environment where (1) supervisors have an incentive to circumvent formal resolution procedures and (2) it is possible to accustom investors and markets to such procedures, thus reducing their stigma effects. Conversely, shadow resolutions are less of an issue for larger banks: this is an environment where (1) supervisors are more reluctant to favor rescue mergers due to their systemic risk implications and (2) bailouts are hard to hide and often the functional equivalent of formal resolutions – capital injections being accompanied by the setting-up of a bad bank and depositor indemnification.[23]

Making formal resolutions the dominant approach

To argue that, in good times, jurisdictions should subject (smaller) failing banks to formal rather than shadow resolutions may well sound

[23] The recent bailout of Banco Espírito Santo provides a good example: see *Financial Times* (August 5, 2014: 13): "Post Mortem Begins into BES's Fall from Grace"; *Wall Street Journal* (July 21, 2014: 1) "Espírito to Reimburse its Retail Customers."

unrealistic. To make the proposal credible from an implementation perspective, one must provide evidence that: (1) it is feasible for a jurisdiction with a strong shadow resolution tradition to shift to a formal resolution approach; and (2) jurisdictions will not just find it always preferable on expediency grounds to circumvent formal resolution procedures when they matter most – that is, in good times.

The Japanese experience demonstrates that a switch to formal resolutions is possible in a jurisdiction with a tradition of shadow resolutions. During the economic recovery decades that followed World War II, the government routinely intervened and arranged for rescue mergers whenever banks faced financial troubles. The practice became so entrenched that it persisted well beyond the post-war recovery period. By the early 1990s, Japanese authorities still dealt with the occasional failure of a smaller bank by encouraging healthier institutions to absorb it[24] – the acquirer's absorption costs being offset by a "bonus" amounting to an overlook of bank regulation infringements. However, the real estate and equity crisis that started in 1997 made the shadow resolution approach unsustainable. With the financial sector in disarray and a number of banks failing, bailouts had to be accompanied by formal resolutions. In total, 11 banks were put into financial administration – 6 in 1999 and 5 in the 2000–2002 period.[25]

No formal resolution took place in the following non-crisis years until the failure of the Incubator Bank of Japan (IBJ), a lender for small and midsize companies which went bust on September 10, 2010. That event attracted significant media attention due to depositors suffering losses after having been fully indemnified by the Deposit Insurance Corporation of Japan (DICJ) in previous resolutions. The difference in treatment is sometimes attributed to the introduction of an indemnification cap in 2005, but that overlooks the fact that pre-existing limits were disregarded in the 1999–2002 resolutions.[26] The more likely explanation is that Japanese authorities were trying to signal their determination in fighting moral hazard – which is likely to have been a real issue given that no formal resolution had taken place since 2002 – but underestimated the resulting outcry.

[24] Nelson and Tanaka 2014: 36

[25] See Deposit Insurance Corporation of Japan (December 26, 2011): *Resolution of Failed Financial Institutions*: www.dic.go.jp/english/e_katsudo/e_hatanshori/; of these 11 institutions, 7 were banks, 2 regional cooperative (shinkin) banks and 2 credit cooperatives.

[26] Tanaka 2010: 18.

The IBJ debacle generated various regulatory and administrative practice reforms.[27] It is too early to evaluate their impact, as no formal resolution has taken place since. The reforms could mark the end of the decade-old formal resolution practice, especially given the lack of transparency and the controversies[28] surrounding the December 26, 2011 transfer of IBJ assets to AEON Bank (an affiliate of the nation's leading supermarket chain operator). Alternatively, the fact that IBJ was subject to formal resolution in good times and the publicity the case attracted may have caused sufficient ambiguity to keep moral hazard at an acceptable level.[29]

The sustainability of formal resolutions when shadow resolutions remain an option is demonstrated by the United States' experience. Let us start with crisis times. Data collected by the Federal Deposit Insurance Corporation (FDIC) shows that a large number of banks were subject to formal resolution during the Savings & Loans (S&L) crisis and the credit crisis. There were 924 FDIC S&L resolutions in the vicinity of the Savings & Loans crisis (1986–1992)[30] and 424 FDIC commercial bank resolutions in the aftermath of the credit crisis (2008–2011).[31] This is substantial, and provides evidence of the important role played by formal resolutions when financial distress is widespread.

What about non-crisis times? The number of FDIC resolutions logically declines but remains significant during recovery periods, with 54 taking place in 1993–1994 and 91 in 2012–mid-2014. In contrast, only a small number of banks (4–5 per year) were subject to FDIC resolution during the 1995–2007 period.[32] There are two ways to read this result. One is to conclude that formal resolutions give way to shadow resolutions as soon as the economy is doing well. The other is that banks are much less prone to failure in normal times. The proper interpretation is probably in the middle. On the one hand, political and reputation considerations favor shadow resolutions in some situations. On the other hand, the mere existence of a few formal resolutions is evidence of the

[27] For a detailed description, see DICJ, Annual Report 2012–2013, 40–44. See also *Financial Times* (June 13, 2013: 24): "Investors to share bank losses under new Japanese rules."

[28] *The Asahi Shimbun* (October 1, 2011): "Aeon to take over Incubator Bank though doubts remain."

[29] See Freixas 1999.

[30] See Bennett and Unal 2010.

[31] FDIC: Failed Bank List: www.fdic.gov/bank/individual/failed/banklist.html [continuously updated].

[32] See Cowan and Salotti 2013.

operational advantages of the Purchase and Assumption (P&A) favored in FDIC resolutions.[33]

Summing-up, formal resolutions should prove palatable and sustainable in an environment where supervisory forbearance is not pervasive and formal resolution procedures properly designed. This is precisely the current environment within the European Union following the set-up of the Banking Union, which provides a unique opportunity for replacing shadow resolution practices with a formal resolution approach.

Getting rid of shadow resolutions under the Banking Union framework

The post-crisis awareness of moral hazard issues has accelerated efforts to give European institutions a central role in bank supervision and resolution. The Single Supervisory Mechanism (SSM) empowers the European Central Bank (ECB) to supervise all of the approximately 6,000 euro-area banks.[34] It will have direct responsibility for "significant" banks – approximately 130 credit institutions, representing almost 85% of total banking assets in the euro area.[35] National supervisors will remain involved in the day-to-day supervision of these 130 banks and, more importantly for our purposes, directly supervise less significant banks.

The Single Resolution Mechanism (SRM), for its part, has subtracted crucial powers from national authorities by empowering the Single Resolution Board (SRB) to resolve significant banks.[36] National resolution authorities remain competent for the resolution of less significant banks, provided their resolution does not require any use of the Single Bank Resolution Fund.[37] However, as we show below, this does not mean

[33] The credit crisis provides evidence of the operational advantages of the P&A: 302 shared-loss agreements had been entered into by June 30, 2013, allowing for estimated savings of $41 billion compared to outright cash sales of assets; FDIC, Loss-Share Questions and Answers: www.fdic.gov/bank/individual/failed/lossshare/.

[34] See Council Regulation (EU) No 1024/2013 of October 15, 2013, [2013] OJ L287/63 conferring specific tasks on the European Central Bank concerning policies relating to the prudential supervision of credit institutions (hereafter SSM Regulation). See also Regulation (EU) No 468/2014 of the European Central Bank of April 16, 2014, [2014] OJ L141/1 establishing the framework for cooperation within the Single Supervisory Mechanism between the European Central Bank and national competent authorities and with national designated authorities (hereafter SSM Framework Regulation).

[35] ECB (2014): List of Supervised Entities Notified of the ECB's Intention to Consider them Significant, Last Update of the List: June 26, 2014.

[36] Article 6a(2), SRM Regulation. [37] Article 6a(3), SRM Regulation.

that smaller banks are unlikely candidates for ECB's or SRB's intervention as both institutions are in charge of the overall "effective and consistent functioning" of the SSM and the SRM.[38]

These reforms do not merely allocate the supervision and resolution of major banks to European-level institutions. They also harmonize procedures for dealing with failing banks in general, via provisions on early intervention, private sector solutions and formal resolutions. On the books, no room appears to be left for shadow resolutions as resolution authorities are empowered to approach potential buyers only in preparation for the adoption of a resolution scheme. Nevertheless, shadow resolutions cannot just be ruled out by legislative fiat. Supervisors may still resort to them and push for a private sector solution behind the curtain, while also relying on the legal provisions stating a preference for pre-resolution alternative private sector measures.[39]

Formal resolution incentives

In practice, the ECB and the SRB have significant incentives to favor formal over shadow resolutions – at least for banks that are not too big to fail. First of all, as already noted, the awareness of moral hazard issues arising from rescue mergers is currently strong among supervisors everywhere. That is especially the case in Europe, where the political choice to save Irish and Spanish banks amplified the euro crisis. Second, as newly set-up supervisory authorities with no prior record to defend, the ECB supervisory arm and the SRB cannot be blamed for having been asleep at the wheel if they force a failing bank into formal resolution. Third, letting some smaller, non-viable banks fail would provide an ideal opportunity to both establish their newly minted authority and test the new resolution regime.

We cannot rule out that, at a later stage, the ECB may nevertheless tolerate shadow solutions. And even in the early days of the Banking Union, it may not object to national supervisors arranging shadow resolutions so as to have an easier hand at them itself at a later stage.

[38] Article 6(1), SSM Regulation; Article 6a(1), SRM Regulation.

[39] Article 32, Directive 2014/59/EU of May 15, 2014, [2014] OJ L173/190 establishing a framework for the recovery and resolution of credit institutions and investment firms and Preamble, Recitals (46) and (53) (hereafter Recovery and Resolution Directive). See also Articles 16(1)(b) and 18(2)(b), SRM Regulation, and Preamble, Recitals (16), (26), (27a) and (29). For anecdotal evidence of political interference regarding failing banks in the UK, see Davies 2013.

The SRB, on the other hand, is less likely to tolerate shadow resolutions. Its supervisory powers are limited and, given its institutional competence, it will be commended rather than blamed for the use of formal resolution proceedings. In addition, to establish its status and reputation, the SRB will have a positive interest in making formal resolutions less rare an event from the outset, lest the formal tool remains associated with a stigma that will make it harder for the SRB to do its job.

National Competent Authorities (NCA), on the other hand, should continue to have a preference for shadow resolutions. They are likely to have made pre-Banking Union supervisory mistakes that need to be covered-up, they are vulnerable to domestic politics and are keen to avoid giving the impression that their member state's banking system is weaker than those of other member states. National authorities' incentives to solve their (less significant) banks' troubles via rescue mergers may even prove stronger at the start of the Banking Union due to a collective action problem. No member state wants to be singled out as the one with failing banks, and whether other member states will opt for formal over shadow resolutions is impossible to anticipate. In such an environment, individual authorities may have an even more intense preference for shadow resolutions.

Overall, the new cultural and institutional environment should allow EU authorities to counter national bank supervisors' incentives, at least at the outset of the Banking Union. In other words, the Banking Union's early days will provide a unique window of opportunity to get rid of shadow resolution practices. Let us analyze in more detail how the ECB and the SRB may exploit it.

Implementation strategy

If the ECB and the SRB do embrace an anti-shadow resolution policy, they could state it explicitly and require national competent authorities to stick to it as well. In particular, that could be done pursuant to SRB's power to issue guidelines and general instructions to national resolution authorities regarding tasks performance and resolution decisions.[40] By drafting regulatory technical standards that specify a minimum set of triggers for the use of early intervention measures, the European Banking Authority (EBA) could also enhance the use of formal resolutions.[41]

[40] Article 31(1)(a), SRM Regulation.
[41] Articles 29(1), SRM Regulation, and 27(4), Recovery and Resolution Directive.

As noticed, national authorities' incentives will diverge from those of EU institutions in this matter and there can be no assurance that they will not still steer rescue mergers behind the curtain. Hence, an active oversight over mergers between stronger and ailing less significant banks will be needed to detect deviations from the stated policies. Prompt corrective action should take place once such deviations are spotted. In the absence of carrots within the Banking Union framework,[42] a number of sticks are available, which may be used following a step-by-step approach.[43]

To begin with, the ECB can intensify its requests for information about less significant banks and its general investigations and on-site inspections.[44] Moreover, when exercising the power to conduct an on-site inspection – a supervisory tool which national supervisors have traditionally been jealous of – the ECB decides who composes the on-site inspection team and whether to draw the head of team from the ECB or the National Competent Authority (NCA) staff.[45] The ECB can thus punish deviating NCAs by putting them on the sidelines when it comes to inspecting its less significant banks.

If needed, the ECB can push one step further and take over direct supervision over any less significant bank, using its powers to do so when it is "necessary to ensure consistent application of high supervisory standards."[46] Alternatively, and even more effectively, the ECB retains a power of life and death on each and any of the euro-area banks, because it has the exclusive power, which it may exercise upon request from the national supervisor or on its own initiative, to withdraw a bank's authorization.[47] To be sure, there are limits to the ECB's exercise of such power. First, when acting on its own initiative, it has to consult with the national supervisor at least 25 working days before the date it plans to withdraw the authorization (5 days, in case of urgency).[48] Second, the national resolution authority (whether distinct from the national banking supervisor or the same entity and so long as resolution powers are not entrusted with the Single Resolution Board[49]) may object to the proposal

[42] See Tröger in this volume ("The Single Supervisory Mechanism – Panacea or Quack banking regulation?" Chapter 8).

[43] Needless to say, the mere expectation of ECB and SRB's use of sticks ex post will greatly increase the effectiveness of European authorities' stated policy against shadow resolutions: national authorities' preference for them over formal resolutions will be reduced.

[44] Article 6(5)(d), SSM Regulation. [45] Article 144, SSM Framework Regulation.

[46] Article 6(5)(b), SSM Framework Regulation.

[47] Articles 14(5) and 16(3)(a) SSM Framework Regulation.

[48] Article 82(2), SSM Framework Regulation.

[49] See below, note 49 and accompanying text.

of withdrawing authorization, in which case the ECB and the resolution authority have to "agree on a time period during which the ECB shall abstain from proceeding with the withdrawal of the authorization."[50] However, after that time period elapses and further consultation with national authorities has taken place, the ECB may withdraw the authorization even against the advice of national authorities, if it holds that "proper actions necessary to maintain financial stability have not been implemented by national authorities."[51]

Hence, the ECB can de facto force national authorities to opt for a formal rather than shadow resolution. It should prove impossible for national authorities to arrange for a rescue merger once a procedure for authorization withdrawal is pending. The prospect of getting involved in a conflict between the ECB and national supervisors is likely to discourage would-be acquirers. Moreover, it will prove difficult for national authorities to credibly claim that any deal they may be able to arrange is not a liquidation transaction and thus subject to formal resolution procedures.

The SRB, for its part, may at any time decide to extend the exercise of its powers to banks for which national resolution authorities are otherwise competent.[52] As is the case for the ECB, the power to request information and to conduct investigations and on-site inspections gives the SRB discretion regarding the role of national authorities.[53]

In sum, within the Banking Union's new legal framework for supervision and resolution, European institutions have broad formal and informal powers to ensure that national authorities will not use shadow resolutions as a tool to solve individual bank crises. The ECB and the SRB also have the incentives to effectively use these powers. They may intervene both ex ante, via formal and informal guidelines, and ex post, by punishing deviating national supervisors in various indirect ways: by cold-shouldering national authorities in the formation of inspection teams, by taking over their powers over less significant banks, by intrusively exercising their direct powers over all banks, and so on.

Provided this strategy is effectively implemented in the Banking Union's early stages, the member states' collective action problems will be minimized as all are held to the same standards. One can also expect

50 Article 84(1), SSM Framework Regulation.
51 Article 84(3), SSM Framework Regulation.
52 Article 7(4)(b), SRM Regulation.
53 Articles 34–36, SRM Regulation.

the negative stigma attached to formal insolvencies to disappear – or, at least, to be manageable. This, in turn, should curtail the risk of market participants overreacting to resolution announcements, especially if the latter are accompanied by ECB and SRB statements of support.

Summary

A common way to deal with failing banks is for supervisory authorities to arrange rescue mergers that are private transactions in form but not in substance: while no public money is used and no formal authority is exercised in their respect, supervisors use their moral suasion powers to obtain private buyers' consent to the transactions, via carrots (more favorable supervisory stance in the future) or sticks (the threat of supervisory measures negatively affecting a bank's profitability and growth opportunities).

Such shadow resolutions can be detrimental for the overall stability of a banking system, as they increase systemic risk by making the too-big-to-fail problem more serious, may weaken healthy banks, distort competition, and give formal resolutions a bad name.

We have thus argued that a policy favoring formal over shadow resolutions is preferable, at least so long as smaller banks are concerned. We have also shown that a transition from a system managing banking crises via shadow resolutions to one relying on formal resolutions is practicable, as seen in the Japanese experience. Finally, we have highlighted that at the initial stage of the European Banking Union, the European authorities in charge of banking supervision and bank resolution are uniquely placed to ensure that shadow resolutions are kept to a minimum within the Union. They have all the formal and informal powers that are needed to move the system in that direction and should have sufficient incentives to do so.

References

Bennett, Rosalind L. and Haluk Unal (2010). "The cost effectiveness of the private-sector resolution of failed bank assets." *University of Maryland, Robert H. Smith School of Business, Working Paper* No. RHS-06-143.

Carletti, Elena and Philipp Hartmann (2002). "Competition and stability: what's special about banking?" *ECB Working Paper* 146.

Carnell, Richard S., Jonathan R. Macey, and Geoffrey P. Miller (2009). *Banking law and financial regulation.* Aspen Publishers, 4th edition.

Claessens, Stijn, Simeon Djankov, and Daniela Klingebiel (1999). "Financial restructuring in East Asia: halfway there?" *World Bank Financial Sector Discussion Paper* 3.

Cowan, Arnold R. and Valentina Salotti (2013). "The resolution of failed banks during the crisis: acquirer performance and FDIC guarantees, 2008–2011." *Working Paper Series*, available at SSRN: http://ssrn.com/abstract=2117574.

Croci, Ettore, Gerard Hertig, and Eric Nowak (2014). "Decision-making during the crisis: why did the treasury let commercial banks fail?" *European Corporate Governance Institute (ECGI) – Law Working Paper*, available at SSRN: http://ssrn.com/abstract=2557717.

Dam, Lammertjan and Michael Koetter (2012). "Bank bailouts and moral hazard: evidence from Germany." *Review of Financial Studies* 25: 2343.

Davies, Alan (2013). "Bank resolution in the UK: creating a culture of early intervention." *Working Paper, mimeo.*

Drummond, Paulo, Andrea M. Meachler, and Sandra Marcelino (2007). "Assessing competition and efficiency in the banking system." *IMF Working Paper* 26.

Ferran, Eilis (2014). "European Banking Union: imperfect, but it can work." *Cambridge Legal Studies Research Paper* 30.

Freixas, Xavier (1999). "Optimal bailout, conditionality and constructive ambiguity." *LSE Financial Market Group Discussion Paper* 237.

Garicano, Luis (2012). "Five lessons from the Spanish Cajas debacle for a new euro-wide supervisor." In Thorsten Beck (ed.), *Banking Union for Europe, risks and challenges.* Centre for Economic Policy Research.

Garrido, Jose M. (2012). *Out-of-court debt restructuring.* World Bank.

Hall, Maximilian J.B. (2009). "The Sub-Prime Crisis, the credit crunch and bank 'failure': an assessment of the UK authorities' response." *Journal of Financial Regulation and Compliance* 17(4).

Hawkins, John and Philip Turner (1999). "Bank restructuring in practice: an overview." *BIS Policy Paper 6.*

Hoggarth, Glenn, Jack Reidhill, and Peter Sinclair (2004). "On the resolution of banking crisis: theory and evidence." *Bank of England Working Paper* 209.

Hüpkes, Eva (2003). "Insolvency: 'why a special regime for banks.'" In IMF (eds.), *Current developments in monetary and financial law*, Vol. 3. Washington DC: IMF.

Micossi, Stefano, Ginevra Bruzzone, and Jacopo Carmassi (2013). "The new European framework for managing bank crises." *Centre for European Policy Studies, Policy Brief* 304.

Milhaupt, Curtis J. (1999). "Japan's experience with deposit insurance and failing banks: implications for financial regulatory design." *Washington University Law Quarterly* 77.

Nelson, Benjamin and Misa Tanaka (2014). "Dealing with a banking crisis: what lessons can be learned from Japan's experience." *Bank of England Quarterly Bulletin* 36.

Nobel, Peter (2002). *Swiss finance law and international standards.* Straempfli: Bern.

Perotti, Enrico C. and J Suarez (2002). "Last bank standing: what do I gain if you fail?" *European Economic Review* 46(9).

Sapir, André and Guntram B. Wolf (2013). "The neglected side of banking union: reshaping Europe's financial system." *Note presented at the informal ECOFIN, 14.9. 2013, Vilnius*, Bruegel.

Swiss Federal Banking Commission (2008). *Bank insolvency, the situation in Switzerland and internationally.* January 2008 Report.

Tanaka, Naoki (2010). "Deposit insurance cap heralds new system for 21st century Japan." *The Nikkei Weekly* September 20.

8

A political economy perspective on common supervision in the Eurozone

Observations on some strengths and weaknesses of the SSM

TOBIAS H. TRÖGER[1]

The context: phasing-in the banking union

The Single Supervisory Mechanism (SSM)[2] was launched as the first step toward an extensive supranationalization of banking regulation in the euro area. The sequels came with the promulgation of the Single Resolution Mechanism (SRM)[3] and an intensified harmonization of national deposit guarantee schemes.[4] The initiative followed increasing and persistent sovereign and private sector imbalances as signs of a critical disintegration of the European Monetary Union (EMU) during the summer of 2012.[5]

1 Professor of Private Law, Trade and Business Law, Jurisprudence, Goethe University Frankfurt am Main, Germany. Principal Investigator at SAFE and Fellow at the CFS. The author wishes to thank symposium and workshop participants at McGill University, University of Ottawa, Jesus College Oxford, the University of Frankfurt, and the Joint Seminar of the German Bar Association and the Bar Council of England and Wales. Comments and critique from Giovanni Dell'Ariccia, Mathias Dewatripont, Guido Ferrarini, Gérard Hertig, Jan Pieter Krahnen, Katja Langenbucher, Patrick Leblond, Ashoka Mody, Helmut Siekmann, Eddy Wymeersch, and Chiara Zilioli were particularly beneficial.

2 Council Regulation 1024/2013, Conferring Specific Tasks on the European Central Bank Concerning Policies Relating to the Prudential Supervision of Credit Institutions, 2013 O.J. (L 287) 63 [hereinafter: SSM Regulation].

3 Regulation 806/2014 of the European Parliament and of the Council Establishing Uniform Rules and a Uniform Procedure for the Resolution of Credit Institutions and Certain Investment Firms in the Framework of a Single Resolution Mechanism and a Single Bank Resolution Fund and Amending Regulation 1093/2010 [hereinafter: SRM Regulation].

4 Directive 2014/49/EU of the European Parliament and of the Council of 16 April 2014 on deposit guarantee schemes, 2014 O.J. (L 173) 149.

5 Return spreads for euro area government bonds widened and money and capital market rates incrementally diverged across the euro area, European Central Bank 2012a: 17–28, 31–5.

These developments encumbered the implementation of a uniform monetary policy within the EMU, as, for instance, slashes in monetary policy rates had little or no effect in certain Member States.[6] This loss of a level playing field for the provision of financial services in the internal market was a function of the general deterioration of confidence in the viability of the banking sector that brought Member States' bail-out capacity to the fore.[7] As banks' cost of doing business and thus their capacity to provide liquidity to the economy hinged incrementally on their home Member State's fiscal strength, breaking the pro-cyclical link between private and sovereign borrowing costs arguably required a "big" counterstrategy that would establish credible fiscal backstops at the European level.[8] To avert moral hazard that looms large where national banking sectors can rely on supranational aid, such mutualization of systemic risks obviously called for an incentive alignment that could only be achieved by supranationalizing prudential supervision and resolution as well.

Political leaders' disposition to establish a European banking union[9] which shall ensure an impartial and uniform implementation of a stringent regulatory and supervisory framework for all euro area banks could, if ultimately fulfilled, lead to reinforced monetary and financial stability within the EMU.[10] Regardless of the desirable elements of a complete banking union[11] and its capacity to correct current

[6] For the ECB's assessment see European Central Bank 2012b; see also Goyal et al. 2013: 6 figures 2 and 3; Pisani-Ferry and Wolff 2012: 7–12.

[7] Angeloni and Wolff 2012.

[8] Such a mutualization of systemic risks would allow adequate provisioning of impaired assets, thus buying time for their value-preserving, post-crisis liquidation, and hence contributing to severing the bank–sovereign link with its negative externalities at the lowest cost for society: Goyal et al. 2013: 9–10, 20–1, 26; for a similar proposal, see Pisani-Ferry et al. 2012: 16–7. Some commentators have voiced fierce criticism with regard to the introduction of common backstops, albeit without addressing the macro-economic issues and pointing inter alia to the perils of common funded, indirect monetary budged financing instead: Schneider 2013: 452–7.

[9] The catchword refers to a centralization of pivotal instruments of banking policy on the supranational level to preserve and advance the integration of the European (euro area) banking system; for an early proposal, see Fonteyne et al. 2010. For the broader political vision of the European "four presidents," see van Rompuy et al. 2012.

[10] On the general desirability of a euro area banking union, see e.g. Goyal et al. 2013: 7–10; Pisani-Ferry et al. 2012: 3–4; Véron 2012. For pre-sovereign solvency crisis contributions that argued for adding a banking component to the EMU model, see Čihák and Decressin 2007; Véron 2007: 4–6. For a skeptical assessment of the project's political feasibility, see Elliot 2012: 45–6.

[11] For an analysis of the individual components an ideal banking union should feature, see Goyal et al. 2013: 7–8, 12–20, Pisani-Ferry et al. 2012: 6–15; see also Wymeersch 2014.

distortions,[12] for regulatory intervention to advance the goal of creating a more resilient financial system, its foremost feature has to be its effectiveness as judged with particular regard to its stringent implementation and enforcement.[13] Only the latter will reaffirm lost confidence in the financial system's stability, which is the indispensable basis for sustainable credit-funded growth going forward.

This chapter is primarily concerned with the new supervisory architecture's prospects to foster the steady state in the long run. In this respect, increased centralization does not represent a value in itself.[14] In fact, the new rules carry the burden of proof that they constitute the superior option to promote the overall stability objectives. A closer analysis of the institutional structure of the SSM creates doubts as to whether the first pillar of the banking union will be effective. The events that broke the political opposition against an extensive supranationalization of bank regulation are responsible for a regime[15] that provides sharp tools to discipline reneging national competent authorities (NCAs) and at the same time relies heavily on their cooperative input for the proper functioning of the new supervisory framework (see "Distribution of competences and supervisory powers within the SSM"). From the perspective of the political economy of bureaucracy, the institutional framework's inherent mistrust vis-à-vis (captured)[16] national supervisors coupled with a lack of integrative elements that could induce optimal cooperation between the ECB and non-opportunistic national supervisors may prove problematic and requires a careful fine-tuning of

[12] How existing debt overhangs (legacy assets) will be treated once the SSM commences its operations is an unresolved issue. SSM Regulation, art. 33(4), prescribes an entrance exam in which the ECB currently assesses those banks' balance sheets that will henceforth fall under its direct supervision; cf. ECB 2013. However, despite the acknowledged urgent case for transparency (ibid.: 10–1; Pisani-Ferry et al. 2012: 15–6), it is unclear how those risks that have been incurred under national supervision, will be eliminated or hedged once the ECB has uncovered them. The Council's pledge that national backstops will be in place (European Council 2013: 10) doesn't help much where Member States' budgets are strained.

[13] Goyal et al. 2013: 8; Huertas 2012: 3; Wymeersch 2012: 4.

[14] Goyal et al. 2013: 22 acknowledge that an "incoherent banking union" could result in "an architecture that is inferior to the current national-based one." See also Pisani-Ferry et al. 2012: 6.

[15] For an account of the interdependence between the SSM's institutional structure and the Spanish and Cypriot sovereign debt crises, see Tröger 2013a: 9–11.

[16] The concept describes how and when interest groups dominate regulatory decision processes Laffont and Tirole 1991; with a particular view to banking regulators Hardy 2006.

incentive structures within the SSM (see "The need to complement sticks with carrots").

Distribution of competences and supervisory powers within the SSM

Financial institutions today typically operate across national borders.[17] As a consequence, their supervision raises specific challenges as sovereign authorities are bound to exchange information and cooperate closely. For the euro area the SSM constitutes an island solution because it provides a degree of centralization on the supranational level unavailable elsewhere.[18] In order to predict the effectiveness of the new regime and identify the mechanics that will prove important when it comes to fine-tuning the supervisory apparatus, this section scrutinizes relevant features of the SSM. With regard to supervision in the euro area, the ECB will become the predominant institution vested with broad powers to determine and oversee supervisory practices (see "The ECB's role in prudential supervision"). Yet, in day-to-day operations it will also depend in important respects on the input and commitment of NCAs (see "The ECB's position vis-à-vis NCAs").

The ECB's role in prudential supervision

The compelling advantage of tasking the ECB with supervisory obligations is that it rests on a relatively sound constitutional basis in the founding Treaty.[19] Moreover, vesting supervisory competences and powers with the ECB, instead of another supranational authority, will arguably create synergies with its mandate for monetary policy and lender of last resort duties within the Eurosystem.[20] Yet, this is

[17] On the efficiency rationale, see Moskow 2006: 4–5; Fiechter et al. 2011: 5. For evidence on the potentially positive effects of internal capital markets in cross-border banking groups, see also Haas and van Lelyveld 2010; Cremers et al. 2011.

[18] For an overview of the system of shared competences in EU banking supervision outside the SSM, see Tröger 2013a: 12–4.

[19] Treaty on the Functioning of the European Union, art. 127(6), Mar. 30, 2010, 2010 O.J. (C 83) 47 [hereinafter: TFEU], Wymeersch 2012: 6–7, 8–9; Ferran and Babis 2013: 256; but see also Carmassi et al. 2012: 3–4.; Wymeersch 2012: 24, who challenge the SSM's openness to non-euro area Member States on legal grounds.

[20] Pisani-Ferry et al. 2012: 11; Goyal et al. 2013: 14. It has to be noted, though, that emergency liquidity assistance (ELA) as a non-specified function of a central bank will remain sourced through national central banks on their own responsibility and liability

ambivalent, as the ECB's dual mandate is also a source for difficult policy trade-offs that account for convoluted governance arrangements (see "Internal decision making procedures").

From the outset, the SSM should not, and will not, cover all institutions subject to prudential regulation and supervision under CRD IV/CRR.[21] Despite the significantly broader scope of TFEU art. 127(6) that also pertains to financial institutions,[22] SSM supervision will be limited to credit institutions as defined in EU legislation.[23] Furthermore, even those credit institutions' activities not covered by supranational prudential regulation will not fall within the remit of the SSM.[24] This contradicts lessons from the financial crisis of 2007/08 that exposed risks for financial stability that reside outside the traditional banking sector[25] which led both the US and the UK to more encompassing and flexible approaches in prudential supervision.[26] The SSM's constriction to deposit-taking institutions may in part be attributed to the fact that it is primarily geared toward intercepting the European feedback loop between banks and

with the ECB's role limited to restricting ELA operations if they interfere with the Eurosystem's objectives, cf. Protocol (No. 4) on the Statute of the European System of Central Banks and of the European Central Bank, art. 14(4), 2012 O.J. (C 326) 320 [hereinafter: ESCB and ECB Statute].

21 The pertinent European rules on prudential supervision cover mainly deposit-taking credit institutions (CRR, art. 4(1)(1)) and investment firms (CRR, art. 4(1)(2) and European Parliament and Council Directive 2004/39 on Markets in Financial Instruments Amending Council Directives 85/611/EEC and 93/6/EEC and Directive 2000/12/EC of the European Parliament and of the Council and Repealing Council Directive 93/22/EEC, art. 4(1)(1), 2004 O.J. (L 145) 1 (EC) [hereinafter: MiFID]), yet only the authorization of credit institutions, cf. CRD IV, arts. 8, 49. With regard to their banking affiliates, financial holding companies (CRR, art. 4(1)(20)), mixed financial holding companies (CRR, art. 4(1)(21)) and mixed-activity holding companies (CRR, art. 4(1)(22)) are included in consolidated supervision; cf. CRD IV, arts. 119 et seq. Financial firms that are included in national prudential bank regulation and supervision remain outside the EU's regulatory grip. For a critical assessment, see Verhelst 2013: 15.

22 Although secondary legislation cannot bind the interpretation of the TFEU, it is indicative that CRR, art. 4(1)(26) defines the latter as "undertaking other than an institution, the principal activity of which is to acquire holdings or to pursue one or more of the" banking activities listed in CRD IV, Annex I, points 2–12 and 15.

23 SSM Regulation, art. 1 subpara. 2. Commentators have pointed to possible tensions in consolidated supervision where the remit of national prudential banking regulation also encompasses, for instance, non-deposit taking institutions that grant credit: Wymeersch 2012: 5; Schneider 2013: 455.

24 For example, activities as central counterparties are explicitly exempt; SSM Regulation, art. 1 subpara. 2.

25 Gorton 2009a, 2009b; Adrian and Ashcraft 2012; Gorton and Metrick 2012.

26 Ferran and Babis 2013: 259; see also Wymeersch 2012: 17–8.

sovereigns. The broader agenda of implementing a regulatory framework for sustainable finance that is attuned to the lessons of the global financial crisis is pursued in parallel and may correct some of the current architecture's shortcomings.[27]

Originally, the Commission intended to establish the ECB as an omnipotent supranational watchdog at least for euro area credit institutions. According to the Commission's concept, the ECB should be in charge of all the major tasks in prudential supervision – that is, licensing and authorizing credit institutions, ensuring compliance with own funds requirements, monitoring internal capital adequacy assessment processes, verifying internal governance arrangements,[28] stress-testing, and so on,[29] with regard to all euro area banks. However, it was clear from the outset that the ECB would be in no position to brave the gargantuan challenge of supervising the more than 6,000 banks in the euro area on a stand-alone basis.[30] Instead, the Commission Proposal acknowledged that "within the SSM national supervisors are in many cases best placed to carry out such activities, due to their knowledge of national, regional, and local banking markets, their significant existing resources and to locational and language considerations, and therefore enable[d] the ECB to rely on national authorities to a significant extent."[31] Yet, with the ECB's pervasive power to issue instructions vis-à-vis national competent authorities,[32] the latter were basically relegated to providing auxiliary

[27] For the initiatives regarding the shadow banking sector, see European Commission 2012; European Commission 2013.

[28] Sapir et al. 2012: 4 have argued that vesting the competence to supervise banks' internal governance structures will be critical for the SSM's overall effectiveness.

[29] Commission Proposal SSM Regulation, art. 4(1). Wymeersch 2012: 15 alludes to confusion if "matters will show up … that are not in the remit of the ECB." However, supervisory responsibilities and related powers not explicitly conferred on the ECB remain at NCAs, SSM Regulation, art. 1(5), and arguably do not require centralization. *E contrario*, where supervisory responsibilities are indeed conferred on the ECB, no such responsibilities and related powers under national law persist in parallel. Overlapping or duplicated competences, as assumed by Ferran and Babis 2013: 266, cannot occur as a matter of law, although disputes over the precise delineation of competences can certainly arise in practice. See also "Bureaucrats' incentives."

[30] But see also Goyal et al. 2013: 12 arguing that a banking union should aim at supranational supervision of *all* banks, "regardless of size, complexity and cross-border reach"; for an assessment that advocates the centralized definition of baselines but allows differences in "size, activity and business model" to be accounted for in supervisory practices and competences, see Wymeersch 2012: 17.

[31] Commission Proposal SSM Regulation, Explanatory Memorandum: 5.

[32] Commission Proposal SSM Regulation, art. 5(4).

Table 8.1 *Direct ECB supervisory competence according to SSM regulation*

Characterization of financial institution	SSM regulation	Precondition for direct ECB supervisory competence
significant	art. 6(4) subpara. 5	participating Member States' three largest banks
significant	art. 6(4) subpara. 2	(alternatively) bank's i. large size (presumed if total assets > € 30 bn) ii. importance for EU/Member State's economy (presumed if total assets to GDP-ratio > 20% and total assets > € 5 bn) iii. ECB confirmation of participating Member State notification indicating significance for domestic economy
significant	art. 6(4) subpara. 3	ECB decision if bank has subsidiaries in at least two participating Member States and substantial cross-border activities (foreign to total assets/ liabilities ratio)
significant	art. 6(4) subpara. 4	direct EFSF/ESM recapitalization
less significant	art. 6(5)(b)	ECB decision after consultation/on request of NCA if insufficient oversight (particularly, in case of indirect EFSF/ESM recapitalization)

assistance,[33] policing money laundering prohibitions, and enforcing consumer protections.[34]

During the legislative process the ECB's role in direct supervision was confined to the euro area's most important financial institutions (Table 8.1) and a stronger role for participating Member States'

[33] For a detailed description, see Wymeersch 2012: 13–4.

[34] Commission Proposal SSM Regulation, recital 22; Ferran and Babis 2013: 2645. Wymeersch 2012: 5, 15–6 points to overlaps where aiding and abetting money laundering or pervasive miss-selling may imperil confidence in a bank.

competent authorities within the SSM was re-installed under a "hub and spokes" arrangement for less significant banks.[35]

Table 8.1 indicates that the rather nested manner in which the SSM Regulation distributes the supervisory competences within the SSM should not blur the ECB's considerable pull as the primary supervisor: 120 top financial institutions that, according to slightly overstating preliminary estimates, account for 80–91 percent of the assets held by the industry in the euro area will fall under direct ECB supervision.[36]

It is a consequence of the sub-optimally coordinated phasing-in of the banking union in a rugged political process that the adequacy of the criteria applied to categorize banks (Table 8.1) cannot be judged conclusively by analyzing the SSM alone. The policy considerations that should drive the decision on which banks to include in direct supranational oversight are largely dependent on the function and design of the other institutions of a banking union (resolution regime, deposit insurance, backstops).[37] Yet, it should be noted that the relevant criteria do not necessarily link direct ECB oversight to a bank's significant cross-border operations – that is, do not align it with comparative informational advantages a supranational supervisor necessarily has from cross-country comparisons and a generally broader database, although, of course, size can be regarded as a rough proxy for transnational operations and interconnectedness.

For all less significant banks, the system of NCAs' shared responsibilities in prudential supervision under CRR/CRD IV[38] in principle remains untouched within the SSM.[39] Notably, both the authorization of credit institutions and the assessment of notifications of acquisitions and disposals of qualified holdings is conferred on the ECB regardless of an applicant's or target's significance.[40] Similarly, the ECB, as a consequence

[35] For a detailed description see Wymeersch 2014: 28–32; Schuster 2014: 4–6; Lackhoff 2013; Schiavo 2014: 126–32.

[36] European Central Bank 2014a: 13; the estimates of total assets were based on the assumption that up to 180 banks would fall within the ambit of ECB supervision; cf. Wolff and De Sousa 2012; Goyal et al. 2013: 15.

[37] For a discussion see Pisani-Ferry et al., 2012: 9–10.

[38] See note 18.

[39] SSM Regulation, art. 6(6).

[40] SSM Regulation, arts. 4(1)(a) and (c), 6(6). The ECB will grant bank licenses as proposed by NCAs in a "no objection" procedure; SSM Regulation, art. 14(2). It can withdraw authorizations on a proposal from the NCA or on its own initiative; SSM Regulation, art. 14(5). In the latter case, as long as no SRM is in operation, NCAs can object to the ECB withdrawal decision if a delay is necessary so as to orderly resolve the institution or/and maintain financial stability; SSM Regulation, art. 14(6). Similarly, the ECB ultimately decides on whether to oppose a share acquisition after an extensive review by NCAs on

of its mandate and expertise in financial stability issues, will have the power to deploy macro-prudential tools (capital buffers increased risk-weights etc) with regard to all euro area banks, even against NCAs' objections.[41]

However, even where no primary ECB competence is established, ECB coordination and oversight is supposed to ensure enhanced consistency and integration of supervisory practices – that is, in relation to the NCAs the ECB shall safeguard the implementation of the supervisory approach that it observes in direct supervision.[42] To that end, the ECB will be empowered to issue regulations, guidelines, or general instructions to NCAs.[43] Hence, it will have extraordinary clout to shape NCAs' actual supervisory practices in great detail.[44] The ECB-formulated framework will compel NCAs to notify the ECB in advance of any material supervisory procedure, further assess these procedures if the ECB so requests, and forward draft supervisory decisions for comments to the ECB.[45] As a matter of law, the ECB will thus be able to control and influence supervisory practices virtually at the grass-roots level. Moreover, it will have to make exhaustive use of these competences, as monitoring of the SSM's proper operation is one of the core tasks conferred on the ECB under TFEU art. 127(6).[46] To facilitate this assignment, the ECB can not only react to ex ante approaches from NCAs, but also proactively request information concerning the performance of their supervisory tasks.[47] Furthermore, it can verify or complement the information received by using its investigatory powers vis-à-vis euro area banks that allow inter alia information requests, general investigations, off-site diligence and (judicially authorized) onsite inspections.[48]

Finally, NCAs will also be coerced to cautiously maneuver within the ECB-set framework for the prudential supervision of the euro area's less significant banks, as they will face the permanent and pervasive threat

the grounds of their proposal; SSM Regulation, art. 15. For a detailed description of the ECBs supervisory powers, see Wymeersch 2014: 45–6.

41 SSM Regulation, art. 5(2), (4). For a critical assessment of such a centralization that contradicts NCAs' idiosyncratic expertise in judging local markets, see Véron 2012: 6.

42 Ferran and Babis 2013: 264. 43 SSM Regulation, art. 6(5)(a).

44 Ferran and Babis 2013: 265 observe that if the ECB-defined framework takes the form of "prescriptive supervisory rules" it will annul most of the leeway to supervise in a judgment-led manner that accounts for local idiosyncrasies.

45 SSM Regulation, art. 6(7)(c). 46 SSM Regulation, art. 6(5)(c).

47 SSM Regulation, art. 6(5)(e).

48 SSM Regulation, arts. 6(5)(d), 10–3. For a detailed description of the ECBs supervisory powers, see Wymeersch 2014: 42–4.

of being ousted as competent supervisor by the ECB. SSM Regulation art. 6(5)(b) vests power with the ECB to assume at any time on its own initiative the competence to directly supervise less significant banks if their supervision falls short of the consistent high supervisory standards the SSM is supposed to adhere to, particularly where these institutions benefit from indirect recapitalizations with funds from supranational coffers.[49]

The pertinent features of the legal set-up add to the overall picture that sees the ECB as the sole guarantor of the consistent, impartial and stringent supervision of euro area financial institutions and exhibits a general mistrust toward NCAs.[50] In sum, as the SSM's primary supervisor the ECB will be provided with heavy sticks, yet the carrots for NCAs seem to be missing.

The ECB's position vis-à-vis NCAs

Even though the humongous challenge the Commission's proposal of direct ECB supervision of all euro area banks (see "The ECB's role in prudential supervision") would have meant has been superseded by a more modest concept, the sizeable responsibilities conferred on the ECB suggest that much of the supervisory legwork will have to be performed "close to the ground." It is at least comprehensible that the novel supervisory architecture seeks to integrate NCAs in order to capitalize on their knowledge of national, regional, and local banking markets, their longstanding expertise particularly with regard to the interpretation and application of (harmonized) national banking regulation,[51] and their advantages with regard to location and language skills. As a consequence, the ECB is tasked with devising a general "framework to organise the practical modalities" of the interplay between itself and the NCAs not only with regard to the supervision of less significant institutions

49 The wording of SSM Regulation, art. 6(5)(b) could be interpreted as empowering the ECB to exercise supervisory powers in individual incidents. Yet, to ensure the proper functioning of the SSM where NCAs are in charge, the ECB can already rely on its right to instruct NCAs to make use of their powers under national law; SSM Regulation, art. 9(1) subpara. 3 (see "The ECB's position vis-à-vis NCAs"). Hence, the provision should be read as a broad power and obligation to preempt NCAs completely. For a similar view, see Wymeersch 2014: 33.

50 On the causal link of this observation to the events that brought about the sweeping institutional reforms, see note 15.

51 See also "Relevance of NCAs' contributions."

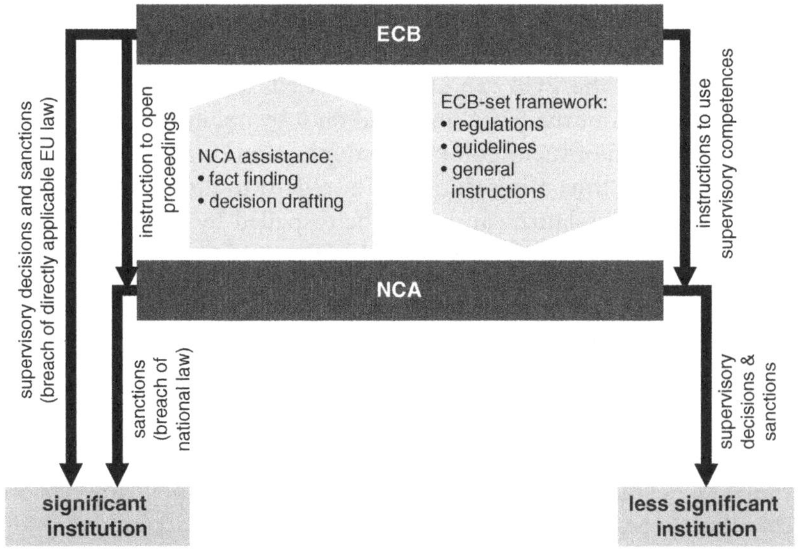

Figure 8.1 ECB/NCA interplay within the SSM

(see "The ECB's role in prudential supervision"), but also with regard to that of the euro area's biggest banks that fall under its direct oversight.[52] Yet, first and foremost, NCAs will also be tightly involved in the supervision of significant institutions, starting with uncovering the factual basis for various ad hoc or ongoing supervisory measures (e.g. onsite-verifications, evaluation of internal risk models),[53] up to and including drafting decisions for the ECB.[54] Moreover, the ECB will have to rely on NCAs when it comes to enforcing prudential regulation as it can impose administrative sanctions autonomously only if banks breach directly applicable EU law[55] – that is, violate regulations (TFEU art. 288(2)) – but can only require NCAs to open

[52] SSM Regulation, art. 6(7). This general framework has recently been adopted; cf. European Central Bank Regulation 468/2014 establishing the Framework for Cooperation within the Single Supervisory Mechanism between the European Central Bank and National Competent Authorities and with National Designated Authorities [hereinafter: SSM-Framework Regulation], 2014 O.J. (L 141) 1. For an overview, see Lackhoff 2014.

[53] It is this involvement of NCAs which – if it was effective – could largely mute concerns that ECB supervision would be "too distant"; cf. Schneider 2013: 454.

[54] SSM Regulation, art. 6(7)(b).

[55] SSM Regulation, art. 18(1) allows for a punitive disgorgement of actual or estimated profits.

proceedings if banks violate (harmonized) national law, thereby coercing reluctant NCAs into quasi-representative actions.[56]

More generally, the ECB can always push NCAs to take the actions necessary to carry out the tasks conferred on it by issuing instructions.[57] However, any form of such "compelled cooperation" makes daily operations arduous and thus raises doubts with regard to the effectiveness of the new regime. The latter can hardly be dispelled by reference to the anemic legal obligation to cooperate within the SSM.[58]

The need to complement sticks with carrots

The literature that seeks to evaluate the new supervisory structures generally dwells on the tacit assumption that the specific supervisory tasks will be performed seamlessly along the lines of competence defined by the SSM Regulation. However, experience with national supervision teaches that, in reality, frictions occur where inter-agency cooperation is required, and that interfaces between hub and spokes constitute potential fault-lines. To conceptualize expected losses in the system's overall effectiveness, it is useful to draw lessons from the political economy of administration and look at top-level bureaucrats' incentives,[59] particularly of those in NCAs (see "Lessons from the political economy of administration: bureaucrats' incentives"). From this perspective, it is important that the supervisory architecture provides not only sticks but also carrots. The SSM certainly supplies the ECB with a heavy club to discipline NCAs. Yet, the perks that could integrate their top personnel in order to induce optimal voluntary efforts are less pronounced and ultimately hinge on developing a common organizational culture within the SSM. Moreover, integrative elements partly have the potential to hamper swift supervisory decision making (see "Integrative prospects of internal

[56] SSM Regulation, art. 18(5). For a pessimistic assessment, see Ferrarini and Chiarella 2013: 57. On the modes of enforcing prudential regulation within the SSM, see also Witte 2014; Schneider 2014.

[57] SSM Regulation, art. 9(1) subpara. 3. On the precise scope of the ECB's supervisory powers, see also Schuster 2014: 6–9.

[58] SSM Regulation, art. 6(2) subpara. 1. For a more optimistic assessment, see Ferrarini and Chiarella 2013: 54.

[59] The underlying assumption is that the internal organization of public authorities allows motivating the rank and file to act – by and large – in accordance with the agencies general policies as determined by its top executives. In any case, optimizing the internal governance and incentive structures does not pose a problem unique to the context of inter-agency cooperation.

decision making procedures, ECB-set framework, and NCA-ECB career paths").

Lessons from the political economy of administration: bureaucrats' incentives

Relevance of NCAs' contributions

NCAs will perform at least preparatory or auxiliary services in establishing the factual grounds for supervisory decision making (direct ECB supervision), or they will execute prudential supervision for less significant banks within the ECB-defined supervisory framework, under the permanent threat to be ousted (indirect ECB supervision).[60] Obviously, the critical proposition underpinning such an institutional framework is that national supervision is generally more hospitable toward detrimental domestic interests, and that hence the ECB has to be established primarily as a "whipper-in" for NCAs who are seen with inherent mistrust.[61]

It has been suggested elsewhere that the emphasis on strong powers for the hub vis-à-vis the SSM's spokes is explicable by availability heuristics that look mainly at the most recent events which triggered the reform efforts and indeed exhibit egregious cases of captured and thus forbearing NCAs.[62] Understandably, this focus becomes even more pronounced, as direct supranational recapitalizations through the ESM will be made expressly available,[63] because the move arguably contributes to calming markets[64] but also exacerbates the potential for moral hazard.

As a prima vista intuitive consequence,[65] political leaders have determinedly embarked on a trajectory of more centralization in prudential supervision. However, it should be kept in mind that the new structure of semi-strong centralization with (critical) NCA involvement has the potential for problems that may not only cancel out some of the

[60] See "The ECB's role in prudential supervision," "The ECB's position vis-à-vis NCAs," and Figure 8.1.

[61] For this rationale for centralization on the supranational level, see "The context: phasing-in the banking union." But see also "Bureaucrats' incentives" and "Conclusion."

[62] Tröger 2013a: 9–11.

[63] On the ESM's approved direct bank recapitalization instrument, see Eurogroup 2013; European Stability Mechanism 2013.

[64] See note 8.

[65] But see also Tröger 2013a: 24, arguing that learning effects and political pressure from burdened taxpayers would have improved national supervision.

benefits of centralization, but also make its key advantage – forestalling forbearance of captured NCAs – partly unachievable. Both legislators[66] and scholars[67] recognize that tapping local knowledge about domestic markets, administrative practices, law, and so forth that resides in NCAs is important. If the contribution of NCAs is indeed vital for the SSM's overall effectiveness, the query becomes whether public officers at NCAs – that is, those agents who actually discharge the duties vested with their supervisory authorities, who either offer or refuse to exchange information and to collaborate with due diligence – are sufficiently incentivized to contribute to high-quality supervision.[68]

Bureaucrats' incentives

To posit that the success of the SSM depends on the incentives of (top-level) bureaucrats in charge at the competent authorities dwells on the realistic assumption that the public agencies involved should not be treated as black boxes that generate flawless output in implementing policy goals. From this perspective, it is important to remember the motivating forces identified in the line of research that applies methodologies from organizational theory to the political and administrative process.[69] Methodologically, the object of investigation can be scrutinized by using the analytical inventory of agency theory: bureaucrats constitute agents who not only have some discretion that allows them to adapt to unforeseen contingencies,[70] but which also grants them leeway to take hidden action and pursue their own interests, because bounded rationality of principals – ultimate (citizens) or intermediate (legislators) – prevents the writing of complete contingent constitutions and laws that would secure the untainted pursuit of the common good.[71] In fact, the intrinsic motives that are commonly identified as driving agency personnel in their exercise of office account for actions that serve the principals' interest only sub-optimally.[72]

[66] See note 31.

[67] Sapir et al. 2012: 3; Goyal et al. 2013: 15; Ferran and Babis 2013: 265; Neumann 2014: 11.

[68] Goyal et al. 2013: 14 recognize the importance of "incentive compatibility" between the ECB and NCAs.

[69] Programmatic contributions include Tullock 1965, Weingast and Marshall 1988 and Moe 1991.

[70] On the positive aspect of "adaptive efficiency," see North 1990.

[71] For an overview of various political agency models, see Besley 2006.

[72] See generally Stigler 1971, Prendergast 2007. For the role of cognitive biases that tend to aggravate the deviation from desirable outcomes, see Choi and Pritchard 2003. For an

According to standard analysis, bureaucrats are driven by a desire to increase their personal power and to augment their prestige.[73] They thus seek to enlarge their agency's size, competence, and right to intervene in the affairs of those falling within the scope of its mandate. They will discharge their duties in a way that allows them to acquire a favorable reputation among their peers, in the general public, and in the media. Moreover, opportunities to advance their future career in administration, politics, or the private sector motivate their behavior, which makes them prone to promoting the interests of those who offer the most desirable job opportunities in the long term and can result in regulatory capture.[74] Finally, agency personnel seek to avoid liability for false actions or forbearance and will consequentially have a proclivity to follow approved practices that can be verified in any review, even if new developments occur.

To be sure, these observed preferences do not necessarily warrant a pessimistic perception of bureaucrats' effectiveness,[75] but they highlight that these individuals are not robots that are automatically programmed to serve the public interest by quasi-mechanically enforcing prudential regulation, along the lines of legally devised competences, and free of self-interest.

Analyzed from this vantage, the incentives to contribute to supervisory efforts within the SSM are potentially suboptimal, particularly from the perspective of "subordinate" NCAs. Both the preparatory and information-gathering services in direct ECB supervision and the ECB-framed oversight of less significant credit institutions represent anything but a gain in power or prestige for thus far independent NCAs – particularly because they will be deprived of the competence to supervise systemic institutions.[76] Ceding ground to the ECB may occur only reluctantly – turf wars loom large.[77] Moreover, professional and/or political upward mobility on the national level is rather unlikely to result

analysis with a particular view to the governance of financial supervisors, see Enriques and Hertig 2011.

[73] Niskanen 1971: 36–42. [74] See note 16.

[75] For at least ambiguous assessments of the complex web of incentives and its inherent trade-offs, see Levine and Forrence 1990, Tullock 1984.

[76] Tröger 2013b: 218.

[77] It is indicative in this respect that the Bundesbank – which participates in banking supervision in Germany – stresses that the SSM is based on the "principle of decentralization" (!) and points to its network character, and thus, at least rhetorically, augments the position of NCAs; Bundesbank 2013: 16.

from good "auxiliary services" discharged in the background. Vice versa, it may not constitute the most attractive or career-boosting task that ECB bureaucrats will perform with utmost diligence, to supervise a tiny euro area Member State's three largest banks.

In sum, incentives to voluntarily contribute with ample commitment to ECB-led, high-quality supervision are not immediately apparent. To be sure, the problem will not be an open blockade or outright sabotage of the ECB's efforts, but a lack of incentives to do more than work-to-rule and go the extra mile instead certainly impends. Proposals for an effect-based regulation that aligns supervisory competences as closely as possible with bureaucrats' incentives, as long as political realities do not allow the avoidance of thickets of inter-agency cooperation altogether, have sought to address precisely the lurking lack of positive motivations.[78] They are based on the insight that improving the supervisory architecture does not only hinge on devising clear responsibilities and hierarchies to compel close cooperation and dense exchange of information by law.[79] To be sure, the ECB can rely on a set of tough enforcement tools in relation to NCAs[80] and does not have to put its hope in informal institutions that normally provide the only available sanctions for non-cooperative behavior in transnational contexts.[81] But they only can be brought to bear where the ECB has detected or suspects deficits in an NCA's supervisory practice. If bureaucrats in NCAs are not positively incentivized to voluntarily unveil shortcomings that their idiosyncratic know-how allows them to detect, then even the most plausible advantage of supranational supervision – forestalling forbearance as a function of NCA's "home bias" – is endangered. The ECB will simply lack the resources to generally investigate daily supervisory practices of NCAs.[82]

[78] Pistor 2010; Tröger 2013b: 220–1. See also FSA 2009 and the "lead supervisor model" as developed in European Financial Services Roundtable 2005: 26–8.

[79] But see Goyal et al. 2013: 14, 15, who focus exclusively on "clear responsibilities" and "strong oversight and accountabilities" of NCAs and argue that ECB's early intervention powers "provide incentives for cooperation" (ibid., p. 23), again relying exclusively on the stick for motivation.

[80] See "The ECB's role in prudential supervision" and "The ECB's position vis-à-vis NCAs."

[81] For an account of the self-enforcing mechanisms that international law normally has to rely on, see Guzman 2008: 33–48.

[82] Ferran and Babis 2013: 265.

Integrative prospects of internal decision making procedures, ECB-set framework, and NCA-ECB career paths

Organizational theory has long embraced the importance of the top level's benign reputation for respecting the legitimate concerns of subordinates as a centerpiece in inducing optimal commitments and efforts from a firm's employees.[83] Translated into the SSM context, the ECB's legally defined lead role within the SSM requires complements that integrate NCAs and translate into a commonly embraced supervisory identity within the SSM.

Internal decision-making procedures

An important aspect of the integrative prospects that help achieve the goal of providing positive incentives for NCAs to contribute voluntarily to optimal supervisory efforts within the SSM may flow from their representation in SSM decision-making bodies, most importantly the ECB Supervisory Board.[84] This newly established body will plan and execute the ECB's supervisory tasks[85] and will be composed of a Chair (external candidate) and a Vice-Chair (Member of ECB Executive board),[86] four ECB representatives not directly involved in monetary tasks, and one representative from each participating Member State's NCA.[87] This composition makes for an overweight of NCAs in the Supervisory Board, because at least 18 of the 24 full members of the Supervisory Board will be delegates from Member States' supervisors. It translates into an NCA-dominance of the Board's decision making. Although voting weights had been favored for all Board decisions during the legislative process,[88] the inclusive and plain solution prevailed: decisions will be taken with simple majority under a one-member one-vote rule, with a casting vote for the Chair in case of a draw.[89] A weighted voting process only applies under

[83] Kreps 1990: 93, 125.

[84] Its creation is owed to legislators' vow to strictly separate monetary policy and supervisory functions of the ECB; SSM Regulation, recital 65 and 73, art. 25.

[85] SSM Regulation, art. 26(1).

[86] SSM Regulation, art. 26(1), (3). The goal is to further separate supervisory and monetary policy functions by limiting overlaps in top personnel; cf. SSM Regulation, recital 66; Ferran and Babis 2013: 269.

[87] SSM Regulation, art. 26(1), (5). Where the NCA is not the central bank, a central bank representative can also be brought to Supervisory Board meetings. However, such twin-attendance does not impact on voting rights; SSM Regulation, art. 26(1) subpara. 1.

[88] The proposals were driven by the desire to reflect the sizes of national banking sectors; Barker et al. 2012.

[89] SSM Regulation, art. 26(6).

SSM Regulation, art. 26(7), where regulations are to be adopted.[90] Quite importantly, ECB representatives on the Board will have a voting capacity equal to the median of NCA representatives and will hence not be in a position to command these decisions either.[91] Furthermore, a Steering Committee with ten members and up to seven NCA representatives will technically prepare Supervisory Board decisions (draft the drafts, and so forth).[92]

In sum, despite the allocation of the most important supervisory powers at the ECB, the decision-making process of the newly created Supervisory Board makes ECB-led supervision essentially a common activity of Member States. At first glance, this gives it significant integrative potential that could induce voluntary collaboration within the SSM. Yet, at least for bureaucrats from those NCAs that thus far supervised a significant banking sector autonomously, the mere participation in the decision-making process on the supranational level arguably does not compensate the visual loss in power and prestige, despite the larger geographic scope of the new activities. Moreover, even the feeble integrative moment comes at the price of a rather bloated size of the Supervisory Board which raises doubts regarding its ability to act in a swift and determined manner.[93]

Moreover, the integrative capacity of internal decision-making procedures is also attenuated, as constitutional concerns arguably compel Governing Council involvement in each and every ECB supervisory decision. This follows from the Governing Council's character as the ECB's ultimately responsible decision-making body.[94] The ultimate legislation has not subscribed to the view that the relation between the Supervisory Board and the Governing Council is a matter of the ECB's internal organization and thus grants leeway to limit the decisions that have to be brought before

[90] SSM Regulation, art. 4(3) subpara. 2 allows the ECB to adopt regulations "only to the extent necessary to organize or specify the arrangements for carrying out of the tasks conferred on it" by the SSM Regulation.

[91] SSM Regulation, art. 26(7).

[92] SSM Regulation, art. 26(10). The Committee will consist of the Supervisory Board's Chair, its Vice Chair, one more ECB representative, and up to seven NCA representatives, according to a rotation scheme to be determined by the Supervisory Board.

[93] Goyal et al. 2013: 29; Ferran and Babis 2013: 270.

[94] The latter has constitutional status as it is codified in TFEU arts. 129(1), 283(1) and ESCB and ECB Statute, arts. 9(3), 10(1). For a detailed discussion of the resulting conflict between well-designed supervisory institutions and Treaty pre-settings that largely override expediency considerations, see Ferran and Babis 2013: 267–8; Véron 2012: 6–7.

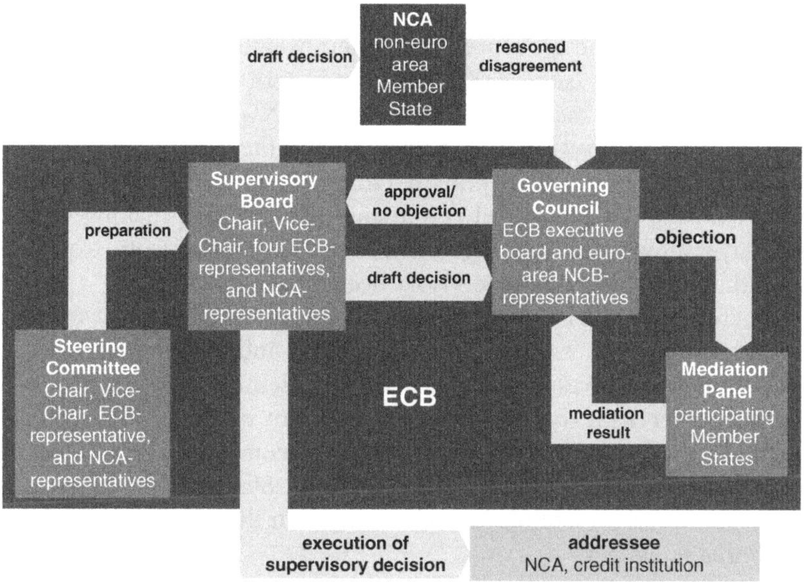

Figure 8.2 ECB supervisory decision making

the Council.[95] SSM Regulation, art. 26(8) provides for a procedure that seeks to uphold the separation of monetary policy and supervisory functions but also reflects the constitutional requirements. It demands that the Governing Council object explicitly to the draft decisions submitted by the Supervisory Board in writing, stating monetary policy concerns in particular, within 10 days during normal times and 48 hours in crisis situations.[96] If the Council objects, a mediation panel will try to resolve the diverging views among participating Member States, SSM Regulation, art. 25(5). However, regardless of the outcome of the mediation, ultimately the Governing Council's decision will prevail – that is, in order to reach a supervisory decision the result of the mediation has to be adopted by the Governing Council (see Figure 8.2). Of course, at least euro area Member

[95] Wymeersch 2012: 7, 10, 11 note 35, 12. Commission Proposal SSM Regulation art. 19(3) allowed the Governing Council to delegate clearly defined supervisory tasks and related decisions regarding individual or a set of identifiable credit institutions to the Supervisory Board.

[96] The Governing Council can only approve or object to Supervisory Boards draft decisions, it cannot amend and shape them according to its own perceptions.

States[97] also dominate the Council.[98] Yet, it is not NCAs and their top-level bureaucrats who are representing their Member States, even where prudential banking supervision is vested with NCBs, because the Governing Council assembles the heads of NCBs' monetary policy arms. Hence, the invariable involvement of the Governing Council weakens both the integrative potential that the internal decision-making process holds, the speed and resoluteness of decision-making in the multi-layer governance arrangement,[99] and the supervisory expertise that ultimately flows into supervisory decisions.[100]

The critical aspect is that the internal decision-making process holds integrative potential, as it provides for a broad and meaningful involvement of representatives from all participating Member States' NCAs. Yet, this – together with the invariable requirement of Governing Council approval – makes arriving at an outcome quite cumbersome. In any case, at least from the perspective of large Member States with a significant banking sector, a perceptible loss of relevance for their NCAs and its top-level bureaucrats persists.

ECB-set framework and NCA-ECB career paths

The SSM's capacity to integrate NCAs and provide proper incentives for their bureaucrats ultimately depends on the ECB-set framework for the cooperation between ECB and national competent authorities and particularly how it is animated in day-to-day supervisory practice. It is a good sign that the Supervisory Manual, which will be the backbone of the organization of common supervision, was prepared by joint ECB/NCA committees and working groups.[101] Furthermore, mixed

[97] On the situation of participating Member States whose currency is not the euro, see Tröger 2013a: 38–9.

[98] Again, the relation is 6 to 18: the President, the Vice-President and four other Members of the Executive Board on the ECB-side, together with the 18 governors of NCBs; TFEU art. 283(1), (2) and ESCB and ECB Statute, arts. 10(1) and 11(1).

[99] The process becomes even more complicated where participating Member States whose currency is not the euro disagree with draft decisions of the Supervisory Board. For a detailed description of the applicable procedure cf. Figure 8.2 and Tröger 2013a: 38–9.

[100] Ferran and Babis 2013: 268. Commentators have expressed concerns that the Supervisory Board will be a practically powerless advisory body; Wymeersch 2012: 12. Yet, this need not be true. Some of the weaknesses in the governance structure may be "corrected" in practice: as the supervisory expertise will reside in the Supervisory Board and its working-level staff – that is, the ECB's supervisory department – benefits from specialization and routinization may accrue if the Governing Council's ultimate responsibility is executed by rubber-stamping draft supervisory decisions in normal times.

[101] European Central Bank 2014b 8–13.

teams[102] may provide an excellent opportunity to incentivize NCAs adequately and induce them to feed their expertise into common supervision.[103] To achieve that goal, they have to be set up in such a way that NCA representatives do not only serve as drudges for the ECB gentry. Unfortunately, the SSM Framework Regulation structures the joint ECB–NCA supervisory teams in a way that once again bolsters the unfettered ECB dominance and implicitly expresses mistrust vis-à-vis NCAs. In particular, the coordinator of the teams necessarily has to be an ECB representative[104] and the ECB at all times has the right to reject NCA representatives as joint team members.[105]

Against this background it becomes all the more important that the exchange and secondment of staff could,[106] if carefully designed, provide career opportunities for NCA bureaucrats, thereby inducing them to cooperate from the start. More generally, career paths should be designed in such a way that good supervisory performances at NCAs may translate into upward mobility to the ECB, turning the SSM into a true unit for promotion purposes. As long as NCA bureaucrats' can procure their next job within the public sector only from their domestic minister of finance, it is clear where their loyalties lie and that the latter may not militate in favor of stringent supervisory practices where national champions are targeted.

Conclusion

The evaluation of the SSM ultimately depends on where the most virulent problems impeding effective prudential supervision are seen – to wit, whether it is indeed the avoidance of regulatory forbearance triggered by NCAs' "home bias" that should shape the institutions of normal-times supervision. However, even if avoiding capture is key and supranationalization is thus heralded as the patent remedy,[107] its institutional set-up seems suboptimal (see "Lessons from the political economy of administration: bureaucrats' incentives") and requires carefully designed integrative elements that provide the carrots to complement the sticks (see "Integrative prospects of internal decision-making procedures, ECB-set framework, and NCA-ECB career paths"). Moreover, it has to be kept in

[102] SSM Regulation, art. 31(2) provides for an ECB arranged, mixed composition of supervisory teams.

[103] Goyal et al. 2013: 15, 27.

[104] SSM Framework Regulation, art. 3(1).

[105] SSM Framework Regulation, art. 4(3).

[106] SSM Regulation, art. 31(1).

[107] E.g. Ferrarini and Chiarella 2013: 40.

mind that it obviously becomes harder for local interests to capture a supra-local supervisor.[108] Yet, this doesn't say much for instances where the interests of agents themselves are broader and may thus lead to potentially more devastating capture on a higher level.[109]

In sum, the institutional design of the SSM suffers from severe structural shortcomings that probably will not all be entirely solvable in supervisory practice once the system becomes operational. Generally, an improved institutional arrangement requires the much dreaded change of the TFEU[110] that would open up political accountabilities of a different kind. However, in its current state, the SSM will certainly not be the much longed-for panacea for Europe's current woes. To become more than a quack policy-maker's initiative to display problem-solving capacity,[111] substantial efforts to ultimately achieve what arguably could not be accomplished under conceived time-pressure in the first round will remain inevitable.

References

Agarwal, Sumit, Amit Seru and Francesco Trebbi (2012). "Inconsistent regulators: Evidence from banking." *National Bureau of Economic Research Working Paper* 17736.

Angeloni, Chiara and Guntram B. Wolff (2012). "Are banks affected by their holdings of government debt?" *Bruegel Working Paper* 7.

Bainbridge, Steven M. (2011). "Dodd-Frank: Quack federal corporate governance round II." *Minnesota Law Review* 95: 1779–1821.

Barker, Alex, Peter Spiegel and Miles Johnson (2012). "Germany demands more power on banking." *Financial Times 9.10.2012.*

Besley, Timothy (2006). *Principled agents?* Oxford: Oxford University Press.

Bundesbank (2013). "European Single Supervisory Mechanism for banks – A first step on the road to a banking union." *Bundesbank Monthly Report* July: 13–31.

Carmassi, Jacopo, Carmine Di Noia and Stefano Micossi (2012). "Banking Union: A federal model for the European Union with prompt corrective action." *Center for European Policy Studies, Policy Brief* 282.

108 Agarwal et al. 2012 show that US federal supervisors observe more stringent supervisory practices than state authorities.

109 See e.g. Macey 2013: 231–50 for a deeply pessimistic account of the SEC being captured by Wall Street.

110 See also Schneider 2013: 454, citing Jeroen Dijsselblom and hinting that the banking union was introduced, accepting breaches of EU law.

111 The picture of a quack regulator originates with Romano 2005 and was carried over to financial regulation in Bainbridge 2011.

Choi, Stephen J. and Adam C. Pritchard (2003). "Behavioral economics and the SEC." *Stanford Law Review* 56: 1–74.

Čihák, Martin and Jörg Decressin (2007). "The case for a European banking charter." *IMF Working Paper* 173.

Cremers, Martijn, Rocco Huang and Zacharias Sautner (2011). "Internal capital markets and corporate politics in a banking group." *Review of Financial Studies* 24: 358–401.

ECB (2013). "Note Comprehensive Assessment October 2013." Available at www.ecb.europa.eu/pub/pdf/other/notecomprehensiveassessment201310en.pdf

Elliot, Douglas C. (2012). "Key issues on European banking union: Trade-Offs and some recommendations." *Global Economy and Development Working Paper* 52.

Enriques, Luca and Gérard Hertig (2011). "Improving the governance of financial supervisors." *European Business Organization Law Review* 12: 357–378.

Eurogroup (2013). "ESM direct bank recapitalisation instrument." Available at www.eurozone.europa.eu/media/436873/20130621-ESM-direct-recaps-main-features.pdf.

European Central Bank (2012a). "Financial integration in Europe." Available at www.ecb.eu/pub/pdf/other/financialintegrationineurope201204en.pdf.

European Central Bank (2012b). "Monetary and fiscal policy interactions in a monetary union." *Monthly Bulletin* 51(7/12). Available at www.ecb.eu/pub/pdf/mobu/mb201207en.pdf.

European Central Bank (2014a). "Guide to banking supervision." Available at www.bankingsupervision.europa.eu/ecb/pub/pdf/ssmguidebankingsupervision201411.en.pdf?404fd6cb61dbde0095c8722d5aff29cd.

European Central Bank (2014b). "Progress in the operational implementation of the Single Supervisory Mechanism regulation." *SSM Quarterly Report* 1. Available at: www.ecb.europa.eu/pub/pdf/other/ssmqr20141en.pdf.

European Commission (2012). "Green paper shadow banking." COM 102 final (Mar. 19, 2012).

European Commission (2013). "Communication to the council and the European Parliament: Shadow Banking – Addressing new sources of risk in the financial sector." COM (2013) 604 final (Sept. 4, 2013).

European Council (2013). "European Council – Conclusions." EUCO 104/2/13 REV 2. Available at http://europa.eu/rapid/press-release_DOC-13-5_en.htm.

European Financial Services Roundtable (2005). "Report on the lead supervisor model." Available at www.efr.be/documents%5Cpublication%5C22676EFRlsvfinal-June2005.pdf.

European Stability Mechanism (2013). "FAQ on the main features of the future ESM direct bank recapitalisation instrument." Available at www.esm.europa.eu/pdf/FAQ%20Direct%20Bank%20Recapitalisation%20280620131.pdf.

Ferran, Eilis and Valia Babis (2013). "The European Single Supervisory Mechanism." *Journal of Corporate Law Studies* 13: 255–287.

Ferrarini, Guido and Luigi Chiarella (2013). "Common supervision in the Eurozone: Strengths and Weaknesses." *European Corporate Governance Institute Law Working Paper* 223.

Fiechter, Jonathan, Inic Ötker-Robe, Anna Ilyina, Michael Hsu, André Santos and Jay Surti (2011). "Subsidiaries or branches: Does one size fit all?" *IMF Staff Discussion Note* 4.

Financial Services Authority (2009). "The Turner review 99." Available at www.fsa.gov.uk/pubs/other/turner_review.pdf.

Fonteyne, Wim, Wouter Bossu, Luis Cortavarria-Checkley, Alessandro Giustiniani, Alessandro Gullo, Daniel Hardy and Sean Kerr (2010). "Crisis management and resolution for a European banking system." *IMF Working Paper* 70.

Gorton, Gary (2009a). "The panic of 2007." In the Federal Reserve Bank of Kansas City (eds.), *Maintaining stability in a changing financial system*, 131–262.

Gorton, Gary (2009b). "Information, liquidity, and the (ongoing) panic of 2007." *American Economic Review* 99: 567–572.

Gorton, Gary and Andrew Metrick (2012). "Securitized banking and the run on repo." *Journal of Financial Economics* 104: 425–451.

Goyal, Rishi, Peya Koeva Brooks, Mahmood Pradhan, Thierry Tressel, Giovanni Dell'Ariccia, Ross Leckow, Ceyla Pazarbasioglu and IMF Staff Team (2013). "A banking union for the Euro Area." IMF Staff Discussion Note 13(01).

Guzman, Andrew T. (2008). *How international law works: A rational choice theory.* Oxford University Press.

Haas, Ralph and Imam van Lelyveld (2010). "Internal capital markets and lending by multinational bank subsidiaries." *Journal of Financial Intermediation* 19: 1–25.

Hardy, Daniel C. (2006). "Regulatory capture in banking." *IMF Working Paper* 34.

Huertas, Thomas F. (2012). "Banking union: What will it mean for Europe?" *LSE Financial Markets Group Paper Series Special Paper* 213.

Kreps, David M. (1990). "Corporate culture and economic theory." In James E. Alt and Kenneth A. Shepsle (eds.). *Perspectives on positive political economy.* Cambridge University Press: 90–143.

Lackhoff, Klaus (2013). "Which credit institutions will be supervised by the Single Supervisory Mechanism?" *Journal of International Banking Law and Regulation* 28: 454–462.

Lackhoff, Klaus (2014). "The framework regulation for the Single Supervisory Mechanism (SSM) – An overview." *Journal of International Banking and Regulation* 29: 13–28.

Laffont, Jean-Jacque and Jean Tirole (1991). "The politics of government decision making: A theory of regulatory capture." *Quarterly Journal of Economics* 106: 1089–1127.

Levine, Michael E. and Jennifer L. Forrence (1990). "Regulatory capture, public interest and the public agenda: Toward a synthesis." *Journal of Law, Economics and Organization* 6: 167–198.

Macey, Jonathan R. (2013). *The death of corporate reputation: How integrity has been destroyed on Wall Street*. New Jersey: Pearson Education, Inc.

Moe, Terry M. (1991). "Politics and the theory of organization." *Journal of Law, Economics and Organization Special Issue* 1991, 7: 106–129.

Moskow, Michael H. (2006). "Cross-border banking: forces driving change and resulting regulatory challenges." In Gerard Caprio, Jr., Douglas D. Evanoff and George G. Kaufman (eds.), *Cross-border banking: Regulatory challenges*. Singapore World Scientific Publishers.

Neumann, Kerstin (2014). "The supervisory powers of national authorities and cooperation with the ECB – a new epoch of banking supervision." *Europäische Zeitschrift für Wirtschaftsrecht: EUZW Beilage* 25: 9–14.

Niskanen, William A. Jr. (1971). *Bureaucracy and representative government*. The University of Chicago Press.

North, Douglas C. (1990). *Institutions, institutional change and economic performance*. Cambridge University Press.

Pisani-Ferry, Jean, Andre Sapir, Nicolas Veron and Guntram B. Wolff (2012). "What kind of European banking union?" *Bruegel Policy Contribution* 12.

Pisani-Ferry, Jean and Guntram B. Wolff (2012). "Propping up Europe?" *Bruegel Policy Contribution* 7.

Pistor, Katharina (2010). "Hosts dilemma: Rethinking EU banking regulation in light of the global crisis." *European Corporate Governance Institute Working Paper* 286/2010.

Prendergast, Canice (2007). "The motivation and bias of bureaucrats." *American Economic Review* 97 (1): 180–196.

Romano, Roberta (2005). "The Sarbanes-Oxley Act and the making of Quack corporate law. *Yale Law Journal* 114: 1521–1612.

Rompuy, Herman Van, José Manuel Barroso, Jean-Claude Juncker and Mario Draghi (2012). "Towards a genuine economic and monetary union." Available at www.consilium.europa.eu/uedocs/cms_data/docs/pressdata/en/ec/134069.pdf.

Sapir, André, Martin Hellwig and Marco Pagano (2012). "A contribution from the chair and vice chairs of the Advisory Scientific Committee to the discussion on the European Commission's banking union proposals." *Report of the Scientific Advisory Committee*.

Schiavo, Gianni Lo (2014). "From national banking supervision to a centralized model of prudential supervision in Europe." *Maastricht Journal of European and Comparative Law* 21(1): 110–140.

Schneider, Sven H. (2014). "Sanctioning by the ECB and national authorities within the Single Supervisory Mechanism." *Europäische Zeitschrift für Wirtschaftsrecht: EUZW Beilage* 25: 18–24.

Schneider, Uwe H. (2013). "Inconsistencies and unsolved problems in the European banking union." *Europäische Zeitschrift für Wirtschaftsrecht: EUZW* 12: 452–456.

Schuster, Gunnar (2014). "The banking supervisory competences and powers of the ECB." *Europäische Zeitschrift für Wirtschaftsrecht: EUZW Beilage* 25: 3–9.

Stigler, George J. (1971). "The theory of economic regulation." *Bell Journal of Economics and Management Science* 2: 3–21.

Tobias, Adrian, and Adam B. Ashcraft (2012). "Shadow banking regulation." *Federal Reserve of New York Staff Reports* 559.

Tröger, Tobias H. (2013a). "The Single Supervisory Mechanism – Panacea or quack banking regulation?" *SAFE Working Paper* 27.

Tröger, Tobias H. (2013b). "Organizational choices of banks and the effective supervision of transnational financial institutions." *Texas International Law Journal* 48: 177–221.

Tullock, Gordon (1965). *The Politics of Bureaucracy*. Washington, DC: Public Affairs Press.

Tullock, Gordon (1984). "A (partial) rehabilitation of the public interest theory." *Public Choice* 42: 89–99.

Véron, Nicolas (2007). "Is Europe ready for a major banking crisis?" *Bruegel Policy Brief* 3.

Véron, Nicolas (2012). "Europe's Single Supervisory Mechanism and the long journey towards banking union." *Bruegel Policy Contribution* 16.

Weingast, Barry R. and William J. Marshall (1988). "The industrial organization of congress." *Journal of Political Economy* 96: 132–163.

Witte, Andreas (2014). "The application of national banking supervision law by the ECB: Three parallel modes of executing EU law?" *Maastricht Journal of European and Comparative Law* 21: 89–109.

Wolff, Guntram B. and Carlos De Sousa (2012). "A banking union of 180 or 91% ?" *Bruegel Blog*. Available at: www.bruegel.org/nc/blog/detail/article/965-a-banking-union-of-180-or-91-percent/.

Wymeersch, Eddy (2012). "The European banking union, a first analysis." *Financial Law Institute Working Paper Series Working Paper* 2012–07.

Wymeersch, Eddy (2014). "The Single Supervisory Mechanism or 'SSM', part one of the Banking Union." *National Bank of Belgium Working Paper* 255.

Verhelst, Stijn (2013). "The European Single Supervisory Mechanism: A sound first step in Europe's banking union?" *Egmont Royal Institute for International Relations Working Paper*.

PART II

Investor and borrower protection

9

Keeping households out of financial trouble

MICHAEL HALIASSOS[1]

> The basic mission of finance is to set up arrangements whereby people may pursue risky opportunities without themselves being destroyed by this risk, and arrangements that incentivize people to behave in a socially constructive manner.
>
> Robert Shiller (2012)

Introduction

The quote by Robert Shiller highlights the conflict inherent in financial innovation: on the one hand, it provides opportunities to save and to borrow in order to achieve household objectives and help them manage risks; on the other hand, it creates the possibility that households will be destroyed by the risks entailed in these new and often complicated instruments. Finance should guide financial firms in their production of instruments. Regulation should be brought in to protect households from the excesses of the financial sector that ultimately cause exploitation of household ignorance or behavioral biases, but also to protect households from using new financial instruments in counterproductive ways.

This chapter starts by describing, in "Opportunities offered by financial innovation," some of the opportunities that financial innovation offers for managing risks households face. The third section, "Getting into financial trouble," takes up the issue of how households can get into trouble, in view of recent findings in the household finance

[1] Professor for Macroeconomics and Finance at Goethe University, Frankfurt. I would like to thank the editor in charge of the paper, Andreas Hackethal, as well as participants in the June 2014 Frankfurt workshop devoted to the volume for very helpful comments. I am especially indebted to my discussant, Hans Christoph Grigoleit, who contributed very useful insights from a legal scholar perspective. I alone remain responsible for any errors or omissions.

literature. "Why is regulation needed?" discusses why regulation is needed. "How to regulate?" presents criteria on which regulation can be based. "Challenges with different forms of regulation" analyzes challenges with different forms of regulation and presents some recent developments on the regulatory front that relate to the points raised in the chapter. The final section offers concluding remarks.

Opportunities offered by financial innovation

Modern households face a number of challenges in financial behavior, some of which are new, but they also have access to innovative financial instruments with which to face these challenges. Surprisingly, many of these instruments are heavily underutilized.

The demographic transition has meant that dependency ratios in developed economies have risen, while life expectancy has also risen. Both factors prevent social security systems, based on contributions from the young to support the elderly, from providing adequate retirement funding. In response to this, several western governments, led by the US, encouraged the development of individual retirement accounts and gave citizens tax incentives to start using them, mainly in the form of tax deferrals. Funds accumulated in these accounts by the start of retirement can be used to purchase annuities, which help households handle longevity risk – that is, the risk of outliving one's resources. Financial innovation has also contributed deferred annuities, which are cheaper, but start paying pension income only after a certain age is reached. Despite the usefulness of various types of annuities for managing longevity risk, they tend to be underutilized by households, to an extent that has been termed the "annuity participation puzzle."

Financial innovation prior to the US subprime crisis created technologies for refinancing mortgages, from higher- to lower-interest rate ones, as well as home-equity loans and lines of credit. The former can be used to economize on interest costs, while the latter effectively allow households to liquidate part of their home in order to buffer consumption from income or expenditure shocks. During the subprime crisis, mortgage refinancing and home equity loans were used by households as a means for raising loan-to-value ratios to almost 100 percent. This reckless use of financial innovation exposed mortgage holders to the risk of negative equity – that is, the house price dropping below the outstanding amount of the mortgage. Indeed, the ensuing house price drop created widespread incidence of negative equity, contributing to the US subprime crisis.

Inflation risk plagued fixed-rate lenders, including long-horizon private and institutional investors, until the creation of inflation-indexed bonds– that is, bonds that provide payoffs indexed to inflation. Although a number of countries now issue these bonds, investors underutilize them (see Campbell, Shiller, and Viceira 2012). Other instruments that would allow management of house price risk, such as the ETFs introduced by Case and Shiller to the New York Stock Exchange, had to be withdrawn after a little more than a year, due to lack of investor interest and liquidity. The ETFs were giving the opportunity to those who expect house price increases to trade with others who expect house price falls (see Greenwood and Viceira 2012).

These examples illustrate some of the wide range of risk management and wealth creation opportunities recently created through financial innovation, but also the limited or inappropriate use to which these have been put by investors. In the next section, we discuss some of the possible reasons for inappropriate use of financial innovation by households.

Getting into financial trouble

Financial illiteracy, lack of awareness or familiarity, bad advice

Households can get into financial trouble in a number of ways. In view of the demographic transition, many households are forced to make financial decisions they cannot handle. As the State passed on the task of adequate provision for old age from ailing social security systems to households and allowed them to reap the wealth generation potential of risky assets, it forced large demographic groups without prior exposure to, or adequate expertise in, financial matters to make decisions that would shape their well-being in retirement. In case of failure to make adequate provisions and to moderate exposure to financial risk, however, households are likely to discover their mistake at a late stage in their life, when they cannot easily adjust their labor supply or access loans markets.

There is now considerable evidence in household finance literature of widespread financial illiteracy among households around the world, which tends to be associated with suboptimal financial behavior.[2]

[2] Contributions include Campbell 2006, Calvet et al. 2007, Lusardi and Mitchell 2007, Lusardi and Tufano 2009, Christelis et al. 2010, Choi et al. 2011, Grinblatt et al. 2011, Hastings et al. 2013, van Rooij et al. 2011, and van Rooij et al. 2012.

Illiteracy does not only refer to advanced topics in graduate finance courses, but also to fundamental concepts such as interest compounding, the difference between real and nominal interest rates, and the concept of risk diversification through holdings of a suitable portfolio of risky assets rather than of one or two such assets. Lusardi and Mitchell (2007) considered a sample of US households at an advanced stage of their life cycle (aged 51–56) and found that only 18 percent of them could calculate two-year interest compounding correctly. Of those who could not, only 43 percent simply failed to compound interest: the majority was completely off the mark. The authors showed that the problem of financial illiteracy is particularly acute in certain demographic groups, such as the less educated, minorities, and women.

The existing literature has been able to establish a positive correlation between financial literacy and good aspects of financial behavior, such as planning for retirement, having higher wealth, and gaining access to the equity premium through stockholding. Although financial illiteracy tends to be associated with inferior financial outcomes, establishing a clear, and policy relevant, line of causality from illiteracy to outcomes is econometrically very challenging.

In addition to being financially illiterate, many households are not even aware of the full asset and debt menu that could be relevant to their needs. Guiso and Jappelli (2005) studied a sample of Italian households and found that only about one-third of those were simultaneously aware of the existence of stocks, mutual funds, and managed accounts. There is also evidence that, within a given asset class, households tend to be drawn to those most familiar to them, even if such a preference is not warranted on the basis of objective asset features, such as expected returns and risk. Familiarity with a subset of the assets in a given class thus tends to contribute to home equity bias or a preference for local stocks (see Feldstein and Horioka 1980, Coval and Moskowitz 1999, Huberman 2001).

Rapidly moving financial innovation raises another familiarity issue. Households are often given the opportunity to participate in a financial product class with which they have little or no previous familiarity, but that may be held by people in their economic environment. In principle, one might expect two kinds of trouble to occur. It is possible that lack of familiarity will make households jump into assets or debts they do not understand and develop levels of exposure that they later regret. Alternatively, households may be overly cautious and delay or cancel their participation in financial instruments with which they are unfamiliar, foregoing useful opportunities for wealth generation, consumption smoothing, or the management of important risks.

In order to evaluate the potential for trouble induced by lack of familiarity, one needs to study the relationship between familiarity with a certain class of financial products and participation in them. This is not straightforward, given the fact that participation causes familiarity (raising the econometric problem of reverse causality) and the possibility that unobserved factors make households both more likely to be familiar with novel financial products and to be participating in them, without familiarity per se causing participation ("unobserved heterogeneity"). Indeed, it is not even clear how the applied researcher can observe and measure familiarity with a particular product class, so as to run the appropriate econometric tests.

Fuchs-Schuendeln and Haliassos (2015) utilize the incident of German reunification as a unique field "experiment" to test the relationship between familiarity and participation in the presence of a knowledgeable and well-incentivized financial sector. Starting with pre-war Germany, a certain subset of Germans, namely those in the East, were randomly and exogenously deprived of access to "capitalist" financial products, while West Germans were exposed to those. Then, both were exogenously put together (following reunification), while West German banks and other financial institutions made East Germans quickly aware of the expanded asset menu available in the unified country. One can compare the asset and debt participation behavior of East Germans following reunification to that of West Germans with similar observable characteristics.

Surprisingly, the authors found that neither of the two a priori plausible kinds of trouble noted above appears to have taken place. East Germans proved equally as ready as comparable West Germans to participate in securities (stocks and bonds), and even more likely to participate in consumer debt previously unfamiliar to them. Despite this, the authors found no evidence of regret, as would be signaled by exodus from these markets shortly after entry. The authors conclude that lack of familiarity can be overcome by a knowledgeable and well-incentivized financial sector, as was the West German financial sector after reunification. In turn, this suggests that regulatory focus may need to be shifted away from denying access to the unfamiliar and towards regulating financial practitioners.

Households can be enticed by irresponsible financial advisors to use financial products that are inappropriate for them. A rapidly growing literature, starting with Inderst and Ottaviani (2009) and Hackethal, Haliassos, and Jappelli (2012), focused on the advice given to households of different characteristics, and on the conflicts of interest present under different advisory models. Conflicts of interest, as well as poor matching between advisors and clients in greatest need of good advice lie behind a growing number of incidents of "mis-selling" in various financially developed countries.

Bad influence of social interactions

Social interactions contribute not only to the spread of information about available financial instruments, but also to behavior that creates prospects for financial distress. Kuhn et al. (2011) used data from the Dutch zip code lottery to show that winners of the lottery are not the only ones to exhibit greater probability of buying a new car or engaging in consumption expenditure: so are their neighbors, who feel the need to keep up with the winners. Charles et al. (2009) studied the tendency of US minorities to spend considerably more on jewelry than others. They document a tendency of minority households to want to signal to the world that they are not as poor as the typical member of their (observable) minority. Thus, they cut back on other important items in order to spend more on conspicuous luxury items, which can signal higher wealth status to their social environment.

Studying the effects of social interactions on financial decisions, rather than on consumption choices, is particularly challenging because household financial data are typically provided without location information in order to preserve respondent anonymity. One approach has been to focus on a particular financial product for which locational information is readily available. Duflo and Saez (2002) and Kaustia and Knüpfer (2012) show that households tend to be influenced by the choices of others in their environment in their decision on whether to hold particular financial products that are novel or complicated. Duflo and Saez compare librarians located in different libraries on the campus of a large US university. As they were hired according to the same criteria, they share many observable characteristics, but they differ crucially in the number of co-workers who have decided to enroll in a particular retirement plan. The authors find that librarians with greater number of co-workers participating in the plan are themselves more likely to participate.

Another approach to dealing with the lack of locational information is to focus on the process of social interactions rather than on a specific product. Hong, Kubik, and Stein (2004) found that simply being more sociable raises one's probability of investing in information-intensive, widely held financial assets. This is consistent with fixed-cost models of stockholding participation: interacting with others provides information, often at no additional cost, and thus lowers the fixed costs otherwise required for stock market entry and participation.

Assessing the role of social interactions in debt participation and in debt amounts outstanding, conditional on participation, faces not only a lack of location information, but also the additional challenge that people tend to be more willing to talk about or exhibit their consumption and assets, but less forthcoming in disclosing methods of financing, including debts outstanding. A recent contribution by Georgarakos, Haliassos, and Pasini (2014) documents for the first time the effects of social interactions on debt behavior. Using population-wide Dutch data (the DNB Survey) that includes responses on how households perceive attributes of their social circle, the paper shows that those who perceive themselves as having lower incomes than the average of their peers are more likely to be in debt, more likely to have larger outstanding debt amounts conditional on borrowing, and are also at greater risk of financial distress. The authors conduct a number of tests to demonstrate that causality runs from associating with richer peers to deciding to borrow, even at the cost of heightened prospects of financial distress.

Why is regulation needed?

The description of ways in which households can get into financial trouble does not lead inescapably to the conclusion that we need financial regulation, let alone that financial regulation is the best way to deal with these issues. One could imagine that financial illiteracy can be addressed through financial education programs, so that households can fend for themselves. Lack of awareness could perhaps be addressed by large-scale information campaigns, spreading information on newly available financial innovations, and enriching the asset menu perceived by households. Maybe the lack of good financial advice could be addressed by the market itself: good financial advisors could find it profitable to seek households in need of advice, and could outperform and eventually eradicate bad financial advisors. Any bad influence of social interactions might also be addressed by financial education campaigns and good advice not to get carried away by the example of others more knowledgeable with financial products, or by a desire to emulate the living standards of richer friends.

Unfortunately, such straightforward remedies to the tendency of households to get into financial trouble are not readily available. The literature on financial literacy has managed to establish the widespread nature of illiteracy and its negative association with good financial outcomes, but it has not yet provided a fully convincing story on causality from illiteracy to bad outcomes. The typical approach to resolving the thorny econometric issues has been to seek "instruments" by going back in time to early life events likely to be exogenous to the financial outcomes of today.[3] Although endogeneity seems far less of an issue with these instruments, one also needs to ensure that the sole channel through which these early-life variables affect today's financial outcomes is via their effect on financial literacy (or that any other channels are controlled for). Early life events, however, are likely to affect financial behavior through many different channels, and there is no guarantee that these can be observed and controlled for.

Another challenging issue with financial education is the time horizon of appropriate action. To the extent that causality from financial literacy to good financial outcomes is established, the optimal timing of acquisition of financial knowledge is far from clear. One does not become automatically wealthier once a financial education program is completed: rather, a whole process is set in motion for putting newly acquired knowledge to work and for exploiting the wealth generation potential of certain investments. It seems logical that early intervention would give maximal time to households to utilize their enhanced knowledge in their accumulation of wealth, but it is far from clear what the optimal time for such intervention is and whether financial education programs cease to have any value after a given stage in the life cycle.

Taken together, the results of Guiso and Jappelli (2005) and Fuchs-Schuendeln and Haliassos (2015) seem to imply that the private sector can be relied upon to provide campaigns to promote awareness of financial products to households. After all, it was the desire to sell financial products that was behind the efforts of West German banks to approach potential East German clients. However, the German reunification experiment was characterized by West German banks highly experienced with the financial products made available to East Germans, and by products that were quite standard (securities and consumer debt) rather than exotic or difficult to price. Given the

[3] Examples of such instruments include education of parents (van Rooij, Lusardi and Alessie 2011), self-reported strength in math when teenager (Jappelli and Padula 2013), and self-reported share of full-time education devoted to finance, economics, and business prior to labor market entry (Disney and Gathergood 2013).

apparent tendency of East Germans to make full use of the opportunities for securities and to be even more heavily involved in consumer debt than West Germans, we should be careful before arguing that the private sector could be trusted to market novel, unproven instruments to households unfamiliar with them in a way that is not subject to regulatory checks.

How about financial advice? Can we rely on an unregulated free market to provide adequate financial advice both to those who need it because of ignorance and to those who use it as a time-saving device?

Inderst and Ottaviani (2009) highlighted a number of conflicts of interest in the provision of financial advice. First, there is conflict of interest between advisors and customers arising from the dual role of advisors in selling products and providing advice on which product is appropriate for the client. Second, there is conflict of interest between advisors and firms producing financial products, arising from the potential for advisors to increase their commissions through larger sales volume, while the brokerage firm or bank has the responsibility to handle client complaints and claims. Hackethal, Haliassos, and Jappelli (2012) considered two different samples – one from an online brokerage dealing with independent financial advisors and another from a bank that provided advice to its customers through its employees. They were the first to show that advised accounts offer, on average, lower net returns and inferior risk-return tradeoffs (Sharpe ratios), controlling for account holder characteristics. Trading costs contribute to outcomes, as advised accounts feature higher turnover, consistent with commissions being the main source of advisor income. Their findings were stronger for bank advisors than for independent financial advisors, consistent with greater limitations on advisory services imposed by the bank.

Hackethal, Haliassos, and Jappelli (2012) identified a second issue arising in the market for financial advice, namely that those who tend to be matched with financial advisors are not the disadvantaged groups needing advice the most, but investors who are wealthier, older, and more experienced. It is reasonable to suppose that part of this has to do with the compensation packages of financial advisors: if compensation is in the form of commissions based on sales of financial products (e.g., of mutual funds), then it may be natural for advisors to direct their efforts toward attracting richer and more experienced clients, who are likely to have bigger accounts. On the one hand, this lowers the probability that ignorant customers will be taken advantage of by bad financial advisors, but on the other hand it leaves many households alone in the face of pressing financial choices that can affect their future (e.g., retirement).

Poor matching between financial advisors and potential investors should not be blamed completely on incentives faced by financial advisors. Bhattacharya et al. (2012) argued forcefully that clients themselves may not be willing to accept – let alone follow – financial advice, even when this is unbiased and is provided at no cost. A German brokerage house made a random offer of unbiased financial advice to its clients, but only 5 percent accepted the offer. Those who accepted tended to be male, older, wealthier, and more financially sophisticated. Those who needed the advice most were least likely to accept the offer. An even smaller subset followed the free advice they received, although this would have objectively helped improve their account performance.

One can go beyond these findings and wonder also whether matching can be inhibited by the behavioral bias in need of correction. For example, if an investor is overconfident, then this bias makes the investor less likely to seek advice from others. Thus, intervention may be needed to ensure both that the sick go to a doctor willing to accept them and that, once they are there, the advice given to them is sound.

How to regulate?

Regulating household use of financial products has many useful analogues to regulating use of medicines, but also some important differences. Some financial products can be dangerous for, or even detrimental to, household wealth when sold to people for whom they are inappropriate. This is analogous to drugs being sold to patients with low tolerance for them or to those not suffering from the disease for which the drug is intended. Other drugs, though suitable for the patient, could be lethal when administered in doses larger than prescribed. The analogy to overexposure to financial risk, exposure to the risk of negative home equity, as well as over-indebtedness seems obvious. Only qualified doctors should prescribe dangerous drugs, so that such problems can be avoided. The closest analogue here would be financial advisors, but this requires considerable thought, especially in view of the points reviewed above that concern conflict of interest. Producers of medicines very much like to standardize their products and make them available to a large-scale market, for example via supermarkets or drugstores. Correspondingly, producers of financial products sometimes find it optimal to standardize and popularize their innovations, so as to operate in a lower-cost, wider-access environment. In both cases, open access could lead to inappropriate use, with concomitant consequences.

Based on this analogy to medical practice, one could imagine four types of financial regulation as relevant for regulating use of financial products by households, distinguished by the entity being regulated: product-based regulation, user-based regulation, and two types of practitioner regulation, namely regulation of financial advisors prescribing and selling financial products, and of producers designing and marketing such products.

A natural way to proceed with product-based regulation would be to set up an FDA (Food and Drug Administration) for financial products. The idea is that such an FPA (Financial Product Administration) would test any financial innovation before it hit the market to uncover its risks, worst-case scenario, appropriate horizon and holding period, but also to identify contraindications and harmful interactions with other financial products. Such an FPA could ban lethal products, very much like the ban on the sale of structured products to households that was imposed recently in Belgium, but would also come up with a set of instructions to financial advisors and to households considering the purchase and appropriate use of the financial product.

User-based regulation would proceed by checking client characteristics that could influence the appropriateness or use of the product and making sure that the financial product is given only to the "right" households. One could imagine that relevant characteristics would include income/wealth levels and variability, occupation, unemployment risk, family structure, age, education, and financial literacy. It could also extend to identifying the rest of the portfolio, any committed recurring expenditures (such as mortgage payments, tuition fees, and rental payments), and indicators of potential financial distress, such as debt-service-to-income and loan-to-value ratios. Finally, characteristics could extend to preferences (e.g., with respect to risk), stated motives for saving or borrowing, and past practices (e.g., frequency of trading, tendency to fall behind in payment obligations). It might be possible to then issue a "license to invest" document, with different classes, as is customary for drivers' licenses that differentiate between normal cars and larger vehicles, such as trucks, or vehicles that expose many to danger of poor driving, such as buses.

The third type of regulation could refer to the background and practices of the financial advisor recommending use of the financial product. Beyond certification of financial advisors, one could monitor and disclose the types of incentive schemes according to which they are paid, and even to tie these schemes to the kinds of financial products advisors are allowed to recommend and/or sell. For some financial products, it may make sense to separate completely the functions of advice and sale, so that advisors do not reap the benefits of certain recommendations over others. In other cases, it may be feasible to align compensation schemes as much as possible to the interests of the user, so as to reduce the conflict of interest between advisors and clients.

The fourth type of regulation is addressed to the financial institutions engaged in financial innovation and in its marketing to consumers. One could imagine a range of measures designed by regulators in order to help contain systemic risks arising from financial innovation, but here we are focusing on the immediate direct effects on consumers of producing and marketing products mismatched to their needs and risk absorption capacities. An important part of producer regulation could be to require the provision of adequate information to consumers and financial advisors in a relevant, user-friendly, and effective way. Rather than maximizing the available amount of information, which could result in wrong decisions due to information overload, producers of financial products could be asked to focus on features salient to the customer, describing the full range of possibilities (worst–best outcome), and the risks involved.

From a legal perspective,[4] the distinction tends to be based on who initiates the sanctions rather than on who is being regulated. On the one hand, there are institutional sanctions, executed by government agencies, that include bans, licensing schemes, fines and other public law sanctions; and on the other, individual sanctions, executed by the investor and normally involving contract law or other private law remedies. In terms of content, sanctions can either be "definite," in the form of explicit and general personal requirements or bans limiting the marketing and use of financial products; or "flexible," taking the form of requirements on the types of information that need to be disclosed to the investor and regulator. In the case of individual sanctions, for example, definite sanctions can include cancellation of sale and restitution, while flexible sanctions include information requirements sanctioned by damages (e.g., prospectus liability, or requirements on the banks to give sufficient advice

[4] This and several subsequent comments on the legal perspective were inspired by the discussion of H.C. Grigoleit, to whom I am grateful but who should not be held responsible for any errors.

based on product features and the characteristics of the individual investor).

Challenges with different forms of regulation

These different forms of regulation present a number of challenges, some smaller and others bigger. In this section, we will discuss household finance research relevant to identifying these challenges and their potential importance. The discussion is meant to shed some light on the relative effectiveness and practicality of different approaches. This is relevant not only from a policy design perspective, but also from a legal one: sanctions are often legally justified when other types of sanctions prove to be ineffective.

Product-based regulation

Perhaps the biggest challenge faced by product-based regulation is that it is very difficult to predict how a particular financial product, especially a new one, will actually be used. Even if the product design is well grounded in financial theory, there is no guarantee that actual use will conform to the intentions of the financial innovator and producer. An apt example seems to be securitization, which was quite central to the subprime market crisis of 2007 in the United States. In theory, securitization of mortgages and their breakdown into different risk classes that could be disseminated to those willing to take the risks was totally sound. Yet the way this theoretically sound process was implemented in practice led to serious valuation problems and eventually to lack of investor appetite for asset-backed securities.

European Union law stipulates that product bans can be imposed by ESMA or EBA, based on product attributes. The legal perspective seems to take a somewhat different angle: products could be banned or restricted if their attributes interfere with the legally required levels of disclosure. An example of such an attribute is complexity, which could obscure cost elements or commissions, such as costs of refinancing a structured product, cost components of equity funds, or unusually high commissions.

Indeed, creating structured products of increased complexity, which can confuse consumers, may be a strategic action on the part of some producers of innovative financial products in the face of increasing competition. Celerier and Vallee (2014) studied 55,000 retail structured products issued in 17 European countries since 2002 and found that financial complexity has been steadily increasing, even after the financial crisis, especially among producers with a less sophisticated investor base. By comparing market price to the fair value of a number of these products, the authors find that the hidden markup in a product is an increasing function of its complexity. They also find that complexity intensifies when competition increases.

When strategic use of financial complexity is confronted with financial illiteracy, or at least limited ability of households to acquire the necessary information in order to value products accurately, an obvious regulatory response is the prohibition of sales of structured products to households, as in the Belgian case. Given the theoretical advantages of access to structured products, however, one wonders whether a set of regulatory measures can be designed so that households do not forego the potential benefits from access to such products because of informational considerations. Truthful revelation of fair values and associated formulas, as well as of hidden risks, costs, and commissions, would seem to be necessary ingredients of such regulation. Regulatory requirements on information disclosure should be strict and aim at removing creation of hidden markups from the set of motives for raising product complexity.

A second problem with product-based regulation is that observation of how a particular financial product was used in the past does not reveal how it will be used in the future. It is interesting, for example, that the precursors of asset-backed securities were German covered bonds, which effectively survived for about 300 years prior to playing a central role in a major financial crisis. This observation can also be turned on its head: having experienced inappropriate use of a financial product in the past does not necessarily imply that it should not be used in the future. The current rekindling of interest in asset-backed securities, only shortly after the end of the subprime crisis, is a case in point.

Related to this is a third problem. Observation of how a particular financial instrument (e.g., stocks) is being used in one type of account ("location") is not necessarily a sufficient statistic for how the same instrument will be used in a different type of account.

A telling example is the juxtaposition of findings regarding household stock trading between the finance and the economics literature. The seminal papers by Barber and Odean (2000, 2001) and a voluminous literature following those focused on stocks located in discount brokerage accounts. These are traded without financial advice being provided by the broker. The key finding of this literature is that households overtrade stocks, suffering unnecessary wealth reductions due to heavy transactions costs, and that these overtrading tendencies are more pronounced among men than among women. The average household in the sample turns over 75 percent of its portfolio annually and earns net stock portfolio returns substantially below market, because of transactions costs. Men trade 45 percent more than women.

In direct contrast to these findings, researchers who focused on stockholding in retirement accounts found signs of extreme inertia on the part of account holders (see, for example, Agnew, Balduzzi, and Sundén 2003, Ameriks and Zeldes 2005). Ameriks and Zeldes looked at 10 years of trading in TIAA-CREF retirement accounts owned typically by faculty of US universities and colleges and at two types of (essentially costless) trading decisions account holders can make. These are to change existing allocations of funds between stocks and bonds, and to change declared preferences for allocation of future premia. Ameriks and Zeldes found that, over a ten-year period, 61 percent of account holders made no change in flow allocations or only one change, and 87 percent made none or only one reallocation of accumulated funds.

Bilias, Georgarakos, and Haliassos (2010) used two population-wide data sets to assess the overall importance of overtrading of stocks in the US economy. Using PSID, they found that, over long periods (1994–99, 1999–2003), less than 30 percent of US households traded stocks, despite significant stock market fluctuations and substantial increase in stock market participation over the period. Using SCF, they documented that, in all SCFs over the period 1989–2004, the percentage of brokerage account owners who had traded in the year prior to the survey was above 65 percent. However, the percentage of households that owned a brokerage account was consistently less than 20 percent, and those who traded through brokerage accounts represented less than 14 percent of US households.

Had researchers looked only at stock trading in discount brokerage accounts, they could have concluded that stocks are dangerous instruments to allow in retirement accounts because they induce households to overtrade and waste part of their wealth on transactions costs. Yet, this would have precluded willing households from taking advantage of the equity premium for the purpose of generating greater retirement wealth.

All in all, predicting future use of a financial instrument on the basis of the theory behind its construction, its overall history of use, and especially the history of its use in one particular asset or debt "location" is at best problematic and most likely misleading.

Unpredictability of future use implies that regulation simply based on financial product characteristics is unlikely to be feasible or advisable. While this sounds discouraging, it does share common features with the regulation of medicines: this involves not only the nature (composition) of the product but also the users (patients) for whom it is suitable, the appropriate way of using it (dosage instructions), and the practitioners (doctors and pharmacists) allowed to prescribe and sell the product.

The question is whether such a comprehensive approach to regulation is more difficult in the case of financial products than in the case of medicines. Before exploring issues related to user-based and practitioner-based regulatory measures, we should note two issues. First, it is unlikely that an FPA will be able to come up with the right "dosage" for any given financial product that can be printed on a folded piece of paper, as is done with medicines. Optimal use and exposure to a product seems to depend on a number of client characteristics and preferences, and it is difficult to see how instructions can be prepared that go beyond a very general set of guidelines.

Second, willingness to deviate from any set of instructions is a function of perceived costs of over-exposure. While there is considerable risk of deviations from prescribed use in the case of addictive drugs, for example, it is fair to suppose that most patients would not risk their life or health in order to experiment with deviations from prescribed use of medicines that they are not scientifically qualified to assess. In the case of financial products, over-exposure is not perceived as lethal, while finance is not as daunting to non-specialists as Medicine is. While this second consideration points to a need for stricter rules or instructions, the first one suggests that the task of defining such rules for financial product use is highly non-trivial. Taken together, these observations suggest that more weight should be placed on making financial products available to households with appropriate characteristics and on making sure that users have access to sound financial advice. We take up these two issues in the following sections.

User-based regulation

User-based regulation is premised on the idea that households with certain characteristics, if left to their own devices, would be likely to choose assets and debts not suitable for them and expose themselves to risks they cannot bear. By conditioning access on not having those characteristics, regulation might prevent erroneous participation decisions and combat mis-selling by irresponsible financial advisors and producers.

The idea behind user-based regulation is consistent with much of the existing literature on household finance. As this literature has shown, investor and borrower characteristics correlate with or influence financial behavior. These include resources (wealth, income, occupational status), knowledge (education, financial literacy, awareness, cognition, familiarity), attitudes and preferences (willingness to take risk, patience, investment horizon, reasons for saving and for borrowing, behavioral biases such as overconfidence), expenditure commitments (e.g., arising from household size, mortgage or other installment obligations), and access to credit (borrowing constraints, ability to raise funds at short notice).

Yet, user-based regulation raises important philosophical and legal issues. Precluding households with certain characteristics from using particular financial products could be construed as paternalism or even discrimination. After all, there is free access to gambling, or to the purchase of luxury goods that could be detrimental to certain households. Denying access to risky products may also deprive disadvantaged household groups from the chance to attain prosperity through higher expected returns.

In practice, it is often the case that one particular consumer aspect, such as knowledge and experience with the particular investment product or investment class under consideration, can preclude participation on the basis of existing regulation (in this example, MIFID). Preventing access based on failure with respect to any single criterion on a list may be simpler than a multivariate approach that weighs different factors, but it can be misleading. If outcomes such as stock market participation or having invested in retirement plans cause households to become more financially sophisticated, then by denying participation to those who are unsophisticated or were never exposed to the product, we are also depriving them of the chance to improve their financial literacy and sophistication.

Moreover, the signal provided by current financial literacy or sophistication can be misleading. Calvet, Campbell, and Sodini (2007) studied the behavior of Swedish households and have confirmed that those who are more sophisticated tend to exhibit a favorable risk-return trade-off (Sharpe ratio) compared to those who are less sophisticated. Nevertheless, more sophisticated households tend to exhibit greater shortfalls in returns from the efficient frontier, because sophistication makes them more confident to undertake larger risks. By contrast, the less sophisticated are more likely to realize their shortcomings, limit their risk exposure, and be closer to the efficient return frontier for the chosen level of risk. Indeed, Fuchs-Schuendeln and Haliassos (2015) showed that immediate participation by households with no previous familiarity with risky assets or consumer debt does not necessarily lead to regrets and exits when combined with awareness campaigns and proper advice, such as that provided by the West German financial sector to the East Germans immediately following reunification. "Smarter" regulation that would not focus exclusively on households' lack of previous exposure but would also consider their intended investment or borrowing level and actions taken to limit downside risks and to seek good financial advice could allow profitable access.

There is also a problem with allowing access simply on the basis of having previously used an instrument located in a different type of account. This is not necessarily indicative of the use to which this instrument will be put when placed in a different type of account. Bilias, Georgarakos, and Haliassos (2010) showed, for example, that US owners of brokerage accounts engaged in heavy trading with the stocks in those accounts, but they also tended to invest a small fraction of their financial assets in brokerage accounts, with a median of only 9.3 percent between 1989 and 2004. This is consistent with the view that at least some brokerage account holders view those accounts as "play money" and trade heavily in the hope of earning high excess returns, even if they do not want to subject the bulk of their financial wealth to this treatment.

Despite limitations of micro-econometric models in predicting household financial behavior, refining existing household finance models could serve the purpose of identifying candidates for suboptimal use of a particular financial product. Indeed, credit-scoring methods for households can be considered (poorer) cousins of such a broader characteristics-based approach.

Given all the problems mentioned above, however, it may be more promising to devote efforts to designing measures that ensure the potential for good use by all rather than to block use by some. From a legal perspective,[5] this could take the form of standardized, product-focused information requirements (e.g., classification of product risks with regard to certain groups of investors or definition of particular target markets under EU-law reform), or individualized, investor-focused information

[5] I owe this proposal to H.C. Grigoleit.

requirements (e.g., EU and German law on information requirements related to marketing of financial instruments requiring individual advice). Some recent developments on this front are reported in "Recent regulatory measures", below. Ensuring the flow of easy-to-understand information and the provision of sound financial advice can also contribute to greater diversification, as households get advice that they can trust on how to build a portfolio of assets or a sound balance sheet. Nevertheless, provision of information is not a sufficient condition for optimal behavior. There is empirical evidence that disclosure of conflicts of interest can have unintended side effects (Lowenstein, Cain, and Sah 2011) or that information fails to have any noticeable effects on behavior (Beshears, Choi, Laibson, and Madrian 2013).

Regulation of practitioners

There are two types of practitioners relevant for our analysis: financial advisors, and producers of financial instruments intended for use by households. There can be multiple objectives in regulating those, including financial stability and containment of systemic risk, but the focus of this chapter is on minimizing the chances that households will get into financial trouble through erroneous decisions regarding participation and levels of holdings.

There is a voluminous literature, starting long before the development of household finance as a field, which raises the question of whether financial analysts and advisors have sufficient knowledge to provide useful advice.[6] It seems obvious that an important aspect of regulation of professional financial advisors is to ensure that they have a minimum level of training in finance and experience in investing before they are allowed to provide financial advice to households. Rather than simply imposing costs on the financial advice sector, such regulation enhances the reputation of financial advisors and the chances that households will turn to them for advice, despite the fact that financial (unlike medical) advice is often provided for free by members of the social circle of the household.[7]

Given the conflicts of interest in the provision of financial advice noted above, regulation needs to consider the payment schemes and financial

[6] Indeed, one of the very first papers asking this question appeared in the first volume of Econometrica and was written by Alfred Cowles (1933).

[7] On financial advice, see also Chapter 11 by Hackethal, this volume.

incentives governing the practice of financial advisors. It may be argued that the conflict between selling products and advising individuals on what is best for them to buy is not unique to the profession of financial advisors. Even medical doctors face some conflict of interest, given the fact that their major conferences are organized by powerful pharmaceutical companies eager to sell their brand name medicines instead of generics, for example.

However, the medical profession has two institutions not directly available to the finance profession. The first is the Hippocratic oath, which prevents medical doctors from knowingly abusing patients. There is no known equivalent to this in the finance profession. The second is the existence of an elaborate system of malpractice procedures, which discourages less-than-diligent medical doctors from mistreating their patients. In principle, this could have an analogue in the finance profession, in the form of a well-developed system of investor and borrower protection. However, this is yet to be developed, and it will certainly take some years before it comes in full force and practitioners and households alike appreciate what it can offer.

Even in the presence of these two institutions, but a fortiori in their absence, it may make good sense for regulation to distinguish and separate the provision of financial advice from the act of selling a financial product. After all, even medical doctors do not produce or sell medicines themselves, and pharmacists are only asked to provide limited medical advice to patients, despite the existence of the two important institutions mentioned above. Some direct support for this proposal can be provided by the findings of Hackethal, Haliassos, and Jappelli (2012): negative effects of financial advice were found to be less pronounced for independent financial advisors than for bank employees under pressure to push the products of their bank onto clients seeking advice.[8]

It will not be straightforward to ensure independence of advice and to handle conflicts of interest by means of law alone, and it can prove to be too costly, in particular for small investors. Separation of functions, to the extent it can be monitored, may be an important first step in handling the issue of mismatch between financial advisors and households discussed early on in this chapter. The merits of separation of functions relative to

[8] Indeed, EU and German laws support independent advice by regulation of firms claiming to be acting as independent advisors. This support comes in the form of requirements of pluralistic information and prohibition of third party commissions.

an alternative scheme, which allows advisors a dual role but requires them to declare their commissions, need to be assessed.

If an important reason that financial advisors are typically matched with wealthier, more experienced investors is that they are paid sales commissions, then removing this feature from their remuneration scheme can only help redirect them toward smaller potential investors in need of good advice. The bias, however, can still remain if inexperienced, small investors or disadvantaged borrowers are less knowledgeable about, or less eager to take advantage of, available financial advice. Incentive schemes may need to be developed to encourage financial advisors to reach out to those less likely to approach them for advice.

Producers of financial instruments themselves have a role to play in encouraging less eager households to contact a financial advisor. Pharmaceutical companies do precisely that when they advertise new medicines and encourage patients to "consult their doctor" about them. Producers of financial products could be required to include such nudges in the information materials accompanying their products.

Information materials and promotional activities for financial instruments should be closely monitored by regulators for clarity and transparency, but also for appropriateness for the customer in question. It does not seem reasonable to apply to information the principle of "the more the merrier." Salient information should be provided regarding expected outcomes, the range of possible outcomes, appropriateness for households with specific characteristics, and contraindications including inappropriate combinations with other financial instruments held by the household. Moreover, the information should be provided in different "languages," depending on the level of financial literacy of households for which the particular financial instrument is intended.

To date, there is limited evidence on how financial advisors tailor their advice to observable characteristics of their clients. Some evidence was provided by Mullainathan, Noeth, and Schoar (2012). They sent "mystery shoppers" with scripts regarding the current location of their funds to visit a number of different financial advisors and to seek advice on where to invest. In this first visit, financial advisors exhibited dramatic bias toward active management rather than index funds, evidence of catering to the initial portfolio, but also differentiation of advice to observable characteristics of the mystery shoppers, including gender and age. The evidence collected is consistent with such differentiation being aimed at serving the different needs of heterogeneous clients rather than at exploiting vulnerabilities and ignorance. As more users from disadvantaged demographic groups are encouraged to obtain financial advice, the potential for exploitation and discrimination is unlikely to diminish and might well increase. Breaking the link between advice and sales could counter this natural tendency.

Recent regulatory measures

As this chapter is being finalized for publication, there is considerable activity on the regulatory front, reshaping the framework regulating the marketing of financial products, the nature and remuneration of financial advice offered, the information that needs to be provided to investors, and the access restrictions that can be imposed by regulators.

Here are some important examples, which also link to the discussion of principles above. In July 2012, the European Commission proposed a legislative package with three main parts. The first regulates the content and format of "Key Information Documents" (KIDS) for packaged retail investment products (PRIPS). The second revises the Insurance Mediation Directive (IMD) to ensure that the same level of consumer protection will apply to all purchasers of insurance products regardless of the channel through which these are purchased; that consumers will be provided with clear information on the professional status and remuneration provisions for the salesperson; and that insurance product sales will have to be accompanied by honest professional advice. The third part is intended to ensure that the duties and liability of asset-keeping entities for investment funds are clear and uniform across the EU. On April 15, 2014, the European Parliament adopted the political agreement reached between the European Parliament and the Council, namely the Regulation on KIDS for packaged retail and insurance-based investment products ("PRIIPs Regulation").

On June 12, 2014, the texts of the MIFID II Directive (2014/65/EU) and the Markets in Financial Instruments Regulation (Regulation 600/2014) (MiFIR) were published in the Official Journal of the EU. Member states have two years to transpose the new rules, which will be applicable from January 2017. The overall objective of the new framework is to make financial markets more efficient, resilient and transparent. In our context, the revised MIFID enhances investor protection through new organizational and conduct requirements or powers for management bodies. In addition, it increases the role and supervisory powers of regulators and establishes powers to prohibit or restrict the marketing and distribution of certain products.

Following the concept of "independent investment advice" proposed by MIFID II, Germany passed an Act on Fee-Based Investment Advice, which introduced the occupational title of "fee-only" (financial) advisors, on August 1, 2014. Such advisors provide financial advice remunerated by transparent fees, but they cannot receive any commission or inducement of other form in selling such products. If they work in a company that also provides commission-based services, they must be organizationally and functionally separated from that other type of advice. If the financial instrument they sell is available only through the payment of inducements, such payments must be transferred to the client. The German legislator assumes that the scope of the German Act is broader than the provisions of MIFID II, and thus requires EU investment firms conducting cross-border services in Germany to obtain licenses.

Concluding remarks

This chapter considered some opportunities provided by financial innovation, and documented ways in which households can get into financial trouble, the criteria for regulating the use of financial instruments, and various difficulties in designing and implementing such regulations. It is fair to say that regulation alone will not be sufficient to keep households out of financial trouble. Improvements in financial education, primarily at an early age so that sufficient time is given for wealth accumulation and the repayment of debts, can enable households to make better use of financial instruments but also of financial advice and product-related information, so as to make better decisions. Promoting transparent products, appropriate default options (in the sense of what happens if no boxes are checked by the consumer), financial advice targeted at disadvantaged groups, and product awareness can complement efforts on the regulatory front.

Appropriate use of novel or complex financial instruments is a process rather than an event that can be determined by a simple financial literacy test or product familiarity check. Indeed, such simple tests or checks can get in the way of promoting household risk management through use of new products. Household finance research can provide useful guidance in predicting mismatches between household characteristics, preferences, attitudes, and constraints on the one hand and financial product features on the other.

Finally, developing an elaborate legal framework for investor and borrower protection, at the same level of sophistication and coverage as existing frameworks for consumer protection and discouragement of medical malpractice, seems indispensable for allowing households to make use of a growing array of financial products designed to enhance wealth, smooth consumption, and manage risks, without actually being destroyed by them.

References

Agnew, Julie, Pierluigi Balduzzi, and Annika Sundén (2003). "Portfolio Choice and Trading in a Large 401(k) Plan." *American Economic Review* 93(1): 193–205.

Ameriks, John and Stephen Zeldes (2005). "How Do Household Portfolio Shares vary with Age?" *mimeo.*

Barber, Brad M. and Terrance Odean (2000). "Trading Is Hazardous to Your Wealth: The Common Stock Investment Performance of Individual Investors." *The Journal of Finance* 55(2): 773–806.

Barber, Brad M. and Terrance Odean (2001). "Boys Will Be Boys: Gender, Overconfidence, and Common Stock Investment." *Quarterly Journal of Economics* 116(1): 261–292.

Beshears, J., J. J. Choi, D. Laibson, and B. C. Madrian (2013). "Simplification and Saving." *Journal of Economic Behavior and Organization* 95: 130–145.

Bhattacharya, Utpal, Andreas Hackethal, Simon Kaesler, Benjamin Loos, and Steffen Meyer (2012). "Is Unbiased Financial Advice to Retail Investors Sufficient? Answers from a Large Field Study." *Review of Financial Studies* 24: 975–1032.

Bilias, Yannis, Dimitris Georgarakos, and Michael Haliassos (2010). "Portfolio Inertia and Stock Market Fluctuations." *Journal of Money, Credit and Banking* 42(4): 715–742.

Campbell, John Y. (2006). "Household Finance." *Journal of Finance* 61(4): 1553–1604.

Campbell, John Y., Robert J. Shiller,and Luis M. Viceira (2012). "Understanding Inflation-Indexed Bond Markets." In Michael Haliassos (eds.), *Financial Innovation: Too Much or Too Little?* Cambridge, MA: MIT Press.

Calvet, Laurent, John Y. Campbell, and Paolo Sodini (2007). "Down or Out: Assessing the Welfare Costs of Household Investment Mistakes." *Journal of Political Economy* 115: 707–747.

Celerier, Claire and Boris Vallee (2014). "What Drives Financial Complexity? A Look into the Retail Market for Structured Products." *mimeo.*

Choi, James J., David Laibson, and Brigitte C. Madrian (2011). "$100 Bills on the Sidewalk: Suboptimal Investment in 401(k) Plans." *Review of Economics and Statistics* 93(3): 748–763.

Christelis, Dimitris, Tullio Jappelli, and Mario Padula (2010). "Cognitive Abilities and Portfolio Choice." *European Economic Review* 54(1): 18–38.

Coval, Joshua D. and Tobias J. Moskowitz (1999). "Home Bias at Home: Local Equity Preference in Domestic Portfolios." *Journal of Finance* 54(6): 2045–2073.

Disney, Richard and John Gathergood (2013). "Financial Literacy and Consumer Credit Portfolios." *Journal of Banking and Finance* 37: 2246–2254.

Duflo, Esther and Emmanuel Saez (2002). "Participation and Investment Decisions in a Retirement Plan: The Influence of Colleagues' Choices." *Journal of Public Economics* 85: 121–148.

Feldstein, Martin and Charles Horioka (1980). "Domestic Saving and International Capital Flows." *Economic Journal* 90: 314–329.

Fuchs-Schuendeln, Nicola and Michael Haliassos (2015). "Product Familiarity and Household Financial Behavior." *mimeo*.

Georgarakos, Dimitris, Michael Haliassos, and Giacomo Pasini (2014). "Household Debt and Social Interactions." *Review of Financial Studies* 27(5): 1404–1433.

Greenwood, Robert and Luis Viceira (2012). "MacroMarkets and the Practice of Financial Innovation." In Michael Haliassos (eds.), *Financial Innovation: Too Much or Too Little?* Cambridge, MA: MIT Press.

Grinblatt, Mark, Matti Keloharju and Juhani Linnainmaa (2011). "IQ and Stock Market Participation." *Journal of Finance* 66(6): 2121–2164.

Guiso Luigi and Tullio Jappelli (2005). "Awareness and Stock Market Participation." *Review of Finance* 9(4): 537–567.

Hackethal, Andreas, Michael Haliassos, and Tullio Jappelli (2012). "Financial Advisors: A Case of Babysitters?" *Journal of Banking and Finance* 36(2): 509–524.

Hastings, Justine S., Brigitte C. Madrian, and William L. Skimmyhorn (2013). "Financial Literacy, Financial Education, and Economic Outcomes." *Annual Review of Economics* 5: 347–373.

Hong, Harrison, Jeffrey D. Kubik, and Jeremy C. Stein (2004). "Social Interaction and Stock-Market Participation." *Journal of Finance* 59: 137–163.

Huberman, Gur (2001). "Familiarity Breeds Investment." *Review of Financial Studies* 14: 659–680.

Inderst, Roman and Marco Ottaviani (2009). "Misselling Through Agents." *American Economic Review* 99(3): 883–908.

Jappelli, Tullio and Mario Padula (2013). "Investment in Financial Literacy and Saving Decisions." *Journal of Banking and Finance* 37(8): 2779–2792.

Kaustia, M. and S. Knüpfer (2012). "Peer Performance and Stock Market Entry." *Journal of Financial Economics* 104(2): 321–338.

Kerwin, Charles, Erik Hurst, and Nikolai Roussanov (2009). "Conspicuous Consumption and Race." *Quarterly Journal of Economics* CXXIV(2): 425–467.

Kuhn, Peter, Peter Kooreman, Adriaan Soetevent, and Arie Kapteyn (2011). "The Effects of Lottery Prizes on Winners and Their Neighbors: Evidence from the Dutch Postcode Lottery." *American Economic Review* 101: 2226–2247.

Loewenstein, G., D. Cain, and S. Sah (2011). "The Limits of Transparency: Pitfalls and Potential of Disclosing Conflicts of Interest." *American Economic Review* 101: 423–428.

Lusardi, A., and O. Mitchell (2007). "Baby Boomers Retirement Security: The Role of Planning, Financial Literacy and Housing Wealth." *Journal of Monetary Economics* 54: 205–224.

Lusardi, Annamaria and Peter Tufano (2009). "Debt Literacy, Financial Experience and Overindebtedness." *mimeo*.

Mullainathan Sendhil, Markus Noeth, and Antoinette Schoar (2012). "The Market for Financial Advice: An Audit Study." *NBER Working Paper* 17929.

Shiller, Robert (2012). "Inventors, Products, and Investors in Finance." In Michael Haliassos (ed.), *Financial Innovation: Too Much or Too Little?* Cambridge, MA: MIT Press.

van Rooij, Maarten, Annamarie Lusardi, and Rob Alessie (2011). "Financial Literacy and Stock Market Participation." *Journal of Financial Economics* 101(2): 449–472.

van Rooij, Maarten, Annamarie Lusardi, and Rob Alessie (2012). "Financial Literacy, Retirement Planning, and Wealth Accumulation." *Economic Journal* 122(5): 449–478.

10

Financial market governance and consumer protection in the EU

NIAMH MOLONEY[1]

The retail interest and the crisis era

It is a truism that since the outbreak of the Global Financial Crisis in 2008, EU financial system regulation has undergone a radical transformation. This transformation has been institutional and substantive. The institutional reform has taken the form of, first, the new European System of Financial Supervision (ESFS), composed of national competent authorities (NCAs), the three European Supervisory Authorities (ESAs) (the European Securities and Markets Authority (ESMA), the European Banking Authority (EBA), and the European Insurance and Occupational Pensions Authority (EIOPA)), and the European Systemic Risk Board (ESRB); and, second, sitting somewhat uneasily alongside/within the ESFS, Banking Union (composed, institutionally, of the Single Supervisory Mechanism (SSM, composed of the ECB and NCAs) and the Single Resolution Mechanism (SRM, based on a complex institutional arrangement which includes the ECB, the Single Resolution Board and Fund, and national resolution authorities)). The substantive reform relates to the massive "single rule-book" which now governs banking, securities, and insurance markets in the EU.[2] By the time the crisis-era Commission and European Parliament terms closed in mid-2014, and following the plethora of final reforms adopted by the European Parliament on "Super Tuesday" on April 15, 2014, EU financial system regulation, and its related institutional architecture, had changed beyond all recognition from the pre-crisis period.

The support of pan-EU financial stability has been the defining concern of this period. But how have retail investor interests been

[1] Professor of Financial Markets Law, London School of Economics and Political Science. This discussion reflects the law and policy as at Summer 2014.

[2] For a recent policy assessment see European Commission 2014 (COM (2014) 279).

addressed?[3] The US and Australia, to take examples from two major retail investment markets, have engaged in wide-ranging crisis-era reforms to retail market intervention, which embrace institutional and substantive reforms.[4] Even at the international level, where there are few incentives to engage with the retail interest given the local nature of retail markets, there is evidence of a concern to address longstanding and intractable retail market failures: the Seoul 2010 G20 meeting led to the crisis-era global agenda somewhat belatedly engaging with the retail interest and to the related November 2011 adoption by the Cannes G20 meeting of the G20/OECD High Level Principles on Consumer Protection.[5]

But it was never obvious that the EU crisis-era agenda would embrace the retail markets. The history of EU intervention in retail financial markets is a troubled one.[6] Progress has been slow and political/institutional interest variable: retail interests have regularly been side-lined or used as political cover for national interests.[7] The careful empirical assessment essential to effective retail market regulatory design – given, in particular, the challenges which deeply rooted industry incentive structures and the behavioural vulnerabilities of retail investors pose to the adoption of effective regulation[8] – has often been absent.[9] And, perhaps above all, it has never been clear that there is a strong case for EU harmonization in this area. A growing body of evidence suggests that the EU retail investor requires significant regulatory support.[10] But it is not clear that the EU should act as regulator. Retail market regulation is not easy to design or apply.[11] It is all the more difficult in the EU.

[3] The focus of this discussion is on the retail investment markets and the distribution of "household" investment products.

[4] See, e.g., Kingsford Smith and Dixon 2015.

[5] See recently OECD, Draft Effective Approaches to Support the Implementation of the Remaining G20/OECD High Level Principles on Financial Consumer Protection: Informal Consultation, May 14, 2014.

[6] See generally Moloney 2010a.

[7] As was the case, e.g., with respect to the febrile negotiations on the liberalization of order execution in the EU by the Markets in Financial Instruments Directive I 2004 (MiFID I) (Directive 2004/39/EC OJ [2004] L139/1). Such "masking" is not confined to the EU: see Roe 1991.

[8] For recent crisis-era assessments see, e.g., Campbell et al. 2009 and Kingsford Smith 2009.

[9] See further Moloney 2010b.

[10] For two major recent empirical assessments see Chater et al. 2010 and Synovate 2011.

[11] See, e.g., the persistence of large-scale mis-selling in the UK despite repeated cycles of scandal and reform, which led to the UK implementing a major structural reform of the distribution industry in 2012 (under the Retail Distribution Review which, inter alia, prohibits commission-based payments to investment advisers).

Investment patterns vary considerably across the Member States.[12] Market structures often diverge.[13] Retail market risks in the EU market tend to be local, cross-border activity is very limited,[14] and the optimum regulatory response is likely to be one deeply rooted in the local market. Nonetheless, the EU has, over the crisis era, moved decisively into the retail market space.

Immediately prior to the financial crisis, the harmonized EU retail market rule-book had become more sophisticated, but it was incomplete. Advances had been made with respect to distribution regulation (primarily under the 2004 MiFID I), but regulatory arbitrage risks were considerable in what was a silo-based regime which organized distribution regulation according to whether it was broadly oriented to the banking, securities, or insurance markets – although retail investment products in the EU typically sit across these silos.[15] Similarly, important outcome-driven reforms had been made with respect to retail market summary/short-form disclosure, but only with respect to the "UCITSs" investment fund. More generally, the EU policy focus remained trained on downstream distribution and disclosure regulation, despite the well-documented and longstanding difficulties with these forms of intervention. Precautionary, upstream product intervention, in particular, was generally limited.

Over the financial crisis, household and individual savers across the EU sustained massive losses.[16] These losses can be associated with market risk – a risk which is not captured (at least directly) by traditional retail market regulation. But they can also be associated with market failures, which are the concern of retail market regulation. The EU retail market is vulnerable to significant market failures arising from: the dominance of complex packaged products as household investments; persistent conflict of interest risk arising from the "financial supermarket" business model (which is based on the distribution of proprietary products) or arising

[12] See, e.g., ECB, The Eurosystem Household Financial and Consumption Survey, Results from the First Wave, Statistics Paper Series No 2 (2013).

[13] Distribution systems and related incentive risks, e.g., vary. In the UK, independent advice is the dominant distribution channel, while across most of continental Europe investment products are distributed as proprietary products through the major bank-based "financial supermarkets".

[14] E.g., European Commission, European Financial Integration Report (2009: 14–17) (SEC (2009) 1702).

[15] Structured securities and deposits, unit-linked insurance products, and collective investment schemes, e.g., are broadly regarded as substitutable in the EU market, although they are regulated differently.

[16] European Commission, Communication from the Commission to the European Parliament and the Council. Packaged Retail Investment Products (2009: 1) (COM (2009) 204) 1.

from the commission-based adviser business model; and limited investor ability to decode complex product disclosures and often opaque and incomplete disclosures related to conflicts of interest. In this environment, the process-based quality of advice rules which applied pan-EU under the cornerstone MiFID I seem to have struggled to support good investor outcomes. In particular, the scale of the incentive risks were highlighted by the mis-selling of structured products and, as the crisis took root, the mis-selling of proprietary products designed to shore up financial institutions' balance sheets (particularly in Spain[17]).

The crisis era would, however, lead to the adoption of a series of important retail market reforms.[18] Distribution regulation has been tightened under the behemoth 2014 MiFID II reforms;[19] further distribution reforms are expected under the Insurance Mediation Directive (IMD) II reforms.[20] Disclosure is being enhanced under the 2014 MiFID II, the 2010 Prospectus Directive summary prospectus reforms,[21] and the cross-sector "packaged retail and insurance – based investment products" (PRIIPs) disclosure reforms (the latter agreed only in April 2014[22]). And, in a major change, product intervention has now become part of the EU's retail market toolbox under the 2014 MiFIR.[23]

There is much that is good and much that is troubling in the new rulebook, which is precautionary and interventionist in style. In particular, it can be associated with a "consumerization" of regulation. While the EU remains committed to the "financialization"[24] of its households,[25] which

17 A major mis-selling scandal arose with respect to the sale by banks of high-risk preference shares to their retail depositors, which shares generated massive losses (Reuters June 15, 2012: "Hard for Spain to share pain with bank bondholders").

18 And particular policy attention from the European Parliament, e.g., its ECON (Economic and Monetary Affairs) Committee produced a wide-ranging report in 2014 on Consumer Protection Aspects of Financial Services (IP/A/IMCO/ST-2013–07).

19 Directive 2014/65/EU OJ [2014] L173/349.

20 COM (2012) 360/2 (although MiFID II brings insurance-related investment products within its scope in some respects).

21 Commission Delegated Regulation 486/2012 OJ [2012] L150/1.

22 Regulation EU No 1286/2014 OJ [2014] L352/1.

23 Regulation EU No 600/2104 OJ [2014] L173/84.

24 The "financialization" of households (or the policy encouragement of households to cover welfare expenditure through long-term, market-based savings), and the related constructions of individuals as independent "financial citizens," is now well-established in the literature as a defining feature of retail market law and policy in major economies globally. See, e.g., Kingsford Smith 2009 and Williams 2007.

25 Well illustrated by the European Commission's 2013 proposal for a Long Term Investment Fund (COM (2013) 462), designed to draw retail funds into illiquid long-term funding vehicles and to support thereby the EU's long-term financing needs.

has long been a driver of EU intervention, the means through which this is being pursued now include more robust regulatory tools than the previously dominant disclosure tools. The extent to which the risks of this more interventionist approach, in an EU retail market characterized by investor, market, and industry difference, will be effectively mitigated depends in large part on EU financial market governance more generally, understood in terms of the institutional architecture which supports rule-making and supervision.

In particular, much depends on how ESMA, a new and influential actor in EU financial market governance, will shape the regime as it is amplified, implemented, and supervised pan-EU. ESMA is not the only EU actor in the ESFS bearing on retail market regulation and supervision. The suite of powers conferred on EBA and EIOPA broadly maps that which ESMA deploys (with some important exceptions), and all ESAs are active in the financial consumer space. Even the ESRB, charged with a pan-EU macro-prudential stability mandate, has engaged with retail market risks, albeit with a close focus on macro-pan-EU stability, rather than on micro investor protection risks.[26] But ESMA, as the EU's nascent markets regulator, is the most closely engaged with the governance of the pan-EU retail market within the ESFS.

ESMA and retail rule-making

EU rule-making, CESR, and ESMA

Retail market rule-making has long been problematic in the EU. It is problematic internationally given the host of complexities engaged, not least among them technical challenges relating to designing outcome-focused rules (including identifying retail investors as a class for the purposes of regulatory design, and addressing deep-rooted incentive and behavioural difficulties); a poorly organized and diffuse retail cohort which can struggle to counter industry lobbies;[27] the difficult balances and compromises engaged, including with respect to where the perimeter of public regulation lies;[28] and acute politicization risks, all of which exacerbate the well-charted weaknesses to which effective rule-making for financial systems generally is prone.[29] But the EU rule-making

[26] Well illustrated by the stability orientation of its 2013 assessment of retailization risks in the EU market (Burkart and Bouveret 2012).

[27] See, e.g., Kingsford Smith and Dixon 2015. [28] E.g., Langevoort and Thomson 2013.

[29] See, e.g., Black 2006 and Black and Gross 2005.

process, with its myriad institutional complexities, its tendency to sclerosis but also over-reaction, its vulnerability to multi-level political horse-trading, and its limited capacity (particularly at European Parliament and Council levels) to engage in impact assessment, is perhaps uniquely poorly equipped to manage the nuanced rule-design required for a fragmented EU retail market. The risks to effective rule-making are exacerbated by the very limited ability of EU retail investors to organize collectively; EU retail investors are not a cohesive group, do not have similar political incentives and interests, and, as has been extensively documented, struggle to influence rule-making.

One well-established response to rule-making challenges is delegation to an expert authority, typically a national financial regulator; the new US Consumer Financial Protection Bureau, however troublesome its gestation, provides a crisis-era example of how an administrative agency can support retail market rule design.[30] An institutional solution to rule-making challenges has also been adopted in the EU, in the form of ESMA. ESMA is not, however, a traditional regulatory agency, much less a consumer protection agency. Its role in EU financial market governance is distinct and has been shaped by the particular Treaty, political, and institutional factors which shape EU governance generally and by the searing influence of the financial crisis.[31]

Prior to the establishment of ESMA in 2011, its precursor – the Committee of European Securities Regulators (CESR), which provided technical advice to the Commission on delegated rule-making and engaged in a range of "soft" supervisory convergence activities designed to support consistency and co-ordination across NCAs – supported EU retail market rule-design through a number of (albeit constitutionally troublesome) channels. For example, it strengthened the Commission's capacity to develop nuanced legislative proposals for the retail markets, notably through its wide-ranging testing activities on the UCITS "Key Investor Information Document"; it adopted a raft of soft law guidance for the retail markets;[32] it developed an innovative retail engagement

[30] See, e.g., Everson 2012 and Barkow 2010.

[31] See, e.g., Busuioc 2013 and Moloney 2011.

[32] Including, e.g., a Q&A on the contested question of whether certain investment products were "non-complex" and so could be sold execution-only under MiFID I (CESR/09–559) and on the definition of "advice" under MiFID I (CESR/10–293); a report on good and poor practices relating to inducements (CESR/10–295); guidance on the treatment of inducements (CESR/07-228b); and guidance on best execution (CESR/07–320).

agenda, including Consumer Days and Workshops; and it developed an investor education programme.

ESMA, however, has injected a new dynamic into EU retail market rule-making. ESMA operates at "level 2" and "level 3" of the EU law-making process for financial markets. As is well known, the co-legislators, the European Parliament and Council, adopt "level 1" "legislative" rules through Treaty-based institutional procedures. Level 1 rules are designed to concretize fundamental political choices, but are rarely in the high-level form that might be expected to follow, given the intensity of national interests in this sphere. Level 2 rules take the form of administrative rules, adopted by the Commission in accordance with a level 1 mandate. ESMA is engaged at level 2 in two ways. With respect to the "standard" Article 290/291 TFEU procedure for administrative rule-making, ESMA provides "technical advice" to the Commission; this technical advice may be taken by the Commission in whole, in part, or not at all, and without any procedural restraint on the Commission. With respect to the adoption of administrative rules in the form of "Binding Technical Standards," ESMA produces a draft standard (BTS) which is subsequently endorsed (adopted) by the Commission (2010 ESMA Regulation,[33] Articles 10–15). The Commission may revise or reject a BTS, but it is subject to a series of procedural constraints, designed to protect ESMA's position as quasi "expert regulator." BTSs are designed to be technical in nature and not to engage strategic decisions or policy choices. But in practice the line between "standard" Article 290/291 rules, where the Commission's primacy is clear, and BTSs, where ESMA, although subsidiary to the Commission, is very closely engaged, is a very fine one. Level 3 relates to the adoption of "soft" measures, designed to support supervisory convergence across the EU's NCAs and to support the consistent application of the "single rule-book." ESMA is heavily engaged at this level through the multiplicity of FAQs, Q&As, Guidelines, Opinions, and other soft measures which it is empowered to adopt under the 2010 ESMA Regulation. In this area, ESMA acts on its own initiative, although level 1 measures can contain directions to ESMA to adopt Guidelines in particular. ESMA Guidelines adopted under ESMA Regulation Article 16, have a strong quasi-binding quality, as a "comply or explain" requirement applies to NCAs in relation to their application.

[33] Regulation (EU) No 1095/2010 [2010] OJ L331/84.

Rule-making

Hitherto, given the pre-occupation of the EU crisis-era reform agenda with stability-oriented reforms, ESMA has not been closely engaged with retail market rule-making. A new "level 1" rule-book is now, however, in place under, for example, the 2014 MiFID I/MiFIR and the 2014 PRIPs Regulation, and extensive delegations to level 2 rule-making have been conferred. ESMA's influence can therefore be expected to be considerable on the related delegated rule-book which should inject nuance, calibration, and differentiation. What, accordingly, might the implications be for retail market rule-design?

The rule-making challenges under the 2014 MiFID II/MiFIR, for example, are considerable. A raft of delegated rules must be adopted with respect to, inter alia, conflict of interest management in distribution and commission payments; know-your-client/suitability disciplines; disclosure requirements; best execution; firm governance; and product governance and product intervention. Careful assessment of national approaches, calibration to different distribution channels, and gathering and interrogation of market data will be required. So too will robust engagement with the industry; resistance to the new delegated rule-book can be expected. And while the new delegated rule-book can draw on the 2004 MiFID I rule-book, many new rules are required.

In principle, and from an EU retail market "output governance"[34] perspective, ESMA can be expected to bring a strong independent, technical capacity to its upcoming advisory and BTS proposal level 2 activities, and to engage in sophisticated consultation practices. Its impact assessment capacity, in particular, is strengthening, as is its ability to gather retail market data to inform its rule-making activities. The retail market coverage of its biannual "Trends, Risks, and Vulnerabilities" reports, for example, is markedly strengthening,[35] as its ability to assess retail market risks.[36] So too is its ability to gather intelligence on

[34] The output/input legitimacy distinction distinguishes between, e.g., legitimacy based on direct representation and legitimacy based on the achievement of particular (technical) goals or outcomes (Esty 2006).

[35] Trends with respect to retail structured product sales and retail investment trends are tracked in its regular Trends, Risks, and Vulnerabilities Reports (TRVs). e.g., ESMA (2013: 22, Report on Trends, Risks, and Vulnerabilities 2/2013 (ESMA/2013/1138)), reporting on returns on a representative portfolio of retail investor wealth, and the subsequent first report for 2014 (containing more detail, including on participation rates and investor trust (ESMA/2014/0188, 26–28)).

[36] E.g., ESMA (2013), Retailization in the EU (ESMA/2013/326).

regulatory practices and market behaviour from its member NCAs. With respect to "input governance," ESMA is making efforts to strengthen retail engagement, although much needs to be done. As required by the 2010 ESMA Regulation (Article 37), it consults its Securities and Markets Stakeholder Group, which contains a number of consumer representatives.[37] With EBA and EIOPA it also engages in regular "Consumer Days"; while such events are unlikely to be of major substantive import, they serve a useful symbolic function. But ultimately, ESMA's enhancement of retail rule-making is more likely to reflect the output-oriented legitimacy associated with expert agencies; input-oriented legitimacy remains elusive.

Over its first three years (2011–2013), immediately prior to the Commission's 2013–2014 ESA/ESFS Review, ESMA's quasi-rule-making activities were almost entirely focused on the development of the crisis-era rule-book and on financial-stability-oriented measures. The evidence from this period points to a very strong technical capacity, and to a related ability to corral and assess quantitative data, to build international relationships with regulators and standard-setters, and to construct strong communication lines to the market.[38] ESMA's ability to defend the retail interest against what can be an industry clamour as to the costs of regulation should, even as the regulatory sine curve moves into a "down-cycle"[39] and as the pre-occupation with costs increases, therefore be considerable.[40] The Commission's 2013–2014 review of the ESAs/ESFS has suggested generally strong support for ESMA's quasi-rule-making activities, which augurs well for the cycle of retail-oriented rule-making which will shortly commence.[41] Early indications from the 2014 MiFID II/MiFIR administrative rule-making process suggest that the new rule-book will benefit from careful ex ante preparation. In May 2014, ESMA launched a massive consultation relating to the development of its technical advice and proposed BTSs under MiFID II/MiFIR.[42]

37 Four (of 30) members represent the consumer interest. A perceived lack of support for consumer representatives was, however, a theme of the 2013–2014 ESFS Review (Demarigny et al. 2013 – often referred to as the "Mazars Report"). Consumer representation on the ESA stakeholder groups more generally has been problematic, and the subject of a challenge to the European Ombudsman: Case 1966/2011.

38 See, e.g., Moloney 2014: chapter 10. 39 See Coffee 2012.

40 Its approach to its MiFID I guidance activities, e.g., was noticeably robust: ESMA (2013), Guidelines on Remuneration Policies and Practices (MiFID) (ESMA/2013/606).

41 E.g., Demarigny et al. 2013.

42 ESMA/2014/549 (Consultation Paper on its technical advice) and ESMA/2014/548 (Discussion Paper on its proposed BTSs).

A number of subsequent consultations are planned, as are Open Hearings, while external contractors have been engaged to support ESMA in the extensive impact assessment and data gathering exercises which will be required.

On the other hand, there are countervailing factors. Despite its independence guarantee and its technical capacity, ESMA cannot, reflecting the *Meroni* ruling,[43] adopt rules; the Commission remains the constitutional location of delegated rule-making power. This disjunction between the Commission as the constitutional location of rule-making power and ESMA as the location of technical expert capacity is troublesome. The Commission has significant incentives to protect its institutional primacy, and, accordingly, to reject and revise technical advice/proposed BTSs from ESMA, notwithstanding that these are typically prepared by ESMA after lengthy consultation and impact assessment. In practice, the first cycle (2011–2013/14) of delegated rule-making under the crisis-era rule-book suggests that an effective working relationship has developed between ESMA and the Commission. But there have been three cases where the Commission has rejected ESMA BTSs, in each case triggering some ESMA and market disquiet. It remains to be seen whether the second cycle of delegated rule-making, which will include the major level 1 retail market measures, leads to increased tensions or to further efficiencies in the pivotal Commission/ESMA relationship.

Initial signs are somewhat troubling in this regard. On the Council's May 2014 adoption of the 2014 MiFID II/MiFIR regime, the Commission made a formal statement that amendments over the inter-institutional MiFID II/MiFIR negotiations of the basis of many of the mandates for delegated rules from the "standard" Article 290/291 process, to the BTS process (over which ESMA has more control and related procedural protections), did "not respect the limitations set out [in the ESMA Regulation] in so far as technical standards can only cover aspects requiring technical expertise and cannot imply strategic decisions or policy choices".[44] The Commission accordingly appears acutely sensitive to its constitutional prerogatives, and can be expected to become more so as the implications of Banking Union, and a powerful ECB/SSM, become clearer. The ESMA/Commission dynamic can be expected to remain unstable as a result. Treaty restrictions and political realities make it

[43] Case 9/56 *Meroni v. High Authority* [1957–1958] ECR 133.

[44] ECOFIN, Statements by the Commission on Adoption of MiFID II/MiFIR, 7 May 2014 (9344/14).

unrealistic to call for ESMA to be conferred with rule-making powers in the interests of outcome-based governance efficiencies – the important January 2014 ruling from the Court of Justice on the validity of certain of ESMA's powers under the 2012 Short Selling Regulation certainly underscores that the Court has little appetite to revisit the *Meroni* ruling in light of recent changes related to the "agencification" of the EU's institutional environment.[45] Nonetheless, there is a governance instability at the heart of the EU's delegated rule-making process which weakens the EU's ability to adopt retail market rules effectively.

Beyond the rule-book: shaping the regulatory environment

The extent to which ESMA will embrace a retail market agenda when operating outside the procedural formalities of the level 2 sphere and in adopting own-initiative "soft" measures at level 3, and will thereby shape the wider EU retail agenda, is unclear.

As a nascent actor, finding its institutional place in an increasingly fragile institutional ecosystem given Banking Union, the financial stability agenda may afford ESMA the most potential to strengthen its capacity.[46] This agenda has a number of attractions, including its political prominence; its novelty in the securities and markets sphere;[47] the institutional complexities and related opportunities for capacity-building (particularly in relation to Banking Union's SSM – see section "Institutional design: an EU consumer agency?"); the acuteness of the need for technical expertise; the clear pan-EU externalities at stake; and the opportunities for international influence. The shadow banking agenda, with its multiple entry points for a securities markets regulator (including with respect to money market funds and securities financing transactions) is a case in point.[48] Financial stability is all the more likely to compel ESMA's attention as its primary objective is to "protect the public interest by contributing to the short, medium, and long-term

[45] Case C-270/12 *UK v Council and Parliament*, January 22, 2014 (not yet reported).

[46] The notion of capacity is associated with a supervisor's ability to achieve outcomes and depends on, inter alia, reputational capital, resources, expertise, relationships with the regulated sector and the nature of the regulated sector, and enforcement and supervisory powers (Black 2003). For a nascent regulator such as ESMA, operating with a limited set of powers, the acquisition of capacity is key to its legitimacy, effectiveness, and resilience.

[47] See, e.g., IOSCO (2011), Mitigating Systemic Risk – A Role for Securities Regulators.

[48] ESMA has seized the shadow banking agenda in a number of respects, notably with respect to money market funds. e.g., ESMA, Peer Review Money Market Funds (2013) (ESMA/2013/476) and ESMA Money Market Funds Guidance Q&A (ESMA/2012/113).

stability and effectiveness of the financial system, for the Union economy, its citizens and businesses" (ESMA Regulation, Article 1(4)). The retail agenda, by contrast, is messier (although consumer protection is one of ESMA's subsidiary objectives (Article 1(5)): the market failures are not as technically problematic as in the financial stability sphere, but arguably are more intractable; the need for local discretion is considerable, given the lack of pan-EU activity; and NCAs, while broadly supportive of the EU retail agenda, are likely to be reluctant to cede all control over politically sensitive retail market issues.

But assuming ESMA has sufficiently strong incentives to pursue a retail agenda, it can effectively deploy soft law in a number of ways, including: to provide guidance to NCAs and the market on the retail market rule-book; to provide an informal corrective dynamic, where difficulties emerge with harmonized rules; and to shape the development of EU retail market policy "upstream" by shaping NCA co-operation and initiatives, and thereby shaping future EU retail market policy initiatives. All of these activities also have the potential to strengthen ESMA's institutional capacity more generally and might accordingly be predicted to be pursued by ESMA, despite the attractions of the stability agenda. In addition, ESMA is a securities market regulator and as such would be expected to engage closely with retail market risks.

There is some support under the ESMA Regulation for a strong retail market agenda. ESMA Regulation Article 9 contains a number of retail-market-oriented obligations and was inserted by the European Parliament, which has since shown a commitment to monitoring the exercise of these powers.[49] Article 9 requires ESMA to "take a leading role" in promoting "transparency, simplicity, and fairness" in the market for consumer financial products, including by examining consumer trends, reviewing and co-ordinating financial literacy initiatives, developing training standards, and contributing to the development of common disclosure rules. It also empowers ESMA to issue warnings where a financial activity poses a serious threat to its objectives, requires ESMA to monitor financial innovation (through a dedicated Committee) in order to achieve a co-ordinated approach, and contains the enabling power for product intervention. ESMA has accordingly, and for the first time within EU rule-making governance, been conferred with an express, own-initiative retail market mandate.

[49] Hearing of the Chairs of the European Supervisory Authorities. September 19, 2012. Written Questions from ECON Coordinators. Joint Answers from the ESAs (JC 2012 090).

There are some indications that ESMA is pursuing an own-initiative retail agenda.[50] Its "soft rule-book", for example, includes robust and practical guidelines on MiFID I remuneration and suitability requirements,[51] which underline ESMA's publicly-expressed commitment to addressing mis-selling risks,[52] as well as "Q&As", supervisory briefings, and Opinions.[53] ESMA has been quick to use its Article 9 power to issue warnings.[54] Similarly, a number of governance initiatives have been taken to embed ESMA's coverage of retail market risks. An Article 9 "Implementation Task Force" has been established to ensure ESMA is equipped to fulfil its Article 9 responsibilities; its early work includes an assessment of the different approaches taken by national NCAs to the retail markets.[55] ESMA has also established a permanent Operational Working Group to promote common practices in investor protection.

Nonetheless, the Commission's 2013–2014 Review of the ESAs/ESFS suggested some concern as to the more limited attention given by ESMA to retail market matters, as compared to financial-stability-related matters.[56] In some "softer" but influential areas ESMA has been somewhat less active. These areas include investor education, in relation to which its initial attempt was somewhat formulaic, despite the need for enhanced investor education in the wake of the financial crisis and the co-ordination role ESMA could play in this regard.[57] They also include research, where ESMA has yet to develop the wide-ranging agenda which could respond to

[50] ESMA's first Annual Report suggested a commitment to the retail markets and highlighted ESMA's Art. 9 responsibilities: Annual Report (2011: 12).

[51] ESMA/2013/606 (MiFID I remuneration) and ESMA/2012/827 (MiFID I suitability).

[52] E.g., ESMA Chairman Maijoor, Speech, ESMA Investor Day, December 12, 2012 (ESMA/2012/818).

[53] E.g., MiFID I Q&A (investor protection and intermediaries (ESMA/2012/328), Supervisory Briefings ESMA/2012/851 (appropriateness and execution only) and ESMA/2012/850 (suitability), and an Opinion on product governance processes for structured retail products (ESMA/2014/332)

[54] Including with respect to: foreign exchange products (ESMA/2011/412); online investing (ESMA/2012/557); contracts for difference (ESMA/2013/267); and the risks posed by complex products (ESMA/2014/154).

[55] ESMA Annual Report (2011: 35).

[56] E.g., Response by EuroFinuse to the 2013 Commission Consultation on Review of the ESFS (responses available at http://ec.europa.eu/internal_market/consultations/2013/esfs/contributions_en.htm). The IMF similarly noted that stronger information-gathering in the products sphere would allow ESMA to make a "qualitative leap" in this area: IMF, Financial Sector Assessment Program. ESMA. Technical Note, March 2013, 26–26.

[57] Its first initiative was a traditional Guide to Investing (ESMA/2012/682), which was relatively unsophisticated as compared to financial literacy efforts at national level in the EU.

the continuing difficulties relating to the availability of empirical data on the EU retail market. While ESMA has been engaged in data collection with respect to complaints, thematic work, and product sales, and with respect to the drivers of investment behaviour,[58] it has produced only one major report on the retail markets which addressed the sale of complex products to retail financial consumers.[59] Similarly, retail investor engagement efforts, while not absent, have been somewhat muted.[60]

This relative lack of prioritization can, however, be related to the monumental weight of the crisis-era administrative rule-making agenda.[61] A more vibrant agenda might be expected as the massive crisis-era reform agenda recedes, not least given the political attractions the retail agenda might hold for ESMA: the European Parliament, long a supporter of enhanced powers for ESMA, was, over its 2009–2014 term, a strong advocate for retail market protection. The attractions of the financial stability agenda and complex dynamics of Banking Union (see section "Institutional design: an EU consumer agency?") may, however, have a de-stabilizing effect.

The retail markets and supervision

ESMA and supervision

Much of the EU's crisis-era reform agenda has been concerned with how to achieve optimal supervisory organization, and has focused on the institutional reforms necessary to ensure pan-EU financial stability and orderly recovery and resolution of financial institutions as necessary. While Banking Union represents the zenith of the institutional reforms, the ESFS generally has led to a reorientation of supervision and to greater centralization, albeit that (outside Banking Union) the NCAs remain the default supervisors.

58 ESMA, Annual Report (2012: 27).

59 ESMA, Retailization in the EU (2013) (ESMA/2013/326). Trends with respect to retail structured product sales and retail investment trends generally are, however, tracked (in outline) in its regular "Trends, Risks, and Vulnerabilities" reports (TRVs).

60 While the Securities and Markets Stakeholder Group supports engagement with the retail sector, ESMA has as yet not actively supported engagement with this sector by means of, e.g., retail-friendly summaries of consultations of particular interest to the retail sector (by contrast with EIOPA).

61 E.g., Statement by ESMA Chairman Steven Maijoor, ECON Public Hearing, September 20, 2013 (ESMA/2013/1363).

ESMA has been conferred with limited powers of direct intervention in three exceptional cases where it is empowered to address/recommend decisions to NCAs and, in the absence of an appropriate response, to impose decisions on market actors (breach of EU law (2010 ESMA Regulation Article 17); binding mediation (Article 19); and in emergency situations (Article 18)). It has also been conferred with direct supervisory powers over rating agencies and trade data repositories, and, more generally, with respect to short selling and, under the 2014 MiFID II/MiFIR, in relation to product intervention and position management. ESMA can also deploy a host of softer supervisory convergence powers, including with respect to peer review (Article 30) and the adoption of guidance and similar measures (Articles 16 and 29).

In the retail markets, any significant moves towards centralization of supervisory powers are problematic given the domestic orientation of retail investors. Local supervision, which responds to domestic risks, investor expectations, and market features, provides the means through which an increasingly prescriptive EU rule-book can be calibrated to local markets. National supervisory techniques, such as the UK Financial Conduct Authority's "Treating Customers Fairly" supervisory strategy, for example, can be used to address local market risks and to target problematic market segments.[62] Local supervision also provides a means for incubating supervisory strategies and techniques, and for ensuring that a healthy degree of experimentation and innovation, and a capacity for supervisory learning, remains within the EU's governance of financial markets. The need to align supervisory incentives also suggests that effective retail market supervision will be primarily local in nature. There is, however, a role for ESMA in developing and promoting supervisory best practices. But the more ESMA's powers move up the spectrum from co-ordination and support to direct intervention, the greater the risks to effective retail market supervision.

Thus far, there are few signs of ESMA disrupting NCA-based local supervision. Of its exceptional 2010 ESMA Regulation Article 17–19 powers of intervention, ESMA's powers in relation to breach of EU law are most likely to be deployed (Article 17); retail market supervision is unlikely to implicated in any Article 18 emergency action; and the Article 19 binding mediation power is most likely to be used to cut through supervisory differences in cross-border "college of supervisor" contexts. ESMA's Article 17 powers in relation to breach of EU law sit, however, at

[62] See, e.g., Georgosouli 2011.

the apex of a group of powers (soft and hard) which ESMA can use to ensure that NCAs comply with EU law (including peer review), and, in practice, wilful breach of EU retail market rules by NCAs is unlikely to be a regular occurrence.

Of more practical significance to the embedding of strong supervisory practices in the retail markets are ESMA's peer review powers (Article 30) and the other soft tools (Articles 16 and 29) which it can deploy to raise supervisory standards and to support supervisory learning. In particular, peer review procedures, which identify and embed good practices, are likely to be pivotal. The IMF, for example, has called on the ESAs to play a significant role in the dissemination of best practices, including through intrusive and publicly disclosed peer review.[63] The Article 30 peer review regime requires ESMA periodically to organize and conduct peer review analyses of NCAs' activities to further strengthen consistency in supervisory outcomes.[64] ESMA's initial approach was based on self-assessment by NCAs and on benchmarking by the ESMA Review Panel, but a more robust approach can be expected in the future given the autumn 2013 reforms to ESMA's Peer Review Methodology which are designed to move peer review away from peer/NCA assessment and towards independent assessment by ESMA, and to remove the risk that NCA interests could distort the outcomes of peer review.[65] The commitment to robust peer review augurs well for the enhancement of retail market supervision in the EU. One of the lessons of the crisis era is that retail market rules, and notably distribution/selling rules, are difficult to embed and can struggle to achieve outcomes, absent strenuous supervision and enforcement.[66]

ESMA also has a key role to play with respect to guidance and similar measures (Articles 16 and 29). Here, the initial indications augur well. ESMA's 2012 Guidelines on the MiFID I suitability regime,[67] for

[63] IMF 2013 Report, n 56, 14.

[64] Peer review is carried out through a Review Panel (composed of NCAs) and in accordance with the ESMA Protocol and Methodology on Peer Review (ESMA/2011/BS/229) and ESMA Review Panel Methodology (ESMA/2013/1709).

[65] A risk which was raised in Demarigny et al. (2013: 100–101), which called for a more independent approach, akin to the IMF's "Financial Sector Assessment Program" reviews.

[66] For an extensive analysis of how the MiFID I suitability requirement has applied in practice (and its weaknesses) across the EU, see Synovate (2011). On the need for robust supervision see, e.g., FSA, Assessing the Quality of Investment Advice in the Retail Banking Sector. A Mystery Shopping Review (2013).

[67] ESMA/2012/387.

example, are detailed, practical, and robust.[68] ESMA has also taken targeted action in relation to the distribution of complex products, with an Opinion on the application of the MiFID I regime to the sale and marketing of complex products.[69] Similarly, its own-initiative decision to adopt Guidelines on remuneration practices under MiFID I augurs well for its commitment to addressing incentive risks in distribution. The 2013 Guidelines are designed to ensure the consistent application of the MiFID I requirements on remuneration policies[70] and are notable for their close focus on quality of advice risks and their strongly operational dimension.[71]

Product intervention and ESMA

ESMA has also, however, been conferred with potentially radical direct powers of intervention under the 2014 MiFIR with respect to the prohibition of products (and services); its range of powers accordingly have moved up the spectrum in terms of level of intervention and risk to local market supervision.

In one of the most striking aspects of crisis-era retail market policy, product-related intervention has come to the fore within many NCAs as an additional tool for addressing retail market risk and in response to persistent mis-selling risks.[72] A range of product-related techniques are now being deployed by NCAs, including oversight of the product development process and prohibitions on the marketing of certain products. The 2014 MiFID II/MiFIR reforms have followed this striking trend. A new product governance regime (which requires firms to put in place procedures governing the development and approval of products) has been adopted, but so too – and more radically – has a new product intervention/prohibition regime.

The new 2014 MiFIR product (and services) intervention regime confers product intervention powers on NCAs, and similar temporary

68 And include warnings, e.g., with respect to the fitness for purpose of online suitability assessment tools and practical guidance as to how the risk tolerance of clients can be established.

69 ESMA/2014/146.

70 ESMA Guidelines on Remuneration Policies and Practices (MiFID I) (2013) (ESMA/2013/606).

71 The Guidelines contain detailed practical examples of good and bad practices.

72 For a summary of product-related failures across the EU see ESMA, EBA, EIOPA (2013), Joint Position of the ESAs on Manufacturers' Product Oversight & Governance Processes (JC-2013–77) Annex 1.

intervention powers on ESMA. They are designed as "last resort" powers which should only be deployed where organizational and conduct rules have failed. ESMA's temporary intervention powers, which mark a significant ratcheting-up of ESMA's direct powers, are similar to the NCA powers, albeit that tighter conditions apply (MiFIR Article 40)[73] that are designed to limit ESMA's discretion and thereby to ensure compliance with the *Meroni* restrictions on agencies, and to respect NCAs' competences in this new and sensitive area. ESMA, where the relevant MiFIR conditions are fulfilled, may temporarily prohibit or restrict in the EU the marketing, distribution, or sale of certain financial instruments or a type of financial activity or practice. Action by ESMA prevails over any previous action taken by an NCA; the potential for conflict, in a highly charged context (given the political attention which large-scale retail market mis-selling often attracts), therefore arises. Less controversially, ESMA is also conferred with co-ordination powers relating to the NCAs' powers (MiFIR Article 43). A parallel suite of powers are conferred on EBA with respect to structured deposits. While this silo-based approach reflects the allocation of banking and financial market competences to EBA and ESMA respectively, it underlines the risks of the EU's sectoral approach to regulation and the need for close co-ordination between ESMA and EBA in this nascent area.

ESMA appears ready to embrace these new powers, although it is likely to deploy them cautiously, not least given the strict conditionality which applies.[74] Auguring well for the necessary ESMA/EBA co-ordination, and, more broadly, for an enhancement in investor outcomes, product oversight generally has been a priority for the ESA Joint Committee (see section "Institutional design: an EU consumer agency?")[75] which has adopted Principles on product oversight and governance processes within product providers.[76] The ESAs (including ESMA) are to develop

[73] Including that ESMA may act only where the proposed action addresses a significant investor protection concern, or a threat to the orderly functioning and integrity of financial markets or commodity markets, or to the stability of the whole or part of the financial system in the EU, and regulatory requirements under EU law applicable to the financial instrument or activity do not address the threat. In addition, NCAs must not have acted or taken inadequate action.

[74] E.g., ESMA Executive Director Verena Ross welcomed the proposed powers as a "major leap forward": Speech on "Strengthening Investor Protection", 5 December 2011.

[75] The Joint Committee [of ESMA, EBA and EIOPA] has established a subgroup to deal with product-related issues: Joint Committee (2013) Work Programme (JC-2013-002).

[76] ESMA, EBA, EIOPA Joint Position No. 71.

sector-specific provisions based on these Principles.[77] While these Principles relate to product governance/oversight more generally, they suggest there are some grounds for optimism in relation to ESMA/EBA-led supervisory learning and co-ordination across NCAs in this new area.

There are, however, risks to the EU retail market and to ESMA as a nascent retail regulator. While ESMA is likely to tread carefully, not least given the constitutional sensitivities arising from the *Meroni* ruling and the related restrictions on discretionary action by EU agencies,[78] an overly ambitious and heavy-handed approach could generate tensions with NCAs and unwelcome uncertainty in the retail markets. As a nascent regulator with limited resources, ESMA can ill afford to become enmeshed in complex, detailed, and resource incentive assessments of products, with the attendant moral hazard and political risks. Although delegated rules will amplify the conditions which apply, making a determination as to whether a product is not suitable for distribution will still demand of ESMA nuanced choices as to the optimum levels of risk and choice in national and cross-border retail markets. While the new intervention power is constrained, it is likely to generate expectations of action.[79] Execution risk is accordingly significant unless considerable (scarce) resources are applied to the consideration of when products are likely to be problematic, and carefully designed safeguards apply. But ESMA's product intervention power may come to generate more light than heat. ESMA's major contribution in this area is more likely to relate to support of NCAs and of supervisory learning than to direct intervention. The new powers may, however, come to ensure that a high priority attaches to retail market issues within ESMA, notwithstanding the gravitational pull of the financial stability agenda.

Institutional design: An EU consumer agency?

ESMA cannot be characterized as a retail market regulator. Functionally, as an EU agency, forged in the crucible of the financial crisis, and carrying

[77] An ESMA Opinion on product governance for structured retail products followed (ESMA/2014/332).

[78] Although the Court's January 2014 Short Selling ruling (n 43) seems to protect ESMA's product intervention powers.

[79] A recurring theme of the ESFS/ESA Review (particularly from consumer stakeholders) was that ESMA had not taken action in relation to products under ESMA Regulation Art 9 (although ESMA had not, by then, been conferred with the necessary enabling power, which would follow under MiFIR).

the imprint of the multiple compromises which the organization of pan-EU financial system supervision requires, it does not have the suite of powers typically associated with retail market regulators. Institutionally, it is very far from having retail market interests imprinted on its "institutional DNA".[80] While the incentives for it to pursue a vigorous retail agenda may increase, the financial stability agenda may, for some time, afford ESMA more opportunities to increase its capacity and to secure its institutional position.

But there are few grounds for arguing for a specialized EU financial consumer agency, given the current fragmented state of the notional "EU retail market", the limited extent of pan-EU retail market failures and externalities (although these may increase), the still incomplete nature of the retail market rule-book, and the unresolved nature of the appropriate location of regulatory/supervisory power with respect to the retail markets. At the very least, the constitutional hurdles are significant; it is not clear, given the current state of the retail markets, and the need for local regulatory and in particular supervisory discretion, that the conditions of Article 114 TFEU (the Treaty competence deployed in support of the ESAs) relating to the establishment and functioning of the single market could be met, even in light of the Court's generally facilitative Article 114 jurisprudence.[81] Neither is it clear how a new agency might strengthen governance significantly, given the *Meroni* restrictions which apply to agencies. Nonetheless, might a more ambitious institutional design be canvassed? Certainly, coherent pan-EU retail market regulation/supervision is ill-served by the sector-specific, three-ESA organizational model, given the cross-sectoral nature of retail market risk and, in particular, the prevalence of substitutable securities-, insurance-, and deposit-based investment products in the EU market, and of related regulatory arbitrage and investor confusion risks. The location of regulatory/supervisory powers relating to structured deposits within EBA rather than ESMA, for example, underlines the potential stresses and gaps. It is also the case that consumer protection is not always within

80 The DNA metaphor has been vividly deployed by Professor Howell Jackson to characterize the depth of the US SEC's commitment to retail investor protection (Jackson 2007: 110).

81 See, e.g., Case C-376/98 *Germany v Parliament and Commission* [2000] ECR I-8419; Case C-491/01 *British American Tobacco (Investments) Limited and Imperial Tobacco v Secretary of State for Health* [2002] ECR I-1453; and Case C-58/08 *Vodafone, O2 et al v Secretary of State* [2008] ECR I-4999. A facilitative approach to Art. 114 and ESMA's powers was also adopted in the January 2014 Short Selling ruling (n 45).

the mandates of all the NCAs which sit on the ESAs, increasing the risks of poor co-ordination and of weak pan-EU consistency.

The "ESA Joint Committee", required under the three ESAs' founding Regulations (2010 ESMA Regulation, Articles 54–57), and which co-ordinates the work of ESMA, EBA, and EIOPA, provides some mitigation. It has established retail-market-focused subgroups, including for consumer protection generally, product oversight and governance, and with respect to the "PRIIPs"' reforms. The operational quality of its agenda thus far[82] suggests that it has the potential to support a co-ordinated approach to retail market risk across the EU. But difficulties remain. Unhelpful competitive, "first mover" dynamics may emerge across the ESAs which may not be fully managed by the Joint Committee. In some respects, a degree of competition is healthy. EBA, for example, has shown itself to have embraced the retail market agenda enthusiastically and to be sensitive to current issues,[83] and was an early champion of strengthening research.[84] A "race to the top" between the three ESAs could prove productive. But where an ESA adopts a retail market initiative which cannot easily be refined to reflect the particular dynamics of the markets over which the other ESAs have oversight, difficulties may emerge. The ESA product governance strategy provides a good example of how a high-level ESA-wide approach can subsequently be finessed to reflect the risks of different market segments, but "first mover" incentives could prove troublesome in other areas.

More radical institutional reforms can be imagined. In particular, the establishment of Banking Union's SSM, and the location of prudential supervision of euro-area banks within the ECB (broadly speaking), might suggest some policy momentum towards a "twin peaks" institutional structure, and the possible location (ultimately) of parallel conduct/investor-protection related supervision/regulation in a distinct EU agency.[85]

[82] Its consumer protection subgroup, e.g., has focused on cross-selling and complaints handling: 2013 Work Programme of the Joint Committee (JC-2013-002) and 2014 Work Programme (JC-2013–051).

[83] It has, e.g., signalled its intention to address the sale by banks of complex, convertible bank debt: *Financial Times* (May 20, 2014): "European Regulators Seek to Limit Retail Sales of Bank Debt".

[84] e.g., EBA, Financial Innovation and Consumer Protection. An Overview of the Objectives and Work of the EBA's Standing Committee on Financial Innovation (SCFI) in 2011–2012 (2012) and EBA Consumer Trends Report (2014).

[85] Some support for a twin peaks (SSM/ECB; and another conduct/investor protection actor) arrangement came from the Responses to the Commission's ESFS Consultation, e.g., from (from the consumer sector) BEUC and EuroFinuse and (from the public

Certainly, the retail market interest is at risk of being overlooked within the ESFS as it adjusts to the new SSM/ECB dynamic. Something of a battle for territory between NCAs, ESMA, and the ECB can be predicted with respect to risk-related issues, and with respect to the interface between market conduct supervision (NCAs/ESMA) and prudential supervision (ECB/SSM). The 2013 ECB/SSM Regulation[86] excludes investment firms and financial institutions covered within the prudential supervision of a banking group, and allocates only identified prudential tasks to the ECB/SSM. But it is an axiom of the crisis era that risks must be addressed in a cross-sectoral manner. Accordingly, careful co-ordination will be needed between NCAs concerned with market conduct and the ECB/SSM with respect to the supervision of multi-function banking groups with significant market operations, whether carried out by group credit institutions or group investment firms. The need for co-ordination is acknowledged in Article 3(1) of the 2013 ECB/SSM Regulation, which provides for the ECB to enter into agreements with NCAs "responsible for markets in financial instruments".[87] In this institutionally complex environment, it is not unlikely that ESMA will become the natural forum for co-ordinating NCAs' positions in ECB discussions with respect to the sensitive prudential/conduct interface, and for co-ordinating other related dealings with the ECB/SSM. While there are risks to ESMA in carrying out such a delicate role, the need for co-ordination may allow ESMA to strengthen its position in EU financial market governance, and to operate as a counterweight to the ECB institutionally.[88] The retail interest may accordingly become side-lined.

The outcome of the Commission's 2013/2014 review of the ESFS/ESAs remains to be seen. Overall, however, while some refinements to support the retail interest (for example, a strengthening of the ESA Joint Committee) are possible and desirable, more radical institutional change is unlikely, given current political, institutional, and constitutional realities, and premature, given market conditions.

sector) the Finnish Ministry of Finance. These calls are longstanding. In 2009, FIN-USE (then the EU's major retail market stakeholder), in the context of the ESFS discussions, called for a European Financial Users Authority (FIN-USE, Communication on Financial Supervision (2009)).

[86] Council Regulation (EU) No 1024/2013 [2013] OJ L287/63.

[87] Similarly, rec. 33 to the 2013 ECB/SSM Regulation calls for agreements between the ECB and NCAs for markets in financial instruments which describe how these actors will co-operate in their performance of supervisory tasks.

[88] The European Parliament, e.g., has been concerned to shore up the powers of the ESAs within the SSM and in relation to the ECB: European Parliament, Resolution on the European System of Financial Supervision, March 11, 2014 (P7_TA-PROV(2014)020).

References

Barkow, E. (2010). "Insulating agencies: Avoiding capture through institutional design". *Texas Law Review* 89: 15–79.

Black, B. and J. Gross (2005). "The elusive balance between investor protection and wealth creation". *Pace Law Review* 26(27): 27–38.

Black, J. (2003). "Enrolling actors in regulatory processes: Examples from UK financial services regulation". *Public Law* [Spring]: 62–90.

Black, J. (2006). "Involving Consumers on Securities Regulation". Report for the Taskforce to Modernize Securities Regulation in Canada.

Burkart, O. and A. Bouveret (2012). "Systemic risk due to retailization?" *ESRB Macro-prudential Commentaries* 3.

Busuioc, M. (2013). "Rule-making by the European financial supervisory authorities: Walking a tight rope". *European Law Journal* 19(1): 111–125.

Campbell, J., H. Jackson, B. Madrian, and P. Tufano (2009). "Consumer financial protection". *Journal of Economic Perspectives* 25(1): 91–114.

Chater, N., S. Huck, R. Inderst, and Online Interactive Research Ltd. (2010). "Consumer decision making in retail investment services: A behavioural economics perspective". Final Report. Decision Technology Ltd.

Coffee, J. (2012). "The political economy of Dodd-Frank: Why financial reform tends to be frustrated and systemic risk perpetuated". Cornell Law Review 97: 1019–1082.

European Central Bank (2013). The Eurosystem Household Financial and Consumption Survey, Results from the First Wave, Statistics Paper Series 2.

Demarigny, F., J. McMahon, and N. Robert (2013). "Review of the new European system of financial supervision. Part 1: The work of the European supervisory agencies". Study for the ECON Committee (IP/A/ECON/ST/2012–23).

Esty, D. (2006). "Good governance at the supranational scale: Globalizing administrative law". *Yale Law Journal* 115: 1490–1563.

Everson, M. (2012). "A technology of expertise: EU financial services agencies". *LEQS Working Paper* No 49/2012.

Georgosouli, A. (2011). "The FSA's 'treating customers fairly' (TCF) initiative: What is so good about it and why it may not work". *Journal of Law and Society* 38(3): 405–427.

IOSCO (International Organization of Securities Commissions) (2011). "Mitigating Systemic Risk. A Role for Securities Regulators". *Discussion Paper*.

Jackson, H. (2007). "A system of selective substitute compliance". *Harvard International Law Journal* 48: 105–110.

Kingsford Smith, D. (2009). "Regulating investment risk: Individuals and the global financial crisis". *University of New South Wales Law Journal* 32(2): 514–546.

Kingsford Smith, D. and O. Dixon (2015). "The consumer interest and financial markets". In N. Moloney, E. Ferran, and J. Payne (eds.). *The Oxford Handbook of Financial Regulation*. Oxford University Press, in press.

Langevoort, D. and R. Thomson (2013). "IPOs and the Slow Death of Section 5". *Working Paper*, available at http://ssrn.com/abstract=2316858.

Moloney, N. (2010a). *How to Protect Investors. Lessons from the EC and the UK*. Cambridge University Press.

Moloney, N. (2010b). "Regulating the retail markets: Law, policy, and the financial crisis". *Current Legal Problems* 63(1): 375–447.

Moloney, N. (2011). "The European securities and markets authority: A tale of two competences. Part (1) rule-making". *European Business Organization Law Review* 12(1): 41–86.

Moloney, N. (2014). *EU Securities and Financial Markets Regulation*. 3rd Edition. Oxford University Press.

Roe, M. (1991). "Political elements in the creation of a mutual fund industry". *University of Pennsylvania Law Review* 139: 1469–1511.

Synovate (2011). Consumer Market Study on Advice within the Area of Retail Investment Services – Final Report. Prepared for: European Commission, Directorate-General Heath and Consumer Protection.

Williams, T. (2007). "Empowerment of whom and for what? Financial literacy education and the new regulation of consumer financial services". *Law and Policy* 29(2): 226–256.

11

Financial advice

ANDREAS HACKETHAL[1]

Introduction

Financial advice should aid households in making better financial decisions. Yet, the market for financial advice might not work in full favor of households. Financial advice is a credence good, where service quality is difficult to observe and advisors often face conflicted interests. As a result, there might be too much of one type of financial advice that does not improve household decision making and too little of another, more beneficial type of advice. And, possibly, those households that would benefit most from good advice do not take any advice or they take the wrong advice.

Without question, financial advice plays an important role in financial decisions by households on both sides of the Atlantic. The estimated size of the financial planning and advice industry in the United States was US$39 billion in 2010,[2] and, according to survey data, at least one in two European households regularly turns to a financial advisor.[3]

Financial decisions of households – and the professional financial advice that influences many of these decisions – affect wealth accumulation, wealth distribution and financial market stability in an economy. On the asset side, household savings translate into funds for real investments so that the household portfolio composition affects capital allocation. If households shift funds from bank deposits into stock investments, this also alters the risk allocation in an economy. Moreover, financial

[1] Professor of Personal Finance, Goethe University. I thank Michalis Haliassos and Tabea Bucher-Koenen for very helpful comments.

[2] www.ibisworld.com/industry/default.aspx?indid=1316.

[3] Chater et al. (2010) report a number of 58 percent for Europe; Hackethal and Inderst (2011) find an even higher number of 75 percent for Germany.

transactions of households can affect securities prices.[4] On the liability side, mortgage and consumer loans leverage household investment risk and make household insolvency more likely. Credit defaults impair the asset quality of financial intermediaries. Financial advice that leads to better individual decisions should therefore lead to better outcomes not only for the private household sector, but also for the financial system and the economy at large.[5]

The next section presents selected observations on investment mistakes of households who do not take advice, but act self-directedly. I will then discuss (in the third section) possible fixes for these mistakes and I will focus on financial advice as the most promising fix. The fourth section summarizes empirical evidence on the actual impact of financial advice on household portfolios and, against this background, assesses the latest regulatory initiatives around investor protection. The fifth section presents three selected ideas of how to better seize the welfare potential of financial advice. The sixth section sketches out promising avenues for future research on advice. The last section concludes the chapter with policy implications. I will focus on household investments into risky assets throughout the chapter because this is the area which boasts the most empirical evidence. Most results and conclusions, however, will carry over to liquidity management, borrowing and purchasing insurance.

Individual investor behavior in the absence of financial advice

Transaction records and portfolio data from online broker clients allow us to study the investment behavior of those households who do not seek advice but who trade self-directedly. The results are therefore not affected by advisor recommendations.[6] Figure 11.1 plots the investment

[4] Shleifer and Summers (1990) develop "the noise trader approach to finance" and argue that changes in investor sentiment are not fully countered by arbitrageurs and so affect security returns. Barber et al. (2009) are motivated by this theory and find that for small stocks, and over short horizons, retail investor trades move markets.

[5] Gennaioli et al. (2012) show in their model how trust-mediated financial advice can also impede arbitrage and as a consequence destabilize financial markets.

[6] The findings for online broker clients do not necessarily carry over to all retail investors who refuse to take advice. Online broker clients might refuse advice primarily due to overconfidence. Other self-directed investors might lack awareness of advice or access to advisors. Yet, online broker clients are the largest and therefore also the most relevant group of self-directed investors in Germany.

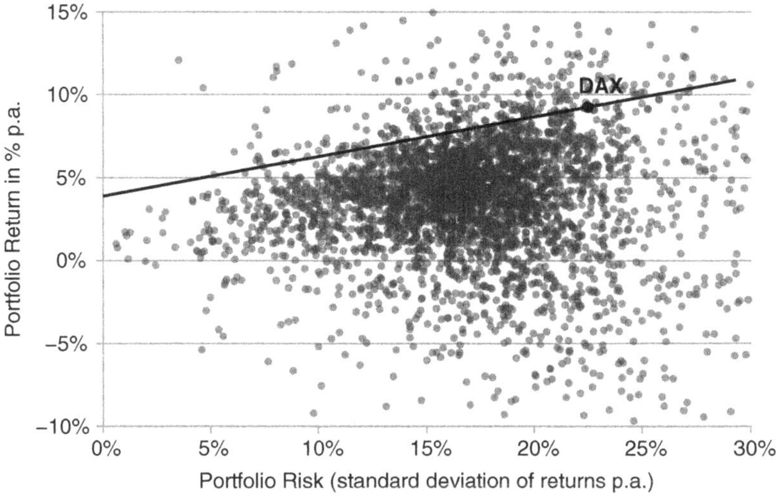

Figure 11.1 Portfolio return and risk profiles for 3,400 online broker clients (2003–2012)

performance of 3,400 clients of a German online brokerage throughout the 10-year period from 2003 to 2012.[7] The vertical axis measures annualized portfolio returns net of cost and the horizontal axes measures the annualized standard deviations of portfolio returns. Net portfolio performance differs widely among self-directed retail investors. When measured by the Sharpe Ratio, 81 percent of investors end up below the German Stock Index DAX and 72 percent of investors end up below the MSCI World Index in Euro terms (not shown in Figure 11.1). The figure also indicates that underperformance is not trivial, and for many investors it amounts to over 5 percentage points per year.

Meyer et al. (2012) apply bootstrapping simulations introduced by Fama and French (2010) to disentangle skill and luck in portfolio performance measurement. They find that over 90 percent of the online brokerage clients in their dataset incur below-market portfolio returns not because of bad luck, but because they suffer from investment biases and repeatedly make costly investment mistakes. Average abnormal portfolio returns amount to −8 percent after costs and per annum. The stark underperformance of German retail investors due to negative

[7] For further details on the dataset, see Weber et al. (2014).

investment skills echoes the results in Barber et al. (2009) for Taiwanese investors.

What are the likely causes of this skill-based return gap? There is abundant evidence that individual investors make investment mistakes (see e.g. Barber and Odean 2011) and a few papers also measure the cost of these investment mistakes (see e.g. Calvet et al. 2007). Barber and Odean (2000) show that some investors overtrade – that is, the extra trading costs exceed any extra returns by more than 2 percentage points per year on average. More recently, Weber et al. (2014) have simultaneously analyzed the impact of multiple investment patterns on portfolio performance. They regress individual portfolio performance on ten measures of investment patterns proposed in the literature, among them the disposition effect, trade clustering, trend chasing, the home bias, and lottery stock preference. They find that most patterns do not impact performance significantly. For example, quite a few investors exhibit a strong disposition effect and also trend chasing behavior, but over the years they did not perform differently from the average sample investor. The only three patterns that turned out to significantly diminish performance were excessive trading (as measured by portfolio turnover), under-diversification (as measured by the fraction of diversifiable risk in total portfolio risk), and the propensity to hold stocks with lottery-like characteristics (low price, high idiosyncratic volatility, and high idiosyncratic skewness). Investors who fell prey to these patterns suffered from risk-adjusted return losses of more than 6 percentage points per year, as compared to a group of investors for whom these patterns could not be observed. It might seem surprising that under-diversification not only affects portfolio risk but also abnormal returns (–4 percent on average). The authors suggest that their under-diversification variable picks up all kinds of noise trading behavior, such as trading on uninformed opinions and signals. For example, Etheber (2014) finds that quite a few retail investors seem to use technical trading rules (e.g. based on the 200-day moving average price) to initiate trades and that these investors do not use a diversified basket of stocks to implement the respective strategy but rather single stocks. Even though under-diversification might not be the root cause of the return gap, improving diversification should still help in closing the gap because it assists investors in avoiding various types of costly trading strategies.

The fact that costly under-diversification is so prevalent among retail investors indicates broader deficiencies of retail investors in dealing with

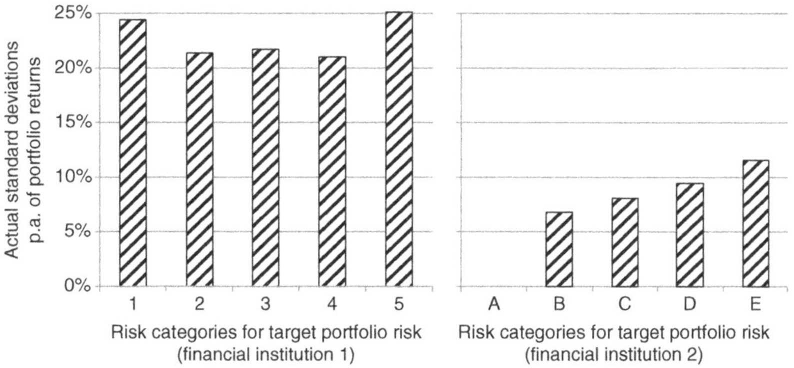

Figure 11.2 Comparison of stated risk preferences and average actual portfolio risk
Note: The bar charts in both panels show average annual standard deviations of portfolio returns for five client groups. Standard deviations were calculated based on weekly returns for the period 1/2007–12/2008 (left panel) and for the period 5/2009–4/2010 (right panel), respectively. Clients were divided into groups according to their ex ante choice of desired portfolio risk. Portfolios in category 1 (A) are typically referred to as "conservative" portfolios and those from category 5 (E) are typically referred to as "speculative" portfolios. Reading example: The portfolio returns of self-directed clients of financial institution 1 who reported ex ante that they prefer risk level 2 ("moderate risk") had an average standard deviation p.a. of 21.5 percent in 2007 and 2008. The left panel shows data for 14,063 self-directed clients of financial institution 1. The right panel shows data for 384 advised clients of financial institution 2. Both institutions use broadly similar questionnaires to guide clients toward their desired risk level.

investment risk.[8] For investors that do not adhere to one of the most basic rules of sound investment – namely, eradicating idiosyncratic risk in their portfolios – it is likely that they also fail to manage overall portfolio risk to be in line with their preferences. The left panel in Figure 11.2 shows anecdotal evidence consistent with this conjecture. Clients of German online brokers are required to state their target risk level for their portfolio. Most brokers use similar questionnaires to give their clients guidance in setting their desired risk levels. In our example, the questions cover investment horizon, income, age, financial literacy and risk aversion and clients have to check one out of five boxes that run from "very conservative" to "speculative." We found the questionnaire sensible and presume that client choice is positively correlated to their true desired risk level.

[8] Lusardi and Mitchell (2014) indicate that financial literacy is particularly low among households around the world when it comes to risk diversification. Over 30 percent of US, German, Italian and Dutch households are not familiar with this concept.

The left panel Figure 11.2 reports average standard deviations of portfolio returns for five client groups according to their desired portfolio risk level. We should expect that average portfolio risk is much lower for conservative investors than for aggressive investors. The data, however, speaks another language. Average portfolio risk is not very different across the five groups, indicating either that retail investors do not care for managing portfolio risk or that they lack the necessary information and the skills to gauge the risk of their holdings. As a consequence, retail investors might not only face a return gap, but might also face a discrepancy between desired portfolio risk and actual portfolio risk.

Taken together, the results suggest that retail investors suffer from systematic investment mistakes and that fixes for the resulting return gap should specifically address over-trading, lottery stock trading and under-diversification. Because under-diversification is much more prevalent among retail investors than over-trading and lottery-stock trading, fixes should especially address under-diversification. Any fix for the return gap needs to take into account poor risk management skills on the side of retail investors and should ideally help them in steering their portfolio risk better.

Potential fixes for investment mistakes

There are three groups of potential strategies to remedy investment mistakes and, in particular, to close the return gap. Fixes from the first group aim at improving financial literacy and equipping investors with more and better information so that they can avoid mistakes on their own.[9] This liberal approach builds on autonomy, self-governance and freedom of choice. Most regulators around the world have advocated this general approach, which is often referred to as the "information model."[10]

Fixes from the second group take the decision away from investors or confine their choice set substantially. Examples are mandatory public pension schemes and outright product bans (direct investments into hedge funds are not permitted for German retail investors). Fixes from the third group build upon financial advice, be it in the form of full

[9] Lusardi and Mitchell (2014: 5) define financial literacy as "people's ability to process economic information and make informed decisions about financial planning, wealth accumulation, debt, and pensions."

[10] See Chapter 14 in this volume on household finance and the law by Katja Langenbucher.

delegation of investment decisions to a portfolio manager, ad hoc investment recommendations, or some online investment tool that uses algorithms to turn investor input into automatic advice.

Educating households

Fernandes et al. (2014) summarize the extant empirical evidence on fixes from the first group. They conducted a meta-analysis of over 200 empirical studies that measure the impact of financial literacy on financial behavior. The average effect of financial education programs is very small across all studies and even the learning effects from multiple day trainings appear to erode very quickly.[11] Plus, any significant correlations between literacy and behavior reported in these studies might to a large extent be merely due to an omitted variable bias.[12] Once psychological traits such as confidence in the value of information search and the propensity to make long-term financial plans are included as controls the coefficient for literacy becomes insignificant. In concluding, the authors advocate "just-in-time" financial education measures – possibly embedded into trustworthy recommender systems – when the decision at hand is consumer-specific, and they champion nudges in the spirit of Thaler and Sunstein (2008) when the optimal decision is homogenous across investors.[13]

When going through the same decision process multiple times, investors might learn, and when repeatedly observing adverse outcomes from their decisions they might want to adapt their behavior. So perhaps plain practicing is the best education program of all, and accumulating experience works even better than "just-in-time" education. The study by Köstner et al. (2012) casts doubt on the general efficacy of the experience

[11] Both Hastings et al. (2012) and Lusardi and Mitchell (2014) acknowledge substantial disagreement in the surveyed literature over the efficacy of financial education programs. Lusardi and Mitchell (2014) presume that extant cost-benefit analyses have not done enough justice to the endogeneity of household investment into financial literacy (human capital approach) and the ensuing heterogeneity among households in financial knowledge and financial behavior. They suggest that financial education programs be targeted to the specific needs of household groups and that education programs should be viewed as complements to stricter regulation and product simplification.

[12] Clark et al. (2014) find that investors with better financial knowledge have higher expected risk-adjusted returns than their less knowledgeable peers. However, they observe no correlation between knowledge and diversification and they cannot explain the precise causal link between knowledge and portfolio profitability.

[13] Cole et al. (2011) conducted a field experiment in Indonesia and document that small pecuniary incentives had a much stronger impact than targeted education programs.

channel.[14] The authors measure the propensity of online brokerage clients to make investment mistakes during an eight-year period. Although the average trader had made over 300 trades in more than 80 different securities over this period, average portfolio diversification did not improve and the disposition effect did not diminish to any meaningful degree. Only portfolio turnover and, as a consequence, trading costs declined. The fact that trading costs are easier to observe and more salient than the efficiency loss from poor diversification suggests that learning is not a function of experience alone, but requires easy-to-understand feedback on individual behavior.

In summary, existing evidence negates a strong case for broader financial education programs or for learning-by-doing in today's trading environments. Rather, for education exercises to be effective they should be context-relevant, applied in small doses and extremely easy to comprehend. One obvious option for financial institutions that want to help their (self-directed) clients to make better decisions is to rigorously simplify their trading process and to integrate just-in-time cues and intuitive guidance (see "Three ideas on how to enhance the value of financial advice" for some examples).

Patronizing households

Evidence on the merits of paternalistic measures from the second group of fixes is scarce. Yet, the paper by Bhattacharya et al. (2014) allows the drawing of some inferences on how a hypothetical policy that obliged investors to purchase only well-diversified products would bear on investment behavior. They analyze how portfolio performance changes when online brokerage clients reallocate their funds from actively managed mutual funds and single stock investments into passively managed index funds. Surprisingly, overall portfolio performance remains unaltered for most investors, and even deteriorates for some investors through the usage of index funds. The positive effects from portfolio diversification are counterbalanced by a surge in poor market timing activities. Because index funds track market indices, users of these instruments seem to be more tempted to time that very market than when they use actively managed funds that cut across several market segments.

[14] Seru et al. (2010) found that learning from trading works predominantly through realizing that one's own trading skills are poor and that one should rather stop trading altogether.

Although the group of early ETF-adopters scrutinized by Bhattacharya et al. (2014) is probably not representative for all retail investors, this finding still demonstrates that paternalistic measures can have unintended consequences for the behavior and welfare of particular investor groups. Moreover, paternalistic measures always run the risk of curbing welfare-enhancing innovation.

Ultimately, if neither broad financial education programs nor learning-by-doing hold the promise to fully fix investor mistakes, and if paternalistic measures are not acceptable, then we should focus on the third group of fixes – namely, financial advice.

The role of financial advice

Hackethal et al. (2012) compare the long-term portfolio performance of self-directed clients to that of advised clients from the same German bank. The bank earns inducements from product providers for the products that bank advisors sell to clients. On average, advised clients underperform self-directed clients. The authors also document that advised clients are older, wealthier and more experienced than self-directed investors. Although the authors cannot fully rule out omitted variable biases and endogeneity issues, they feel confident to conjecture that this underperformance stems from the mediocre quality of advice. Generally speaking, financial advisors are similar to babysitters, in that they are hired for a job that their clients could do better but want to delegate to save precious time.

At face value, the mediocre performance of advised portfolios suggests that when the quality of advice is improved, the performance of clients will also improve. Many policymakers around the world seem to subscribe to this view, and I will discuss recent policy measures in the next subsection.

The problem of low investor adherence to good advice

Bhattacharya et al. (2012) demonstrate that such regulation might not be sufficient to close the return gap of advised clients. In a field study design they investigated what happens to the portfolio performance of clients when a bank introduces a fee-only advisory model. The advisory model had been designed by the bank according to textbook prescriptions on building efficient portfolios that match client risk preferences. The right panel in Figure 11.2 above shows the portfolio risk implied by the recommendations. Clients who stated that they target high portfolio risk (category E) obtained recommendations that directed them toward a portfolio with about twice the standard deviation of portfolios from category B, which were recommended to clients with higher risk aversion. Yet, when Bhattacharya et al. (2012) measured the actual performance of clients who opted into the new fee-only model, they obtained results reminiscent of those in Hackethal et al. (2012). Advised clients do not perform better than self-directed clients. The simple explanation for these results, championed by the authors, is that clients do not adhere to advisor recommendations. In fact, they document that not a single advisory client fully implemented the advice she or he received. Some clients even purchased *more* of the securities that the bank advised them to sell. This is despite the fact that adherence would have paid off for almost all clients in the sample. There is a positive correlation between advice adherence and performance improvement.[15] This result teaches an obvious and important lesson: good financial advice will serve as an effective fix for investment mistakes only if clients adhere to this advice.

Recent work by Germann (2014) on the determinants of client satisfaction with professional advice points toward a delicate challenge for advisors who strive for high client adherence to their advice. Client satisfaction was retrieved through randomized surveys subsequent to advisory meetings. Covariates include the number of recent advisory meetings, the product usage of the client (including loan and insurance products) and demographic variables such as age, income, wealth and financial literacy. Also included as covariates are portfolio characteristics, such as transaction fees, portfolio volume, portfolio turnover, abnormal portfolio returns, standard deviation of past portfolio returns and the share of idiosyncratic risk in total portfolio risk. Maybe not surprisingly, Germann finds a negative relation between total portfolio risk and client satisfaction. Much more surprisingly, however, he finds a significantly positive relation between the idiosyncratic portfolio risk and client satisfaction. Advisory clients seem to be looking for "safe bets" that promise moderate total risk but still allow for a substantial upside. That presents advisors with a dilemma. If advisors cater to these preferences they

[15] Hackethal et al. (2012) analyzed data from two other financial institutions and found no such positive relation between adherence to advice and portfolio performance. This suggests that for these two institutions, poor client performance is driven more by the poor quality of advice than by poor client adherence to high-quality advice.

reinforce their clients' misperceptions about risk and returns and clients will most likely end up with inefficient portfolios and a return gap. If advisors attempt to de-bias their clients they run the risk of low customer satisfaction scores and perhaps of losing the client to another advisor.[16]

There are important parallels with the health sector. According to a broad study by the World Health Organization from 2003, approximately half of individuals with chronic diseases did not adhere to the therapies recommended to them by their doctors. Non-adherence has dire and sometimes lethal consequences for many patients. The World Health Organization infers from this result that the health sector should focus less on inventing new therapies and instead redirect resources into finding instruments that improve adherence.

What are the likely causes for poor adherence to professional financial advice? I suspect that investors believe that they would not benefit from the advice either because they distrust the advisor or because they are overconfident in their own skills. Alternatively, they might subscribe to the general benefits of advice but then find it too arduous or costly to implement all recommendations. Those obstacles need to be tackled differently. If a lack of trust or overconfidence is the main driver then the key may lie in confronting clients with facts on their current performance and on how much they would benefit from adherence. If implementation costs are the main drivers then we need to think about ways to simplify adherence and to help people stick to their plans. Recent empirical work on the role of self-control in building up financial wealth suggests that the lack of self-control might in fact play a key role when it comes to sticking to financial plans. Using US survey data, Biljanovska and Palligkinis (2014) find a strong correlation between household wealth and three constituents of self-control (ability for goal-setting, monitoring, and committing to earlier set goals). People who do not set goals, who do not check their finances regularly and who easily fall victim to temptations are ceteris paribus less wealthy than people with better self-control.[17]

[16] Mullainathan et al. (2012) used an audit methodology to reveal that participating advisors reinforced client biases. Some of those advisors might have used these tactics primarily to achieve client satisfaction.

[17] People can display low levels of self-control for many reasons. Some people might have a preference for low control levels and others might expect to incur prohibitively high costs from self-control. Institutions that want to help their clients in achieving more self-control therefore need be careful to devise and communicate the right instruments to the right client groups.

In conclusion, at least two necessary conditions need be in place for financial advice to add value for clients: high quality of advice (in essence, matching clients with well diversified portfolios that reflect their risk preferences), and high adherence to advice. Both in Europe and the US, investor protection regulation has focused almost exclusively on the quality of advice, but hardly at all on measures that ensure adherence to high-quality advice.[18]

The efficacy of recent investor protection regulation

The following quote from the European Commission's recast proposal (2011, p. 27) for a directive on markets in financial instruments (MiFID II) is symptomatic:

> The continuous relevance of personal recommendations for clients and the increasing complexity of services and instruments require enhancing the conduct of business obligations in order to strengthen the protection of investors. ... In order to give all relevant information to investors, it is appropriate to require investment firms providing investment advice to clarify the basis of the advice they provide, notably the range of products they consider in providing personal recommendations to clients, whether they provide investment advice on an independent basis and whether they provide the clients with the on-going assessment of the suitability of the financial instruments recommended to them. ... In order to strengthen the protection of investors and increase clarity to clients as to the service they receive, it is appropriate to further restrict the possibility for firms to accept or receive inducements from third parties, and particularly from issuers or product providers, when providing the service of investment advice on an independent basis and the service of portfolio management.

In this very spirit, the UK and the Netherlands have recently imposed general bans on product inducements for all financial advisors. Germany has banned inducements only for those advisors who wish to carry the title "fee-only advisor" ("Honoraranlageberater"). Such advisors must also provide their clients access to the full spectrum of suitable products in the market. All other advisor types may still accept inducements and pick products from a narrow menu, but they are now obliged to hand out standardized product brochures to clients each time they present a

[18] For an overview of these regulatory measures, see Hackethal and Inderst (2013).

product and to prepare detailed minutes for each advisory meeting. Each individual advisor needs to be registered with the financial services authority and he or she must demonstrate certain minimum qualifications. All client complaints need to be relayed to the authority. Finally, financial institutions that want to offer both fee-based advice and commission-based advice must fully separate both models in their organization and must clarify to the client which model she obtains.

Available empirical evidence casts some doubt on the efficacy of regulatory measures that exclusively focus on the quality of advice. Germann (2014) used a difference-in-difference research design to measure the impact of mandatory advisory meeting minutes on the composition and performance of some 3,000 client portfolios of a German retail bank.

He failed to find any significant effect. One explanation is that clients find these minutes too difficult to absorb and, in particular, that clients are not able to connect their individual investment results to the minutes of a particular meeting. In this case, banks have no incentive to adapt their recommendations in response to the obligation to produce minutes.

Beshears et al. (2009) conducted experiments on how the presentation of product information influences investor decisions. They found that summary prospectuses on mutual funds did not lead to different purchasing decisions than much more detailed (and complex) statutory prospectuses for the same products. Moreover, the studies surveyed in Loewenstein et al. (2011) cast doubt on the effectiveness of mandatory disclosure of advisor conflicts of interest. When advisors placed a warning sign on their desk, they felt more comfortable giving biased advice and the adherence rate of clients actually went up.

The available evidence thus suggests that recent regulatory measures have not been conducive to close the return gap of retail investors. A straightforward explanation for this failure would likely be that none of these measures address adherence to good advice. Plus, there are technical issues that preclude incumbent players from embracing the new advisory models advocated by policymakers. For example, the mandatory internal separation of fee-only advice from commission-based advice might prove a serious impediment for financial institutions to introduce the model across the board. Because not all clients will want to opt into fee-only advice, and because the same advisor must not offer both types of advice to clients, many clients would need to be re-assigned to a new advisor. Interference with long-term client relationships is risky, and this risk will probably make many financial institutions shy away from offering strictly regulated fee-only advice. Incumbent players will instead attempt to steer their wealthier clients into portfolio management services that entail full delegation of investment decisions from the client to the financial institution in exchange for a fee proportional to portfolio size. The same financial institutions might pull out of conventional investment advice and steer less wealthy clients into execution-only models or savings and insurance products. The separation of advice imposed by recent regulation might therefore result in less advice across the board, and especially in less advice for the people who need it most.

In anticipation of these market reactions, regulators will probably need to give consideration to alternative measures when they aim to narrow the return gap experienced by retail investors. These alternative measures should directly or indirectly address the lack of trust, the lack of self-control and the perceived implementation costs to both financial institutions and clients.

Three ideas on how to enhance the value of financial advice

In what follows I sketch out three selected measures that each address one or more of the obstacles identified above – that is, the lack of trust (sometimes combined with overconfidence), the lack of self-control, and perceived high implementation costs.

Smart portfolio disclosure

The first measure proceeds from the observation that most clients do not observe and therefore do not know the risk and return profile of their holdings (see also Glaser and Weber 2007). This is not surprising given the fact that very few banks and brokerages in Europe report portfolio performance in a meaningful way to their clients. For example, the owners of the portfolios depicted in Figure 11.1 do not get any information about the location of their own portfolio in the diagram from their brokerage. Moreover, computing returns and their standard deviations from the available information at hand is virtually impossible for most clients. Therefore, most clients can be assumed to be ignorant about their own return gap compared to a market benchmark or compared to a reasonable peer group of investors. They are most likely also ignorant about their total portfolio risk and about the fraction of diversifiable risk in total risk. Without all this information there is too little impetus for self-directed investors to adapt their investment behavior, and there are too few reference points to judge the quality of advice, for example, in terms of steering portfolio risk.

Clear, simple and salient portfolio reports that feature a few standardized indicators are a possible fix for this problem. As part of a commissioned study for a large German consumer protection organization a team of researchers from Goethe University tested several such indicators and alternative graphical depictions with several thousand participants in an online survey, and with a smaller group of participants in structured discussion groups. The feedback from these exercises suggests that the three key indicators that help investors in building an opinion about the appropriateness of their portfolio are the absolute change in portfolio value over the past period (due to price changes, dividends, coupon payments, and product/transaction cost), time-weighted average portfolio returns net of cost, and portfolio risk. Most investors had problems understanding and comparing risk measures such as standard deviations of returns or value at risk, and they had problems inferring the risk in their portfolio from graphs that showed daily or weekly portfolio value fluctuations.

Participants in the discussion groups seemed to comprehend risk profiles much better when they were confronted with simple graphical scales that sorted portfolios into risk categories according to their historical return distributions. The maximum number of categories that people seemed to be willing to accept for assessing portfolio risk was six, and the preferred graphical representation was symbols instead of numbers. Hackethal and Inderst (2011) demonstrate that the choice of risk measure that is used to map portfolios into risk categories hardly affects the sorting of portfolios. Most portfolios of individual investors exhibit fairly symmetric return distributions so that standard deviation, value at risk and lower partial moments yield identical categorizations for over 90 percent of the portfolios in their large sample.[19]

In order to ensure comparability across periods, portfolios and institutions, all return and risk indicators for such simplified portfolio reports must be computed the very same way across all financial institutions. Such minimum standards for producing portfolio risk and return indicators must therefore be stipulated by an official authority. The standard

[19] Hackethal and Inderst (2011) also suggest adding a note to the portfolio risk profile which indicates whether the portfolio contains significant shares of instruments with high credit risk (not necessarily picked up by past return variability) or of instruments with nonlinear payout profiles that imply skewed or fat-tailed return distributions.

indicators have to be reported on a separate page and must not be buried in a convolute of extra information and data points. Of course, financial institutions would be free to use and enrich the standard indicators for the purpose of customized additional reports, just-in-time financial education measures or incentive-compatible advisor remuneration schemes.

A small but possibly powerful technical extension of standardized portfolio reports is to complement these reports with a data file containing the raw data that were used to calculate the return and risk indicators. Such a data file should include all individual transaction logs as well as portfolio balances and should be saved in a standardized format so that it is machine-readable. This approach is in the spirit of a "smart disclosure" of data which was recently promoted by the Obama administration (see the report from May 2013 on smart disclosure and consumer decision making commissioned by the National Science and Technology Council).[20] Computer-savvy investors could use the raw data for additional own analysis. The majority of investors, however, would probably rather upload the file to specialized websites (an example of what Richard Thaler calls choice engines) that facilitate further analyses and comparisons. For example, such analyses could include the computation of value-weighted averages of past portfolio returns (instead of time-weighted average returns) and the decomposition of total portfolio risk into systematic risk and diversifiable risk (both reported on a standardized scale).

Peer comparisons could further help put an investor's individual portfolio results into perspective. In particular, investors might find it helpful to learn how other individual portfolios from the same risk category performed over the past.[21] What has been the average performance in this category and in other categories? How much portfolio risk did other investors from a peer group with comparable age, wealth and family status bear over the observation period? How well diversified were the portfolios of investors with above-median portfolio performance? Ideally, investors infer from these results whether their portfolio risk was in line with their preferences, whether they earned a fair return on that risk and whether portfolio risk was perhaps inflated because of poor diversification. Self-directed (and possibly overconfident) investors,

[20] Loewenstein et al. (2013) discuss evidence on the various factors enhancing the effectiveness of disclosure policies.

[21] If uploading the data is voluntary, the choice engine must thoroughly deal with potential selection biases. One possible solution would be to stratify the sample by inviting investors from under-represented investor groups and institutions.

who are confronted with a return gap relative to their peers and with undesired levels of portfolio risk, might take this evidence seriously and adapt their behavior or seek advice as a consequence. Clients of advisors can use this evidence to assess whether their advisor kept his promises in terms of total portfolio risk, diversification levels and long-term returns net of advisory fees and product costs. Advisors themselves could use these data from their clients' portfolios to demonstrate their skills to existing and potential new clients.[22] Repeated solid performance would probably instill more trust among clients into the skills of the particular advisor and possibly increase adherence to advisor recommendations.

For clients with low adherence, advisors could also use the reports ex post to demonstrate how much the client would have benefited if she had followed their recommendations. For example, the advisor could open up an extra virtual portfolio for the client that is strictly managed according to the advisor's recommendations. At the end of the period the risk and return profile of that virtual portfolio (full adherence) could be compared to the risk and return profile of the actual portfolio (low adherence). Any performance differentials must be due to incomplete client adherence to advice plus execution-only transactions by the client. Extant empirical evidence on the poor portfolio performance of self-directed retail investors (see, for example, Figure 11.1) suggests that such comparisons would equip advisors who recommend efficient portfolios with convincing arguments for better client adherence.

I also expect websites to emerge that collect a large number of portfolio reports or corresponding data files from the clients of different banks and brokerages and then report aggregate portfolio results per institution. Based on these reports, banks and their advisors could be ranked according to risk management skills and long-term after-cost returns for client portfolios.[23] This newly gained transparency on the results of the advisory process possibly changes the credence good character of financial advice and also has the potential to induce higher adherence rates.[24] Once key aspects of financial advice are no longer obfuscated but get measured more accurately, financial institutions might focus more on

22 Choice engines would perhaps offer a service to verify advisor performance and thereby add credibility to such claims.

23 Already today, most if not all German banks track for each and every retail client transaction whether it was initiated by an advisor or whether it was execution-only. This transaction flag would allow banks to report aggregate portfolio indicators separately for high-adherence clients and for low-adherence clients.

24 This also allows for new pricing schemes for advice that tie fees to verifiable outcomes.

these aspects. As a result, competitive forces should increase the average quality of advice in the market.

Pension claim aggregation

The second measure is particularly concerned with retirement savings and aims at reducing the implementation costs of sound financial decision making. It provides investors access to already existing but dispersed and difficult to access data and can hence be viewed as another form of smart disclosure. When investors decide on how much to save and how much financial risk to bear, they need to take into account their current wealth situation. This applies in particular to saving for retirement, as saving for old age is a key savings and investment motive for most people in Europe's aging societies with their overburdened public pension schemes. Yet, only a few people know their pension claims on the public pension scheme and how much their savings in occupational or private pensions are worth today. In principle, they could collect that information from the paper reports which they obtain from their pension providers. But finding the right number on each report and aggregating the data into a consolidated claim is difficult because reporting standards differ widely. Translating current claims into future pensions is even more difficult because investment risk and cost are not transparent and knowing the math necessary for this kind of financial planning might be asking too much. Sweden (www.minpension.se) and Denmark (www.pensionsinfo.dk) have therefore established internet platforms that allow households to view all their pension claims from participating providers in one place so that they can use this information as a direct input into their investment decisions. By these means, households learn how much they have saved for retirement over the previous year, how much total savings have been accumulated over the entire past and how high the pension annuity can be expected to be under standard assumptions.

Of course, there are several prerequisites for these systems to work. A unique personal identifier is required that links clients with each contract they have with any pension provider. Data security and data confidentiality issues need to be resolved and a common data standard needs to be in place so that pension information can be retrieved and compiled automatically. Finally, standardized contract information with regards to administrative cost and investment risk are required to make forecasts as accurate as possible. The examples of the Scandinavian countries prove that the technological and data security issues are surmountable. The biggest challenge is probably the coordination of the large number of institutions involved, including insurance companies, pension funds and employers that administer unfunded pension schemes. Governments that like to install such a pension information platform in their country have to take the responsibility for initiating and coordinating the implementation process.

Portfolio management for the less wealthy

Currently, innovative financial services firms (so called fintechs and robo advisors) are mushrooming on both sides of the Atlantic. These firms use technology and insights from behavioral economics to help their clients in achieving their financial goals faster. They radically simplify the investment process and relay typical behavioral patterns of investors toward decisions in line with finance theory and individual long-term savings goals.[25] Product selection is limited to a set of low-cost index funds and investor guidance is not focused on product selection or market timing but on gauging portfolio risk and adapting saving patterns to consumption plans. The investment process itself is construed to minimize the chance of investment mistakes and to promote investor self-control.

Examples of such innovative offers include betterment from the US, nutmeg from the UK and vaamo from Germany.[26] All of these companies offer their clients an "all-inclusive solution" to invest according to textbook prescriptions and in particular according to the two-fund separation concept. There is only one risky asset that comprises stocks, bonds and real estate from all over the world. This ensures a high degree of diversification and precludes investments in lottery stocks or home bias. In their portfolio, clients then blend the risky asset with a quasi risk-free asset, so that it matches their preferences and risk capacity. This allows savers to select and manage the market risk of their investments more rigorously. Finally, clients have the opportunity to stipulate specific

[25] These new retail investment models can also be viewed as portfolio management services for the less wealthy. As mentioned above, incumbent players might shun the increasing regulatory costs of investment advice and steer their wealthier clients into portfolio management while pulling out of costly investment advice to the less wealthy clients. The new model might fill this void.

[26] Vaamo is a startup company supported by the incubator of Frankfurt University. I, as the author of this chapter, have an interest in the company and I act as the chairman of its supervisory board.

savings goals and to monitor the progress in achieving them. For example, a client can open a dedicated subaccount to save for the college education of her children. She is then asked to define the target amount, the target date and the target risk level for that savings goal. She can then deposit an initial investment into this particular account and start a monthly savings plan. Installments are set so that she will most likely reach the savings goal before the target date. As future scenarios unfold, she can obtain constant feedback on whether she is on track or whether she should adjust monthly savings or the risk level of her savings. Because there is only one underlying risky investment vehicle, the investments for all individual savings goals (if the client stipulated multiples of them) can be easily aggregated into total savings and total risk, equal to the weighted average risk across all savings goals.

These new financial services tackle at least three important behavioral patterns. First, and most importantly, they help investors to avoid underdiversified portfolios. They redirect investor attention away from seeking single investment opportunities from the huge menu of available financial instruments and toward seeking guidance on how to set and pursue higher-ranking savings objectives. Second, they help investors to gain more self-control when dealing with their personal finances. Goal setting and progress monitoring were found to be essential for successful long-term investment and both are integral to the investment process designed by the startups.[27] Third, the concept to save for specific goals also tackles the inclination of many people to compartmentalize their financial activities into mental accounts. A negative side effect of mental accounting is that the aggregate of all accounts is difficult to observe and therefore also difficult to optimize. People might pursue a high-risk strategy with their play money but invest overly conservatively when it comes to long-term savings. Their total portfolio might then end up poorly diversified and with a risk profile that does not match their overall preferences and goals. With goal-based, single-product saving the aggregate risk and return

[27] There are other tools that aid investors combating a third cause of self-control failure, namely yielding to spontaneous temptation. Impulse purchasing is a phenomenon where short-term satisfaction undermines achievement of long-term goals. An app launched by Austrian Erste Sparkasse in 2012 allows savers to engage in "impulse saving" as a response to the urge to purchase a nice-to-have product immediately. When urged, users can pull out their phone and push a single button that initiates the transfer of a pre-set amount from the transaction account to a savings account. Each savings account is dedicated to a specific long-term savings goal. The app makes the trade-off between impulse purchasing and long-term savings goals more tangible. See Mullainathan (2013) for further examples on how to make trade-offs more tangible for people that face slack as opposed to scarcity.

profile is directly observable and can be regularly checked against overall preferences and goals. The transparency of incurred risk and realized returns on, both the level of individual savings goals (possibly with different risk profiles) and the level of total savings should allow savers to better learn over time how different risk levels and savings patterns bear on achieving their financial goals.

The goal-based, single-product saving concept of the new services might in addition facilitate social interactions in the financial decision making process. With the high degree of standardization of the investment process, investment vehicle and reporting of investment outcomes, social interaction can be leveraged to achieve individual goals. In today's world of retail finance, it is virtually impossible for individual investors to discuss their investment strategy and the outcome of that strategy with their friends in a meaningful way. If neither investment risk nor investment outcomes are observable on a portfolio level, most such discussions will necessarily remain on a product or transaction level and therefore will remain incomplete or imprecise. Smart (and standardized) disclosure of portfolio results would already greatly facilitate such a discussion, but the implementation of insights gained from such discussions is much easier when both investors also share an investment process and investment vehicle.

Avenues for future research

Most empirical studies on the role of financial advice have either used an experimental research design or a field study design in conjunction with administrative data. Surveys are typically not rich enough when it comes to the ramifications of the financial decision at hand, and stated decisions can of course deviate from actual decisions and actions.

In my opinion, the next frontier for empirical research on financial advice is the combination of administrative data and survey data from the same group of individual investors. One such option is to build a large "hybrid" dataset that combines transaction data and account balances for many thousands of retail bank clients with their responses to a detailed questionnaire akin to the Eurosystem Household Finance and Consumption survey. Such a hybrid dataset would permit microscopic analyses of the composition and the determinants of financial balance sheets of a large number of households.

A second option is to build and administer a panel dataset that combines administrative bank data with responses from multiple waves of quick client surveys. Such client panels would permit researchers to run quasi experiments with real clients and on real-life financial decisions.[28] For example, the hypothesis formulated above – that investors would appreciate smart disclosure of their own portfolio data and that they would react in a sensible manner to this information – can be validated by sending reports with different styles to different client groups. One group would receive plain return and risk figures, another group would receive a graphical representation of their portfolio's risk and return, and yet other groups would receive extra benchmark data or extra information on the degree of portfolio diversification. A control group of investors would continue to receive the standard report of that bank. One could then compare subsequent transactions across the recipients of different report formats – controlling for a whole battery of variables from bank data and from survey data (including individual portfolio risk assessments after receiving the reports). This would allow inferring the marginal effect of specific report features on investor behavior. Such a client panel research design can of course be generalized to analyze all kinds of interventions and innovations that attempt to de-bias investor behavior.

A third option is to capitalize on the user data produced by young internet firms that aid clients in exerting more self-control over their own savings behavior. Administrative user data could again be complemented by client responses from quick context-specific questionnaires. This would help in elucidating the potential of online tools to substitute for personal financial advice in the long-term.

Conclusion and policy recommendations

This chapter has argued that most private households need sound financial advice to improve their financial wellbeing. Today, financial advice is widespread around the globe, but the available evidence suggests that it does not yet exploit its welfare potential. Recent investor protection initiatives by policymakers have focused on input factors to the production of financial advice, and most notably tried to tackle conflicted advisor incentive schemes and obfuscated product information. It appears that these initiatives have had no substantial positive impact on investor welfare. I hypothesize that this is mainly due to the fact that such

[28] As with all client surveys, selection bias can be a serious issue and researchers need to pursue a sound sample stratification strategy.

measures have not helped households in identifying high-quality financial advice and that they have not addressed the main obstacles to adhering to good financial advice: the lack of trust, the lack of self-control and the perception of high implementation costs. I suggest changing course and refocusing investor protection policies. Instead of confronting investors with general information on the input to advice and on all single products in the initial choice set, investors should instead be equipped with relevant data on the individual output of advice. "Smart disclosure" of past portfolio return and risk can steer investor and advisor attention away from product selection and toward the very aspects of financial advice that add value to clients: matching individual characteristics with efficient portfolios, and, more generally, managing a client's personal balance sheet in accordance with her long-term financial goals. The role of authorities in the context of smart portfolio disclosure would only be to set technical reporting standards and to enforce implementation. The disclosure of client portfolios' return and risk profiles should create better incentives for clients to adhere to good advice and to abandon poor advice. Disclosure should give advisors who persistently achieve good results a competitive edge and it should promote new remuneration schemes for advice, for which the price of advice is a function of the benefits from advice. I therefore consider smart disclosure of individual financial results as a core policy measure that should spark off a series of new retail financial services and business models with clear value propositions for specific consumer groups. For example, I would expect business models catering to households with little financial literacy to proliferate in the future. These models would offer an easy-to-implement, low-cost investment process, helping clients to avoid costly investment mistakes while at the same time focusing on achieving the clients' financial goals.

Smart disclosure also qualifies as a swift alternative measure to the strict legal ramifications of fee-only advice. As argued above, the mandatory organizational separation of fee-only advice from commission-based advice will likely preclude large incumbent players from embracing fee-only advice. Alternatively, regulators could liberate financial institutions from this organizational separation and in exchange require them to disclose portfolio returns net of cost and portfolio risk in a standardized format to all their clients. This newly gained transparency on the actual value of different advisory models might have a much stronger impact on the efficacy of the market for financial advice than further restrictions on the production of advice.

References

Barber, B. M. and T. Odean (2000). "Trading is Hazardous to Your Wealth: The Common Stock Investment Performance of Individual Investors." *The Journal of Finance* 55(2): 773–806.

Barber, B. M. and T. Odean (2009). "Do Retail Trades Move Markets?" *Review of Financial Studies* 22(1): 151–186.

Barber, Brad M. and Terrance Odean. (2011) "The Behavior of Individual Investors." Available at SSRN 1872211.

Barber, B.M., Y. T. Lee, Y. J. Liu and T. Odean (2009). "Just How Much Do Individual Investors Lose by Trading?" *Review of Financial Studies* 22(2): 609–632.

Barberis, N. and R. Thaler (2003). "A Survey of Behavioral Finance." In G. Constantinides, M. Harris and R. Stulz (eds.), *Handbook of the Economics of Finance.* Vol. 1. Amsterdam: North-Holland, 1053–1128.

Beshears, J., J. J. Choi, D. Laibson and B. C. Madrian (2009). "How Does Simplified Disclosure Affect Individuals' Mutual Fund Choices?" *NBER Working Paper* 14859.

Beshears, J., J. J. Choi, D. Laibson and B. C. Madrian (2013). "Simplification and Saving." *Journal of Economic Behavior and Organization* 95: 130–145.

Bhattacharya, U., A. Hackethal, S. Kaesler, B. Loos and S. Meyer (2012). "Is Unbiased Financial Advice to Retail Investors Sufficient? Answers from a Large Field Study." *Review of Financial Studies* 24: 975–1032.

Bhattacharya, U., B. Loos, S. Meyer and A. Hackethal (2014). "Abusing ETFs." Available at SSRN 2022442.

Biljanovska, Nina and Spyros Palligkinis (2014). "Control thyself: Self-control failure and household wealth." Available at http://dx.doi.org/10.2139/ssrn.2341701.

Calvet, L. E., J. Y. Campbell and P. Sodini (2007). "Down or Out: Assessing the Welfare Costs of Household Investment Mistakes." *Journal of Political Economy* 115(5): 707–747.

Campbell, J. Y., H. E. Jackson, B. C. Madrian and P. Tufano (2011). "Consumer Financial Protection." *Journal of Economic Perspectives* 25(1): 91–114.

Chater, N., S. Huck and R. Inderst (2010). "Consumer Decision-Making in Retail Investment Services: A Behavioural Economics Perspective – Final Report." November.

Clark, R. L., A. Lusardi and O.S. Mitchell (2014). "Financial Knowledge and 401 (k) Investment Performance." *NBER Working Paper* 20137.

Cole, S., T. Sampson and B. Zia (2011). "Prices or Knowledge? What Drives Demand for Financial Services in Emerging Markets?" *Journal of Finance* 66(6): 1993–1967.

Etheber, Thomas, Andreas Hackethal, and Steffen Meyer. (2014). "Trading on Noise: Moving Average Trading Heuristics and Private Investors." *Available at SSRN 2520346* (2014).

European Commission (2011). "Proposal 2011/0298 for a Directive of the European Parliament and of the Council on markets in financial instruments repealing Directive 2004/39/EC (MiFID II)."

Fernandes, D., J.G. Lynch and R. G. Netemeyer (2014). "Financial Literacy, Financial Education, and Downstream Financial Behaviors." *Management Science* 60(8): 1861–1883.

Gennaioli, N., A. Shleifer and R. W. Vishny (2012). "Money doctors." *NBER Working Paper* 18174.

Germann, F. (2014). "The Effect of Advisory Minutes on the Portfolios of German Investors." *Working paper, mimeo.*

Germann, F. (2014). "Looking for Safe Bets – Revealing the Dilemma between Investment Advice and Customer Preferences." *Working paper, mimeo.*

Glaser, M. and M. Weber (2007). "Why Inexperienced Investors Do Not Learn: They Do Not Know Their Past Performance." *Finance Research Letters* 4(4): 203–216.

Hackethal, A., M. Haliassos and T. Jappelli (2012). "Financial Advisors: A Case of Babysitters?" *Journal of Banking and Finance* 36: 509–524.

Hackethal, A. and R. Inderst (2013). "How to Make the Market for Financial Advice Work." In O. S. Mitchell and K. Smetters (eds.), *The Market for Retirement Financial Advice.* Oxford University Press, 213–228.

Hackethal, A. and R. Inderst (2011). "*Messung des Kundennutzens der Anlageberatung, Report to the German Ministry of Consumer Affairs (BMELV).*" Berlin: BMELV.

Hastings, J. S., B. C. Madrian and W. L. Skimmyhorn (2012). "Financial literacy, financial education and economic outcomes." *NBER Working Papers* 18412.

Kahneman, D. (2011). *Thinking, Fast and Slow.* London: Allen Lane.

Koestner, M. (2012). *Essays in Household Investment Behavior.* PhD Thesis, Goethe University Frankfurt.

Loewenstein, George, Cass R. Sunstein, and Russell Golman. (2013). "Disclosure: Psychology changes everything." Available at http://dx.doi.org/10.2139/ssrn.2312708.

Loewenstein, G., D. Cain, and S. Sah (2011). "The Limits of Transparency: Pitfalls and Potential of Disclosing Conflicts of Interest." *American Economic Review* 101: 423–428.

Meyer, Steffen, Maximilian Koestner, and Andreas Hackethal. (2012). "Do Individual Investors Learn from Their Mistakes?" Available at SSRN 2122652.

Meyer, S., D. Schmoltzi, C. Stammschulte, S. Kaesler, B. Loos and A. Hackethal (2012). "Just Unlucky? – A Bootstrapping Simulation to Measure Skill in Individual Investors' Investment Performance." *Working Paper, mimeo.* Available at SSRN: http://ssrn.com/abstract=2023588.

Mullainathan, S., M. Noeth and A. Schoar (2012). "The Market for Financial Advice: An Audit Study." *NBER Working Paper* 17929.

Mullainathan, Sendhil, and Eldar Shafir (2013). *Scarcity: Why Having too Little Means so much.* Macmillan.

Shleifer, A. and L. Summers (1990). "The Noise Trader Approach to Finance." *The Journal of Economic Perspectives* 4(2): 19–33.

Seru, A., T. Shumway and N. Stoffman (2010). "Learning by Trading." *Review of Financial Studies* 23: 705–739.

Thaler, R. H. and C. R. Sunstein (2008). *Nudge: Improving Decisions about Health, Wealth, and Happiness.* New Haven: Yale University Press.

Weber, J., S. Meyer, B. Loos and A. Hackethal (2014). "Which Investment Behaviors Really Matter for Individual Investors?" *Working paper, mimeo.* Available at SSRN: http://ssrn.com/abstract=2381435.

12

U.S. financial regulation in the aftermath of the Global Financial Crisis

HOWELL E. JACKSON[1]

With the outbreak of the Global Financial Crisis now more than a half decade in the past and the passage of the Dodd-Frank Wall Street Reform and Consumer Protection Act of 2010 heading toward its fifth anniversary in July of 2015, the time is ripe for a retrospective on the changes these events have brought to the regulation of financial institutions and financial markets in the United States. In this chapter I offer such a review. I begin with a brief description of market dynamics and dominant regulatory paradigms in U.S. financial regulation during the decades leading up to the Global Financial Crisis. I then identify ten features of the reformed regulatory structure in the United States that distinguish our new regulatory landscape from that which preceded it.

The analysis that follows is, of necessity, skeletal and impressionistic. Many critical components of the post-Crisis regulatory regime are still in flux, with key regulations only recently adopted and the implementation of many new statutory requirements not to be completed for another few years. Still, one can begin to discern the general outline of an approach to financial regulation in the United States that has a substantially different feel than that of the regime in place before 2008. Assumptions about central regulatory challenges have shifted and the mechanisms of supervision have evolved in a number of ways that an observer back at the turn

[1] James S. Reid, Jr., Professor of Law, Harvard Law School. The ideas expressed in this chapter benefit from discussions with and research conducted by my students at Harvard Law School, as well as collaborations with my co-authors Michael Barr and Margaret Tahyar. Many of the themes introduced here about the structure of post-Crisis regulation in the United States are explored in greater detail in Barr, Jackson and Tahyar (2016). This chapter benefited from comments by Helmut Siekmann as discussant and questions from conference participants at the "SAFE Workshop on Financial Regulation." All opinions expressed in this chapter are my own and do not represent the views of any organizations or entities with which I am affiliated.

of the millennium would have been unlikely to predict. The chapter attempts to highlight the chief points of differentiation between internal logic of the ancien régime and the new financial regulatory landscape that is growing up around us.

The internal logic of ancien régime

Within the popular press – and some recent academic work as well – there's often a tone of befuddled amazement in looking back on the regulatory policies advanced in the United States and other leading jurisdictions in the decades leading up to the Global Financial Crisis. The liberalization of New Deal strictures, most notably aspects of the Glass-Steagall Act, appears in retrospect to be a series of incomprehensible or at least ill-advised choices to those who were first introduced to the challenges of financial regulation during the market turmoil of 2007 and 2008. What, the general public asks, were the responsible authorities thinking? In fact, a combination of market developments and shared assumptions as to proper goals of public policy contributed to the background understanding of public officials, academics, and practitioners engaged in the area of financial regulation in the latter half of the twentieth century. These considerations explain, to a large degree, the logic of the deregulatory efforts of the 1980s and 1990s, and also serve as a helpful baseline against which to measure the new orientation that characterizes financial reform over the past five years.[2]

Growth in capital markets and rise of market-oriented intermediaries

Perhaps the most striking economic phenomenon in post-World War II U.S. financial markets was the growth in capital markets and the subsequent rise of a new class of market-oriented financial intermediaries. This growth came at the expense of traditionally regulated financial intermediaries, including insurance companies but most noticeably depository institutions. In 1950, for example, financial assets held by depository institutions in the United States – chiefly commercial banks and thrift institutions – constituted nearly two-thirds of all financial

[2] The analysis presented in this section is drawn to a considerable degree from Jackson and Symons (1999), which presented an overview of the regulation of financial institutions in the United States at the turn of the millennium.

assets held by regulated financial intermediaries. By 2000, the market share of depository institutions had fallen to 28.6 percent. Over the same period, pension plans saw their market share grow from 4.2 percent to 27.0 percent and investment companies enjoyed growth from 1.9 percent to 22.6 percent. Both pension plans and investment companies were primarily oriented toward capital market investments – both debt and equity – and contributed to the emergence of major new classes of institutional investors. At the same time, individual investors were increasingly moving away from direct holdings of equity and debt instruments and into intermediated means of investment, those same pension plans and mutual funds.

The deepening of U.S. capital markets and concurrent developments in information technologies and data processing increased the range of borrowers capable of accessing capital markets directly, rather than being dependent on depository institutions for sources of credit. Even short-term working capital requirements could be met through burgeoning commercial paper markets in the 1970s and 1980s. By the end of the last century, individual borrowers could also, in effect, access capital markets through securitization vehicles and other sorts of asset-based financing. In terms of savings vehicles, money market mutual funds and other deposit-substitutes, such as guaranteed investment contracts from insurance companies, offered new and vigorous competition for traditional savings accounts and certificates of deposit.

Competitive responses to the erosion of bank dominance

Much of the evolution of banking regulation in the decades leading up to the Global Financial Crisis can be understood as responses to the mounting pressure from capital market expansion. The earliest challenges to the Glass-Steagall Act were designed to allow commercial banks to compete in offering mutual-fund substitutes, commercial paper, and retail brokerage services. Relatively quickly, the banking industry expanded its efforts to participate in sponsoring asset securities and eventually underwriting markets. Similarly spirited efforts on the part of banks to enter insurance markets encountered temporary setbacks in Congress until the Gramm-Leach-Bliley Act of 1999 allowed commercial banks full access to all financial sectors, including insurance, provided the activities were undertaken in separate affiliates. Contemporaneous efforts to facilitate geographic expansion of commercial banks can also be understood as a response to competitive pressures during this period, and resulted in a national market for banking services, initially through regulatory accommodation but eventually with congressional blessing in the Reigle-Neal Interstate Banking and Branching Efficiency Act of 1994.

Portfolio theory infused into prudential regulation

While competitive pressures explain the push toward expanded banking powers from the perspective of industry participants, there was also an academic account for the liberalization of the Glass-Steagall Act and the elimination of geographic constraints on expansion. Modern portfolio theory, introduced to academic audiences in the 1950s, was being grafted into regulatory policies by the end of the 1970s, and offered a compelling intellectual foundation for activities liberalization in the decades that followed. The introduction of new financial products allowed regulated entities to push out the efficient frontier, thereby increasing returns without assuming additional risk. The S&L crisis of the 1980s offered further corroboration of the fragility of single-line-of-business financial intermediaries limited to credit exposures in local markets, and the apparent success of universal banking models operating in other developed countries presented additional evidence that the cramped constraints of New Deal limitations did not represent the only viable approach to regulatory design. The notion that diversified lines of business operating across a national or at least regional market might enhance the stability of financial institutions was not a difficult sell – either in the academic community or policy making circles – and routinely carried the day when additional activities – from retail securities brokerage to derivatives trading to merchant banking – were proposed as new lines of business for commercial banks and their affiliates.[3]

Functional supervision based on traditional financial sectors

As activities restrictions on depository institutions fell in the 1980s and 1990s, questions of supervisory jurisdiction came to the fore.[4] Once financial conglomerates broke through traditional boundaries between

[3] A separate intellectual justification for activities liberalization in this era was concern that prior restraints were inhibiting competition within markets and across financial sectors. The then-recent deregulation of airlines and telecommunications stood as influential exemplars of potential benefits to be derived through the elimination of state-mandated market segmentation.

[4] For an overview, see Jackson (2009).

banking, insurance, and securities, government officials had to determine how these consolidated entities were to be overseen. While other jurisdictions responded to similar transformations through the consolidation of regulatory functions into unitary or sometimes the adoption of "twin peaked" regulatory systems with specialized market conduct and prudential authorities, the fragmentation of financial supervision in the United States, plus our national aversion to centralized authority, made radical reforms of this sort a political non-starter. Instead, and as exemplified most clearly in the Gramm-Leach-Bliley Act of 1999, the United States opted for a system of "functional" regulation under which existing sectoral authorities would retain their traditional supervisory responsibilities for elements of financial conglomerates – ideally organized into separate affiliates – where the relevant activities took place. Thus, the SEC would oversee securities affiliates, state insurance commissioners would monitor insurance affiliates, and banking authorities, such as the OCC, would police banking affiliates. Even where the Federal Reserve Board retained enterprise-wide responsibilities for financial conglomerates under the Banking Holding Company, the Gramm-Leach-Bliley Act clearly specified that deference to functional regulators, to the extent practical, was the order of the day. And, of course, activities such as securitization and OTC derivatives trading, which were not subjected to distinct regulatory regimes, were allowed to proliferate within or outside financial conglomerates under the same lax supervisory standards otherwise applicable to those financial activities in the United States.

Capital-based activities restrictions

The pre-Global Financial Crisis regulatory regime in the United States was not, however, entirely deregulatory. Indeed, for much of the era, there was a heavy emphasis on capital and capital-based regulation. As early as 1983, Congress had identified the desirability of countering the secular decline in capital reserves that had been underway since the banking reforms of the 1930s and the creation of the FDIC. The savings and loan crisis (and the lesser banking crisis that followed) clearly demonstrated the dangers of thinly (or negatively) capitalized financial institutions, and by the 1990s federal authorities were unambiguously focused on raising capital standards for all depository institutions. Activities liberalization, moreover, was increasingly premised on capital adequacy, and the dramatic liberalization of commercial banking activities sanctioned in the Gramm-Leach-Bliley Act of 1999 was expressly limited to financial holding companies that were "well-capitalized," as well as "well-managed." On top of that, reforms begun in the United States in the 1980s and then popularized for the rest of the world through the Basel Committee on Banking Supervision mandated additional risk-based capital requirements that increased the capital reserves of firms engaged in higher risk activities, while lowering requirements for those engaged in low risk activities. Capital was also hard-wired into supervisory standards for distressed U.S. depository institutions with the creation of prompt corrective action requirements in 1991, specifying a cascading array of regulatory sanctions to be imposed on institutions that failed to meet capital requirements, culminating in mandatory closure if tangible capital ratios fell below 2 percent. For those who lived through the Global Financial Crisis with its unambiguous evidence of the inadequacy of capital reserves throughout the financial system, it is easy to forget that capital was king in supervisory circles for at least a decade and a half before the Crisis unfolded.

Expansion of information technology in finance and financial regulation

A final defining characteristic of the pre-crisis regulatory structure was the expanding role of information technology and data processing. As mentioned earlier, technological advancement contributed to the growth of capital markets in the second half of the twentieth century, but it also transformed the content of financial regulation itself. Perhaps the most striking example was the complexification of capital requirements. Moving from the relatively crude risk-based capital measures of Basel I, the Basel II regime developed highly elaborate internal models for producing capital requirements for larger, more sophisticated firms. Credit rating agencies employed similar techniques to produce ratings for asset-backed securities. Based on statistical modeling and Monte Carlo simulations, both developments required large quantities of PhDs and other technical personnel to review historical data and devise computer programs to simulate future events. These developments brought a degree of complexity and sophistication to financial regulation and risk management that would have been unimaginable in earlier times. But these innovations also seemed essential and unavoidable in addressing the mounting complexity of the modern financial services industry. As firms themselves invested larger and larger sums into information systems and risk management protocols, regulatory authorities had little choice but to emulate the development of new regulatory standards.

Ten critical and unanticipated features of the new financial landscape

I now turn to the post-Global Financial Crisis structure of financial regulation in the United States, as it is now evolving, and attempt to identify the critical features of that regulatory landscape that knowledgeable observers at the beginning of the millennium would not have anticipated as likely directions for regulatory evolution before the outbreak of the Crisis. This standard of foreseeability is, to be sure, a subjective one, and isolated individuals may have predicted or advocated for some of these features I associate with the post-Global Financial Crisis landscape.[5] My claim, however, is that the common wisdom, circa 2005, would not have considered these critical features of the new financial landscape as either inevitable or in some cases even likely.

Superimposing modified twin peaks on sectoral foundations

I will start with regulatory structure. While it is sometimes said that the Dodd-Frank Act side-stepped efforts to consolidate or otherwise reform the organization of financial regulation in the United States, that assessment is not, in my view, accurate. While the Act did retain almost all of the key front-line prudential regulators[6] – and somewhat ignominiously failed even to consider combining the CFTC and SEC – the legislation did superimpose a novel form of twin peak organization on top of existing regulatory structures. The new Consumer Financial Protection Bureau (CFPB) serves as a sort of limited-purpose market-conduct regulator for most credit, savings, and payment functions in the United States, and operates in conjunction with a combination of prudential regulators, such as the OCC, FDIC, and state banking regulators, under traditional

[5] Indeed, some of my own pre-Crisis writing could be seen as generally supportive of elements of the post-Crisis regime, particularly the creation of the Financial Stability Oversight Council (Jackson 2008).

[6] The Dodd-Frank Act did eliminate one supervisory agency, the Office of Thrift Supervision, which was merged into the OCC. On the other hand, it created a new Federal Insurance Office with a quite limited policy remit.

sectoral mandates.[7] Similarly, the Financial Stability Oversight Council (FSOC) constitutes a limited-purpose, macro-prudential authority superimposed on top of the entire American financial system with a roving mandate that potentially (and controversially) extends beyond the traditional regulatory perimeter.[8] These dual innovations in organization reflect the American genius for proliferating governmental agencies in the aftermath of financial turmoil, but also represent unanticipated responses to the specific imperatives of the events of 2007 and 2008: the stupendous scale of consumer abuse that the subprime crisis evinced and the massive systemic fallout that the Crisis engendered. While numerous pre-Crisis studies had proposed new models of regulatory reform for the United States, none proposed the superimposition of functional, twin-peak-style models on top of our fragmented sectoral arrangement. But that is what the Dodd-Frank Act did.

Diversification reconsidered

Another dramatic shift in regulatory philosophy following the Global Financial Crisis was a reconsideration of the benefits and risks of diversification. Perhaps the poster child for this development is the Volcker Rule, which prohibits banking organizations from engaging, either directly or through affiliates, in proprietary trading and certain other investments. While far from a full reinstitution of the Glass-Steagall Act prohibitions of yesteryear, restrictions such as the Volcker Rule represent a major shift in direction in U.S. regulatory policy, and one that has endured a painful and protracted gestation period since the passage of the Dodd-Frank Act in the summer of 2010. By some accounts, the Volcker Rule constituted nothing more than a concession to populist sentiments against Wall Street interests, and certainly there is ample evidence that elements of the Obama administration's economic team were unenthusiastic about this feature of financial reform.[9] But there has also emerged

[7] The emergence of the CFPB as an agency dedicated to consumer financial protection in the United States is consonant with the trend towards a greater focus on consumer finance in the European Union, as explored in by Haliassos (Chapter 9), Langenbucher (Chapter 14) and Moloney (Chapter 10) in this volume.

[8] The UK and the EU also created specialized macro-prudential bodies in the aftermath of the Global Financial Crisis. This trend towards macro-prudential regulation is chronicled in Chapter 1 by Faia and Schnabel.

[9] Former Secretary of the Treasury Geithner's recent memoire chronicles this ambivalence in some detail (Geithner 2014).

an analytical defense of heightened activities restrictions, a defense that represents a coherent counterweight against the logic of modern portfolio theory. One aspect of this defense focuses on the cultural impact of allowing trading desks – as opposed to lending functions – a central role in banking organizations. When capital-market risk-taking rather than the underwriting of commercial loans becomes the dominant perspective in the executive suite, the nature of banking organizations changes and volatility inevitably increases. Under this view, the diversification benefits of portfolio trading are more than offset by a weakening of internal prudential restraints. Another plank of the new case against broad banking powers is a recognition that regulatory firewalls, such as sections 23A and 23B of the Federal Reserve Act or accounting practices designed to define the boundaries of balance sheet exposures, are invariably imperfect and under-enforced. As a result, even the segregation of functions in separate affiliates cannot guarantee insulation for core banking functions (and government backstops).[10] Together, these and related considerations have tempered U.S. policy makers' previously unalloyed enthusiasm for activities liberalization. To be sure, the old logic of modern portfolio theory still has some force, which is one of the reasons why regulators found it so difficult to define how (bad) proprietary trading was to be distinguished from (good) hedging of positions, hence the multi-year rulemaking process for the Volcker Rule, which has only recently come to closure. Still, in the new regulatory landscape, greater diversification is not invariably seen as a salutatory direction.

Pivoting from moral hazard to systemic risk (and the uneasy role of public support in future systemic crises)

As described above, the ancien régime developed a system of tiered supervision based on capital levels and designed to solve a moral hazard problem by conditioning the liberalization of activities on the adequacy of capital reserves. The post-Crisis reforms in the United States have

[10] Interestingly, U.S. skepticism regarding the capacity of regulators to isolate core banking functions from corporate affiliates is not shared by policy makers in other financial markets. For example, the Vickers Report contemplated for British financial conglomerates largely unrestricted securities activities outside of a ring-fenced business unit focused on retail deposit-taking and limited lending activities (Independent Commission on Banking 2011).

superimposed a second system of tiering based on an assessment of the systemic risks associated with particular firms.[11] This tiering is most apparent in new Federal Reserve Board oversight requirements for banking organizations with more than $50 billion of assets, but is also evident in the authority of FSOC under Title I of the Dodd-Frank to designate certain non-banking financial institutions as systemically important and therefore subject to additional prudential supervision by the Federal Reserve Board. Updated capital standards in the United States, building on but also extending Basel III reforms, also embrace a number of surcharges for systemically important institutions. Thus, both portfolio restrictions and capital standards in the United States are now calibrated to systemic importance.[12] Whereas systemic risk was traditionally something that regulatory authorities were to resolve on an ex post basis through lender of last resort operations or application of the FDIC's systemic risk exception, our reformed regime moves systemic risk regulation into an ex ante posture. By enhancing regulation of systemically important institutions on the front end, it is contemplated, the need for public interventions on the back-end will be reduced. Of course, one of the difficult (and impolitic) questions to ask is whether the United States has retained sufficient ex post capabilities to deal with systemic risks should our new ex ante mechanisms fail to perform as planned.[13] In certain respects, the Dodd-Frank Act deactivated, or at least complicated, our ex post toolkit for systemic risks, and there is an active debate in academic circles whether this hand-tying to prevent future bailouts has gone too far (or not far enough).[14] But a new and defining feature of post-Crisis financial regulation in the United States is adoption of a regulatory structure that is increasingly contingent upon ex ante systemic risk assessments.

[11] This new tiering of regulation based on systemic risk assessments is trumpeted in a recent speech by Federal Reserve Board Governor Daniel Tarullo (Tarullo 2014).

[12] In the other direction, smaller banking institutions are sometimes exempt from supervisory standards, such as direct oversight by the Consumer Financial Protection Bureau, in part based on an assumption that these institutions are less likely to pose systemic risks.

[13] See Guynn 2012.

[14] See Committee on Capital Market Regulation (2014). Of course, certain U.S. analysts remain concerned that supervisory authorities retain too much discretion to assist failing financial institutions. See Republican Staff of the House Committee on Financial Services (2014). This view reflects similar concern expressed by Enriques and Hertig (Chapter 7 in this volume) with respect to smaller bank bail-outs in the European Union.

Doubling down (and doubling back) on risk-based capital requirements

Enhanced capital regulation has the peculiar distinction of being a defining feature of both the ancien régime and the new regulatory landscape. Even as the crisis was unfolding, the Basel Committee announced its initial plans for Basel III reforms in December of 2009, identifying many of the critical elements – such as leverage requirements, new rules for securitization, counter-cyclical buffers, and liquidity standards – that would ultimately be incorporated into the final Basel III rules adopted in 2012 and the U.S. reforms that followed.[15] So higher and more finely tailored risk-based capital standards characterize both eras. But what is distinctive about the new regulatory landscape is a mounting and profound discomfort with the logic of risk-based approaches to capital standards. The Basel Committee itself reflects this sentiment by including – in the face of opposition in some quarters – development of parallel leverage requirements, which do not depend on risk adjustments. The Collins Amendment within the Dodd-Frank Act reflects a similar skepticism, with its stipulation that crude Basel I capital rules set a floor on capital reserves beneath which more advanced risk-based capital measures cannot lower. Finally, in both academic writing and policy-maker speeches, one sees increasing skepticism that the complexification of risk-based capital requirement developed in Basel II and expanded in Basel III is worth the candle, with the alternative being the rough justice of simple leverage rules and the intuitions of seasoned regulators, as revealed through stress testing and on-site examination.[16] While the Basel capital process always drew critics, this growing disenchantment with the most developed and often heralded area of international financial regulatory cooperation is a striking and unexpected turn of events.

Recalibrating oversight of financial conglomerates

Greater attention to the regulation of organizational structure, particularly within financial conglomerates, is also a hallmark of the new

[15] For an overview of the development of international capital standards, see Financial Stability Board (2014b). The proliferation of capital stress tests, as explored in the European context by Orphanides (Chapter 3 of this volume) is an important element of the heightened emphasis on capital requirements in the post-Crisis environment.

[16] Haldane (2012) is perhaps the foremost illustration of this view, but Governor Tarullo's writings have a similar flavor, as does a mounting body of academic commentary (Sunstein 2013).

regulatory landscape in the United States. Motivated by the difficulty authorities faced in dealing with problems at Lehman Brothers and AIG, the Dodd-Frank Act establishes elaborate new requirements for the oversight of systemically important financial firms and abandons (or at least moves away from) the prior regime's bias in favor of deference to functional oversight of affiliates based on traditional sectoral divisions. But these reforms go well beyond additional prudential oversight, as the Dodd-Frank Act and regulations being adopted under its authority contemplate a much more intrusive role for supervisory authorities in shaping the structure of financial conglomerates. Through the review of living wills (also known as recovery and resolution plans) and other statutory levers, federal authorities have the capacity to force organizational changes in structure of financial conglomerates, streamlining operations and potentially jettisoning lines of business that might complicate resolution in times of financial stress. More profoundly, the FDIC, working in combination with the Federal Reserve Board, is implementing a "single-point-of-entry" approach for dealing with systemically important firms.[17] Once fully implemented, this strategy will have radical implications for how financial holding companies are structured and interact with their downstream affiliates.[18] A new system of convertible debt requirements will likely be imposed and regulatory authorities may also institute mandatory requirements with respect to inter-affiliate extensions of credit designed to pre-position capital infusions to downstream affiliates in times of financial distress. This expanded role of supervisory authorities in shaping the structure of financial conglomerates is a far cry from the Fed-lite approach of the Gramm-Leach-Bliley era, and represents a significant reorientation of the relationship between regulatory authorities and financial firm management.

Capturing systemic risks beyond banking

Another defining characteristic of the new regulatory landscape in the United States is an effort to broaden the regulatory perimeter. To a degree, this phenomenon is a delayed response to the explosion of capital market innovations of the decades preceding the Global Financial Crisis. The provisions of the Dodd-Frank Act dealing with the OTC derivatives

[17] See Bipartisan Policy Center (2013). The development of bail-in clauses, as discussed by Krahnen and Moretti (Chapter 6 of this volume) is a closely related phenomenon.

[18] See Financial Stability Board (2014a).

and the securitization of financial assets represent areas where regulatory oversight has been light or non-existence in the pre-Crisis era, and legislation brings them squarely and unambiguously within the regulatory perimeter. But the Dodd-Frank Act also contemplates the imposition of additional prudential oversight for elements of the financial system – even those traditionally overseen by sectoral authorities such as the SEC or state insurance commissions – on the grounds that those elements pose potential systemic risks.[19] This, of course, is another example of systemic risk contingent regulation, but it is an example that poses special legal challenges. To begin with, there is the inter-personal dilemma of one group of officials – those sitting on the FSOC – coming to the conclusion that one of their colleagues has not been sufficiently attentive to systemic risk concerns. Interactions between FSOC and the SEC on the oversight of money market mutual funds is an excellent illustration of this tension.[20] Next, the statutory language of the Dodd-Frank Act is awkwardly worded in defining exactly which activities can be designated as systemically troubling and how much flexibility the Council has in interpreting its mandate. (And, of course, the politics of such designations can be tricky as well.) Finally, and perhaps most profoundly, there are serious questions regarding how the Federal Reserve Board, which under the Dodd-Frank Act has the dubious honor of overseeing systemically important non-banking financial institutions, should go about restraining systemic risk in those entities. Much of the Board's prudential toolkit, such as capital requirements and activities restrictions, is designed to police the risks posed by depository institutions, and it is far from clear how those tools should be rejigged, if at all, for asset managers or other areas of shadow banking. So, while the Dodd-Frank Act is quite clear that federal authorities should capture and curtail systemic risks outside of the banking sector, it offers very little guidance on how authorities are to accomplish that assignment.

Policing a disaggregated financial services industry

Another characteristic and distinctive feature of the post-Crisis regulatory landscape in the United States is the amount of effort being expended in developing a new system of legal rules to govern a financial

[19] For a recent and controversial illustration of this trend, see Office of Financial Research (2013), exploring potential systemic risks posed by large asset management concerns.

[20] See Securities and Exchange Commission 2014.

services industry that has disaggregated the elements of credit extension and debt collection. This phenomenon is most visible in the area of asset securitization where discrete financial functions – from credit scoring to loan origination to asset pooling to capital raising to bond rating to servicing to debt collection – are all farmed out to specialized entities, commonly unaffiliated with each other. In simpler times, local banks and thrifts combined all these activities within a single entity, which could oversee credit extensions and loan workouts in a coordinated and integrated manner. The Global Financial Crisis revealed that modern securitization practices, sometimes derided as the originate-to-distribute model, were rife with agency costs and moral hazard problems. But rather than forcing credit extensions fully back on to the balance sheets of traditional financial institutions, the Dodd-Frank Act and its implementing regulations have taken up the challenge of devising new requirements for almost every component of the securitization process. In the past few years, we have seen the adoption of new regulations governing mortgage origination, compensation of mortgage originators, securitization risk pooling, credit rating agencies, and mortgage servicers. In addition to adding to the proliferation of new regulations, this approach has forced regulatory authorities to face the difficult task of defining discrete and hopefully market-improving rules for individual cogs of a much larger machine.[21] Whether the resulting apparatus proves to be a workable and welfare enhancing refinement of past securitization practices remains to be seen.[22]

Imperatives of coordination: foreign and domestic

A separate legacy of the Global Financial Crisis has been an explosion of coordination and collaboration. As the Crisis demonstrated the interconnectedness of financial sectors and the infirmities of regulatory oversight built upon functionally isolated supervisory agencies, reform efforts have placed unprecedented demands on regulatory officials in the United States to coordinate amongst themselves. This requirement is most visible in the creation of FSOC, where all major regulators plus the Secretary of the Treasury and representatives of state insurance commissions are literally

[21] For an illustration of this phenomenon with respect to the oversight of second mortgages, see Been, Jackson and Willis 2012.

[22] An entirely separate line of reforms directed at government sponsored enterprises, such as Fannie Mae and Freddie Mac, are still languishing in Congress, awaiting a politically viable compromise.

called upon to sit down together and make collective decisions (albeit with relatively limited capacity to make those decisions stick).[23] At a more operational level, key judgments as to whether to invoke the FDIC's new Orderly Liquidation Authority or some of the Federal Reserve Board's powers to provide liquidity in times of distress must be made by an amalgamation of decision-makers.[24] In addition, much of the most complicated rulemaking required under the Dodd-Frank Act – including the eponymous Volcker Rule – must be promulgated as a joint exercise of multiple agencies, a practice that is not common under U.S. administrative law and one that poses numerous challenges, both legal and practical. The framers of the Dodd-Frank Act also crafted a variety of dispute resolution mechanisms for fitting the CFPB on top of existing prudential regulators and astride other consumer protection activities operating out of the FTC and state agencies. With the challenges of regulatory arbitrage and the complexities of overseeing financial conglomerates on a global basis, the need and scale of coordination on an international level is, if anything, more profound. While the development of regulatory networks in the field of finance was well underway before the Crisis struck, the extent and intensity of international coordination has ballooned. Under the G-20 structure, and overseen by a reformulated and energized Financial Stability Board operating out of Basel, the number of substantive areas in which national authorities are called upon to approach or achieve regulatory harmonization has dramatically expanded.[25] Disputes over regulatory coordination – whether in aligning home-host requirements or resolving the extra-territorial application of domestic laws – have proliferated, especially as regulatory authorities extend their reach into capital market activities such as OTC derivatives, which enjoyed the supervisory equivalent of benign neglect in the years preceding the Crisis. The manner in which the Global Financial Crisis has transformed the scope and goals of financial regulation has elevated the necessity of regulatory coordination, although sadly it has not enhanced the capacity of regulatory authorities answering to local polities and resource constraints to achieve cross-sectoral or cross-jurisdictional accommodations in a timely or painless manner.

23 See, e.g., Financial Stability Oversight Council (2014). Some of the complexity of coordination in the post-Crisis European environment are explored by Pagano (Chapter 2) and Tröger (Chapter 8) in this volume.

24 See Bipartisan Policy Commission (2013).

25 For an overview of FSV reform efforts through Fall of 2014, see Financial Stability Board (2014b).

The rising tide of compliance professionals

Yet another distinctive and surprising feature of post-Crisis financial regulation is the increasing prominence and authority of compliance professionals, a term I use to include lawyers but also to embracing the every growing body of service providers from accounting firms to compliance specialists who support the financial services industry in their interactions with regulatory authorities. In part, this growing prominence relates to the sheer volume of new statutory requirements and implementing regulations that have been adopted over the past few years (and are continuing to be adopted). In the United States, these compliance professionals have played a major role in shaping legislation and regulatory proposals, but they also play an ever-prominent role in explaining and interpreting the new rules for their clients (and sometimes for the regulators who authored the rules). With increased emphasis on enforcement, the secular rise in the level of sanctions, and renewed attention to improving the corporate culture within financial conglomerates, compliance professionals are also playing an ever more significant role in monitoring firm behavior, whether through the expansion of internal audit and compliance functions or through the use of outside firms to perform "mock" examinations in preparation for actual supervision in the future. The implications of this development are, in my view, far from clear. While an emphasis on compliance seems altogether salubrious in light of widespread rule violations uncovered in the financial crisis, the rise of compliance professionals comes at a real cost, and the possibility exists that the interests of those professionals may not always align with public policy or even the long-term interests of their industry clients. While mock examinations and other supervisory cleanups may improve the underlying compliance of financial services firms, these practices may also make it more difficult for supervisory authorities to detect actual violations, perhaps creating a system of Potemkin examinations where all unpleasantness has been swept away before official visitors arrive. All of this is, of course, mere speculation, but the rise of the compliance professional is a development in the new regulatory landscape worth tracking.

Edging toward and stepping back from genuine paradigm shifts

A final unexpected consequence of the Global Financial Crisis is how little has actually changed in terms of paradigm shifts in regulatory design and substantive mandates. In the face of the tremendous costs of the Global Financial Crisis – with economic consequences that linger more than half a decade after the crisis unfolded – the extent of fundamental change in our regulatory structure is relatively limited. To be sure, a number of radical ideas have been bandied about and still emerge from time to time in the speeches and opinion pieces of thought leaders. But we have neither nationalized our financial institutions (save the GSEs, which now seem headed back to privatization) nor given serious consideration to breaking up our major financial institutions. While commentators have proposed dramatic increases in capital requirements[26] along with serious constraints on executive compensation[27] and Tobin taxes on financial transactions,[28] none of these ideas has gained traction in policy circles. Even the CFPB, which was launched with visions of a dramatically new system of consumer protection built around novel insights from behavioral economics, has largely relied upon traditional disclosure strategies and activities restrictions in its initial rulemakings. But while radical agendas have not, for the most part, been adopted, these proposals are all now on the table, as it were, for potential consideration in the future. A host of novel ideas about financial regulatory design are percolating along at the working paper/roundtable level.[29] And, were we to face another major financial crisis in the next few years, politicians and the general public would have a much more extensive array of interventions to choose along with White Papers, statutory language, and policy entrepreneurs all dressed up and ready to go. Should there be another widespread financial crisis in the not too distant future, more than a few paradigms may well end up broken.

Conclusion

The evolution of regulatory policy is often difficult to detect in real time. The reforms imposed in the United States in the wake of the Great

[26] Admati and Hellwig 2013. [27] Dudley 2014.

[28] Center for Economic and Policy Research 2011.

[29] Beyond those mentioned in the text, some of the more radical proposals that have been vetted in academic papers include supervisory standards that are directly tied to market signals (like movements in CDS prices), public assignment of credit rating agencies to issuers, reforms to inhibit the pace of high-speed trading, and use of public eminent domain powers to take control of troubled financial assets. One could also add in proposals to re-institute something akin to the original Glass-Steagall Act and recommendations to dramatically enhance capital requirements or move towards a system of narrow banking.

Depression – the creation of the SEC and the introduction of the federal deposit insurance – were designed as responses to the excesses of the 1920s, but ushered in an era of capital market development and financial stability that the framers of those reforms would have been unlikely to anticipate. The recent round of financial reforms may have a similar trajectory. The new statutory requirements and regulatory provisions have defined a distinctive new regulatory landscape. Even now, one can articulate how it departs from the ancien régime. But where the new landscape will lead is something that will not be entirely clear for years to come.

References

Admati, A. and M. Hellwig (2013). *The Bankers' New Clothes: What's Wrong with Banking and What to Do about It.* Princeton University Press.

Barr, M.S., H.E. Jackson, and M.E. Tahyar (2016). *Financial Regulation: Law and Policy. Foundation Press, in press.*

Been, V., H.E. Jackson, and M. Willis (2012). "Sticky Seconds: The Problems Second Liens Pose to the Resolution of Distressed Mortgages." *New York University Journal of Law and Business* 9(1): 71–123.

Bipartisan Policy Center (2013). Too Big to Fail: The Path to a Solution: A Report of the Failure Resolution Task Force of the Financial Regulatory Reform Initiative. The Financial Regulatory Reform Initiative.

Center for Economic and Policy Research (2011). Facts and Myths about a Financial Speculation Tax (available at: www.cepr.net/documents/fst-facts-myths-12–10.pdf).

Committee on Capital Market Regulation (2014). What to Do About Contagion? A Report by the Committee on Capital Markets Regulation (available at: http://capmktsreg.org/reports/what-to-do-about-contagion/).

Dudley, W.C. (2014). Enhancing Financial Stability by Improving Culture in the Financial Services Industry, *Speech*, October 20, 2014 (available at: www.ny.frb.org/newsevents/speeches/2014/dud141020a.html).

Financial Stability Board (2014a). Adequacy of Loss-Absorbing Capacity of Global Systemically Important Banks in Resolution: Consultative Document (available at: www.financialstabilityboard.org/wp-content/uploads/TLAC-Condoc-6-Nov-2014-FINAL.pdf).

Financial Stability Board (2014b). Overview of Progress in the Implementation of the G20 Recommendations for Strengthening Financial Stability, *Report of the Financial Stability Board to G20 Leaders* (available at: www.financialstabilityboard.org/wp-content/uploads/Overview-of-Progress-in-the-Implementation-of-the-G20-Recommendations-for-Strengthening-Financial-Stability.pdf).

Financial Stability Oversight Council (2014). FSOC 2014 Annual Report.
Geithner, T.F. (2014). *Stress Test: Reflections on Financial Crises.* Crown Publishers.
Guynn, R.D. (2012). "Are Bailouts Inevitable?" *Yale Journal on Regulation* 29(1): 121–154.
Haldane, A. (2012). The Dog and the Frisbee. *Speech given at the Federal Reserve Bank of Kansas City's 36th economic policy symposium "The Changing Policy Landscape," Jackson Hole, Wyoming on August 31, 2012.*
Jackson, H.E. (2008). A Pragmatic Approach to the Phased Consolidation of Financial Regulation in the United States. *Harvard Public Law Working Paper* 09-19.
Jackson, H.E. (2009). "Learning from Eddy: A Meditation Upon Organizational Reform of Financial Supervision." In Michel Tison et al. (eds.), *Perspectives in Company Law and Financial Regulation.* Cambridge University Press.
Jackson, H.E. and E.L. Symons (1999). *The Regulation of Financial Institutions.* West Publications.
Independent Commission on Banking (2011). Final Report: Recommendations.
Office of Financial Research (2013). Asset Management and Financial Stability. US Department of Treasury.
Republican Staff of the House Committee on Financial Services (2014). Failing to End "Too Big to Fail": An Assessment of the Dodd-Frank Act Four Years Later. Report.
Securities and Exchange Commission (2014). Press Release: SEC Adopts Money Market Fund Reform Rules, July 23.
Sunstein, C. (2013). *Simple. The Future of Government.* Simon and Schuster.
Tarullo, D.K. (2014). Rethinking the Aims of Prudential Regulation, *Speech Given at the Federal Reserve Bank of Chicago Bank Structure Conference, May 8.*

13

Risk aversion and financial crisis

LUIGI GUISO[1]

> On the traditional view, an explanation of economic phenomena that reaches a difference in tastes between people or times is the terminus of the argument: the problem is abandoned at this point to whoever studies and explains tastes (psychologists? anthropologists? phrenologists? sociobiologists?). On our preferred interpretation, one never reaches this impasse: the economist continues to search for differences in prices or incomes to explain any differences or changes in behavior.
>
> George Stigler and Gary Becker (1977)

Introduction

Risk preferences are a key parameter for financial decisions. They govern portfolio choice and the demand for insurance, and they are central for mortgage contract choice. More generally, they enter any decision that has an element of risk in it. Economists have long tended to regard risk preferences as a given attribute, possibly invariant over time and age and possibly independent of circumstances. The typical and most diffuse characterization of preferences for risk – the CRRA utility – conforms to this view. Under CRRA, risk tolerance is a constant parameter, independent of age, independent of wealth and of the state of the world, but possibly varying across individuals for reasons that economists have often avoided exploring, partly because, in the classical division of labor across disciplines, economists have chosen to leave the explanation of the origin of preferences and technologies to other interested disciplines and focalize instead on variation in prices and endowments as driving forces of behavior. This traditional view became rooted in

[1] AXA Professor of Household Finance at the Einaudi Institute for Economics and Finance (EIEF) and Fellow at the Centre for Economic Policy Research (CEPR).

Economics after Stigler and Becker (1977) forcefully theorized it by arguing that "The establishment of the proposition that one may usefully treat tastes as stable over time and similar among people is the central task of this essay."

Times have changed, and views too. It is now accepted that economists not only rely on tastes to understand behavior, they also try to understand what drives differences in preferences across individuals and their changes over time, possibly linking these changes to economic phenomena; preferences, far from being part of the data for an economist, become part of the factors used to explain economic phenomena. In turn, changes in the economic environment can alter preferences.

This link is most clear in asset pricing, where the idea that risk preferences are invariant has long been abandoned. Models that assume invariant preferences are in fact unable to account for the observed variation in the prices of risky assets relying only on variation in assets cash flows. Variation in the risk tolerance of individuals is required in order to match the high variability that we observe in assets prices.

But do risk attitudes of individuals actually change over time? If so, what drives variation in individuals' risk preferences? Are they driven by economic factors or by psychological forces? How do preferences for risk evolve dynamically? How enduring are variations in risk attitudes over time? How should time-varying risk preferences be characterized? In this chapter I will tackle these questions. I will discuss these issues, summarizing what we know about individual preferences for risk and motives for them to change over time. I will also provide some evidence on how much and why these preferences changed during the financial crises. This discussion provides some food for thought for a pending but important issue: is there room for policy and regulatory interventions to affect variation in risk preferences, and are interventions of this sort desirable? Needless to say, part of the answer will depend on what drives variation in risk preferences and on the effects of these variations on policy relevant outcomes.

The rest of the chapter is organized as follows. In "Why can willingness to bear risk vary over time?" I review several factors than can lead to changing risk aversion, distinguishing between economic and non-economic drivers. In "Does willingness to bear risk actually vary over time?" I provide evidence of what actually matters for changing risk aversion and show evidence of risk aversion changing during the last financial crisis. Conclusions follow.

Why can willingness to bear risk vary over time?

The risk aversion that matters for assets pricing is the risk aversion of the average investor. This can change over time because the distribution of wealth across individuals with different but constant risk aversion changes or because the risk aversion of the single individual changes. Here, we will focus on changes in the risk aversion of the single investors.

In turn, there are two reasons why the willingness of the individual to bear risk changes over time: because the risk aversion *parameter* of the period utility function evolves, or because the individual endowment evolves and risk preferences are sensitive to the movements of the endowment, which could be the mean or its variance or even higher moments.

Evolving risk aversion parameter

Suppose the utility function is CRRA, so that the period utility is $u(c) = \frac{c^{1-\lambda}}{1-\lambda}$; the individual relative risk aversion is λ. Rather than being a constant, individuals' willingness to bear risk can be made a function of observables z_{it} and $\lambda = \lambda(z_{it})$. The set of observables can vary across individuals and over time. Differences across individuals contribute to creating heterogeneity in risk aversion in a population, and potentially in the aggregate risk aversion, as the distribution of wealth changes. Some of the time variations in z_{it} can be specific to the individual; some can be common to all and thus shift the risk aversion of a whole population in the same direction. The first will normally have no effect on the aggregate risk aversion except when idiosyncratic variations happen to be correlated with the wealth of the individuals (and thus with the weights used to aggregate the individual risk aversions); the second can move the overall risk aversion and can have important effects on assets prices. As we will see, financial crises are episodes of the latter type. The literature has identified several factors of both types.

Time-invariant characteristics

Before discussing them, it is worth noting that several time-invariant, demographic characteristics have been found to correlate with individual risk preferences. Thus, variation over time in the composition of the population across groups with different risk aversion can result in variation over time in the average risk aversion of the population. For instance, several papers find that risk aversion is higher for women than for men.[2] Another robust cross-sectional finding is that education has a positive impact on risk taking (e.g. Vissing-Jørgensen 2002). Recent research has also established strong correlations between measures of risk preferences and individual intelligence. Frederick (2006) finds that, in a sample of students, laboratory measures of risk aversion are negatively correlated with IQ scores. This result extends outside the lab and to non-student samples (Dohmen et al. 2010, Beauchamp, Cesarini and Johannesson 2011 [in a sample of Swedish twins], Grinblatt, Keloharju and Linnainmaa 2011, Anderson et al. 2011). Since IQ seems to have a time trend, this can generate a temporal pattern in the average risk tolerance of the population. But because IQ does not evolve over the business cycle, this channel cannot explain changes in risk aversion at the business cycle frequency.

Interestingly, Anderson et al. (2011) also find that specific components of personality measures, in particular neuroticism (individuals' tendency to experience negative emotional states such as anger, guilt and anxiety), are also correlated with risk aversion. This is interesting because emotional states, such as anger and guilt, are bound to change possibly at high frequency. Anger, in particular, is a sentiment that, as documented by Guiso, Sapienza and Zingales (2013b), is associated with financial crisis and can thus be a cause of increased risk aversion following episodes of financial collapse.[3]

A recent and growing literature aims at assessing the genetic component of financial risk taking by using data on the behavior of twins. Cesarini et al. (2009) estimate that about 30 percent of the individual variation in risk aversion elicited in experiments using hypothetical lotteries is due to genetic variation. They also find that the shared environmental component (due, for example, to upbringing) is very small, and in some specifications close to zero.

Even though there is clear consensus on the existence of a genetic component of risk taking, its magnitude is still under debate. A promising approach is taken by Dreber et al. (2009) and Kuhnen and Chiao (2009) who look directly at the effect of actual genes on risk-taking

2 In experimental settings, e.g. Holt and Laury (2002) and Powell and Ansic (1997). Using field data and surveys, see Hartog, Ferrer-i-Carbonell and Jonker (2002), Dohmen et al. (2011), Guiso and Paiella (2009), Kimball, Sahm and Shapiro (2007), among others. Croson and Gneezy (2009) survey the literature and warn about the bias that only papers finding a gender effect might end up being published.

3 Consistent with these features, Calvet and Sodini (2014) document that twins with depression symptoms tend to have a lower share of financial wealth invested in risky assets.

behavior. They are able to find a positive and significant correlation between risk taking and the lack or presence of specific alleles.

Finally, an emerging literature studies the role of specific biological factors in shaping investors preferences. Particular attention has been given to the effect of testosterone on risk attitudes. A growing number of contributions study the effect of fetus exposure to testosterone during pregnancy, as measured by the 2D:4D ratio, finding, so far, weak effects (Garbarino et al. 2011, Sapienza, Zingales and Maestripieri 2009, Apicella et al. 2008 and Guiso and Rustichini 2011 find none).

Needless to say, while genetic factors and early experiences reflecting differences in family backgrounds help explain persistent cross-sectional differences in risk attitudes, they cannot explain time variation in risk attitudes among adults.

Age

One demographic characteristic that can result in variation in risk attitudes over time is age. Elicited risk aversion parameters tend to be positively correlated with age (e.g. Dohmen et al. 2011, Barsky et al. 1998, Guiso and Paiella 2008); age may contribute to explaining patterns of portfolio choice over the life-cycle, and even trends in risk aversion if the age-distribution of the population changes, but per se cannot explain variation in risk aversion over business cycles and thus the variation in asset prices at the business cycle frequency.

Mood and fear

Emotions can cause changes in people's willingness to bear risk. Loewenstein (2000) argues that decisions are not made only on the basis of anticipated results, as in a standard expected utility framework. Emotions experienced at the time of decision-making (immediate emotions) can also play a role, sometimes a key one. Emotions – such as fear – originate in the brain's limbic system (amygdala, cingulate gyrus and hippocampus) and they are processed and moderated by the frontal cortex (Pinel 2009). For instance, mood may be affected by weather conditions or by exposure to light: people exposed to more light tend to be less risk averse. Because light varies seasonally, this introduces a time variation in risk aversion and in people's financial decisions (Kamstra et al. 2003, Kramer and Weber 2012).

A simple way to embed the role of emotions in the standard utility framework is to assume that emotions can alter some parameter of an individual utility function. That is, fear or some other risk aversion relevant emotions can be thought as a state-contingent increase in the curvature of the utility function.

Insofar as a catastrophic event, either economic or non-economic, triggers an emotional reaction such as fear, it can result in an increase in risk aversion. This may explain why during downturns, and particularly during financial crises, investors who do not lose money directly also become more risk averse, even with respect to known probabilities gambles, as we will show in the second section. The terrifying news appearing on television, interactions with friends who lost money in the market, and the pictures of fired people leaving their failed banks might have triggered an emotional response. Of course, because during financial crises the value of the endowments changes also the hypothesis cannot be tested with our data because it is observationally equivalent to a background risk model. Does the picture of Lehman's fired employees trigger an emotional fear response, or does it increase the subjective probability of a very bad outcome?

Traumas

A large literature in medicine and psychiatry, such as Holman and Silver (1998), documents that exposure to traumas can produce complex and long-lasting consequences on mental and physical health. Shaw (2000) argues that major structural central nervous system changes occur from birth to early adolescence. Traumatic experiences during these critical stages may have a determining effect on brain structural development and sympathetic nervous system responsivity, and the hypothalamic pituitary adrenal axis[4] (see Lipschitz et al. 1998). Therefore, traumas experienced early in life could reasonably affect adults' risk-taking behavior. Indeed, several papers from psychology and neuroscience suggest that risk aversion has a specific neural basis and an important emotional component (e.g. Kuhnen and Knutson 2005).

One strand of literature has focused on *non-economic* traumas – in particular, exposure to natural disasters – as causes of change in people's risk attitudes. For example, Cameron and Shah (2012) find that individuals, who recently experienced a flood or an earthquake in Indonesia during the previous three years exhibit higher levels of risk aversion than

[4] The sympathetic nervous system (one of three major parts of the autonomic nervous system) is responsible for mobilizing the body's nervous system fight-or-flight response. The fight-or-flight response is a physiological reaction that occurs in response to a perceived harmful event, attack or threat to survival.

similar individuals living in villages in the same area who were not touched by the disasters. Others find that, as an immediate reaction to a natural disaster, individuals tend to become *less* risk averse (Eckel et al. 2009, Page et al. 2012). There are still no studies of the long-term consequences of traumatic natural disasters, such as an early-age experience of an earthquake.

Traumas can also be induced by large and unusual shocks, such as the loss of a job or exposure to a financial crisis. One small but influential body of research on the impact of life experiences on risk attitudes has investigated the impact of macroeconomic events, such as financial busts or the great depression, on risk-taking behavior and people's beliefs. Malmendier and Nagel (2011) find that birth-cohorts of people who have experienced low stock market returns throughout their life report greater risk aversion, are less likely to participate in the stock market and, if they participate, invest a lower fraction of liquid wealth in stocks. Their estimates indicate that experiencing macroeconomic events early in life affects risk-taking behaviors, but recent realizations have a stronger impact than distant ones. Fagereng, Gottlieb and Guiso (2013) find similar results in a large panel of Norwegian households: investors who, in "impressionable years" (age 18–23), were exposed to more macroeconomic uncertainty, invest a lower share in stocks over their lifetime.

These effects, though triggered by "bad" economic events, are unlikely to reflect a relation between risk tolerance and wealth. In fact, wealth-induced changes in risk preferences (such as those generated by habit preferences, as we discuss below; see "Evolving endowment and economic environment") should revert quickly as wealth recovers over the business cycle. Trauma-induced changes may instead be long-lasting. Insofar as a financial crisis is a traumatic experience for many, it can induce large changes in risk aversion and, most importantly, this may be long lasting, which may help explain why recoveries from financial-crisis-induced recessions are so slow.

Evolving endowment and economic environment

Risk preferences can change over time, not because the concavity of period utility changes in response to shocks, but because the individual endowment and the economic environment change, and the structure of preferences is such that people's willingness to bear risk is sensitive to variations in the distribution of the endowment or in the structure of the economic environment. Changes of this sort fall in the tradition of economics: variations in willingness to bear risk are caused by changes in economic endowments, and variation in the first can, in turn, affect equilibrium asset prices.[5]

Financial wealth

One key variable is the level of financial wealth. It is widely accepted, and strongly supported by evidence, that the absolute risk aversion of an individual decreases with the level of the endowment. More controversial is the relation between the endowment and the relative risk aversion of an individual. But it is the latter that matters for asset pricing. In order to generate a link between relative risk aversion and the individual financial wealth one needs to depart from CRRA utility. Assume that relative risk aversion depends on financial wealth W_i according to $\lambda = \lambda(z_{it})$

$$\lambda = \frac{\lambda \gamma_i}{W_{it}^{\eta}}$$

where γ is an individual component that captures unobserved risk preferences and may depend as before on a vector z_{it} of time-varying or time-invariant characteristics. A value of $\eta = 0$ corresponds to constant relative risk aversion, and we are back to the previous case in which relative risk aversion can evolve over time because the risk aversion of period utility changes. Positive values of η imply decreasing relative risk aversion. When financial wealth increases people's willingness to bear risk increases, and vice versa. Hence, if $\eta > 0$ movements in personal wealth over the business cycle, for instance caused by a drop or a boom in assets prices, may result in swings in individual willingness to bear risk. Habit persistence models such as those used by Constantinides (1990) and Campbell and Cochrane (1999) have this property and this is the main hypothesis that has been explored by economists. Needless to say, during financial downturns, and even more so during financial crises, asset values drop and the stock of wealth tends to get closer to the stock of habits, causing risk aversion to increase. Hence, in principle, habit models can explain time variation in risk aversion. One type of habit that has been recently emphasized in the literature is consumption commitments – expenditures related to durable goods, such as housing and cars – that involve adjustment costs. Commitments can affect investor risk preferences (e.g. Grossman and Laroque 1990, Chetty and Szeidl

[5] Put differently, the deep preferences for risk do not vary; what changes is the risk aversion of the indirect utility function.

2007, Postlewaite, Samuelson and Silverman 2008). In particular, these papers argue that commitments amplify risk aversion over moderate shocks. Households with housing or expensive cars have an incentive to reduce financial risk exposure to make sure they can continue paying their bills when hit by temporary shocks.

Despite the fact that habit preferences have been the main explanation put forward by economists for time-varying risk aversion, this seems to receive mixed empirical support when tested on micro data. For instance, Brunnermeier and Nagel (2008) find that one key implication of habit models – that the portfolio share invested in risky assets should correlate positively with the level of wealth – does not hold in a sample of US households. Chiappori and Paiella (2011) run a similar test in a panel of Italian households and cannot reject that the risky portfolio share is unaffected by variation in households wealth, leading them to conclude that household preferences are well represented by CRRA utility, and thus to reject the habit model as an explanation for variation over time in preferences for risk.

Lupton (2002) and Calvet and Sodini (2014) find instead evidence that is more consistent with the habit model. They test directly habit formation models on household portfolio allocation decisions by using proxies for habit measured with US and Swedish data. They note that habit formation models carry four testable predictions. The portfolio's risky share should decrease with proxies for habit and increase with financial wealth. Additionally, the financial wealth elasticity of the risky share should not only be positive but also heterogeneous across investors. It should decrease with financial wealth and increase with the habit. Lupton (2002) tests the effect of internal habit on the risky share in the cross section, finding support for habit formation models. Calvet and Sodini (2014) document the same result with Swedish data, and argue that habit has a causal effect on the risky share by using twin regressions. They also find that the financial wealth elasticity of the risky share is decreasing in wealth and increasing in proxies for habit. Finally, Chetty and Szeidl (2008) provide some empirical evidence that households with more commitments follow more conservative financial portfolio strategies.

One issue with this evidence is that, instead of capturing a relation between habits and risk aversion, any correlation between the risky share and wealth may reflect some relation between wealth and other determinants of the portfolio risky share, such as information which may evolve with wealth. To isolate the risk aversion channel, one would require direct measures of risk aversion and of their evolution over time.

Guiso, Sapienza and Zingales (2013b) use a measure of this sort and find mixed evidence. We will return to their evidence below, in "Does willingness to bear risk actually vary over time?"

Background risk and access to credit markets

Background risk is probably the most widely cited environmental factor used to explain heterogeneity in risk attitudes. It can be defined as a type of risk that cannot be avoided because it is non-tradable and non-insurable. Under some regularity assumptions on preferences, background risk makes investors less willing to take other forms of risks, such as investment in risky financial assets. Researchers have identified sources of background risk in wealth components that cannot be fully diversified because of market incompleteness or illiquidity. Human capital (e.g. Bodie, Merton and Samuelson 1992, Viceira 2001, Cocco, Gomes and Maenhout 2005), housing wealth (e.g. Cocco 2005, Yao and Zhang 2005) and private business wealth (Heaton and Lucas 2000) have been used to explain the reluctance of households to invest in risky financial markets. Differently from habits which are concerned with the first moment of the distribution of the endowment, background risk arises in relation to variation in the second moment. The latter in turn may vary over the business cycle, and increase during downturns (Pistaferri and Meghir 2004).

In addition to background risk, Gollier (2006) argues that risk preferences might also be affected by limited access to credit markets since it restricts the ability of households to transfer risk in time. Borrowing constraints make investors more risk averse in anticipation of the possibility that the constraint might be binding in the future (Grossman and Vila 1992). Finally, background risk might also be affected by household size and composition, as the probability of divorce and the random liquidity needs of a larger family with children might discourage financial risk taking (Love 2010). Needless to say, credit market accessibility tends to be more severe during downturns, and even more so during financial crises, when intermediaries restrict credit-granting criteria and credit crunches emerge. Hence, this channel too has a potential for inducing increased risk aversion in downturns and in particular during financial crises.

Empirical evidence on background risk and risk-taking behavior rely mostly on cross-sectional evidence. Guiso, Jappelli and Terlizzese (1996), Guiso and Jappelli (1998), and Palia, Qi and Wu (2014) find that investors with more uncertain labor income, facing tighter borrowing constraints, buy more insurance and tend to participate and invest less in equity markets. Guiso and Paiella (2008) document that households living in areas with more volatile aggregate income growth are more risk averse when offered a hypothetical lottery. Hung et al. (2014) find that in Taiwan, individuals employed at listed companies with greater idiosyncratic return volatilities are less likely to invest in equity in general, and in their employer's stock in particular. Betermier et al. (2011) find that a household moving from an industry with low wage volatility to one with high wage volatility will, ceteris paribus, decrease its portfolio share of risky assets by up to 35 percent. Heaton and Lucas (2000a) find that entrepreneurial households with more private business wealth hold less in stocks relative to other liquid assets. Similarly, they find that workers with stocks in the firm they work for have a lower portfolio share of common stocks. Cocco (2005) and Yao and Zhang (2005) calibrate life-cycle models of optimal portfolio decisions with data from the PSID and document a background risk component of housing wealth that crowds out equity holdings.

The cross-sectional literature cannot distinguish the direct effect of background risk from the extent to which it proxies for latent characteristics. Panel analysis, on the other hand, might be problematic since some forms of background risk, such as human capital, are highly persistent and others, such as housing wealth, might be endogenous to financial decisions. Calvet and Sodini (2014) use twin regressions to shed light on this issue and confirm the importance of background risk on financial risk taking. They verify the cross-sectional findings that self-employed and credit-constrained twins with more volatile income invest less in equity markets.

Persistence and contagion

Persistence

How persistent can changes in risk aversion be over time? Answering this question is important. If changes are (possibly small and) short lived, so are their consequences. Furthermore, individuals may be aware that their attitude is subject to temporary fluctuations and thus act on the expected value of their risk aversion. In this case, the traditional characterization of risk preferences as a stable individual trait may be a reasonable assumption to characterize behavior. If instead departures are (large and) persistent, they may have enduring consequences. And even if individuals understand these swings in their preferences for risk, they may find it difficult to ignore them.

Persistence of changes in risk aversion is likely to differ depending on the cause of the change and the size of the shock. Changes induced by variation in mood, such as those due to light exposure (Kramer et al. 2012), variation in the blood levels of testosterone (Sapienza, Zingales and Maestripieri 2009) or even fear-inducing (though not traumatic) experiences are very likely to revert quickly as the cause of this change reverts too. Variation induced by age is by definition permanent and irreversible. The persistence of scary and traumatic experiences is more problematic to assert. Some early-age traumatic experiences are likely to have permanent consequences. The evidence in Malmendier and Nagel (2011) that birth-cohorts of people who have experienced low stock market returns throughout their life report greater risk aversion, is consistent with long-lived effects of traumatic experiences. Some of these experiences can persist even longer than the lifetime of the individual who has experienced them, if, as shown by Dohmen et al. (2011), risk aversion transmits across generations.

Finally, variation in risk aversion due to changes in the level of wealth in habit models persists for as long as it takes for wealth to revert back to normal. Large drops in wealth may be slow to rebuild, particularly after a financial crisis, implying that increases in risk aversion following a financial depression can be slow to recover. Hence, habit models can explain relatively long-lasting changes in risk aversion but cannot explain changes that last beyond the change in wealth. A similar consideration applies to cyclical changes in background risk and households' access to the credit market.

Contagion

To explain large fluctuations in assets prices, variation in risk aversion must be common to a substantial portion of the investors. This is the case if risk aversion responds to aggregate shocks, such as a drop in wealth due to a financial crisis. Idiosyncratic variations due to, for instance, changes in mood will tend to wash out. Yet, there is evidence that emotions can be contagious, so an event experienced by a fraction of the population that makes them cautious may spill over to others, thereby increasing their cautiousness too. In an experiment on Facebook, Kramer et al. (2014) show that emotional states can be transferred to others through emotional contagion, which leads people to experience the same emotions even without their awareness. Hence, a traumatic experience – such as fear – that hits a relatively large portion of the population and raises their level of risk aversion can have a similar effect on the remaining portion.

The media and social networking (as in the Kramer et al. (2014) experiment) can be the vehicle of contagion.

Does willingness to bear risk actually vary over time?

The observation that the price of risk varies over time is consistent with fluctuations in investors' risk tolerance, but it is no proof of it. A more direct approach is to rely on direct measures of risk aversion elicited in surveys or even experiments. This is the approach that economists are starting to employ. There are two big advantages in using direct measures of individuals' risk aversion. The first is that one can directly document whether individuals' risk aversion has a time-varying component and thus check directly whether it is the risk aversion of the individuals that leads to a change in aggregate risk aversion or whether it is the distribution of wealth that changes, altering the aggregate risk aversion with no change in the risk aversion of the individual investors. The second is that one can test different explanations of what produces the changes and possibly distinguish among the various forces discussed in Section 2. The main shortcoming is that the collection of data on elicited risk aversion has only started recently and there is little panel data.

One useful source that has a relatively long time span is the Survey of Consumer Finances. Since 1989 it has included a question meant to elicit investors' levels of risk aversion. In the SCF each participant is asked: "Which of the following statements comes closest to the amount of financial risk that you are willing to take when you make your financial investment? : (1) Take substantial financial risks to earn substantial returns; (2) Take above-average financial risks, expecting to earn above-average returns; (3) Take average financial risks, expecting to earn average returns; (4) Not willing to take any financial risks." Answers to this question allow the classification of investors according to their level of risk aversion.

In a world where people face the same risk-return trade-offs and make portfolio decisions according to Merton's formula, their risk/return choice reflects their degree of relative risk aversion. In such a world, the answers to the above question can fully characterize people's relative risk preferences. People opting for low-risk/low-return combinations are also individuals with higher risk aversion. Table 13.1 shows the distribution of the answers to these questions in all SCFs where it was asked, including the last one.

Table 13.1 *Evolution of the distribution of risk preferences among US households*

	Year							
	1989	1992	1995	1998	2001	2004	2007	2010
1. Substantial risk and return	4.91	5.08	5.15	6.09	5.8	5.12	5.17	3.51
2. Above-average risk and return	12.24	16.09	18.64	23.34	23.17	20.25	21.42	13.38
3. Average risk and return	42.27	39.69	41.88	40.26	40.1	41.5	42.2	36.76
4. No financial risk	40.58	39.14	34.33	30.31	30.93	33.13	31.2	47.35
Risk tolerant (1 or 2)	17.15	21.17	23.79	29.43	23.75	25.37	26.59	16.89

The table shows the distribution of a qualitative measure of risk aversion in the survey of consumer finances. Investors are asked their preferences about risk and returns when making their portfolio choices. They face four alternatives: 1) Take substantial financial risks to earn substantial returns; 2) Take above-average financial risks, expecting to earn above-average returns; 3) Take average financial risks, expecting to earn average returns; 4) Not willing to take any financial risks. The table shows the frequency distribution of the answers to this question. The last row shows the percentage of people answering either 1 or 2.

There are a number of intriguing features in this table. First, and most importantly, there is substantial increase in risk aversion following the financial crisis. The fraction of risk-tolerant individuals – defined as those answering either (1) or (2) – was 26.6 percent in 2007, before the financial crisis, and drops to 16.9 percent in 2010 after the crisis (last row); similarly, the percentage of individuals that prefer no financial risk, even if this entails very low returns, jumps from 31.2 percent in 2007 to 47.4 percent in 2010, as is made clear in Figure 13.1.

This is consistent with risk aversion changing dramatically during the most recent financial crisis. The second feature is that risk aversion was higher than average in 1989 and then dropped continuously in the subsequent surveys. The share of people answering "no risk" was around 40 percent in 1989 and fell to 30 percent over 11 years. The first SCF following the stock market crash of 1987 was in 1989. Based on the patterns shown by the measure in 2007/2010 it is tempting to conclude

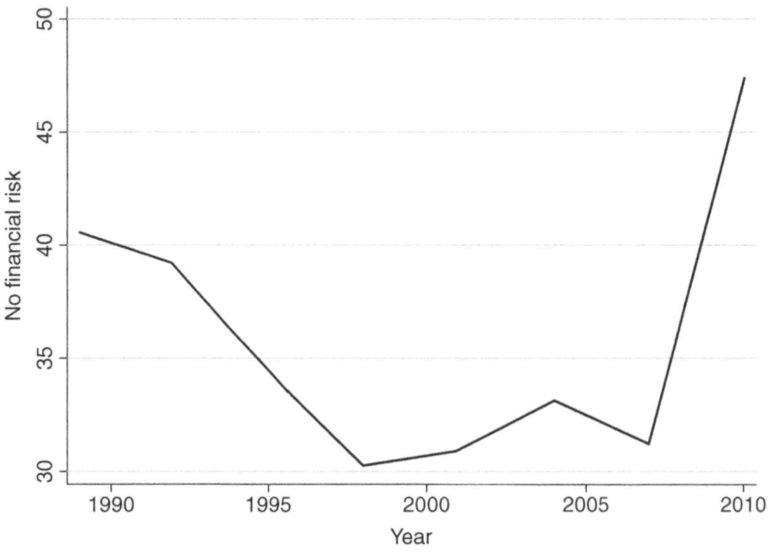

Figure 13.1 Share of highly risk-averse people in the Survey of Consumer Finances [Subtext figure: The figure shows the proportion of people answering "Not willing to take any financial risk" to the risk aversion question asked in the Survey of Consumer Finances described in Table 13.1, year by year.]

that the high level of risk aversion in 1989 reflects an increase due to the financial collapse of 1989. Unfortunately, we cannot prove this; but if this interpretation were true, then it would also show that an increase in risk aversion after a scary episode such as a major financial crisis takes considerable time to revert. Indeed, the fact that investors still show a great reluctance to assume financial risk in 2010 compared to 2007 – that is, two years after the collapse of Lehman Brothers and even after the stock market recovered – suggests that increases in risk aversion of this sort tend to be long-lasting.

The SCF data refer to a sequence of cross-sections, not to panel data. Thus, they are informative of the evolution of the risk aversion of the average investor but not of the risk aversion of the single investor. In addition to this there are two other problems with the SFC measure. First, because of their cross-sectional nature, they cannot easily be used to test different factors that can explain the change in risk tolerance. For instance, with this data it is hard to test whether risk aversion has increased more (or mostly) for those who incurred financial losses during the crisis, as would be predicted by habit models. One could bypass this problem by constructing averages of risk aversion and endowments (and other explanatory variables) for different groups in the years covered by the survey and following them over time (and age) – that is, setting up a pseudo-panel. Clearly, the results would be conditional on the grouping criteria. Second, if people differ in beliefs about stock market returns and/or volatility, these differences will tend to contaminate the answers to the SCF question. This bias would affect not only cross-sectional comparisons, but also inter-temporal ones, possibly revealing a change in risk preferences when none is present.

In a recent paper, Guiso, Sapienza and Zingales (2013b) try to overcome these problems. First, they elicit a measure equivalent to the SCF, but in a sample of Italian investors interviewed before the financial crisis (in 2007), and then after the collapse of Lehman Brothers, in the spring of 2009. For this panel of investors they have several measures of their assets as well as various characteristics and information on their expectations about stock market returns and volatility, allowing them to assess whether the latter played a role in affecting risk attitudes. Being a panel, they can look at correlations between changes in risk aversion and changes in potential determinants.

Second, they obtain an additional measure of risk aversion that is not contaminated by changing beliefs. Each respondent was presented with several choices between a risky prospect, which paid EUR 10,000 or EUR 0 with equal probability and a sequence of certain sums of money. These sums were increased progressively between EUR 100 and EUR 9,000. More risk-averse people will give up the risky prospect for lower certain sums. Thus, the first certain sum at which an investor switches from the risky to the certain prospect identifies (an upper bound for) his/her certainty equivalent, from which they obtain the investor risk premium.

Using these measures, they document a remarkable shift in risk preferences. As in the SCF, the fraction of individuals who answer that they normally are not willing to take any financial risk increases from 18 percent in 2007 to 42 percent in 2009. Similarly, the risk premium the median investor in willing to pay to avoid the secure safe lottery prospect increases from EUR 1,000 in 2007 to EUR 3,500 in 2009. This corresponds to a doubling of the tripling of the median investor risk aversion. They show that the change in the distribution of wealth plays essentially no role in explaining the change in the investors' aggregate risk aversion, which is entirely due to the changes in the risk aversion of the individual investors.

Guiso, Sapienza and Zingales (2013b) try to test various channels that could potentially explain these patterns. Though changes in these measures of risk aversion predict participation rates in the stock market, they do not correlate with changes in investor wealth except for those who experienced very large losses during the financial crisis. But risk aversion increases substantially even among investors who suffered very mild losses and, most importantly, among those who suffered no losses at all because they held no stocks in the summer of 2008 when the crisis began. The latter experienced an increase in risk aversion as large as the former. This evidence is hard to reconcile with pure habit models, though it may be consistent with changes in expected future incomes and background risk. However, Guiso et al. (2013) check whether risk aversion increased more among investors that are less likely to face background risk (such as public employees or the elderly) and find no evidence in support of this either. What, then, has driven the change? They advance a conjecture: fear. People reacted to the crisis by becoming more fearful, and this fear automatically triggered higher risk aversion. This explanation follows evidence in neuro-economics and lab experiments that risk aversion is augmented by panic and fear. Kuhnen and Knutson (2005) find that more activation in the anterior insula (the brain area where anticipatory negative emotions are presumably located) is followed by increased risk aversion. Kuhnen and Knutson (2011) find that subjects exposed to visual cues that induced anxiety were subsequently more risk averse and less willing to invest in risky assets. In support of this view, they find that the increase in risk aversion is correlated with measures of Knightian uncertainty. In addition, to find some indirect confirming evidence, they ran an experiment with a sample of students at Northwestern University, treating half of the sample with a scary movie and then eliciting risk aversion from all participants using the same questions that they asked the sample of investors. They found that people who had watched the movie were systematically more risk averse than those who had not been exposed to the movie. Most importantly, the difference in risk aversion between the two groups was sizeable – as sizeable as was the increase in risk aversion during the financial crisis. While this is no direct proof that the increase in risk aversion during the financial crisis was triggered by fear, it shows that a fear mechanism has the potential to explain large swings in risk aversion such as those documented in the SCF and in the Italian panel.

Conclusions

It is well documented that recovery from financial crises tends to be slow, much slower than recovery from standard recessions. They may also have more persistent effects, even on the level of potential output and long-term growth – an issue that is receiving considerable attention in the US (Hall 2014) and which should be even more relevant in Europe given the extremely slow recovery of the euro area as a whole, particularly among the Southern European economies. The mechanisms generating the slow recovery and the persistent growth effects can be several and they are not yet well understood. In this chapter we have added another channel: increased investors' risk aversion caused by the crises. Increased risk aversion can affect the economic growth performance directly by diverting entrepreneurs' investments from high-growth but risky projects to safer but lower-growth investments; by raising investors' required risk premium, and thus the cost of capital, higher risk aversion can slow down recoveries because it lowers capital accumulation. In addition, because it increases the relative cost of risky capital, it can slow down growth because the relative cost of equity investment increases, discouraging investment in innovative firms which rely disproportionately on equity finance.

We have discussed several mechanisms through which people's risk tolerance can change over time. Some are due to variations in economic variables, in particular the distribution of individual endowments or the access to insurance and credit markets; others reflect psychological forces that trigger fear. The evidence on what leads to changing risk aversion is just starting to accumulate. The available data suggests that both factors – economic and psychological – seem to matter in explaining why risk aversion increases in response to financial crises.

Is there room for policy and regulatory interventions to stabilize people's risk preferences and, if so, for which kind? Can policy makers intervene in the psychological mechanisms that drive risk aversion during a financial crisis? Can governments, for instance, regulate the dissemination of information or its tone through the high-speed channels of today's world, in order to pre-empt the contagion of fear and the propagation of a crisis? We have no answer to these questions, but they are on the table.

References

Anderson, Jon, Stephen Burks, Colin DeYoung and Aldo Rustichini (2011). "Toward the integration of personality theory and decision theory in the explanation of economic behavior." University of Minnesota. *Mimeo.*

Apicella, C. L., A. Dreber, B. Campbell, P. B. Gray, M. Hoffman and A. C. Little, (2008). "Testosterone and financial risk-taking." *Evolution and Human Behavior* 29: 385–390.

Beauchamp, Jonathan, David Cesarini and Magnus Johannesson (2011). "The psychometric properties of measures of economic risk preferences." *New York University Working Paper.*

Betermier, Sebastien, Thomas Jansson, Christine A. Parlour and Johan Waldeny (2012). "Hedging labor income risk." *Journal of Financial Economics* 105(3): 622–639.

Bodie, Zvi, Robert C. Merton and William F. Samuelson (1992). "Labor supply flexibility and portfolio choice in a life-cycle model." *Journal of Economic Dynamics and Control* 16(3–4): 427–449.

Brunnermeier, Markus K. and Stefan Nagel (2008). "Do wealth fluctuations generate time-varying risk aversion? Micro-evidence on individuals' asset allocation." *American Economic Review* 98(3): 713–736.

Calvet, Laurent E. and Paolo Sodini (2014). "Twin picks: disentangling the determinants of risk taking in household portfolios." *Journal of Finance* LXIX(2): 867–906.

Cameron, Lisa and Manisha Shah (2012). "Risk-taking behavior in the wake of natural disasters." *IZA Discussion Paper* 6756.

Campbell, John Y. and John H. Cochrane (1999). "By force of habit: a consumption-based explanation of aggregate stock market behavior." *The Journal of Political Economy* 107(2): 205–251.

Campbell, John Y. and João Cocco (2003). "Household risk management and optimal mortgage choice." *Quarterly Journal of Economics* 118(4): 1449–1494.

Cesarini, David, Christopher Dawes, Magnus Johannesson, Paul Lichtenstein and Björn Wallace (2009). "Genetic variation in preferences for giving and risk-taking." *Quarterly Journal of Economics* 124(2): 809–842.

Chetty, Ray and Adam Szeidl (2007). "Consumption commitments: neoclassical foundations for habit formation." *Working Paper*, University of California, Berkeley.

Chetty, Ray and Adam Szeidl (2008). "Do Consumption Commitments Affect Risk Preferences? Evidence from Portfolio Choice." *Working Paper*, University of California, Berkeley.

Chiapporì, Pierre-Andrè and Monica Paiella (2011). "Relative risk aversion is constant." *Journal of the European Economic Association* 9(6): 1021–1052.

Cocco, Joao (2005). "Portfolio choice in the presence of housing." *Review of Financial Studies* 18(2): 535–567.

Cocco Joao, Francisco Gomes and Pascal Maenhout (2005). "Consumption and portfolio choice over the life-cycle." *Review of Financial Studies* 18(2): 491–533.

Constantinides, George M. (1990). "Habit formation: a resolution of the equity premium puzzle." *Journal of Political Economy* 98(3): 519–543.

Croson, Rachel and Uri Gneezy (2009). "Gender differences in preferences." *Journal of Economic Literature* 47(2): 448–474.

Dohmen, Thomas J., Armin Falk, David Huffman and Uwe Sunde (2010). "Are risk aversion and impatience related to cognitive ability?" *American Economic Review* 100(3): 1238–1260.

Dohmen, Thomas J., Armin Falk, David Huffman, Uwe Sunde, Jürgen Schupp and Gert G. Wagner (2011). "Individual risk attitudes: new evidence from a large, representative, experimentally-validated survey." *Journal of the European Economic Association* 9(3): 522–550.

Dreber, Anna, Coren L. Apicella, Dan T. A. Eisenberg, Justin R. Garcia, Richard S. Zamore, J. Koji J. Lum and Benjamin Campbell (2009). "The 7 R polymorphism in the dopamine receptor D4 gene (DRD4) is associated with financial risk-taking in men." *Evolution and Human Behavior* 30(2): 85–92.

Eckel, Catherine C., Mahmoud A. El-Gamal and Rick K. Wilson (2009). "Risk loving after the storm: A Bayesian-Network study of Hurricane Katrina evacuees." *Journal of Economic Behavior and Organization* 69(2): 110–124.

Fagereng, Andreas, Charles Gottlieb and Luigi Guiso (2013). "Asset market participation and portfolio choice over the life cycle." *CEPR Discussion Papers* 9691.

Frederick, Shane (2006). "Cognitive Reflection and Decision-Making." *Journal of Economic Perspectives* 19(4): 24–42.

Garbarino, Ellen, Robert Slonim and Justin Sydnon (2011). "Digit ratios (2D:4D) as predictors of risky decision making." *Journal of Risk and Uncertainty* 42(1): 1–26.

Grinblatt, Mark, Matti Keloharju and Juhani Linnainmaa (2011). "IQ and stock market participation." *Journal of Finance* 66: 2121–2164.

Grossman, Sanford J. and Guy Laroque (1990). "Asset pricing and optimal portfolio choice in the presence of illiquid durable consumption goods." *Econometrica* 58(1): 25–51.

Grossman, Sanford J. and Jean-Luc Vila (1992). "Optimal dynamic trading with leverage constraints." *Journal of Financial and Quantitative Analysis* 27(2): 151–168.

Guiso, Luigi and Tullio Jappelli (1998). "Background uncertainty and the demand for insurance against insurable risks." *The Geneva Papers on Risk and Insurance Theory* 23: 7–27.

Guiso, Luigi, Tullio Jappelli and Daniele Terlizzese (1996). "Income risk, borrowing constraints and portfolio choice." *American Economic Review* 86(1): 158–172.

Guiso, Luigi and Monica Paiella (2008). "Risk aversion, wealth, and background risk." *Journal of the European Economic Association* 6(6): 1109–1150.

Guiso, Luigi, and Aldo Rustichini (2011). "Understanding the effects of testosterone on preferences for risk, ambiguity and regret." University of Minnesota. *Mimeo.*

Guiso, Luigi, Paola Sapienza and Luigi Zingales (2013a). "The determinants of attitudes toward strategic defaults on mortgages." *Journal of Finance* 68(4): 1473–1515.

Guiso, Luigi, Paola Sapienza and Luigi Zingales (2013b). "Time varying risk aversion." *CEPR working paper.*

Hall, Robert (2014). "Quantifying the lasting harm to the US economy from the financial crisis." *NBER Macroeconomic Annual* 2014/29.

Hartog, Joop, Ada Ferrer-i-Carbonell and Nicole Jonker (2002). "Linking measured risk aversion to individual characteristics." *Kyklos* 55(1): 3–26.

Heaton, John and Deborah Lucas (2000). "Asset pricing and portfolio choice: The importance of entrepreneurial risk." *Journal of Finance* 55 (3): 1163–1198.

Holman, E. Alison and Roxane C. Silver (1998). "Getting 'stuck' in the past: temporal orientation and coping with trauma." *Journal of Personality and Social Psychology* 74(5): 1146–1163.

Holt, Charles A. and Susan K. Laury (2002). "Risk aversion and incentive effects." *American Economic Review* 92(5): 1644–1655.

Hung, Wei, Yu-Jane Liu, Chia-Fen Tsai and Ning Zhu (2014). "Employer stock risk, employee income risks, and portfolio choice: new evidence from Taiwan." National Taiwan University. *Mimeo.*

Kamstra, Mark J., Lisa A. Kramer and Maurice D. Levi (2003). "Winter blues: a SAD stock market cycle." *American Economic Review* 93(1).

Kimball, Miles S., Claudia R. Sahm and Matthew D. Shapiro (2008). "Imputing risk tolerance from survey responses." *Journal of the American Statistical Association* 103(483): 1028–1038.

Kramer, Lisa A. and J. Mark Weber (2012). "This is your portfolio on winter: seasonal affective disorder and risk aversion in financial decision making." *Social Psychological and Personality Science* 3(2): 193–199.

Kramer, Adam, Jamie E. Guillory and Jeffrey T. Hancock (2014). "Experimental evidence of massive scale emotional contagion through social networks." *PNAS* 111(24): 8788–8790.

Kuhnen, Camelia M. and Joan Y. Chiao (2009). "Genetic determinants of financial risk taking." *Plos One* 4(2): 1–5.

Kuhnen, Camelia M. and Brian Knutson (2005). "The neural basis of financial risk taking." *Neuron* 47(5): 763–770.

Kuhnen, Camelia M. and Brian Knutson (2011). "The influence of affect on beliefs, preferences and financial decisions." *Journal of Financial and Quantitative Analysis* 46(3): 605–626.

Lipschitz, Deborah S., Ann M. Rasmusson and Steven M. Southwick (1998). "Childhood posttraumatic stress disorder: A review of neurobiological sequelae." *Psychiatric Annals* 28: 452–457.

Loewenstein, George (2000). "Emotions in economic theory and economic behavior." *The American Economic Review* 90(2): 426–432.

Love, David A. (2010). "The effect of marital status on savings and portfolio choice." Review of Financial Studies 23(1): 385–432.

Lupton, Joseph (2002). "Household Portfolio Choice and the Habit Liability: Evidence from Panel Data." *Working Paper*, University of Michigan.

Malmendier, Ulrike and Stefan Nagel (2011). "Depression babies: Do macroeconomic experiences affect risk taking?" *The Quarterly Journal of Economics* 126(1): 373–416.

Page, Lionel, David A. Savage and Benno Torgler (2012). "Variation in risk seeking behavior in a natural experiment on large losses induced by a natural disaster." *CESifo working paper series* 3878.

Palia, Darius, Yaxuan Qi and Yangru Wu (2014). "Heterogeneous background risks and portfolio choice: evidence from micro-level data." *Journal of Money, Credit and Banking*, forthcoming.

Pinel, John P.J. (2009). *Biopsychology*. Boston, MA: Pearson/Allyn and Bacon.

Pistaferri, Luigi and Costas Meghir (2004). "Income variance dynamics and heterogeneity." *Econometrica* 72(1): 1–32.

Postlewaite, Andrew, Larry Samuelson and Dan Silverman (2008). "Consumption commitments and employment contracts." *Review of Economic Studies* 75(2): 559–578.

Powell, Melanie and David Ansic (1997). "Gender differences in risk behaviour in financial decision-making: an experimental analysis." *Journal of Economic Psychology* 18(6): 605–628.

Sapienza, Paola, Luigi Zingales and Dario Maestripieri (2009). "Gender differences in financial risk aversion and career choices are affected by testosterone." *PNAS* 106(36): 15268–15273.

Shaw, John A. (2000). "Children, adolescents and trauma." *Psychiatric Quarterly* 71(3): 227–244.

Stigler, George J. and Gary S. Becker (1977). "De gustibus non est disputandum." *American Economic Review* 67(2): 76–90.

Viceira, Luis (2001). "Optimal portfolio choice for long-horizon investors with nontradable labor income." *The Journal of Finance* 56(2): 433–470.

Viscusi, W. Kip (2009). "Valuing risks of death from terrorism and natural disasters." *Journal of Risk and Uncertainty* 38(3): 191–213.

Viscusi, W. Kip and Richard J. Zeckhauser (2006). "National survey evidence on disasters and relief: Risk beliefs, self-interest, and compassion." *Journal of Risk and Uncertainty* 33(1): 13–36.

Vissing-Jørgensen, Annette (2002). "Towards an explanation of household portfolio choice heterogeneity: nonfinancial income and participation cost structures." *NBER Working Paper* 8884.

Yao, Rui and Harold Zhang (2005). "Optimal Consumption and Portfolio Choices with Risky Housing and Borrowing Constraints." *Review of Financial Studies* 18(1): 197–239.

14

Household finance and the law – a case study on economic transplants

KATJA LANGENBUCHER[1]

> And the logical method and form flatter that longing for certainty and for repose which is in every human mind. But certainty generally is illusion, and repose is not the destiny of man. Behind the logical form lies a judgment as to the relative worth and importance of competing legislative grounds . . . the very root and nerve of the whole proceeding.[2]

Law and economics have a history. There have been periods of admiration, flirting and courtship, leading to happy marriages and a bunch of children with names such as torts, antitrust, and banking regulation. There have also been language problems, misunderstandings, and passionate fights about who wears the pants, resulting in the law having affairs with dangerous strangers such as Ronald Dworkin. Today, we seem to be witnessing an aging couple, pottering about in harmony, the fights of the past long forgotten. All they quarrel about nowadays is economics' newfound hobby involving a lot of mathematics which the law doesn't understand. May we, then, safely assume that they have agreed on what life is about and how to tackle its challenges? Are they speaking a common language? It is claimed in this chapter that this is not the case.

The argument put forward here concerns a practice I will call "economic transplants".[3] The term denotes the process of identifying

[1] Professor for Private Law, Corporate and Financial Law at Goethe University and Affiliated Professor at SciencesPo/Ecole de Droit, Paris. This chapter forms part of a broader research project on economic transplants. For comments on earlier versions I am much indebted to Scott Brewer, Harvard Law School; to David Kershaw, LSE; to Gunter Teubner, Goethe University; to Mikhail Xifaras, SciencesPo; and to the participants in a 2014 séminaire doctorale at SciencesPo, Paris, and in the 2013 Law & Economics Forum, LSE London. Remaining errors are mine.

[2] Holmes 1897.

[3] The term has been used by David Kershaw (Unpublished PhD thesis, on file at Harvard Law School) and by Lianos (2009).

components of economic theory and integrating them in a legal argument. We have seen substantial collaboration along those lines for a long time. It has been especially popular in financial markets law, where theories such as the efficient capital markets hypothesis, the market for control theory or the capital asset pricing model have had a direct impact not only on legal scholarship, but also on legislators and consequently on the judiciary. Having lost some of their appeal after the financial crisis, behavioural economics approaches have sparked new interest in legal scholars, delivering a new type of "economic transplants". Household finance regulation provides interesting examples of those, making use of their insights for coping with investor's shortcomings via enhanced information or "nudging" techniques.

Despite the apparent ease of the working relationship, there is a surprising lack of methodological reflection upon the ways in which the process of transplanting economic theories into the legal universe is to be carried out. We see lawyers debating intensely on the possibility of "legal transplants" from one legal order to another, wondering to what extent the boundaries of national legal orders may be crossed.[4] No such discussion has yet surfaced as to the possibly more complex endeavour of an economic transplant transgressing the borders of disciplines. This chapter takes a first step, using household finance as a case study (see "Economic transplants at work: household finance"). It provides a rough sketch of the epistemic goals pursued and the techniques used in both disciplines (see "On epistemic motives" and "On techniques"). Some reasons for understanding the growing impact economic transplants have had on legal scholarship are advanced (see "On economics' promise") and areas for further research are highlighted (see "The normative challenge: areas of further research").

Economic transplants at work: household finance

The argument proposed here is not an argument about economics, nor does it concern traditional law and economics scholarship. It tries to understand a less intensely theorized phenomenon which has increasingly shaped financial markets law. Over the last decades, areas such as capital markets law, banking law and insurance regulation have

[4] See, for the debate on "legal transplants", Watson 1974, Kahn-Freund 1974, Legrand 1997, and Teubner 1998: 12.

incorporated economic theories into law-making. This trend has not necessarily subscribed to the broad claims of traditional law and economics theory (see, in more detail, the section "On economics' promise"). Instead, it comes across as a very pragmatic approach, linking for example the economist's finance research on capital markets and their actors to the legal rules that govern them. The more philosophical debate on the legitimacy of traditional law and economics has no equivalent in this new, pragmatic version of law and economics. It has been argued that this is due to critics of law and economics having no interest in business law.[5] Arguably, the assumption that the goals pursued by both disciplines seem to be closely related, if not the same, has contributed to the lack of theoretical research on how to bridge the gap as well.

The legislative history of household finance provides good examples for this new pragmatic approach, ranging from optimistic reliance on theories such as the efficient capital markets hypothesis, seemingly rendering investor protection almost redundant, to transplanting ideas from behavioural economics in order to protect investors from wrong decisions.

A number of earlier European Directives display the belief in efficient markets, and the existence of "correct" prices and rational actors, as well as the importance of providing information to those. We find the conviction that "full and proper market transparency . . . is a prerequisite for trading for all economic actors"[6]. Prices are usually correct, but can also be "at an abnormal or artificial level".[7] "Reasonable investors base their investment decisions on information . . . available to them";[8] hence, the main instrument of investor protection is to give them enough information: "The provision of full information concerning

[5] This point is made by Schwartz (2011: 110).

[6] Recital (15), Directive 2003/6/EC of the European Parliament and of the Council of 28 January 2003 on insider dealing and market manipulation (market abuse); Recitals (7), (58) Regulation (EU) No. 596/2014 of the European Parliament and of the Council of 16 April 2014 on market abuse (market abuse regulation).

[7] Art. 1 para. 2 (a) Directive 2003/6/EC of the European Parliament and of the Council of 28 January 2003 on insider dealing and market manipulation (market abuse); Art. 12 No. 1 (a) (ii) Regulation (EU) No. 596/2014 of the European Parliament and of the Council of 16 April 2014 on market abuse (market abuse regulation).

[8] Recital (1) Commission Directive 2003/124/EC of 22 December 2003 implementing Directive 2003/6/EC of the European Parliament and of the Council as regards the definition and public disclosure of inside information and the definition of market manipulation; Recital (14) Regulation (EU) No. 596/2014 of the European Parliament and of the Council of 16 April 2014 on market abuse (market abuse regulation).

securities and issuers of those securities promotes . . . the protection of investors".[9] The legislator assumes that providing information will "enable them [the investors] to take investment decisions in full knowledge of the facts",[10] as long as the information is "sufficient and as objective as possible".[11]

The financial crisis seems to have shattered some but surely not all of the legislator's optimism as to (then) mainstream economic theories on the efficiency of capital markets. In addition to providing ever more information for the investor, studies with a behavioural and/or empirical background have attracted the lawmaker's interest. It is no longer assumed that investors aspire to full knowledge of the facts and base their decision on an appreciation of these facts. Instead, the legislator realizes that financial products "are frequently combined with insurance coverage or are complex and difficult to understand".[12] Doubts about the investor being capable of processing information adequately show when the legislator claims that "existing disclosures to investors . . . are uncoordinated and often fail to aid retail investors compare between the different products, and in comprehending their features. As a consequence, retail investors have often made investments with risks and costs that were not fully understood by those investors."[13] These insights, along with political pressure after the crisis, have led the legislator to consider new forms of providing information. "To meet the needs of retail investors, it is necessary to ensure that information . . . is accurate, fair, clear and not misleading".[14] "Retail investors should be provided with the information necessary for them to take an informed decision".[15] More radically, reasons for limiting the choice available to investors have

[9] Recital (18) Directive 2004/25/EC of the European Parliament and of the Council of 4 November 2003 on the prospectus to be published when securities are offered to the public or admitted to trading and amending Directive 2001/34/EC.

[10] Recital (19) Directive 2004/25/EC of the European Parliament and of the Council of 4 November 2003 on the prospectus to be published when securities are offered to the public or admitted to trading and amending Directive 2001/34/EC.

[11] Recital (20) Directive 2004/25/EC of the European Parliament and of the Council of 4 November 2003 on the prospectus to be published when securities are offered to the public or admitted to trading and amending Directive 2001/34/EC.

[12] P7_TC1-COD(2012)0169 – Position of the European Parliament adopted at first reading on 15 April 2014 with a view to the adoption of Regulation (EU) No . . . /2014 of the European Parliament and of the Council on key information documents for packaged retail and insurance based investment products (PRIIPs), p. 6, available at: http://register.consilium.europa.eu/doc/srv?l=EN&f=ST%208486%202014%20INIT.

[13] Ibid. p. 6. [14] Ibid., p. 14. [15] Ibid., p. 15.

been advanced, advocating product bans when there are "concerns to investor protection".[16]

On epistemic motives

Finding economic transplants of this kind, we may intuitively expect that both disciplines ask similar questions and speak a common language. This would allow us to frame the law as advancing side by side with economics, adapting progress made in economic research to work out legal rules and institutions. We would assume that the lack of legal rules on investor protection was due to minor flaws in the economic theories transplanted. We would also have an adequate solution at hand, consisting in transplanting "better" economic theory enriched, for example, by behavioural aspects or game theory.[17] However, closer inspection seems to reveal that law and economics differ substantially as to epistemic motives pursued and as to techniques employed. Transplants of economic theory, with or without a behavioural background, seem to carry the risk of misunderstandings and incompatibility. Let us unfold the argument step by step. We will turn to economics first.

On economics' epistemic motives

Defining a discipline's epistemic motive is a tricky endeavour. Not everyone working in this discipline will agree on what it is he is searching for. What is more, epistemic motives change over time and evolve when new methods of scientific research become available[18] or new subdisciplines develop.[19] For the purposes of the argument put forward here, it is not necessary to present a comprehensive account of economics' epistemic motives over time. It will suffice to highlight some core features in order to later pass a judgement on the similarity or dissimilarity with law's epistemic motives.

Arguably, economics started out as *économie politique* (political economy), focusing on processes such as labour, production, sales and markets, as well as the distribution of national wealth by the state.[20] Economics was

[16] See ESMA, 2014 Work Programme, 30 September 2013/1355, p. 10.

[17] Schwartz (2011: 107) on economics in the 1960s, lacking game theory and thus very limited in its contribution to legal problems of private law.

[18] For an example see Akerlof (2007: 6) on the decline of Keynesian economics due to a change in methodology.

[19] Roncaglia 2001: 468ff.

[20] John Stuart Mill 1967.

then closely linked to philosophical investigations about distributive justice and state governance.[21] With the advent of new methods and techniques in the nineteenth century, economics experienced a "scientific turn". It seemed promising to compare its methods to those established by natural sciences and to adopt what seemed promising.[22] Much of modern economics has continued this path, ever more radically focusing on enhancing its scientific credibility, rather than its more political tradition.[23] Moving away from largely verbal explanations of phenomena, economic science has developed a taste for mathematical models and for empirical investigations. Those instruments lend themselves to application in a number of areas, among which we find business and finance but also corporate and state governance, crime prevention, family structures and legal institutions. What makes those investigations belong to the larger family of economics has been a focus on certain techniques and reliance on one or more assumptions, such as efficiency-maximizing behaviour under the premise of stable preferences, rational actors and market equilibrium.[24]

The increasing impact of formal methods and techniques in economic research has led the discipline into quite radically separating "what is and what ought to be".[25] Discussion today[26] is in many ways still shaped by a Milton Friedman essay from the 1950s where he claimed: "Positive economics is in principle independent of any particular ethical position or normative judgments. . . . In short, positive economics is, or can be, an 'objective' science, in precisely the same sense as any of the physical sciences."[27] Even if an economist ventures to make policy recommendations, and hence is practicing "normative economics",[28] this "necessarily rests on a prediction about the consequences of doing one thing rather than another, a prediction that must be based . . . on positive economics".[29]

[21] Hayek 1942: 267. What is left of this branch goes under the heading of "normative economics" and sometimes "welfare economics" (with the former being more open towards a diversity of social goals, cf. Mishan 1981: 3).

[22] Larrère 1992. Very critical on this development, see Hayek (1942: 267f.). On the impact of this development for the law, see Xifaras 2004: 187.

[23] Debreu 1991: 3; Leontief 1982: 104f; with a focus on law and economics, see Schwartz (2011: 105).

[24] Lazear 2000: 99f. [25] Friedman 1953: 2, referring to Keynes.

[26] For a comprehensive account of the current discussion, see Mäki 2009.

[27] Friedman 1953: 2.

[28] On current definitions of "normative" (welfare) economics, see Bergson 1966, Mishan 1981.

[29] Friedman 1953: 5.

Contemporary definitions of the object of economic research differ surprisingly little, framing the goal of economic research as the "attempt to understand, predict, and control the unknown through quantitative analysis"[30] and concluding that "the power of economics lies in its rigor. Economics is scientific".[31] The efforts undertaken by some to point out "that the aggregation or comparison of the different satisfactions of different individuals involves judgments of value rather than judgments of fact, and that such judgments are beyond the scope of positive science"[32] have not resonated much within mainstream economics.[33]

On law's epistemic motives

Framing law's epistemic motives encounters the same difficulties as stating in a few sentences what economics is about. Legal scholars have disagreed most fundamentally about what they are trying to achieve and have said different things when talking about legislative law-making on the one hand and judicial interpretation on the other.[34] Again, the argument proposed here does not require a display of the entire spectrum of theories about the aims pursued by legal scholarship. Instead, a very crude comment on law's motives will suffice.

It is suggested here that the bulk of legal scholarship is about normative rather than positive work.[35] If we remain on a level of considerable abstraction, we might say that the goal of legal scholarship is to contribute to the creation and the interpretation of rules. This is not to say that legal scholars disregard empirical insight.[36] I will address the ways in which they consider descriptions of reality later, when discussing the "synthesizing" methodology of law (see "An exercise in law's techniques", below). However, while the economist's normative statements seem to be a by-product of his positive work (see "On economics' epistemic motives", above), the legal scholar's descriptive work seems to typically serve the normative goal of making suggestions for keeping or altering existing rules.

30 Lo/Mueller (12 March 2010: 1). 31 Lazear 2000: 102.
32 Robbins 1945: vii; in a similar vein, see Hayek (1942: 267).
33 This is not to say that there has not been debate on this topic. For more classic articles, see: Archibald (1959: 316); Heilbroner (1973: 129), reprinted in: Marr/ Raj (1983: 3ff.); Little (1957: 67ff.); Stilwell (1975); more recently, Mongin (2006: 19).
34 Chemerinsky/Fisk (1998–1999: 667), Epstein (2002: 1288).
35 See positions such as Dworkin 1986, Hart (1994: 52f., 70f.); Weinrib (1995: 70ff.). A more current account is to be found in Goldberg (2012: 1656f.).
36 An overview of empirical legal studies can be found in Heise (2002: 822f.).

On techniques

On economics' techniques

The results of scientific research are in many ways shaped by the methodology each discipline employs. As was mentioned earlier ("On economics' epistemic motives"), during the last century economics in general, and its branch "finance" in particular, have moved away from the more verbal tradition of political economy towards measurable quantities, favouring research based on theoretical models and on empirical analysis,[37] more recently including behavioural insights.[38] We might interpret economics' methodology today as a combination of the techniques used in the natural sciences, inductively working out hypotheses on the basis of empirical research, and the methodology of mathematics, formulating abstract hypotheses and deductively applying rigid logical operations to those.[39]

The "scientific method"

The natural sciences have served as the archetypical example of the scientific method, a label developed in philosophy and in the history of science. The scientific method has been understood as working out hypotheses on the basis of inductive inferences from large samples of observable facts. It is characterized by the repeatability of experiments, and in its Popperian version by the falsifiability of its hypotheses. Its initial addressees have been the natural sciences. This accounts for its focus on gathering data and on observing real-life phenomena, as well as on specific, repeatable processes – such as an experiment – which are open to empirical testing. Success, both on purely scientific as well as on political grounds, had fuelled expansive tendencies of the scientific method to take over other sciences.[40] While these attempts were not entirely successful, they did lead to a persistent process of the social sciences and the humanities reflecting upon methodologies characteristic

[37] On the growing impact of empirical research but critical as to quality, see Schwartz (2011: 135f.).

[38] Debreu (1991: 1, 3); Oswald (1991: 75) (who includes sociological insights on career dynamics). Ironically, economists who focus on theoretical models tend to not use empirical research to falsify their findings. Very different is Friedman's (1953: 8f.) approach: "the only relevant test of the *validity* of a hypothesis is comparison of its predictions with experience"); see also: François 2008: 128f.), Morgan (1988: 160–164).

[39] Debreu (1991: 3), Vazquez (1995: 247). Very critical on the transferability, see Hayek (1979: 40–60).

[40] See the overview in Mirowski (1989: 354).

of their own research. Most have found the transfer of the scientific method fruitful. Disagreement remains as to the amendments necessary for accommodating the fact that the object of those disciplines is in part or exclusively human behaviour or human creations.

Economics and the scientific method

Economics' technique today seems to heavily rely on the scientific method as well as on mathematics and theoretical physics.[41] Economists who work with theoretical models make use of the mathematical tradition to set up formal assumptions and deduce their hypotheses according to highly formalized methodologies. Doing so, an economist will often serve two masters. On the one hand, much of his research concerns human behaviour, entailing quite a bit of complexity. Controlled experiments are hard to come by at macro-level and the effects of learning are often complex to integrate. On the other hand, the structure of mathematical models will allow for disregarding substantial parts of empirically perceivable reality or radically simplifying it in order to create an artificial setting, suitable for such models.[42]

On law's techniques

As mentioned in "On law's epistemic motives", legal scholarship's primary epistemic motive lies in the production of a normative statement. The methodology used incorporates features familiar from social sciences as well as from the humanities.

An exercise in law's techniques

Let us picture a legal scholar searching for an answer to a legal problem at hand. We will imagine a retail investor who bought a product which his financial advisor recommended to him. The product is quite risky and it is unclear to what extent the advisor made perfectly clear how risky the product is. The advisor has sold the product in question often and gained a "kick-back" payment from the issuer each time he sold it. May the investor claim damages? A legal scholar's answer to this question will depend upon whether he is asked (1) for the interpretation of a certain

[41] See Debreu (1991: 1) (claiming that theoretical physics precedes mathematization at p. 2); Mirowsky (1989: 354ff.) (skeptical about the existence of a hard and fast scientific method at p. 356).

[42] Passeron (2001: 243); very critical, see Leontieff (1982: 104); in a similar vein, see Adorno (1962: 249f.), Debreu (1991: 4) (linking this to mathematization).

country's existing laws on this point, (2) for the formulation of a rule in an imaginary country with no body of law on this point, or (3) if he is asked for a rule that could be freshly enacted, while fitting in with a certain country's law on this point.

Doctrinal legal scholarship If the legal scholar carries out the doctrinal task of working on the interpretation of a certain country's laws on this point, he will focus primarily on legal texts. His research will include legislatively enacted laws and, if available, judicial precedents. He will ask what the wording of available rules on investor protection, duty of care and independence of advisors suggests. Often, he will analyse how they have been understood in the past and possibly how the legislative body that enacted the relevant norms wanted them to be interpreted. In addition he might ask how a duty to advise a retail investor fits into a coherent reading of an existing country's private law.[43] Possibly, he will also compare relevant rules on investor protection in other countries. His answer will often include a prediction of what a court in this country is likely to decide.

Unrestrained legal scholarship Let us now fast-forward to the unrestrained legal scholar whose focus is on developing a rule on investor protection in an imaginary country without any rule yet enacted. He might remind us of the economist who builds a mathematical model based on features he deems relevant. He treats the legal question at hand in isolation from its "natural surroundings" – for example, from the laws defining a duty of care, a retail investor or a financial product.

What could this unrestrained scholar's methodology be? It will be a combination of many things. He will gather as much information on the phenomena in question as he can. Doing so, he will rely on techniques that are characteristic of other disciplines. Quite probably he will ask economists for their theories on the effects of a high or low level of retail investor protection on capital markets. He might look for psychological and behavioural insight on the retail investor's capacity to process information or on their reaction to transparency about conflicts of interest of financial advisors. He might consider sociological or historical evidence.[44] He will probably formulate possible rules and he might consider testing empirically how these could work out in practice – depending, of

[43] On the notion of "coherent fit", see Dworkin (1986: 268ff.).

[44] On the limits of contributing empirical research, see Vermeule (2006: 153ff.).

course, on how imaginary the world is in our example. He will bring his theories on what is fair and just to bear on the problem. On the basis of such research, he will decide what he considers to be the best legal answer to the substantive problem.

On a more technical level, he will also have to give the wording of possible rules some thought. Throughout the process of drafting a statutory rule, he will strive for linguistically precise and logically stringent rules. The methodologies he employs for this task are closely related to those of the humanities, albeit with some specifics of law. He will work on logically valid and conclusive arguments in order to justify the weight he attaches to each of the many factors under consideration. He will need to explain why he thinks the proposed rule is a good one. In addition, he might work out a coherent set of interrelated rules, defining, for example, a duty of care, the burden of proof when establishing a claim and the damages which may be awarded.

Coherentist legal scholarship Lastly, let us consider the coherentist legal scholar who aims to find a rule to be freshly enacted, while still fitting within the broader scheme of a certain country's existing laws. If we compare him to the first scholar, who was looking for guidance on an interpretation of one country's laws on this point, we find that the latter's leeway of possible rules is considerably broader. The existing body of law limits the coherentist's liberties in coming up with a convincing rule insofar as the proposed rule ideally should not be inconsistent with the bulk of existing rules. If, for example, a duty of care to allow the retail investor to claim damages in comparable situations is a foreign concept in this country, he will advocate a new rule more carefully than if this country's laws have seen a long tradition of investor protection and independence of advisors.

Which technique would this legal scholar employ? First, he does what the doctrinal scholar did. He considers the relevant laws of this country in order to understand the "natural surroundings" any new rule will have to fit into. He might try to offer a convincing case for a reform of a duty of care and discuss to what extent legislative attention is required. In the same way as the doctrinal scholar did, he will keep an eye on legal history and comparative legal studies. He will also work on arranging individual norms into a coherent whole, a practice continental scholars refer to as "systematic interpretation".[45] However, his task differs from the

[45] On Kant's notion of a "system", see Immanuel Kant (1786: IV).

doctrinal scholar's in that he is being asked for genuine, fresh input. He might consider proposing a new duty of care or a novel approach to independence of advisors which does not yet form part of that country's body of law. The methodology he employs in order to produce such fresh input at first glance resembles that of the unrestrained scholar we have considered, who was asked to come up with a rule in an imaginary world. He will gather information provided by other disciplines and evaluate it. He will formulate hypothetical rules; possibly, he might also consider testing them empirically or in a laboratory. He will evaluate them under his understanding of what he considers a fair and just result. However, his discretion is reduced by the fact that he was asked to formulate a rule that fits in with a certain country's existing body of law. Law builds up over time and legal institutions are path dependent. Entirely new, "ahistoric" rules cannot usually be enacted without severely disrupting legitimate expectations. There are many reasons to deplore this somewhat conservative bias of legal scholars.[46] Its advantage lies in enabling a form of "collective reason" – or, economically put, of extensive market tests – to deliver input on the task of formulating adequate rules.

Law's synthesizing capacity

If we compare the sparse comments on economics' methodology advanced here to the equally crude summary of legal techniques, we find a distinct feature of law's technique to be its *synthesizing* capacity.[47] We have said earlier that law's epistemic motive is in many respects a normative one.

Since most legal research does not provide descriptive insights, law is often dependent on input from other disciplines.[48] Criminal laws draw on psychology and criminology. Civil liability rules need input from various disciplines. When regulating actors in financial markets, most legislative bodies consult economic theories. If we wish to regulate investor protection, we need to understand the economic impact of harsh and of lax rules. The task of defining rules on insider trading requires an understanding of the extent to which insider trading "harms the market" and what type of harm we are talking about. If we require stock corporations to disclose specific information to the public we should have a well-founded expectation regarding the effects of

[46] Posner (2002: 1320), Hilgendorf (2010: 918). [47] Passeron (2001: 224) ("synthétique").
[48] Vermeule (2007).

disclosure on professional and retail investors. If we consider harsh sanctions for market manipulation, we should be able to give sound estimates of why those sanctions will help – and so on.

On economics' promise

This chapter started with the premise of law and economics collaborating in the law of financial markets. Having pointed to the marked differences as to epistemic goals and techniques of both disciplines, this premise seems less natural. Why have we seen this cooperation, if law and economics ask different questions and employ different techniques in order to come up with their respective answers? One of many reasons we may advance might be due to the fascination of the "scientific method". Economics' methodological history is clear evidence of the trust placed on the scientific method and of the high hopes for enhancing a discipline's credibility and status through the promise of "scientific" techniques being employed.

Physics envy

The term "physics envy" has been used to describe the attraction physics has had for economics scholars.[49] The nineteenth century saw breathtaking advancements in the natural sciences, most notably in physics, and economists pondering to what extent their methods might be useful in their own discipline.[50] It is in this tradition that economists working with a number of quantitative models have succeeded in applying physics' predictability of future events to an impressive amount of economic problems.[51] However, the rise of behavioural research and the growing awareness of the incompatibility of rigid premises with real-life actors and markets have reinforced scepticism about economics being as "hard" a science as physics.[52]

[49] Cf. Friedman (1953: 2 note 2) (on "prestige and acceptance of the views of physical scientists"), Mirowski (1989: 354ff.); on this book, see De Marchi (1993).

[50] Lakatos (1978).

[51] Listing a number of breakthroughs (game theory, general equilibrium, economics of uncertainty, long-term economic growth, portfolio theory and capital-asset pricing, option-pricing theory, macroeconometric models, computable general equilibrium models and rational expections), see Lo/Mueller (2010: 4f.).

[52] On a comparison of techniques, see Machlup (1961: 173ff.).

Economics envy

While legal scholars do not seem to suffer from "physics envy", there are good reasons to suppose that the strong appeal economics has had for many lawyers goes back to "economics envy".[53] This discipline, while seemingly working in a neighbouring field, boasts attractive features of a hard science, being measurable, precise and capable of predicting future developments.[54] By contrast, law seems to follow techniques characteristic of the humanities, given its emphasis on language, interpretation and discretion.[55] Just as the legal realists of the 1930s hoped for more empirical input, and the 1970s had witnessed a growing impact of sociology,[56] the past decades have seen the rise of economics as the promise of finally doing away with the much deplored indeterminacy and discretion of legal rules.[57] This is one of the areas where the argument put forward in this chapter overlaps with the theoretical debate on *law and economics*: Possibly, some of its appeal goes back to law's "soft" features, which we have just outlined.

Economics' promise to offer clear guidance on legal intricacies comes in both a strong, theoretical version and a weaker, pragmatic version. Its strong, theoretical version has formed the backbone of traditional *law and economics* theory. It suggests a collapse of law's technique into economics' methodology, entirely replacing law's vague standards by economics' benchmark. Let us go back to the three legal scholars we envisaged earlier to illustrate the dynamics of this strong version. It works very straightforwardly for the unrestrained legal scholar proposing norms in an imaginary country. Unencumbered by the restrictions of any legal order, he benchmarks against economic efficiency and looks for economically sound norms. The endeavour is slightly more complicated for the coherentist scholar who was faced with the additional task of fitting a newly to be developed rule into an existing body of law, achieving a good degree of coherence. Should he wish to make use of the "economic promise", he has to subscribe to economic efficiency in order to streamline his new proposition with economics' premises. In addition, he will

53 See Charles Goodhart (1997: 10), focusing more generally on a "social sciences approach"; Samuel (2008: 310).

54 Charles Goodhart (1997: 1f.) ("unashamedly imperialist"); celebrating the imperialist features of economics, see Lazear (2000: 99f.).

55 A good example is provided by the effort of Rubin (1992: 889).

56 Some 70 years earlier: Pound (1907; 1911: 591; 1911/12: 140, 489).

57 Related points are made by Goldberg (2012: 1648f.), Jestaz/Jamin (2004: 141ff.), Samuel (2008: 294f.).

need to reinterpret some of the existing body of law as governed by the guiding principle of economic efficiency.[58] This allows him to produce a coherent fit between the existing legal order and his newly developed norms.[59] The doctrinal scholar faces the most difficult task. He needs to reinterpret most of his legal tradition, arguing that it has been about promoting efficiency all along. He will try to claim precedential and statutory support for legal rules he considers to make most sense under an economic point of view, aiming at replacing traditional arguments of interpretation by economic considerations.

For the argument proposed here, the weaker, pragmatic version of economics' promise is of more interest. It claims that many questions which seem to be legal questions are in fact economic questions.[60] Finance law provides numerous examples for this version. To the seemingly legal question of when corporations should be required to disclose information, the answer is: whenever this makes sense under the assumptions of the efficient capital markets hypothesis. Devising legal rules on remuneration for stock corporation managers is in fact a task for economists, since legal rules need to ensure that long- and short-term incentives are balanced out in an economically efficient way. Ensuring sound risk management in banks needs an economist to figure out efficient procedures, and so forth. The charm of the weak version of the argument lies in its innocent appearance. We do not need to subscribe to the strong claim that law really is about enhancing efficiency. As long as we understand that most of what matters in regulating financial markets is economic research, we may well hold our own views on what law's ultimate goal should be.

Taking this weak pragmatic version of the argument together with the Holmesian lawyer's "longing for certainty and for repose",[61] we understand its strong appeal. Much of the legal discipline is rendered measurable by working with findings based on scientific methodology; many of the problems resulting from the indeterminacy of legal concepts can be ameliorated by this methodology's certainty. I have tried to show that there are good reasons to be hesitant about yielding to this appeal too readily. Law's epistemic motive is as diverse from economics' epistemic motive as are its techniques. While legal scholars are trained in making

58 Probably the most quoted exercise is translating the "Learned Hand" formula (*United States v. Carroll Towing Co.*, 159 F. 2nd. 169, 173 (2d Circ. 1947)) into economic formulae.

59 This is why most proponents of law and economics have indeed tried to show this.

60 See Friedman (1953: 2ff.) for a forceful claim of this nature.

61 See quotation from Holmes at start of chapter.

normative judgements, most economists insist that they are not. Consequently, as tempting as it may be, there is no easy way to profit from economics by indiscriminately transplanting its supposedly "value-free" findings into a legal context.[62] Instead, law faces the normative challenge to process economics' findings through its legal treadmill of argument and counter-argument, its requirements of fit and coherence, of fairness and rights, of path-dependency, political feasibility and the like. Once passed, the transplant has a good chance of working.[63]

The normative challenge: areas of further research

So far, the argument has been quite straightforward. Despite similarities in appearance, law and economics are not as closely related as one might think. Economics has employed "scientific" methodologies, achieving a high degree of testability, sometimes at the expense of a certain artificiality of its assumptions. This method is generally not a scientific venue open to the law. But how can we at the same time be aware of this fundamental difference and claim that many findings of economic research will need to be transplanted into a legal context? I would like to claim that the answer is to be found on the receiving end of the transplant. The law has had a long history of importing findings from other disciplines, be they psychology, sociology or history, implementing and including them in the broader "web" of the law.[64] Along those same lines, it is the legal scholar's task to define how to synthesize economic findings with the requirements of making a legal rule work.

Traditional law and economics theory rests on the assumption that legal scholars need to be educated in economics in order to make the most of potential transplants.[65] The success of this complex interdisciplinary endeavour does not form part of the argument advanced here. Instead, the "filter" considered is a much less ambitious one. It draws on the differences in techniques employed by both disciplines. Transplanting economic thought requires awareness of its "natural surroundings". This includes an understanding of relevant

62 Critical on being "value-free", see Mongin (2006: 269f.).

63 In a similar vein, see Fleischer (2007: 76); from the vantage point of physics, see Schwarcz (1997/98: 87).

64 For the concept of a "seamless web", see Dworkin (1986: 268ff.).

65 On problems this entails due to economics' increasing sophistication, see Schwartz (2011: 101, 103, 111, 115); from a more general viewpoint, see Sneed (1979: 154ff.); Stegmüller (1986 volume II/3); applying the later to legal reasoning, see Canaris (1993: 379).

theoretical assumptions, standard fallacies of experiments and inductive reasoning, and the situations in which an economic forecast is likely to apply.

Premises, models and assumptions

We saw earlier that the economic model of rational actors on capital markets has been heavily criticized following the financial crisis. I would like to make an argument for redirecting this criticism. Rigidity of formal assumptions seems to form part of the way in which much of economics is done today. It defines its "natural surroundings" and has a clearly defined place in which such assumptions work fairly well *for the purposes of the economist.* It seems far from certain that there is a better way given the current status of methods and techniques.[66] Monitoring changes, especially with a behavioural background, in this discipline's techniques which we might – or might not – see in decades to come will certainly be a fascinating undertaking for a historian of science. For the legal scholar, this should not be the key issue. Put differently: there is no reason for him to be overly concerned with the question of whether the success story of mathematical models and formal assumptions will or will not continue in the realm of the economist. Rather, the legal scholar is to focus on the potential of the economist's "work products" to be used for the purposes of setting and interpreting legal rules. There are obvious limits to the legal scholar's competence for intrinsically assessing the quality of such "work products" as a contribution to economic theory. Instead, he will need to determine which economic findings he feels confident transplanting from the artificial world of theoretical premises to the real-life setting he makes rules for. Singling out the relevant premises is one of many endeavours to be undertaken. Another one is to understand that an economist ranking different scenarios as more or less preferable will make a ceteris paribus judgement. Hence, "preferable" means: with regard to one specific criterion, all other relevant factors being equal or of no relevance. Before subscribing to the economist's ranking, the lawyer will have to make sure that for his rule-making endeavours, all other factors can indeed be regarded as equal or of no relevance.

[66] Caplin 2008: 336ff.; Gale 2008: 283.

Inductive and experimental reasoning

Empirical research on the effectiveness of legal rules has been an established part of the work of legal scholars studying techniques of legislating and assessing the success of legislative projects ex post.[67] The European Commission regularly collects data on the transposition of European Directives into the national law of the Member States as well as on their effectiveness in promoting the goals aimed for.[68] In that sense, empirical reasoning is not a new exercise for lawyers, which should make economic transplants relying on induction quite accessible. The opposite is true for laboratory experiments which are becoming fashionable in behavioural economics but have not been in much use by legal scholars.

Enhancing awareness of the fallacies of such reasoning has a more technical flavour than discussing the merits of economics' theoretical premises, even if findings based on experiments share some features of the problem of artificiality with formal models. Before transplanting results of experimental economic reasoning, we will need to raise the legal scholar's awareness of "external validity" issues: the laboratory setting may be a very specific one. The questions asked may point the agents in one direction. The persons taking part in the exercise may not mirror the population as a whole, and so forth.[69]

By contrast, empirical research in economics is being conducted in a real-life setting. Hence, at first glance it resembles the lawyer's "natural surroundings". If we take a closer look, however, quite a number of standard fallacies of inductive reasoning merit the legal scholar's attention before transplanting economic findings.[70] The most common one might be hasty generalization with the notorious "black swan". What has proved successful for one country's capital markets might not be generalizable for another region, displaying a different, path-dependent history.[71] The intricacies of data collection, most notably representativeness and selection biases, seem to be equally important. Data on banks' risk management structures in a certain country or for a specific size of bank only will render interesting results. But before transplanting them into a legal setting, they will need to be carefully checked for their potential for

[67] Emmenegger (2006), Bogdandy (1999); more generally, Heise (2002: 819).

[68] See, e.g., the EU Commission's Insider Trading overviews.

[69] For an introduction, see the textbooks of Creswell (2008), Gorard (2013); as an example for pointing out flaws, see Spamann (2010: 468).

[70] Very critical on empirical legal studies, see Schwartz (2011: 135f.).

[71] On "hasty generalization", see Leddy (1986: 53).

generalizability. Along these same lines, further caution is warranted as to false analogies and fallacies of exclusion. Data on the effects of disclosure might vary according to the type of capital market considered.

Summing up

I have tried to argue that while using findings of economic theory forms a necessary feature of making good law, this collaboration entails significant challenges neither discipline is necessarily aware of. These have become apparent considering the epistemic motives underlying both disciplines as well as their standard methodological techniques. Economics has been described as a positive endeavour, interested in discovery and prediction of real-life phenomena and correlations (see "On economics' epistemic motives"). Its standard methodology has for some decades been "scientific" with a focus on empirical work and mathematical models, lately enhanced by behavioural features (see "On economics' techniques"). Legal work has been seen as primarily normative (see "On law's epistemic motives"). Its techniques have rarely relied on the scientific method. They have been described as an endeavour to rank arguments according to both judicial rules of interpretation (see "Coherentist legal scholarship") and legislative political processes (see "An exercise in law's techniques"). It has been argued here that, due to those differences, findings of one discipline can rarely be indiscriminately transplanted into the other. Instead, a nuanced technique for tackling economic transplants has been called for.

References

Adorno, Theodor W. (1962). "Zur Logik der Sozialwissenschaften". *Kölner Zeitschrift für Soziologie und Sozial-Psychologie* 14(2): 249–263.

Akerlof, George (2007). "The missing motivation in macroeconomics". *American Economic Review* 97(5): 5–36.

Archibald, G. C. (1959). "Welfare economics, ethics and essentialism". *Economica* 26(104): 316–327.

Bogdandy, Armin von (1999). *Gubernative Rechtsetzung*. Tübingen: Mohr Siebeck.

Canaris, Claus-Wilhelm (1993). "Funktion, Struktur und Falsifikation juristischer Theorien". *Juristen Zeitung* 48: 377–428.

Caplin, Andrew (2008). "Economic theory and psychological data: bridging the divide". In Andrew Caplin and Andrew Schotter (eds.), *The foundations of positive and normative economics*. Oxford University Press.

Chemerinsky, Erwin and Catherine Fisk (1998–1999). "In defense of the big tent: the importance of recognizing the many audiences for legal scholarship". *Tulsa Law Journal* 34(677): 667–678.

Creswell, John W. (2008). *Research design: qualitative, quantitative and mixed methods approaches*. Los Angeles: Sage Publications.

Debreu, Gerard (1991). "The mathematization of economic theory". *American Economic Review* 81(1): 1–7.

De Marchi, Neil (1993). "Non-natural social science: reflecting on the enterprise of more heat than Light". *History of Political Economy* 25(5): 978–982.

Dworkin, Ronald (1986). *Law's empire*. Harvard University Press.

Emmenegger, Sigrid (2006). *Gesetzgebungskunst: Gute Gesetzgebung als Gegenstand einer legislativen Methodenbewegung in der Rechtswissenschaft um 1900 – Zur Geschichte der Gesetzgebungslehre*. Tübingen: Mohr Siebeck.

Epstein, Richard A. (2002). "Let the 'fundamental things apply': necessary and contingent truths in legal scholarship". *Harvard Law Review* 115: 1288–1313.

Fleischer, Holger (2007). "Gesellschafts- und Kapitalmarktrecht als wissenschaftliche Disziplin". In Christoph Engels and Wolfgang Schön (eds.), *Das Proprium der Rechtswissenschaft*. Tübingen: Mohr Siebeck, 51–76.

François, Pierre (2008). *Sociologie des marchés*. Paris: Armand Colin.

Friedman, Milton (1953). "The methodology of positive economics". In *Essays in positive economics*. University of Chicago Press: 3–43.

Gale, Douglas (2008). "Revealed preference and bounded rationality". In Andrew Caplin and Andrew Schotter (eds.), *The foundations of positive and normative economics. A Handbook*. Oxford University Press.

Goldberg, John C. P. (2012). "Introduction: pragmatism and private law". *Harvard Law Review* 125: 1640–1663.

Goodhart, Charles (1997). "Economics and the law: too much one-way traffic?" *The Modern Law Review* 60(1): 1–22.

Gorard, Stephen (2013). *Research design: creating robust approaches for the social sciences*. Los Angeles: Sage Publications.

Hart, H. L. A. (1994). *The concept of law*. Oxford: Clarendon Press, 2nd ed.

Hayek, Friedrich August (1942). "Economics and knowledge: scientism and the study of society; Part I". *Economica New Series* 9(35): 267–291.

Hayek, Friedrich August (1979). *The counter-revolution of science: studies on the abuse of reason*. Indianapolis: Liberty Fund Inc.

Heilbroner, Robert L. (1973). "Economics as a 'value-free' science". *Social Research* (40)129, reprinted in: William L. Marr and Baldev Raj (eds.) (1983). *How economists explain*. Lanham, MD: University Press of America.

Heise, Michael (2002). "The past, present, and future of empirical legal scholarship: judicial decision making and the new empiricism". *University of Illinois Law Review* 4: 819–850.

Hilgendorf, Eric (2010). "Bedingungen gelingender Interdisziplinarität – am Beispiel der Rechtswissenschaft". *Juristen Zeitung* 65(19): 913–968.
Holmes, Oliver Wendell (1897). "The path of the law". *Harvard Law Review* 457(10): 465–466.
Jestaz, Phillippe and Christophe Jamin (2004). *La Doctrine*. Paris: Dalloz.
Kahn-Freund, Otto (1974). "On use and misuse of comparative law". *Modern Law Review* 37(1): 1–27.
Kant, Immanuel (1786). *Metaphysische Anfangsgründe der Naturwissenschaft*. Riga: Hartnoch.
Lakatos, Imre (1978). *The methodology of scientific research programmes*. Cambridge University Press.
Larrère, Catherine (1992). *L'invention de l'Économie au XVIIIe Siècle. Du droit naturel à la physiocratie*. Paris: Presses Universitaires de France.
Lazear, Edward P. (2000). "Economic imperialism". *The Quarterly Journal of Economics* 115: 99–146.
Leddy, Thomas (1986). "Is there a fallacy of small sample?" *Informal Logic* 8(1): 53–56.
Legrand, Pierre (1997). "The impossibility of 'legal transplants'". *Maastricht Journal of European Comparative Law* 4: 111–124.
Leontief, Wassily (1982). "Academic economics. Letters". *Science* 217(4555): 104–107.
Lianos, Ioannis (2009). "'Lost in translation': towards a theory of economic transplants". *Jean Monnet Working Paper 08/09*, NYU School of Law.
Little, Ian (1957). *A critique of welfare economics*. Oxford: Clarendon Press.
Lo, Andrew W. and Mark T. Mueller (2010). "WARNING: Physics envy may be hazardous to your wealth!" *MIT Sloan School of Management* 8 (2), Second Quarter 2010, available at http://ssrn.com/abstract=1563882 and http://dx.doi.org/10.2139/ssrn.1563882.
Machlup, Fritz (1961). "Are the social sciences really inferior?" *Southern Economic Journal* 27: 173–184.
Mäki, Uskali (2009). *The methodology of positive economics: reflections on the Milton Friedman legacy*. Cambridge University Press.
Mill, John Stuart (1824). "Essays on economics and society part I". In John M. Robson (eds.), *The Collected Works of John Stuart Mill, Volume IV*. University of Toronto Press.
Mirowski, Philip (1989). *More heat than light*. Cambridge University Press.
Mishan, Edward J. (1981). *Introduction to normative economics*. Oxford University Press.
Mongin, Philippe (2006). "A concept of progress for normative economics". *Economics and Philosophy* 22: 19–54.
Mongin, Philippe (2006). "Value judgments and value neutrality in economics". *Economica* 73(290): 257–286.

Morgan, Theodore (1988). "Theory versus empiricism in academic economics: update and comparisons". *The Journal of Economic Perspectives* 2: 159–164.

Oswald, Andrew J. (1991). "Progress and microeconomic data". *The Economic Journal* 101: 75–80.

Passeron, J. C. (2001). "Formalisation, rationalité et histoire". In Jean-Yves Grenier, Claude Grignon and Pierre-Michel Menger (eds.), *Le Modèle et le récit*. Paris: Éditions de la Maison des sciences de l'homme: 215–243.

Posner, Richard (2002). "Legal scholarship today". *Harvard Law Review* 115: 1314–1320.

Pound, Roscoe (1907). "The need for a sociological jurisprudence". *Green Bag* 19: 607–615.

Pound, Roscoe (1912). "The scope and purpose of sociological jurisprudence". *Harvard Law Review* 25(6): 489–516.

Robbins, Lionel (1945). *An essay on the nature and significance of economic science.* London: Macmillan and Co.; 2nd ed.

Roncaglia, Alessandro (2001). *The wealth of ideas: a history of economic thought.* Cambridge University Press.

Rubin, Edward L. (1992). "On beyond truth: a theory for evaluating legal scholarship". *California Law Review* 80(4): 889–963.

Samuel, Geoffrey (2008). "Is law really a social science?" *Cambridge Law Journal* 67(2): 288–321.

Schwarcz, Steven L. (1997/98). "Is law an autonomous discipline?" *Harvard Journal of Law & Public Policy* 21: 85–87.

Schwartz, Alan (2011). "Two culture problems in law and economics". *Yale Law and Economics Research Paper* 432: 101–138.

Sneed, Joseph D. (1979). *The logical structure of mathematical physics.* University of California.

Spamann, Holger (2010). "The 'Antidirector Rights Index' revisited". *The Review of Financial Studies* 23(2): 467–486.

Stegmüller, Wolfgang (1986). *Probleme und Resultate der Wissenschaftstheorie und analytischen Philosophie* II(3). Berlin: Springer.

Stilwell, Frank J. B. (1975). *Normative economics: an introduction to microeconomic theory and radical critiques.* Rushcutters Bay, N.S.W.: Pergamon Press.

Teubner, Gunther (1998). "Legal irritants: good faith in British law or how unifying law ends up in new divergences". *Modern Law Review* 61: 11–32.

Vazquez, Andrew (1995). "Marshall and the mathematization of economics". *Journal of the History of Economic Thought* 17(247).

Vermeule, Adrian (2006). *Judging under uncertainty: an institutional theory of legal interpretation.* Harvard University Press.

Vermeule, Adrian (2007). "Connecting positive and normative legal theory". *University of Pennsylvania Journal of Constitutional Law* 10: 387–398.

Watson, Alan (1974). *Legal transplants.* Athens, GA: University of Georgia Press.

Weinrib, Ernest J. (1995). *The idea of private law*. Harvard University Press.

Xifaras, Mikhail (2004). "Science social, science morale? Note sur la pénétration de l'économie dans la pensée juridique française au XIXe siècle". In Heinz Mohnhaupt and Jean-François Kervégan (eds.), *Droit, philosophie et économie*. Frankfurt: Klostermann, *Ius Commune*: 185–226.

INDEX

ABN AMRO, 96
AEON Bank, 158
age, risk aversion and, 294
agency theory, 180–182
agents, behavior of, 16–17
aggregate credit, 12
aggregate leverage, 12
aggregate risk, 4
AIG, 281
antitrust laws, 97–103
asset price bubbles
  monetary policy and, 18
  prevention of, 13
Asset Quality Review, 46
asset-backed securities, 207, 208, 276
asset-liability structure, xiv
assets
  liquidity of, xiv–xv
  risk-weighted, 43–45, 46
asymmetric information, 90, 143

background risk, 299–300
bail-in clauses, 110–115, 125–147
  access restrictions, 140–141
  BRRD, 128–132
  conversion, 136–138
  equity and bail-in debt, 142–145, 147
  existing, in EU, 128–135
  experiences with, 134–135
  features of, 136–142
  introduction to, 125–127
  loss absorbing capacity, 145–146
  market-friendly, 136–142
  role of supervisor, 141–142, 146
  SRM and, 132–135
  SSM and, 132–135
  triggers, 138–140
  vs. bailouts, 125
bailouts
  debates over, 150
  of banks, xvi, 8, 24, 25, 37, 41, 95, 111, 126, 134, 167
  vs. bail-ins, 125
Banca Antoniana Popolare Veneta, 96
Banca Nazionale del Lavoro (BNL), 96
Banco Bilboa Vizcaya Argentaria (BBVA), 96
Banco Espirito Santo, S.A., 135
bank failures, xiii, 35–36
  consequences of, xiv
  during financial crisis, 4
  reducing systemic consequences of, xvi–xvii
Bank for International Settlements (BIS), 4, 13
bank forbearance, 34–35
Bank Holding Company Act, 101, 102, 274
bank leverage, 41–46
bank liquidity, 6
Bank Merger Act, 101–102
bank mergers
  antitrust laws and, 100–102
  control of, 95, 97–103
  rescue mergers, 154–156, 161, 164
Bank of England, 63, 116
Bank Recovery and Resolution Directive (BRRD), xvi, 39, 79, 89, 126, 128–132
bank resolution, 62
  BRRD, xvi, 39, 79, 89, 126, 128–132
  debates over, 150
  ELA and, 131
  fiscal backstop and, 83–84, 85
  framework for, xvi–xvii
  in euro area, 75, 83, 89, 113

procedures, 10
regulatory forbearance and, 35–41
Single Resolution Mechanism. *See* Single Resolution Mechanism (SRM)
tools, 113
Banking Communication (2008), 110–115
Banking Communication (2013), 110–115
banking crisis, 78
banking nationalism, 38
banking supervision. *See also* financial regulation, *See also* regulatory frameworks
bank failures and, xiii
by ECB, 59, 78–79, 80–81, 82, 89, 114, 132, 170–173
capital-based activities restrictions, 275
cross-border banks, xiii
ESMA and, 234–237
euro area, 38, 39–41, 58–60, 68, 78–79, 82, 89, 170–186
functional supervision, 274
moral hazard and, 80–81
within SSM, 170–186
banking system
efficiency of, xiii
euro area, 64, 75–78
lack of confidence in, 49
Banking Union, xii, 10, 31, 59, 91, 230, *See also* Single Resolution Mechanism (SRM), *See also* Single Supervisory Mechanism (SSM)
bank-sovereign feedback loop and, 83–84
competition rules and, 118–120
components of, 78, 221
establishment of, 168
goals of, xiii
institutional structure of, 169
lack of, 75
lender of last resort in, 78–79, 80–83
monetary policy in, 61–87
phasing-in of, 167–170, 174
political economy perspective of, 167–192
regulatory environment and, 231–234
removal of shadow resolutions and, 159–164
shock absorption mechanism, 79
Single Resolution Mechanism and, 132–135
state aid and, 118–120
systemic risk and, 127
banks. *See also* financial institutions
antitrust laws and, 98–103
asset-liability structure of, xiv
bail-ins of, 125–147
bailouts of, xvi, 8, 24, 25, 37, 41, 95, 111, 126, 167
balance sheets of, xvi
burden-sharing and, 110–115, 134
capital positions of, 6
commercial, 272, 273
competition, 89–97, 100–103, 273
consolidation of, 274
cross-border acquisitions, 96
cross-border operations of, 38, 39, 174
defaults, 6
deleveraging, 10–12, 53
equity capital, 41–46
European. *See* European banks
funding costs of, 37
funding models of, xiv
home bias, 25, 30, 31, 33, 34, 182, 187
illiquid vs. insolvent, 76–78
interconnectedness of, 6, 8
internal models of, 4
ownership structure of, xv
resilience of, xiv–xv
runs on, 7, 40, 64, 113, 143
shadow, xviii, 231
size of, 8
sovereign debt exposures and, 23–34, 43
state aid and, 105–108
stock returns, 26–29
stress testing, 46, 49–60, 117–118
universal, 39
valuation of, 77
zombie, 35
bank-sovereign feedback loop, xiii, 23–34, 83–84
Banque de France, 63

Basel Committee on Banking
Supervision, 275
Basel I, 276
Basel II, 4, 38, 44, 51, 276
Basel III, xv, xvii, 6, 7, 8, 11, 45, 279, 281
Basel regulatory framework, 3, 6
behavioural economics, 313
Belgium, 27, 30
Bernanke, Ben, 55
Binding Technical Standards (BTS), 227, 230
BIS. *See* Bank for International Settlements (BIS)
black swan events, 330
bonds, inflation-indexed, 197
book capital, xv
book leverage ratio, 41, 45
BRRD. *See* Bank Recovery and Resolution Directive (BRRD)
BTS. *See* Binding Technical Standards (BTS)
bubbles. *See* asset price bubbles
burden-sharing, 90, 104, 110–115, 134
bureaucratic incentives, 178–182

capital
  contingent, 144
  equity, 41–46, 142–145, 147
  hybrid, 43, 112, 138
  Pillar 2, 51
  shortfalls, 46, 132, 134
  Tier 1, 43, 44, 45, 46
  Tier 2, 43
capital buffers, xvii, 6, 11, 89, 174
capital markets
  competition in, 273
  growth of, 272–273
  information technology and, 276
  innovations, 282
  oversight of, 284
capital ratios, 4, 11, 41–43, 44–46
capital regulation, risk-based, 11
capital requirements, xiv, xv, xvii, 6, 7, 89
  Basel III, 45, 281
  complexity of, 276
  euro-area banks, 32, 41–46
  low, 11
  risk-based, 281
  standardized approach to, 45
  systemic risk and, 127
Capital Requirements Directive (CRD), 89
Capital Requirements Regulation (CRR), 89
capital short-fall (SRisk), 9
capital structure, 7
capital-based regulation, 275
carry trades, 30, 31–32
cartels, 92, 102
CCPs. *See* central counterparties (CCPs)
CDS spreads, 12
central banks. *See also* European Central Bank (ECB), *See also* Federal Reserve
  as lender of last resort, 65, 72–78, 81
  credibility of, 74
  euro debt crisis and, 84–85
  financial dominance and, 72–78
  functions of, 116
  national, 68–69, 71, 116–117
  role of, 19, 63–64
  type 1/type 2 error problem of, 77–78
central counterparties (CCPs), 10
centrality indices, 8
CESR. *See* Committee of European Securities Regulators (CESR)
CFPB. *See* Consumer Financial Protection Bureau (CFPB)
Clayton Act, 97, 98, 102
coherentist legal scholarship, 323–324
Collins Amendment, 281
commercial banks, 272, 273
commercial paper markets, 273
Committee of European Securities Regulators (CESR), 226
comparative advantage, of domestic banks, 30, 33
competition
  banking union and, 118–120
  in banking sector, 89–97, 100–103, 273
  laws, 91–93
  retail markets, 241
  shadow resolutions and, 153

state aid and, 92–93, 103–105
U.S. antitrust laws and, 97–103
compliance professionals, 286
comprehensive assessment, 89
conditional joint probability of default, 9
conditional transactions, 102
conditional value at risk, 9
constructive ambiguity, 69, 80
Consumer Financial Protection Bureau (CFPB), 226, 277, 286
consumer protection, 221–242
Consumer Protection Act (2010), 271
contagion, xiv, 6, 7, 10, 75, 78, 83
euro debt crisis and, 24–25
information, 6
risk aversion and, 301
contingent capital, 144
contingent capital certificates, 137
conversion clauses, 136–138
cooperative game theory, 9
countercyclical policy, xvii, 281
countercylical capital buffers, xvii, 6, 11
counterparties, 10, 78
credit
aggregate, 12
pro-cyclicality of, xvii
credit crunch, 6
policy-induced, 55–59
recession and, 56
Crédit Lyonnais, 105–108
credit markets, access to, 299–300
credit rating agencies, 276
credit risk, 4
credit supply, 53, 54, 55–56
creditors, xvi, 135
Crisis Communications, 108, 109
cross-border acquisitions, 96
cross-border banks, xiii
cross-border externalities, 35, 39, 82
cross-border operations, 38, 39, 174
cross-country policy coordination, 17
cross-sectional dimension, 7, 8–10, 19
CRRA utility, 290, 292, 297, 298
Cyprus, 134, 135

Deauville doctrine, 110
debt financing, xv
Debt to Income (DTI) ratios, xviii
debt, maturity structure of, 7
default, statistical indicators of, 12
deleveraging, 10–12, 53
demographic trends, 196, 197
deposit insurance, xvi, 38, 40, 41, 101, 167, 287
Deposit Insurance Corporation of Japan (DICJ), 157
Depository Institution Management Interlocks Act, 102
depository institutions, 272, 273, 274, *See also* banks
deregulation, 3, 272
disclosure, 224, 316
discretion, 80, 131
diversification, 33, 197, 212, 248–250, 278
doctrinal legal scholarship, 322
Dodd-Frank Act, xvi, 81, 271, 277, 278, 279, 281, 282, 283, 284
domestic banks, comparative advantage of, 30, 33
domino effects, 6
Draghi, Mario, 25, 33, 58

East Asian financial crisis, 154
EBA. *See* European Banking Authority (EBA)
Economic and Monetary Union (EMU)
architecture of, 61
breakup of, 25
credibility of, 33
economic growth, xv, 49
economic theory, 313, 317, 331
economic transplants, 313–331
economics
envy, 326–328
epistemic motives, 317–319
law and, 313–331
physics envy and, 325
positive, 318
promise of, 325, 326
scientific method and, 321, 331
techniques in, 320–321, 331
economy, stress tests and, 53–54
efficient markets, 315–317
ELA. *See* emergency liquidity assistance (ELA)

emergency liquidity assistance (ELA), 71, 78, 82, 115, 116
bank resolution and, 131
foundations of, 68–70
state aid and, 117–118
EMIR. *See* European Market Integrity Regulation (EMIR)
emotions, risk aversion and, 294–295
empirical research, 330–331
endogenous aggregate shocks, 6, 7
epistemic motives
of economics, 317–319
of law, 319
equity capital, 41–46
bail-in debt and, 142–145, 147
ESAs. *See* European Supervisory Authorities (ESAs)
ESM. *See* European Stability Mechanism (ESM)
ESMA. *See* European Securities and Markets Authority (ESMA)
ESRB. *See* European Systemic Risk Board (ESRB)
ETFs. *See* exchange-traded funds (ETFs)
EU Directive on Bank Recovery and Resolution, 38
EU Treaty. *See* Treaty on European Union (TEO)
euro area
bank resolution in, 75, 83, 89, 113
banking system, 64, 75–78
economic performance in, 50
interconnectedness in, xii
lender of last resort framework for, 80–83
monetary policy, 167
policy responses to financial crisis in, 49–60
real output in, 49
state aid in, 92–93
stress tests in, 50–60
supervision within, 38, 39–41, 58–60, 68, 78–79, 82, 89, 170–186
euro debt crisis, 23–46
bank forbearance and, 34–35
capital requirements and, 41–46
central banks and, 84–85
contagion dimension of, 24–25
ECB management of, 62–83, 84–85
financial policies and, 62
regulatory forbearance and, 35–41
sovereign debt exposures and, 23–34
state aid in, 108–110
euro-area debt market, segmentation of, 33–34
euro-area periphery, 24, 26
European Banking Authority (EBA), 28, 132, 161, 221, 238, 241
European banks, 64, 75–78, *See also* Banking Union, *See also* banks
capital requirements, 41–46
leverage ratios, 41–46
regulation of. *See* financial regulation
regulatory forbearance and, 35–41
resolution. *See* bank resolution
stress testing, 49–60
ties between politics and, 38
European Central Bank (ECB), 14, 15–16, 19, 24
anti-shadow resolution policy and, 162–164
as lender of last resort, 70–72
as single supervisor, 31
banking supervision by, 59, 78–79, 80–81, 82, 89, 114, 132, 170–173
credit operations by, 64
crisis management by, 62–83, 84–85
ECB-set framework, 186–187
emergency liquidity assistance by, 68–70
fine tuning operations of, 67, 70
functions of, 64
Governing Council, 64, 69, 78, 116, 122, 184–186
internal decision-making procedures, 183–186
marginal lending facility, 67
monetary policy, 62–83
NCA-ECB career paths, 186–187
NCAs and, 175–178, 179–187, 241
pre-crisis management framework, 67–70
shadow resolutions and, 159
state aid and, 117
Supervisory Board, 183–186

European Commission (EC), 89, 90, 330
  Crédit Lyonnais case and, 105–108
  merger control by, 95
  on state aid, 105–110
  recent regulatory measures by, 216
  retail rule-making and, 227, 230
European Council, 227
European Debt Agency (EDA), 33
European Insurance and Occupational Pensions Authority (EIOPA), 221
European Market Integrity Regulation (EMIR), 129
European Monetary Union (EMU), 167
European Parliament, 227
European Safe Bonds (ESBies), 33
European Securities and Markets Authority (ESMA), 221
  financial market governance and, 225
  institutional design of, 239–242
  product intervention and, 237–239
  regulatory environment and, 231–234
  retail rule-making and, 225–234
  supervision and, 234–237
European Stability Mechanism (ESM), 31, 40, 83
European Supervisory Authorities (ESAs), 14, 221, 240–241
European System of Central Banks (ESCB), 116
European System of Financial Supervision (ESFS), 14, 221
European Systemic Risk Board (ESRB), 14–15, 19, 221
European Union. *See also* euro area
  bail-in policy, 126
  bank competition in, 91–97
  bank resolution in, 35–41
  bank supervision in, 38, 39–41
  consumer protection in, 221–242
  financial market governance in, 221–242
  institutional framework in, 13–16
  regulatory environment, 231–234
  retail markets, 221–242
  rule-making process, 225–234
  supervisory mechanism in, 13–16
Eurosystem, 69, 71–72, 122, 170
exceptions, under BRRD, 129–131
exchange-traded funds (ETFs), xviii, 197, 252
exogenous aggregate shocks, 5, 7
exogenous shocks, 4
experimental reasoning, 330–331
external validity, 330
externalities, 4
  cross-border, 35, 39, 82
  fire sale, 4
  internalisation of, xiv
  market distortions and, 90
  network, 6, 95

fear, risk aversion and, 294–295
Federal Deposit Insurance Corporation (FDIC), 38, 40, 101, 142, 158, 275, 284
Federal Reserve, 274
  antitrust assessment by, 102
  as lender of last resort, 81
  banking supervision by, 59
  founding of, 63
  lending by, 64
  oversight by, 282
  policy on asset bubbles, 13
Federal Reserve Act, 63, 278
Federal Trade Commission (FTC), 98
financial advice, 245–267
  enhancement of value of, 258–265
  fee-only, 253, 256, 257, 267
  for less wealthy investors, 263–265
  future research on, 265–266
  investor behavior in absence of, 246–250
  investor protection regulation and, 256–258
  low investor adherence to, 253–256
  pension claim aggregation, 262–263
  policy recommendations for, 266–267
  portfolio disclosure and, 258–262
  role of, 253–258
financial advisors, 201
  commission-based, 223
  conflicts of interest for, 203, 213–215, 223
  irresponsible, 199

financial advisors, (cont.)
regulation of, 205, 213–216, 256–258
to households, 203–204, 213–216, 223
financial conglomerates
global, 284
oversight of, 281, 284
financial contagion. *See* contagion
financial crisis, 18, *See also* euro debt crisis
recovery from, 307
risk aversion and, 290–312
social costs of, 23
financial crisis (2007–2009), xvi
bank failures, 4
financial regulation reform and, 221–225, 271–288
impact of, 19
lessons from, 3
macro-prudential policy and, 3–5
market efficiency and, 316
policy responses to, 49–60
real output following, 49
triggers of, 5
financial cycle
dampening of, 10–13
macro-prudential policy and, xvii–xviii
financial decisions
financial illiteracy and, 197–200
social interactions and, 200–201
financial dominance, 62, 63, 72–78
financial education, 201–202, 250–252
financial fragmentation, xiii
financial illiteracy, 197–200, 201, 208
financial innovations, 4, 195–197, 273
lack of familiarity with, 198–200
opportunities offered by, 196–197
regulation of, 201–218
structured products, 207–208
financial institutions. *See also* banks
capital-based activities restrictions, 275
contagion among, 6
regulation of, 206
supervision of, 234–237
financial integration, xii, xiii
financial intermediaries, 4, 272–273, 274
financial markets, xiv
deregulation of, 3, 272
efficiency of, 3, 315–317
governance of, 221–242
law, 314, 325
prevention of bubbles in, 13
regulation of. *See* financial regulation
self-regulation by, 4
U.S., 271–288
financial policies, national, xii
financial products, 263–265, 273
disclosures about, 316
ESMA and, 237–239
information about, 257
regulation of, 250, 252–253
retail, 221–225
structured, 223
financial regulation, 206, *See also* banking supervision, *See also* regulatory frameworks
aims of, xii
capital-based, 275
challenges for, xix, 207–217
compliance professionals and, 286
consumerization of, 224
coordination of, 284
euro debt crisis and, 23–46
functional, 274
information technology and, 276
institutional structure of, 239–242
lack of paradigm shifts in, 286
macro-prudential. *See* macro-prudential policy/regulation
micro-prudential, 3, 4, 7, 14
need for, 3, 201–204
of advisors, 205, 213–216
of banks' sovereign exposures, 23–34
portfolio theory and, 274
post-crisis, 277–287
product-based, 205, 207–210
recent measures, 216–217
reforms, 4, 89–91, 221–225, 228–234
regulatory environment, 231–234, 277
retail markets, 221–234
to protect households, 195, 201–218, 256–258, 316
U.S., 271–288
user-based, 205, 210–213

financial sector
  consolidation in, 274
  information technology and, 276
  interconnectedness of, 284
  risk-taking in, xix
financial services firms, 263–265
  disaggregation by, 283
  regulation of, 283
financial stability, xii, xiii, 4, 62, 67, 72, 75, 95, 108, 221
  ESMA and, 231, 233, 234
  safeguarding, by ECB, 65
Financial Stability Board, 284
Financial Stability Oversight Council (FSOC), 277, 279, 282, 284
financial supermarket model, 223
financial system, systemic risks in, 5–7
financial wealth, risk aversion and, 297–299
fine tuning operations (FTOs), 70
fire sale externalities, 4
fiscal backstop, 83–84, 85, 167
fiscal dominance, 61, 72
fiscal policy
  euro area, 49
  in monetary union, 61
  US, 49
forbearance
  bank, 34–35
  regulatory, 35–41
formal resolutions, 151, 153
  as dominant approach, 156–159
  incentives, 160–161
France, 30
Friedman, Milton, 318
FSOC. *See* Financial Stability Oversight Council (FSOC)
funding models, xiv

G20/OECD High Level Principles on Consumer Protection, 221
game theory, 9
Garn-St. Germain Depository Institutions Act, 102
General Council (ESRB), 14
German banks, shadow resolutions and, 154, 156
Germany, 58
Glass-Steagall Act, 272, 273, 274, 278
global financial crisis. *See* financial crisis (2007–2009)
globalization, 3
Goodhart's Law, 12
Governing Council, 64, 69, 78, 116, 122, 184–186
Gramm-Leach-Bliley Act, 273, 274, 275, 281
Greece
  debt crisis in, 24
  sovereign debt exposure in, 26
guided discretion, 17

home bias, 25, 30, 31, 33, 34, 182, 187
home equity loans, 196
household finance, law and, 313–331
households. *See also* individual investors
  financial advice for, 245–267
  financial advisors to, 199, 201, 203–204, 213–216, 223
  financial education for, 250–252
  financial illiteracy and, 197–200, 201
  financial trouble for, 195–218
  lack of financial familiarity and, 198–200
  minority, 200
  paternalistic measures to protect, 252–253
  regulation to protect, 195, 201–218, 256–258, 316
  regulatory reform and, 221–225
  risk preferences of, 290–312
  savings by, 245
  social interactions and, 200–201
  stock trading by, 208–209, 245
housing market, 196
hybrid capital, 43, 112, 138

idiosyncratic shocks, 6
illiquidity, 76–78
inaction bias, 17
Incubator Bank of Japan (IBJ), 157–158
index funds, 252, 263
individual investors. *See also* households
  disclosures to, 316

individual investors. (cont.)
factors affecting risk aversion in, 291–302
financial advice for, 253–267
financial education for, 250–252
financial intermediaries and, 272
investment mistakes by, 246–250
paternalistic measures to protect, 252–253
portfolio management for less wealthy, 263–265
regulation to protect, 256–258, 316
risk preferences of, 248, 290–300
smart portfolio disclosure and, 258–262, 266–267
inductive reasoning, 330–331
inflation, 72, 74
inflation risk, 197
information asymmetries, 90, 143
information contagion, 6
information technologies, 273, 276
input-output metrics, 8
insolvency, 76–78, 80
insurance companies, 272
Insurance Mediation Directive (IMD), 216
interbank markets, 6
interconnectedness, 6, 8
interest rates, 18
interlocking directorships, 102
Internal Market, 92–93
internal risk models, 44
International Monetary Fund (IMF), 236
investment mistakes
by individual investors, 246–250
excessive trading, 248
fixes for, 250–253
stock holding, 248
under diversification, 248–249
investor protection regulation, 195, 201–218, 256–258, 316
Ireland
bank bailouts in, 126, 134
debt crisis in, 24
sovereign debt exposure in, 26
Italy, 58
shadow resolutions in, 155
sovereign debt exposure in, 26

Japan, 157–158
joint return distributions, 9

Key Information Documents (KIDs), 216
Krugman, Paul, 25

Large Exposures limits, xviii
law
economic envy and, 326–328
economics and, 313–331
epistemic motives, 319
financial markets, 314, 325
household finance and, 313–331
synthesizing capacity of, 324
techniques in, 321–325
legal scholarship, 319, 322–325, 328–329
Lehman Brothers, 71, 90, 126, 281
lender of last resort
arrangements for, 62, 63
central banks as, 65, 72–78, 81
ECB as, 70–72
framework for, 80–83
in banking union, 78–79
need for, 64
state aid and, 115–118
level playing field, 8
leverage
aggregate, 12
bank, 41–46
excessive, 7
shadow banking and, xviii
leverage ratio, xv, 11, 45–46
liquidity
asset, xiv–xv
bank, 6
by central banks, 64, 65, 70–72
emergency liquidity assistance, 68–70, 71, 78, 82, 115, 116
funding, 62
requirements, 7, 281
shocks, 34
living wills, 134

Loan to Value ratios, xviii
loans, non-performing, 34–35, 41, 53
Lombard Club decision, 94
loss absorbency, xiv–xv
loss absorbing capacity (LAC), 145–146
Lucas critique, 16–17

Maastricht Treaty, 61
macro stress tests, 52–53, 54–60
macroeconomic feedbacks, 6
macroeconomic policy, 17
macro-prudential policy/regulation, xii, 7
  adoption of, 19
  asset bubbles and, 13
  challenges for, xix
  credit booms and, xvii–xviii
  cross-country coordination of, 17
  cross-sectional dimension of, 7, 8–10, 19
  deployment of, xviii
  dimensions of, 7–13
  emergence of, 3
  financial crisis and, 3–5
  financial cycle and, xvii–xviii
  framework for, 5
  goals of, 10
  implementation of, 16–19
  inaction bias and, 17
  institutional framework for, 13–16
  overlaps/conflicts with other policies, 18–19
  rules vs. discretion, 16–17
  shadow banking and, xviii
  supervisory mechanism for, 13–16
  target for, 12–13
  time series dimension of, 10–13, 19
marginal expected short-fall (MES), 9
marinal lending facility, 67
market access, 140–141
market discipline, xvi
market efficiency, 315–317
market failures, 64, 77, 90, 221, 223
market leverage ratio, 46
market risk, 4
market-oriented intermediaries, 272–273
mark-to-market accounting, 6
mental accounting, 264
merger control, 95, 97–103
mergers. *See* bank mergers
Merton's formula, 302
micro stress tests, 51–52
micro-prudential regulation, 3, 4, 7, 14
MiFID I, 236
MiFID II, 216–217, 228, 229, 230, 235, 237, 256
MiFIR, 228, 229, 230, 235, 237
Minimum Requirements of Eligible Liabilities (MREL), xvi, 129, 136
minority households, 200
monetary authority, 19
monetary policy, 18–19
  ECB and, 62–83
  euro area, 49, 167
  in banking union, 61–87
  US, 49
money market funds, 231, 282
mood, risk aversion and, 294–295
moral hazard, xiv, 17, 31, 41, 77, 80–81, 113, 131, 157, 239, 279
moral suasion, 30, 31
mortgage refinancing, 196
mortgage-backed securities, 4
MREL. *See* Minimum Requirements of Eligible Liabilities (MREL)
mutual funds, 272, 273, 282

national central banks (NCBs), 68–69, 71, 116–117
national competent authorities (NCAs), 161, 162, 169, 221
  bureaucratic incentives for, 178–182
  contributions of, 179–180
  ECB and, 175–178, 179–187, 241
  ECB career paths and, 186–187
  ESMA and, 235, 236
  home bias of, 182
  internal decision-making procedures, 183–186
  peer review and, 236
  product intervention and, 237–239
  prudential supervision by, 174–176
  supervision by, 234
national deposit guarantee schemes, 167
negative equity, 196

Netherlands, 30, 256
network centrality, 8
network externalities, 6, 95
neuro-economics, 306
New Deal regulation, 272
non-performing loans (NPLs)
bank forbearance and, 34–35
losses from, 41
recessions and, 53
no-worse-off rule, 130

off-balance sheet risks, 4
online brokers, 248, 252
Orderly Liquidation Authority, 284
organizational theory, 183
Outright Monetary Transactions (OMT), 33
over-the-counter (OTC) derivatives, 274, 284
ownership structure, xv

packaged retail investment products (PRIPs), 216, 224, 228, 241
Padao-Schioppa, Tomasso, 69
pari passu rule, 130
peer review, 235, 236
pension claim aggregation, 262–263
pensions, 196, 197, 250, 272
physics envy, 325
Pillar 2 capital, 51
policy commitment, 17
political economy, 317
political risk, 239
portfolio disclosure, 258–262
portfolio diversification, 32–33, 248–249, 278
portfolio management, 263–265
portfolio risk, 248–250, 254, 258–262
portfolio theory, 274, 278
Portugal
bank bail-in in, 135
debt crisis in, 24
sovereign debt exposure in, 26
positive economics, 318
price bubbles. *See* asset price bubbles
price stability, 61, 63, 64, 69, 72, 74
PRIPs. *See* packaged retail investment products (PRIPs)
Private Sector Involvement (PSI), 57, 110
pro-cyclicality
of capital regulation, 10
of risk measures, 9
product-based regulation, 205, 207–210
profit maximization, 4
Prompt Corrective Act, 275
prudential regulation. *See* financial regulation, *See* macro-prudential policy/regulation, *See* micro-prudential regulation
prudential rules, 95–96
prudential supervision
bureaucratic incentives and, 178–182
centralization in, 179
ECB's rle in, 170–173
public pension schemes, 250
purchase and assumption (P&A) transactions, 151–152, 158

real economy, xiv, 4
real estate prices, 5
recapitalisation, 111, 179
recessions, 53
regulation. *See* financial regulation
regulatory arbitrage, 4, 42, 43–45
regulatory forbearance, 35–41
regulatory frameworks
antitrust laws and, 99–100
Basel, 3, 6
Basel I, 276
Basel II, 4, 38, 44, 51, 276
Basel III, xv, xvii, 6, 7, 8, 279, 281
challenges for, xix
institutional framework, 13–16
regulatory hybrid securities, 137
representativeness, 330
reputational risk, 80, 139
rescue mergers, 154–156, 161, 164
resilience, xiv–xv
resolution. *See* bank resolution
resolvability, xvi–xvii
retail investor interests, 221–225
retail markets
cross-border, 239
ESMA and, 221–242
product intervention and, 237–239
regulatory environment and, 231–234

rule-making, 225–234
soft laws, 226
supervision, 234–237
retailinvestors. *See* individual investors
retirement accounts, 196, 197, 209, 262–263
reverse convertible debentures, 137
Riegle-Neal Interstate Banking and Branching Efficiency Act, 100
risk
aggregate, 4
background, 299–300
credit, 4
endogeneity of, 4
inflation, 197
internal models of, 44
market, 4
off-balance sheet risks, 4
political, 239
portfolio, 248–250, 254, 258–262
pricing of, 138
reputational, 80, 139
sovereign, 24
systemic. *See* systemic risk
tail, 34
risk aversion, 248, 290–312
age and, 294
background risk and, 299–300
contagion and, 301
credit market access and, 299–300
emotions and, 294–295
factors affecting, 291–302
financial crisis and, 303–307
financial wealth and, 297–299
genetics and, 293–294
IQ and, 292
parameter, 292–296
persistence of changes in, 300–301
personality and, 293
time invariant characteristics, 292–294
traumas and, 295–296
variation in, over time, 302–311
risk preferences, 290–300
changes in, over time, 302–311
risk-based capital requirements, 281
risk-shifting incentives, 41
risk-taking, xiv, xv, xvi, xix
risk-weighted assets, 43–45, 46
risk-weighting, 6, 45
Rome Treaty, 92
Roubini, Nouriel, 25
rules vs. discretion, 16–17

savings and loan (S&L) crisis, 158, 274
scientific method, 320, 325
economics and, 321, 331
Securities and Exchange Commission (SEC), 274, 282, 287
Securities and Markets Stakeholder Group, 228
securitization, 44, 207, 273, 274, 283
selection bias, 330
shadow banking, xviii, 231
shadow resolutions, 150–164
appeal of, 154–156
compared with formal resolutions, 151, 153
costs and benefits of, 152–154
defined, 151
implementation strategy for removal of, 161–164
removal of, under Banking Union framework, 159–164
Shapley value, 9
shareholders, xvi
Sharpe Ratio, 246
Sherman Act, 97–98
Shiller, Robert, 195
shock absorption capacity, xii
shocks, 5
endogenous aggregate, 6, 7
exogenous aggregate, 5, 7
idiosyncratic, 6
liquidity, 34
systemic, 66
short-term debt, 143–144
Single Resolution Board (SRB), 132, 150, 159, 162, 163
Single Resolution Fund, 40–41, 132–134
Single Resolution Mechanism (SRM), 10, 38, 40, 78, 79, 89, 114, 150, 221
bail-ins and, 132–135
establishment of, xiii, xvi, 167
solvency assessment and, 82

Single Supervisory Mechanism (SSM), xii, xiii, 13–16, 39, 78, 89, 114, 221
bail-ins and, 132–135
bureaucratic incentives and, 178–182
institutional structure of, 169, 241
political economy perspective of, 167–192
shadow resolutions and, 159–160
supervisory powers within, 170–186
smart portfolio disclosure, 258–262, 266–267
social interactions, 200–201
Social Security, 197
social welfare, 4
sovereign debt
crisis, 78, 84
exposure of banks to, 23–34, 43
sovereign risk, 24, 31
sovereign yield differentials, 25, 29–31, 34
Spain, 58
bank recapitalization in, 31
special purpose vehicles, 4
SRISK measure, 46
SRM. *See* Single Resolution Mechanism (SRM)
SSM. *See* Single Supervisory Mechanism (SSM)
Stability and Growth Pact, 61
state aid, 90
Banking Communication (2013), 110–115
banking union and, 118–120
banks and, 105–108
burden-sharing and, 110–115
competition and, 103–105
control of, 103–118
Crédit Lyonnais case and, 105–108
in crisis period, 108–110
lender of last resort and, 115–118
pre-crisis experience, 105–108
rules on, 92–93
Statute of ECB, 69
stock trading, 208–209, 245
stress tests, 46, 49–60
ELA and, 117–118
euro area, 50–60
introduction to, 49–51
macro, 52–53, 54–60
micro, 51–52
overall economy and, 53–54
successful vs. destructive, 51–53
US, 50–51, 54–60
stressed market leverage ratio, 46
structured products, 207–208, 223
subprime mortgage crisis, 196, 207
supervision. *See* banking supervision
supervisor policy, in Europe, 13–16
supervisor, role of, 141–142, 146
Supervisory Capital Assessment Program, 50, 54–55
Survey of Consumer Finances (SCF), 302–311
Sveriges Riksbank, 63, 81
Swiss National Bank, 81
Switzerland, 156
systemic crisis, 66
systemic risk, xiv, 7, 279
bail-ins and, 127, 129
beyond banking, 282
forbearance and, 35
identification of, 14
individual contributions to, 8
measurement of, 8–10
metrics, 12
mutualization of, 167
regulation and, 10
shadow resolutions and, 164
sovereign exposures and, 25–29
transmission channels of, 5–7
systemic shocks, 66
systemically important financial institutions (SIFIs), 279, 281
capital surcharge for, 8
identification of, 8

tail risk, 34
testosterone, risk aversion and, 294
thrift institutions, 272
Tier 1 capital, 43, 44, 45, 46
Tier 2 capital, 43
time-series dimension, 7, 10–13, 19
TLAC. *See* Total Loan Absorption Capacity (TLAC)

too big to fail principle, 131, 164
Total Loan Absorption Capacity (TLAC), xvi
transparency, 155
traumas, risk aversion and, 295–296
Treaty on European Union (TEO), 62, 69, 91
Treaty on the Functioning of the European Union (TFEU), 90, 170, 240
triggers, 138–140
type 1 errors, 77–78
type 2 errors, 77–78, 130

U.S. financial regulation, 271–288
  broadening of, 282
  capital-based regulation, 275
  compliance professionals and, 286
  coordination of, 284
  Dodd-Frank Act, xvi, 81, 271, 277, 278, 279, 281, 282, 283, 284
  functional supervision, 274
  Glass-Steagall Act, 272, 273, 274, 278
  Gramm-Leach-Bliley Act, 273, 274, 275, 281
  information technology and, 276
  lack of paradigm shifts in, 286
  moral hazard and, 279
  of financial services industry, 283
  oversight of financial conglomerates, 281
  portfolio theory and, 274
  post-crisis, 277–287
  pre-crisis, 272–277
  regulatory structure, 277
  risk-based capital requirements, 281
  systemic risk and, 279
  Volcker Rule, 278
unemployment, 18
United Kingdom, 235
United States
  antitrust laws in, 97–103
  bail-in policy, 126
  bank resolution in, 35–36, 38
  capital markets in, 272–273
  Consumer Financial Protection Bureau, 226, 277, 286
  economic performance in, 50
  financial intermediaries in, 272–273, 274
  financial planning industry in, 245
  financial regulation in. *See* U.S. financial regulation
  formal resolutions in, 158
  mortgage crisis in, 5
  real output in, 49
  savings and loan (S&L) crisis, 158, 274
  shadow resolutions in, 158
  stress tests in, 50–51, 54–60
  subprime crisis in, 196, 207
universal banks, 39
unrestrained legal scholarship, 322–323
user-based regulation, 205, 210–213

value-at-risk models, 4
Volcker Rule, 278

waterfall principle, 129–131

zombie banks, 35

Lightning Source UK Ltd.
Milton Keynes UK
UKOW06n0154170815

257031UK00005B/40/P

9 781107 084261